Transformations

TRANSNATIONAL FEMINIST STUDIES

KAMALA KEMPADOO, SERIES EDITOR
York University, Toronto, Canada

Books in the Series:

The Wages of Empire: Neoliberal Policies, Repression, and Women's Poverty
edited by Amalia L. Cabezas, Ellen Reese, and Marguerite Waller

Transformations: Feminist Pathways to Global Change—An Analytical Anthology
Torry Dickinson and Robert Schaeffer

Forthcoming:

From Hollywood to Bollywood: The Cinema of South Asians Abroad
by Shoba S. Rajgopal

Transformations: Feminist Pathways to Global Change

An Analytical Anthology

TORRY DICKINSON
and ROBERT SCHAEFFER

Paradigm Publishers
Boulder • London

Paradigm Publishers is committed to preserving ancient forests and natural resources. We elected to print *Transformations* on 50% post consumer recycled paper, processed chlorine free. As a result, for this printing, we have saved:

9 Trees (40' tall and 6-8" diameter)
3,808 Gallons of Wastewater
1,534 Kilowatt Hours of Electricity
420 Pounds of Solid Waste
825 Pounds of Greenhouse Gases

Paradigm Publishers made this paper choice because our printer, Thomson-Shore, Inc., is a member of Green Press Initiative, a nonprofit program dedicated to supporting authors, publishers, and suppliers in their efforts to reduce their use of fiber obtained from endangered forests.

For more information, visit www.greenpressinitiative.org

Copyright © 2008 Paradigm Publishers

Published in the United States by Paradigm Publishers, 3360 Mitchell Lane, Suite E, Boulder, CO 80301 USA.

Paradigm Publishers is the trade name of Birkenkamp & Company, LLC, Dean Birkenkamp, President and Publisher.

Library of Congress Cataloging-in-Publication Data

Transformations : feminist pathways to global change : an analytical anthology / Torry Dickinson and Robert Schaeffer.
    p. cm.
  Includes bibliographical references and index.
  ISBN-13: 978-1-59451-355-8 (hardcover : alk. paper)
  ISBN-13: 978-1-59451-356-5 (pbk. : alk. paper)   1. Feminism—International cooperation.
2. Women social reformers—History.   3. Globalization—Social aspects   4. Social change.
5. Social movements.   I. Dickinson, Torry D.   II. Schaeffer, Robert, 1953–
  HQ1155.T73 2008
  305.4201—dc22

                                                                                    2007045360

Printed and bound in the United States of America on acid free paper that meets the standards of the American National Standard for Permanence of Paper for Printed Library Materials.

Designed and Typeset by Straight Creek Bookmakers.

11 10 09 08 07   1 2 3 4 5

Contents

List of Sidebars		*vii*
Credits		*ix*

1 Women-Centered Movements and Alternative Development *1*
Introduction: Women-Centered Movements and Alternative
  Development, 1490 to the Present, 1
Gargi Bhattacharyya, "Violent Endings and New Beginnings," 18

2 Redefining Work, Gender, and Development *24*
Introduction: Redefining Work, Gender, and Development,
  1970 to the Present, 24
Chandra Talpade Mohanty, "Antiglobalization Pedagogies," 39

3 Feminist Pathways to Democracy and Equality *46*
Introduction: Feminist Pathways to Democracy and Equality,
  1990 to the Present, 46
Siriporn Skrobanek, Nataya Boonpakdee, and Chutima Jantateero,
  "From Research to Action," 60
Paulo Freire, "First Letter: On the Spirit of this Book," 73

4 Humanizing Social Relations *77*
Introduction: Humanizing Social Relations, 1990 to the Present, 77
Maria Lugones, "Playfulness, 'World'-Travelling, and Loving
  Perception," 95

5 Restructuring Gender to Promote Alternative Development *105*
Introduction: Restructuring Gender, Sexuality, Age to Promote
  Alternative Development, 1990 to the Present, 105
Yvonne Corcoran-Nantes, "Female Consciousness or Feminist
  Consciousness? Women's Consciousness Raising in Community-
  Based Struggles in Brazil," 123

June Jordan, "A New Politics of Sexuality,"   133

M. Jacqui Alexander, "Pedagogies of Crossing,"   136

6   Feminists Reconstitute Work and Market   **143**

Introduction: Feminists' Reconstitution of Work and Market,
    1990 to the Present,   143

Sharon Ann Navarro, "Las Mujeres Invisibles/The Invisible
    Women,"   159

Namita Datta, "The Significance of the House as Property,"   171

7   Women and the Environment: Regenerative Development   **175**

Introduction: Women and the Regeneration of the Environment,
    1990 to the Present,   175

Marilou Awiakta, "How the Corn Mother Became a Teacher of Wisdom:
    A Story in Counterpoint—Two Mind-Sets, Two Languages,"   195

Farida Akhter, "Seeds in Women's Hands: A Symbol of Food Security
    and Solidarity,"   203

Leigh S. Brownhill and Terisa E. Turner, "Feminism in the Mau Mau
    Resurgence,"   207

8   Feminist Movements for Nonviolence and Peace   **224**

Introduction: Feminist Movements for Nonviolence and Peace,
    1990 to the Present,   224

Margaret D. Stetz, "Representing 'Comfort Women': Activism
    through Law and Art,"   244

Kathleen Staudt and Irasema Coronado, "Human Rights and
    Wrongs"   249

Shelley Anderson, "Crossing the Lines: Women's Organizations
    in Conflict Resolutions,"   258

Andrea Smith, "Heteropatriarchy and the Three Pillars of White
    Supremacy: Rethinking Women of Color Organizing,"   264

**9   Pathfinders: Women-Centered Movements Discover Intersecting
    Routes to Global Change**   **273**

Conclusion: Global Theories, the Historical World-System, and
    Intersecting Women-Centered Movements,   273

About the Editors   *286*

Sidebars

Feminist Perspectives on Subsistence   32
Reversing the Priorities of Development   34
Feminist Approaches to Research   48
Using Participatory Education to Address Power Differences   54
We Are All Connected: Global Workers, Consumers, and Activists   79
Feminist Political Economy and the Global Redistribution of Wealth   89
On Sexuality: Answering Basic Questions   109
The Continuum of Sexes   112
Male and Heterosexual Domination in an Unequal Global Society   115
UPAVIM: Unidas Para Vivir Mejor/United for a Better Life:
    A Guatemalan Women's Fair-Trade Cooperative   153
Engaging Environmentalists and Feminists in Collaborative Change   179
Tourism for Activists   183
Engaging Feminists and Peace Activists in Collective Change:
    "The Women's Action Agenda for a Peaceful and Healthy Planet 2015"   228
Alternative Development Based on Feminist Nonviolence: Paths to
    Genuine Security   238

*To: Rink, Ron, and Derry
and with reflective gratitude to
Thurgood Marshall and the NAACP,
who made possible the* Brown v. Board of
Education *school-integration ruling,
changing education for our generation and
linking together social movements
from the 1960s to the present*

*and in memory of Gregory Walls,
beloved friend, loving soul,
Miller J.H.S. and Cass Tech student
in our class of 1971,
and y/Young b/Black m/Man
who went running to protect his w/White friends
from a pistol-bearing woman-hating racist
("No Jew will sleep with our girl!"/
mom sat outside in the car while the deed was done);
four died that morning in Detroit:
how to change?*

Credits

Gargi Bhattacharyya, "Violent Endings and New Beginnings," in *Traffick: The Illicit Movement of People and Things*. London: Pluto Press, 2005, 189–196. Reprinted with permission of Pluto Press.

Chandra Talpade Mohanty, "Antiglobalization Pedagogies," in *Feminism without Borders: Decolonizing Theory, Practicing Solidarity*. Durham, NC: Duke University Press, 2003, 238–245. Reprinted with permission of Duke University Press.

Siriporn Skrobanek, Nataya Boonpakdee, and Chutima Jantateero, "From Research to Action," in *The Traffic in Women: Human Realities of the International Sex Trade*. London: Zed Books, 1997, 80–97. Reprinted with permission of Zed Books.

Paulo Freire, "First Letter: On the Spirit of This Book," in *Pedagogy of Indignation*. Boulder, CO: Paradigm Publishers, 2004, 15–21, 24–25. Reprinted with permission of Paradigm Publishers.

Maria Lugones, "Playfulness, "World"-Travelling, and Loving Perception," in Gloria Anzaldúa, ed., *Making Face, Making Soul: Haciendo Caras, Creative and Critical Perspectives by Women of Color*. San Francisco, CA: Aunt Lute Press, 1990, 390–402. Reprinted with permission of Maria Lugones, Department of Philosophy, Binghamton University.

Yvonne Corcoran-Nantes, "Female Consciousness or Feminist Consciousness? Women's Consciousness Raising in Community-Based Struggles in Brazil," in Carol R. McCann and Seung-Kyung Kim, eds., *Feminist Theory Reader: Local and Global Perspectives*. New York: Routledge, 2003, 126–137. Reprinted with permission of Taylor and Francis/Routledge.

June Jordan, "A New Politics of Sexuality," in *Technical Difficulties: African-American Notes on the State of the Union*. New York: Pantheon, 1992, 187–193. Reprinted with permission of the June Jordan Literary Trust, San Francisco, CA.

M. Jacqui Alexander, "Pedagogies of Crossing," in *Pedagogies of Crossing: Meditations on Feminism, Sexual Politics, Memory, and the Sacred*. Durham, NC: Duke University Press, 2005, 1–9. Reprinted with permission of Duke University Press.

Sharon Ann Navarro, "Las Mujeres Invisibles/The Invisible Women," in Nancy A. Naples and Manisha Desai, eds., *Women's Activism and Globalization: Linking Local Struggles and Transnational Politics*. New York: Routledge, 2002, 83–98. Reprinted with permission of Taylor and Francis/Routledge.

Namita Datta, "The Significance of the House as Property," from "Joint Titling: A Win-Win Policy? Gender and Property Rights in Urban Informal Settlements in Chandigarh, India." *Feminist Economics* 12, no. 1–2 (January–April 2006): 276–278. Reprinted with permission of Taylor and Francis.

Marilou Awiakta, "How the Corn Mother Became a Teacher of Wisdom: A Story in Counterpoint—Two Mind-Sets, Two Languages," in Marilou Thompson Awiakta, *Selu: Seeking the Corn Mother's Wisdom*. Golden, CO: Fulcrum. Reprinted with permission of Fulcrun.

Farida Akhter, "Seeds in Women's Hands: A Symbol of Food Security and Solidarity," *Development* 44, no. 4 (December 2001): 52–55. Reprinted with permission of Sage Publications.

Leigh S. Brownhill and Terisa E. Turner, "Feminism in the Mau Mau Resurgence," *Journal of Asian and African Studies* (2004): 39–95. Reprinted by permission of Sage Publications.

Margaret D. Stetz, "Representing "Comfort Women": Activism through Law and Art." *Iris: A Journal about Women* (Fall 2002): 26–27. Reprinted with permission of the Women's Center at the University of Virginia.

Kathleen Staudt and Irasema Coronado, "Human Rights and Wrongs," in *Fronteras No Más: Towards Social Justice at the U.S./Mexico Border*. New York: Palgrave Macmillan, 2002, 150–159, 171–173. Reprinted with permission of Palgrave Macmillan.

Shelley Anderson, "Crossing the Lines: Women's Organizations in Conflict Resolution." *Development* 43, no. 3 (2000): 34–39. Reprinted with permission of Sage Publications.

Andrea Smith, "Heteropatriarchy and the Three Pillars of White Supremacy: Rethinking Women of Color Organizing," in Incite! Women of Color against Violence, *Color of Violence: The Incite! Anthology*. Cambridge, MA: South End Press, 2006, 66–73. Reprinted with permission of South End Press.

1

Women-Centered Movements and Alternative Development

INTRODUCTION: WOMEN-CENTERED MOVEMENTS AND ALTERNATIVE DEVELOPMENT, 1490 TO THE PRESENT

In recent years, women, who have multiple and hybrid identities and are positioned in complex and intersecting hierarchies, have assumed prominent roles in social change movements that promote alternative development around the world. By taking action on multiple fronts, women have brought feminist-inspired ideas to many movements that are shaping the direction of global change. To understand women's work in social action groups and social movements, it is necessary to examine women's and men's lives within the context of past and recent developments in the capitalist world-system.

The capitalist world-system, which first took shape in Western Europe 500 years ago, is made up of a set of integrated economic, political, social, and cultural institutions. One of its key economic features is the global division of labor, which divides people and assigns them different economic roles around the world. Although capitalism divides people and assigns them different economic roles, it also joins them together in common projects—growing, making, manufacturing commodities—that stretch around the world. So, for example, the people who produce cotton apparel are divided, one from another. People who grow cotton in Sudan, spin it into yarn in Pakistan, sew it into shirts in China, design seasonal color schemes in New York City, and sell them at retail shops in Des Moines do these jobs separately, under very different conditions, and for very different rates of pay. But even though people are divided, they are also joined together in a common global enterprise, what economists

1

call a "commodity chain," that integrates their separate labors like links on a chain. These links ultimately allow people to change the world at local and global levels.

Global economic divisions are reinforced by political and cultural divisions, which give rise to social identities based on gender and sex, ethnicity, language, religion, class, status, age, ability, citizenship, and residency. Because the system constructs people's identities in relation to all social hierarchies, and groups and individuals reinforce and challenge these processes, people develop *multiple* social identities. As they go through their lives, people develop dimensions of their identities that are shaped "inside" of oppressed groups and "outside" of oppressed groups.[1] All dimensions of multiple social identities, including inside and outside dimensions of identity, provide ways to challenge global hierarchies and other foci of social change.[2]

Take, for example, a woman worker—it could be any of us or it could be a young Latina whose ancestors had always lived in the region that we now know as El Paso, Texas, a city on the U.S. side of the Rio Grande, which directly faces Ciudad Juarez. This young woman, who manages a cell phone company and who may participate in social actions on both sides of the border—perhaps as an employment mentor for El Paso's La Mujer Obrera (The Working-Class Woman; LMO)[3] and a vocal member of Mujeres de Negro[4] (Women in Black) who seeks an end to the murder of Ciudad Juarez women—has a multiple set of social identities, which help shape her worldviews and give her particular kinds of political traction. Not only does she have multiple social identities based on social categories with common, yet differentiated, attributes (gender, age, sexuality, racialized ethnicity, class, global locational), but these identities—which are shaped by social constructions and her self-definitions and actions—may also combine and evolve to form hybrid identities. In this U.S. worker's family (it could be our family, in any country), if her professional, working-class father is of Mayan-Mexican and Euro-American origin and her corporate mother of cross-border indigenous and Afro-Latina descent, her class-"ethnic" identity is a hybrid expression of different identities (just as most of our identities are, because we are connected together). And because she has chosen to relate to and participate in the development of different, overlapping cultures in the United States, Central America, and the Philippines (including subcultures that are strongly influenced by women, age, sexuality, ethnicity, linguistic, class, and cross-national identities), the hybrid character of this imaginary worker's identity (and of our own) is further complicated.

These hybrid identities lie in the region between overlapping, intermingled social categories and heterogeneous social spaces, what some feminists describe as "borderlands."[5] This means that some social categories and social-temporal spaces are less discrete and homogeneous and less constructed by either/or binaries, and some are relatively more homogeneous. Even though there are social constraints, people have the power to shape their identities and to shape the direction that society takes. Borderland identities and social-temporal spaces are highly complicated, mixed, and heterodox. Feminist women and men who shape contemporary movements have multiple and often hybrid social identities, and this prepares them to meet multiple human needs as they develop feminist pathways to global change.

What's more, these diverse social identities are arranged by the capitalist world-system into sets of *complex* and *intersecting* hierarchies. The young worker from El Paso would probably find (or we might find), for instance, that working men receive higher pay for almost identical or comparable work and that men get promoted more quickly than women. This would indicate the existence of an institutionalized "gender" hierarchy that privileges men over women. She might also discover that men defined by top managers as "white" are privileged over men whom executives categorize as recent Asian immigrants, indigenous, Latino, and African American, which would indicate the presence of an "ethnic" hierarchy as well, one that *intersects* or overlaps with gender. But this might be complicated by the fact that even though these hierarchies generally privilege men over women, there might also be a sexual hierarchy that excludes homosexual men from the privileges extended to dominant, heterosexual men in the gender and racialized ethnic hierarchies. As a result, she might conclude (as we might) that identities are subject to complex and intersecting institutional hierarchies, not only at work but in other spheres of her life as well.

Because the capitalist world-system assigns people different economic, social, and cultural roles, women and men develop multiple and hybrid identities and are subjected to complex and intersecting hierarchies.

But hybrid social identities are not simply "given" or assigned by dominant economic and cultural systems and faceless forces of power. They are also "made" by people themselves, the daily decisionmakers at all levels (and this can include us) that choose to maintain intersecting hierarchies or choose to abolish them. The women-centered movements that are bringing change have chosen to disassemble all of these constructed, unequal hierarchies, which arbitrarily classify and place people in groups that end up with lots of money or little money, with lots of food or little food, with the chance to live long or the chance to face early death. As historian E. P. Thompson argued, social identities can be constructed by thoughtful individuals and groups of people who share experiences and ideas and learn from each other.[6] These "situated knowledges," as Donna Haraway called them,[7] emerge from one's individual or collective social experience and enable people to think about their place, really their *places* in the world, their relationships with others, and ways to work with others, through their social connections, to change the world and its systems of identity and hierarchy.

People make the world in different ways, depending on where they're coming from and where they want to go. Their point of origin, what feminist scholars call their "standpoint," is shaped by hybrid identities and intersecting hierarchies. Where women and men want to go is shaped by their situated knowledge, what they make of their experience and how they want to change it.

People's work relations, and their responses to them, emerge within the context of the formation of gender and class and other identities. This process shapes the development of situated knowledge and standpoints. Although both women and men engage in paid and unpaid work relations, women tend to do more work, although much of it is not acknowledged in monetary or public ways. Wage work very rarely covers the cost of reproducing the household unit, even in the North today. Work and income generation that women and men do in the home, in markets, in voluntary neighborhood activities, and through exchanges and transfers within and between households actually accounts for much of the nonmonetized and cash-based value (or income) that is needed for household reproduction. These income sources are combined with wage incomes (whose real and nominal values have decreased since the 1970s) and reduced state transfer payments to create the means for survival.[8] Women's and men's situated knowledge and standpoints develop in different ways, within just these unequally constructed work relations. How women and men feminists participate in movements is greatly affected by these broad work, household, neighborhood, and state-related income-generating and cultural relationships.

Theoretically, people can start with any given combination of identities, located in any given set of hierarchies, and use their situated knowledge to make change. Theorists cannot easily predict which set of identities is likely to produce the kind of situated knowledge that enables people to change economic and social structures. But historical developments can make particular sets of identities salient for people at different times. For example, wars typically make ethno-"national" identities more salient for people in countries that go to war, whereas economic depression makes "class" a salient identity for people impoverished by it. Of course, the impacts of historical development on social identities are complex. After the attacks of September 11, 2001, the national identity of "white" U.S. citizens became more salient for many in the United States, and the ethnic and national identities of other U.S. citizens and residents also became more salient. In some cases, white Anglos' fervent attachment to the "Euro-American" U.S. image led to assaults on other "Americans." Arab Americans who were attacked by fellow "Americans" suddenly discovered that their identity as "Arabs" was more significant or salient than their identity as "Americans," as it was for people who fit this ethnic "profile," such as Sikhs from India or dark brown–skinned Latino/as and Asians. The point is that the social salience or significance of particular identities was shaped by historical developments.

Women's hybrid ethnic, gender, class, and global identities have been shaped within the contexts of both the ongoing development of the global system and the growth of local and global resistance to the system and other forms of domination. The development of the diverse forms of social alternatives creates many rivers of local and global change, which flow side by side and sometimes merge. This sets the stage for profound changes.

In recent years, women have played a prominent role in diverse efforts to promote global social change. Many social change movements are led by economically disadvantaged or poor women, by women assigned to the lower echelons of the global division of labor and located at the bottom of social and cultural hierarchies. One reason women in these movements have been able to work together to promote social change is that their political practice is based on their experience at the bottom of social ladders. For example, women in poor households around the world engage in nonwage labor to survive.[9] It is common practice among the poor to engage in reciprocal relations with other poor households. They pool resources, share knowledge, exchange skills, and cooperate with others to make ends meet.

It should not be surprising, then, that they would take their situated knowledges, based on their shared and differentiated experiences, and use them to change their circumstances. The microcredit lending institutions and small-scale, cooperative business ventures they have developed are based on the kind of relations they had already practiced as poor people. Of course, poor women are not alone in this, as many people have used their situated knowledges to initiate these kinds of changes. Social change movements, of course, are not confined to grassroots forms of economic development. They also engage at a wide variety of political, social, and cultural activities on a global scale. But around the world, in the contemporary grassroots and global social movements that promote "alternative development," women play important roles.

But how can we account for the prominent roles played by women in social change movements around the world? If social change can emerge from any given set of hybrid identities, why should contemporary movements for social change rely on people for whom being a woman is a salient identity? Why should gender be a key component of the complex, hybrid identities that come together in any given movement?

The answer, we think, is that contemporary global economic change, particularly the reorganization of the global division of labor in recent years, has altered gender relations and placed new economic and cultural burdens on women around the world. Women's experiences with post-1975 globalization, and the situated knowledges that grew out of their experiences with structural change, persuaded women to organize and lead social movements with different agendas the world over.

To appreciate why gender has become a salient identity in this period, and why women have assumed prominent roles in alternative development, it is important to review the history of structural economic and cultural change in the postwar period. Then we can see how women, who have hybrid identities and are positioned in intersecting hierarchies, take steps (agency) to change the world (structure) and themselves (identity and hierarchy).

POSTWAR DEVELOPMENT AND GENDER

After World War II, states around the world organized and promoted economic and social "development."[10] Of course, there were important political differences among capitalist democracies in the West (states in Western Europe, the United States, and Japan), communist dictatorships in the East (the Soviet Union and regimes in Eastern Europe and East Asia), and capitalist dictatorships across much of the South (regimes in South Asia, the Middle East, Africa, and Latin America). And these states adopted somewhat different strategies to promote development. Some states "opened" their domestic markets to foreign goods, whereas others practiced "import substitution," which meant restricting the import of foreign goods so they could force domestic consumers to purchase "homemade" products and thereby protect and nurture domestic industries. But whatever their political or economic differences, states around the world promoted the rapid industrialization of the economy and the adoption of green revolution technologies in agriculture to feed rapidly growing populations. They also spent heavily on the military, to protect government from domestic or foreign "threats," and increased spending on public "welfare" programs—providing education and health care and providing subsidies to reduce the cost of food, fuel, and transport for their citizens—to keep consumer demand up and worker protest down.

State-sponsored development had important gender consequences. Because states promoted industrialization, they assigned men an important role as wage workers in factories. To expand the production of "cash crops"—coffee, sugar, cotton, cocoa, which could be sold abroad to raise the money they needed to finance industrial development—states persuaded male farmers in agriculture to adopt green revolution technologies, typically neglecting the women who grew "subsistence" crops or foods that people ate as a staple part of their daily diet.[11] And because states spent heavily on the military, they recruited young men into the armed forces in large numbers. As a result, state-sponsored development in the postwar period was based on expanding work and employment opportunities for men. Women were not expected to play an important role in the development project.

But even though state planners did not assign women a significant role in development, women nonetheless played an important, but unacknowledged, role by engaging in work that sustained households during this period. Some women generated income by working for wages in industry and the service sector. Still, the percentage of women in the paid workforce was relatively small; about one-third of women worked in the labor force in the United States and Soviet Union, fewer elsewhere. Although many people, particularly men, imagine wage work makes them the "breadwinners," households do not live on this "bread" alone.[12] Households also depend for their survival on the nonwage income generated primarily by women but also by children and elders. They engage in "enterprising" work, selling goods and services in the streets; undertake subsistence and reproductive work, making meals and raising children in the home; practice reciprocal exchanges with other households, bartering and exchanging goods and services; and obtain income from intergenerational transfers and rents. Because women, children, and elders engage in nonwage work activities to sustain households, their nonwage work makes it possible for men and women to work for *less* than the cost of reproducing the household as an economic unit. In effect, women's work provides a subsidy to male wage workers and the firms that employ them. Without this subsidy, development would have been more costly, and more difficult, to achieve.

State-sponsored, male-oriented, but female-dependent development promoted rapid economic growth around the world. Development made it possible for states to recover from the effects of the Great Depression and world war and to provide jobs to male workers and farmers in the West, the East, and the South, which decolonized in the period between 1945 and 1970. But it didn't last. During the 1970s, world economic growth slowed and the state-led model of development experienced a serious crisis that would lead, in the 1980s, to its undoing.

THE CRISIS OF DEVELOPMENT

Although it was state promoted, economic growth itself created two problems—increasing competition and rising costs—that ruined the development project and altered gender relations around the world.

The postwar expansion of manufacturing increased the competition among the producers of steel, cars, appliances, and electronics for control of domestic and foreign markets. And by the 1970s, competition began to reduce profits significantly. Then during the mid-1970s, the oil embargo of the Organization of Petroleum Exporting Countries (OPEC) and poor grain harvests in the Soviet Union forced energy, food, and raw material prices to rise sharply, which increased the cost of doing business around the world. Other business costs were rising as well. Wages had risen during the postwar period because labor unions were fairly strong and the demand for labor was high. They rose again in the 1970s as workers demanded higher wages to cover the rising cost of fuel and food. This too increased the cost of doing business. At the same time, state spending on the military, which grew as a result of the Cold War arms race, and on social welfare, which rose as oil, food, and transport soared, increased the direct and indirect costs of doing business. These separate developments contributed to global "inflation."[13]

Initially, the rising prices associated with inflation were "good" for businesses and states in the South, which produced oil, food, and raw materials for the West. But rising prices were "bad" for businesses and states in the West, both because they increased the cost of doing business and because they triggered a general inflation. Inflation was a problem because it is a discriminatory economic process. When OPEC raised oil prices, some companies—oil companies—could raise their prices at the pump, and people paid whatever the oil giants asked. But other businesses couldn't easily raise prices without losing business. Inflation discriminated against businesses that weren't powerful enough to keep pace with rising prices. The same was true for workers. Some workers—government officials, members of strong unions—could demand and get higher wages. But workers who labored in competitive industries without strong unions couldn't easily demand higher wages. So inflation also discriminated against workers who weren't powerful enough to keep pace. What's more, businesses and workers who managed to keep up with inflation still complained about it because although they were keeping up, they weren't getting ahead. So inflation was both an economic and a political problem. It was a discriminatory form of economic development that made everybody mad.

In 1979, U.S. officials took steps to battle inflation by raising interest rates. Rising U.S. interest rates threw the world into a recession and triggered a debt crisis for dictatorships in the East and South, who had earlier borrowed money to accelerate their industrial and agricultural development.[14] When debtor states went bankrupt, first in Latin America, then in Eastern Europe, regimes turned to the International Monetary Fund (IMF) for funds to sustain their economies. In return, the IMF imposed structural adjustment programs to manage the crisis and make sure they would repay their debts. The combination of bankruptcy and structural adjustment triggered the collapse of the dictatorships that had borrowed money to promote development. The collapse, first of capitalist dictatorships in the West and South and then of communist dictatorships in the East (with the important exception of China), brought state-sponsored development projects to an end and contributed to "democratization"—the transfer of political power from dictatorships to elected civilian governments—around the world.[15] But even though rising interest rates triggered important economic and political change, they did not solve the problems associated with increased competition and inflation. So during the 1980s, "globalization" was advanced as a comprehensive solution to both problems.

GLOBALIZATION

The term *globalization* was coined in 1983 by Theodore Leavitt, a business professor at Harvard. It soon became the catchword to describe the "solutions" advanced to deal with the global crisis of the 1970s and 1980s. The term has many rhetorical uses and ideological meanings, but at bottom it describes the group of strategies designed to (1) reduce competition and (2) cut costs. According to the proponents of globalization, if competition is reduced and costs are cut, the profitability of the corporations that survive can be improved, and their profits can be used to finance new economic growth around the world. Since the mid-1980s, efforts to do both have introduced important structural changes that have altered gender relations around the world.

Reducing Competition

Although postwar development resulted in rapid industrialization, it also increased the competition among the producers of steel, cars, consumer goods, and arms. By the mid-1970s, for example, the Big Three car makers found themselves competing with German and Japanese firms for customers in the United States. Increased competition was a problem because it reduced the profitability for all the big auto makers in the West. The solution advanced by proponents of globalization in the 1980s was monopolization: the merger of firms from different countries and the consolidation of whole industries across national borders. In the years that followed, for example, Mercedes bought Chrysler, Ford purchased Volvo and Jaguar, BMW bought Rolls Royce, and Renault merged with Nissan. In 1980, U.S. corporations announced mergers worth about $33 billion. But by 1998, corporations announced mergers worth $40 billion in just one *day*. In the period between 1980 and 2000, U.S. firms arranged 151,374 mergers worth thirteen *trillion* dollars.[16]

This kind of monopolistic behavior had previously been prohibited in the West, both because it violated antitrust law and because foreign control of domestic industry was seen as harmful to the long-term interests of workers, domestic firms, and the state. But in the 1980s and 1990s, government officials refused to enforce antitrust law and instead encouraged monopolistic behavior, arguing that monopolization on a global scale increased efficiency and profitability.

Cutting Costs

During the 1970s, the price of raw materials, wage labor, and military welfare programs rose dramatically. Inflation was a problem for corporations because it increased the cost of doing business and reduced profits at a time when increased competition also squeezed profits. So in the 1980s, proponents of globalization advanced a series of strategies to reduce inflation by cutting the cost of raw materials, labor, and state welfare programs.

Raw Materials. OPEC oil embargoes and Soviet grain shortages in the 1970s drove up the price of energy, food, and raw materials around the world. In the 1980s, proponents of globalization used two strategies—(1) structural adjustment programs and (2) technological innovations—to cut commodity prices.

During the 1970s, dictatorships in the East and South borrowed money to finance economic development. But rising interest rates in the early 1980s forced debtor states into bankruptcy. Lenders in the West then demanded that debtor states allow the IMF to organize debt repayment programs that would allow them to avoid economic collapse and repay their bills. The structural adjustment programs imposed by the IMF required countries to increase their production of raw materials so they could earn the money they needed to repay their loans. Indebted countries did as they were told and increased the production of oil and gas, coffee and sugar, tin and copper. As the supplies of these goods increased, prices fell, which helped lower costs for businesses and consumers in the West. Of course, falling prices made it even more difficult for poor countries to repay their debts, which is why many of them are still laboring to do so, twenty-five years later.

Businesses also used technology to push commodity prices down and lower their costs.[17] During the 1980s and 1990s, fuel-saving technologies in higher-mileage cars reduced the demand for oil, the introduction of fiber optic cable and wireless cell phones reduced the need for raw copper, and the introduction of high fructose corn sweetener and dietary sugars reduced the demand for natural cane sugar. Technologies that reduced the demand for commodities from the South or replaced them with substitutes made in the West helped push down commodity prices and cut costs for business in the West. They also lowered costs for consumers in the West, which meant that they would not be under as much pressure to demand higher wages.

These developments had important gender consequences. Falling commodity prices reduced the income of the men who drilled for oil, mined copper, or grew coffee across the South. It also had consequences for male wage earners in the West. Falling commodity prices meant that workers paid less for energy and food. Because workers paid less, employers could pay workers less, thereby cutting their costs, which was an important goal for proponents of globalization.

Labor. Postwar industrialization relied on male wage workers. (Of course, it need not have done so—World War II demonstrated that women could just as easily have done all but a very few jobs in industry.) Because they were concentrated in large industrial settings and subjected to intense exploitation by technological innovations (Fordist assembly lines) and management practices (Taylorism), male wage workers became aware of their conditions and organized unions, movements, and political parties to advocate on their behalf. During the postwar period, male workers typically avoided making political demands and instead focused on obtaining higher wages, better working conditions, nonwage benefits (health care), and social security. In the West, where unions were strong, comprising one-third of the workforce or more, wages rose substantially between 1950 and 1970. They also rose in the dictatorships in the South and East, though not as fast, because regimes wanted to purchase workers' quiescence and encourage their participation in the development project. But rising wages and benefits increased costs for businesses and for states and contributed to inflation during the 1970s.

In the 1980s, proponents of globalization developed several strategies to cut labor costs: attacking unions and "downsizing," "outsourcing" jobs, and introducing women (lower-cost workers) into the workplace.

As part of their cost-cutting strategy, business leaders and government officials attacked labor unions and took steps to reduce the bargaining power of male wage workers, largely by downsizing the workforce. The monopolization of industry (see above) assisted this process. When firms merged, they only needed one accounting or shipping department, so they could lay off workers made "redundant" by the merger. This "downsizing," or "rightsizing" as the proponents of globalization prefer, increased competition among workers for the jobs that remained, reduced their effective solidarity, and made it difficult for unions to organize effectively or demand higher wages. To assist this process, government officials stopped enforcing antitrust law, making it easier for firms to merge and then downsize their workforce, and eased enforcement of labor laws, making it more difficult for workers to organize unions.

Firms also began to "outsource" jobs by moving factories to countries where labor costs were lower or by subcontracting work to firms based in low-wage settings. Government officials assisted this migration by adopting free trade agreements that made outsourcing possible and inexpensive.[18] Prior to the adoption of free trade agreements in the early 1990s, governments levied tariffs or taxes on imported goods. This made it expensive for businesses to have goods made overseas and then imported into their home country. By eliminating tariffs and other barriers, free trade agreements made outsourcing profitable.

U.S. firms first outsourced jobs to low-wage maquiladoras or sweatshops in Mexico. But during the 1990s, businesses in the United States and throughout the West shifted out of Mexico and began outsourcing jobs to China, a communist dictatorship, where wages were lower still.[19] China can offer workers to Western business at rock bottom prices. But so, too, can India, the world's largest democracy. Still, businesses prefer China, rather than India, by a wide margin. They prefer China because the regime promises to *keep* wages low. They avoid India because the democratic government there cannot prevent low-wage workers from organizing or demanding higher wages. So during the 1990s, Western businesses invested eighty-five times as much money on outsourcing in China as they did in India.

Outsourcing is one way for business to cut labor costs. But when corporations outsource, they not only shift the location of work from a high-wage to a low-wage setting, from democratic countries to a dictatorship, they also typically shift from using male workers to younger, lower-paid, female workers.

Businesses and states also cut labor costs by encouraging or permitting the immigration of workers, male and female, from other countries. In the United States and also in China (where "immigrants" from the countryside evade residency laws and migrate illegally into the cities), immigrants are allowed to enter the country and work illegally because they accept low pay and because their status as "illegals" makes it difficult for them to complain about wages or conditions, much less organize unions and demand higher pay.

Of course, the strategies that cut labor costs—deunionization, outsourcing, the feminization of the paid labor force, and immigration—have important gender consequences. In general, they have contributed to the demasculinization of the wage labor force and to its feminization.[20] Demasculinization and feminization refer to the growing number of increasingly lower-paid women in typically manufacturing or service and other low-paid jobs and not to the replacement of men at the top or the systemically generated overthrow of male domination. The decline of some wage work for men, which has expressed and reinforced their historical power over women, has meant that some men have felt compelled to define their own masculinity in especially violent ways, even though male domination has largely stayed intact. Many more women now participate in wage labor than they did fifty years ago, and women are now employed in professional activities that were once prohibited to them. But although many feminists regard these developments as indicating both new forms of sexism and signs of progress, it is important to recognize the general global decline in wages and to examine impacts of these changes on men and women in households.

Because men have lost jobs or income as a result of cost-cutting efforts, their contribution to household income has stagnated or declined. Women have found wage work to help compensate for the loss of male wages. But because women are paid less than men for the same job, their increased participation in the paid work-force has *not* increased total household income. What's more, women who find paid employment are still expected to perform nonwage work activities, which are important to the survival of households, so women work harder in both capacities to make household ends meet. So while more women are finding paid work, overall household income has not improved.

The State. During the postwar period, states increased military spending and spent more on "welfare" programs.[21] In the West and East, states spent heavily on education, health care, and social security. In the South, regimes subsidized the cost of fuel, food, and transportation. During the 1970s, military spending escalated in the West and East as a result of the Cold War arms race, and welfare spending increased around the world because rising oil, food, and raw material prices drove up the cost of social programs, pensions, and subsidies.

The debt crisis of the 1980s forced capitalist dictatorships from power in the South and then drove communist regimes from power in the East. When civilian governments took power as a result of widespread democratization, they took several steps. First, they cut military spending, which they regarded as unnecessary. Second, they cut social welfare programs and subsidies because structural adjustment programs required states to use the money to repay debt and because proponents of globalization, and IMF managers, believed that welfare programs distorted the market and taught people to act in ways they would not if they had to pay the real "market" price for these goods. And third, they sold state assets—government-owned utility companies, transport systems, heavy industries, retail shops, and housing—a development described by proponents of globalization as "privatization" because it transferred public assets to private hands, sometimes to domestic owners but often to foreign buyers.[22]

The proponents of globalization persuaded or required states to cut spending on the military and on welfare because, they argued, high levels of state spending increased the direct and indirect costs (taxes and regulations) of doing business. And they urged privatization because state-run businesses competed with private business. Recall that reducing competition—competition among firms and competition between firms and states—was one of the central goals of globalization.

Reductions in state spending on the military and on public welfare, and the privatization of state-run assets, had important gender consequences. When states cut spending on the armed forces and the arms industries associated with them, men in uniform and men in the arms industries were thrown out of work. When states cut public welfare, they increased the cost of education, health care, social security, food, fuel, and transport for both men and women in households. And when states privatized public assets, private owners consolidated industries, eliminating "inefficient" firms and eliminating the jobs of the men who worked there. In the East, where fairly large numbers of women worked in state-run industries, women also lost jobs as a result of privatization.

GLOBALIZATION, STRUCTURAL CHANGE, AND GENDER

Globalization was advanced as a solution to the problems associated with the crisis of development in the 1970s and 1980s, chiefly increased competition and inflation. Efforts to monopolize industry and cut costs triggered important structural changes that had a big impact on gender, on both women and men.

The effort to reduce competition by consolidating industry resulted in mergers that frequently laid off male wage workers. Efforts to cut the price of raw materials reduced the income of male farmers and miners or put them out of work. Efforts to reduce the power of unions and outsource jobs to low-wage countries and assign work to poorly paid women resulted both in the demasculinization of wage work in industry and the feminization of wage work in maquiladoras around the world, increasingly in China. Reductions in state spending led to the reduction of armed forces and the exit of men from the military in most countries. Even in the United States, overall troop levels were reduced, whereas the percentage of women in the military increased, a pattern consistent with what has occurred in industry generally. Efforts to cut social welfare programs reduced real incomes for both men and women in households. And the privatization of state-owned assets typically resulted in job loss for men who worked there.

Overall, the pattern is clear. The structural changes associated with globalization resulted in substantial job and income loss for men in industry. Increasing numbers of women have gone to work for wages in industry and in the agricultural and service sectors, both because they have been *asked* to do so and because they *need* to do so to maintain household income levels. But because the women who find wage work are not paid as much as men, which is why businesses invite women to work in jobs once held by men, and because it is difficult for women to increase their wages, the benefits to households of women's entry into paid employment are not as substantial as they might have expected. Instead, real wages and total household incomes have stagnated or fallen, which was the goal of globalization all along. To make ends meet, women not only have worked harder for wages but also have intensified their nonwage work activities. So as a result of globalization, women work harder, both in settings where they work for wages and in settings—in the home, on the streets, and in the field—where they generate nonwage income for households.

GLOBALIZATION AND WOMEN'S AGENCY

During the period of globalization, capitalist firms and state policymakers have assigned women new and more arduous work roles. As a result, women have developed an awareness of their changed roles; have developed feminist orientations that collectively challenge all hierarchies, what is called "feminism";[23] and have organized women-centered, grassroots and global movements to address the problems associated with structural change and develop alternatives to globalization.

Women-centered movements are necessarily diverse. The ideas, research, and actions being developed by women-inclusive groups in different settings challenge structural change and economic and social-cultural hierarchies and promote feminist, environmental, and peaceful change in different parts of the world.[24] Some movements challenge cost-cutting business practices and propose new kinds of "fair trade"; others protest state cutbacks and demand public services essential to the health, education, and security of households. And some develop alternatives outside the state, what might be called "anarchistic" strategies for change. Although *anarchy* is a word now synonymous with *chaos,* it was originally used to describe a politics conducted with*out* the state (anarchy means without government). Anarchists such as Emma Goldman argued that movements for social change should not look to the state for solutions but instead develop cooperative institutions outside the state, what today are called nongovernmental organizations (NGOs), to provide services. Goldman endorsed the International Committee of the Red Cross as an example of a cooperative, service-providing, nongovernmental institution that might be seen as a model for "anarchistic" or alternative development.

Today, many contemporary women-centered movements work outside the state. They do so in part because state-sponsored development during the postwar period did relatively little to assist women and households but instead concentrated its efforts on assisting men in agriculture and industry. They do so in part because privatization has reduced the ability of states to promote public welfare. In parts of the South, the state has collapsed altogether, leaving humanitarian NGOs as the only institutions that provide public welfare. And they do so because many successful development strategies have been organized without government assistance, sometimes even in opposition to the state. So, for example, microcredit and microenterprise groups have promoted alternative development without assistance from the state.

Because these activities are diverse and disparate, it is not always obvious how they are joined together. But think of them as separate streams that might converge, as rivers do, somewhere downstream, sometime in the not-too-distant future.

These women-centered movements are important because globalization has not solved the problems associated with the crisis of the 1970s and 1980s. Indeed, the proponents of globalization have created new problems. Rising prices, particularly of oil but also of other commodities, have reemerged as a problem as a result of conflict in the Middle East and growth in China. In the 1970s, rising energy prices fueled the inflation that created an endemic crisis for capitalism and the state.

The proponents of globalization describe monopolization as a new, more efficient kind of global economic "cooperation" and describe cost-cutting strategies as a way to promote efficient markets that lower prices for consumers. They describe reductions in state welfare programs as a way to cut taxes for workers and argue that globalization promotes open communication through the Internet, democracy, and secular values. But as we have seen, this is the rhetoric, not the reality. Globalization has resulted instead in the consolidation of corporate monopoly power, the immiseration of wage workers and small-scale producers, the recent feminization of especially low-paying wage work and the intensification of work for women and household members, and the destruction of government programs designed to promote public health, education, and security. In globalization's extreme form, structural adjustment and privatization have destroyed states, and where this has occurred, economic marginalization, epidemic disease, and endemic violence have followed in its wake.

Post-1975 globalization has also accelerated cultural and political changes and impacted gender relations in unexpected—often adverse—ways, which has led some men to create new forms of patriarchal domination. The demasculinization of wage work in industry and the military has weakened male identities as "breadwinners" and "protectors." At the level of intimate relations and the household, changing gender roles and identities have contributed to rising divorce rates, domestic violence, and the rise of female-headed, and therefore also poorer, households around the world. At the level of social relations, men have turned in increasing numbers to fundamentalist and orthodox religious movements (orthodox Judaism and fundamentalist Christian, Islamic, Hindu, and Buddhist traditions); to conservative, "family values" political parties, which are often linked to fundamentalist religions; and to violent, militant social movements (gangs, militias, and insurgent groups) as a way to defend male "breadwinner" identities, reassert patriarchal authority in households and society, discipline women, and prevent feminist values and women-centered movements from making headway around the world. The irony is that many male-dominated, fundamentalist and religious groups and conservative political parties (though not all) support globalization, despite the fact that globalization is responsible for the structural changes that reduce most men's wage power and undermine this aspect of patriarchy.

This development means that women-centered movements not only have to address the structural changes associated with globalization, they also have to deal with the patriarchal-fundamentalist male reaction to globalization, which frequently takes a violent form in the household and in society.

SYSTEMIC CRISIS?

Women's efforts are crucial because the world economic system may be undergoing a systemic crisis, not simply a cyclical one, which means that the creation of new institutions, social relations, and sustainable development practices is urgently needed as global systemic relations dissolve.

There is some evidence to suggest that the world-economy is undergoing a systemic crisis.[25] First, throughout its long history, which dates back to its fifteenth-century origins in Western Europe, the capitalist world-economy has *expanded.* Colonialization, the incorporation of people and places, fueled its growth and strengthened core states in the West. But in the last half century, the system reached its spatial limits and, in recent years, has started to *contract.* In parts of Africa, Asia, the Middle East, and Latin America, where states have collapsed or state authority has dissolved, where people are impoverished, where disease is epidemic and violence is endemic, regions and the people in them have been marginalized or pushed out of the world-economy and consigned to a "no-go" external arena, much as they were in the era before colonization. Of course, as the world-economy *contracts,* the opportunities for future growth and development are *diminished.*

Second, the centuries-long expansion of the world-economy was also fueled by the exploitation of the natural world and its bountiful resources. But the intensification of this exploitation, particularly during the last half century, has exhausted natural resources and ecological systems. The intensification of energy use in this period has also contributed to global warming, which threatens to undermine food-production systems around the world.

In coming years, economic and ecological constraints may undermine the ability of the system, which has long relied on expansion and exploitation to fuel development, to grow as it has in the past. Under these circumstances, the development alternatives being advanced by women-centered movements around the world are particularly important and timely.

The next chapter explores how women's movements began addressing global development as a way of reducing poverty and improving society for everyone. As multiple human needs became identified, women and men feminists brought women-centered politics to more local, national, and global movements, contributing to a complex and many-layered process of change.

READING

Gargi Bhattacharyya's concluding chapter to *Traffick: The Illicit Movement of People and Things* looked at globalization in this social-historical moment, when the United States has begun losing its empire and when global capitalist development has been bringing violence to women and men. In these vast and chaotic changes, she argued, major transformations are taking place that will shape the world to come.[26] We explore these changes by examining how feminist pathways are shaping these global transformations.

NOTES

1. Nancy A. Naples, *Feminism and Method: Ethnography, Discourse Analysis, and Activist Research* (New York: Routledge, 2003), 49–66.
2. Torry Dickinson and Robert Schaeffer, *Fast Forward: Work, Gender, and Protest in a Changing World* (Lanham, MD: Rowman and Littlefield, 2001).
3. Sharon Ann Navarro, "*Las Mujeres Invisibles*/The Invisible Women," in Nancy A. Naples and Maniha Desai, eds., *Women's Activism and Globalization: Linking Local Struggles and Transnational Politics* (New York: Routledge, 2002), 83–98.
4. Melissa Wright, *Disposable Women and Other Myths of Global Capitalism* (New York: Routledge, 2006).
5. The writers represented in *Making Face, Making Soul,* along with Audre Lorde, Patricia Hill Collins, and the Combahee River Collective, have helped lead the way in terms of understanding the social construction of overlapping identities and how feminists can use this to remake individual identity, relationships, and society. For example, see Gloria Anzaldúa, ed., *Making Face, Making Soul/Haciendo Caras: Creative and Critical Perspectives by Feminists of Color* (San Francisco: Aunt Lute Books, 1990). Also see Patricia Hill Collins, *Black Feminist Thought: Knowledge, Consciousness, and the Politics of Empowerment* (New York: Routledge, 2000).
6. Edward P. Thompson, *The Making of the English Working Class* (London: V. Gollancz, 1963).
7. Donna Haraway, "Situated Knowledges: The Science Question in Feminism and the Privilege of Partial Perspective," *Feminist Studies* 14, no. 3 (1988): 575–599.
8. Dickinson and Schaeffer, *Fast Forward;* Torry Dickinson, *CommonWealth* (Lanham, MD: Rowman and Littlefield, 1995).
9. In this book our examination of wage and nonwage income and household structures grows out of the research done by the Household Working Group at the Fer-

nand Braudel Center at Binghamton University in New York. We were graduate students in the Sociology Department when the Braudel Center formed, at which we participated in research projects and colloquia. The influence of world-system analysis has been evident in our subsequent work.

10. For a more detailed account, see "The Redistribution and Reorganization of Work in the Core," in Dickinson and Schaeffer, *Fast Forward,* 49–81.

11. See "Technology, Food, and Hunger," in Robert K. Schaeffer, *Understanding Globalization: The Social Consequences of Political, Economic, and Environmental Change,* 2nd ed. (Lanham, MD: Rowman and Littlefield, 2003), 153–190.

12. See "The Meaning of Work," in Dickinson and Schaeffer, *Fast Forward,* 23–35.

13. See "Fighting Inflation," in Robert K. Schaeffer, *Understanding Globalization: The Social Consequences of Political, Economic, and Environmental Change,* 3rd ed. (Lanham, MD: Rowman and Littlefield, 2005), 61–78.

14. See "Debt Crisis and Globalization," in Schaeffer, *Understanding Globalization,* 3rd ed., 79–102.

15. See Robert K. Schaeffer, *Power to the People: Democratization Around the World* (Boulder, CO: Westview Press, 1997).

16. Stephen Lebaton, "Despite a Tough Stance or Two, White House Is Still Consolidation Friendly," *New York Times,* April 6, 1999.

17. See "Falling Commodity Prices," in Schaeffer, *Understanding Globalization,* 3rd ed., 157–192.

18. See "Free Trade Agreements," in Schaeffer, *Understanding Globalization,* 2nd ed., 217–250.

19. See "The Rise of China," in Schaeffer, *Understanding Globalization,* 3rd ed., 193–220.

20. Louis Uchitelle and David Leonhardt, "Men Not Working, and Not Just Wanting Any Job," *New York Times,* July 31, 2006. The authors noted that one of every eight men age thirty to fifty-four in the United States did not work, a development they attributed to downsizing, the entry of women into the workforce, and an unwillingness on the part of men to take jobs that appeared "beneath" their skill. Many of these men relied on working wives to support them, a development that expresses the simultaneous demasculinization and feminization of the labor force.

21. See "Welfare States Cut Benefits," in Dickinson and Schaeffer, *Fast Forward,* 138–158.

22. See "Democracy and Development," in Schaeffer, *Power to the People,* 218–246.

23. Estelle Freedman, *No Turning Back: The History of Feminism and the Future of Women* (New York: Ballantine, 2002), 7–8. After teaching feminist studies for twenty years and doing nine years of research on feminist movements around the world, Freedman concluded that most women's groups see feminism as taking action on at least four basic fronts: promoting the equal worth of women and men, challenging male privilege, addressing all intersecting hierarchies, and promoting change through social movements.

24. See section on "Change and Protest," in Dickinson and Schaeffer, *Fast Forward,* 205–272.

25. See Dickinson and Schaeffer, *Fast Forward,* 275–290.

26. Gargi Bhattacharyya, "Conclusion: Violent Endings and New Beginnings," in *Traffick: The Illicit Movement of People and Things* (Ann Arbor, MI: Pluto Press, 2005), 189–196.

⊛

VIOLENT ENDINGS AND NEW BEGINNINGS

Gargi Bhattacharyya

The world has changed a great deal since I began work on this book. When I started to assemble material for it, the machinery of globalisation appeared triumphant and immovable. There was an increasing awareness of the terms of resistance and protest, and a recognition that alliances were being formed across disparate interest groups, spanning old and new forms of organisation, from well-established trade unions and non-governmental organisations to the new breed of protesters who saw globalisation itself as the enemy and developed their campaigning techniques accordingly. However, there was little sense that global institutions were dented by these protests. Although NGOs and the representatives of poor nations have welcomed the impact that anti-globalisation protests have had on the formal negotiations about the terms of international trade, no one seemed to expect much more than concessions within the terms of the existing system. However much we all wished and believed that another world was possible, few had anything to say about how change on such a dramatic scale could be achieved. In short, although many people were developing a convincing and thoughtful critique of the inequalities and injustice of global processes, no corresponding global agent of change appeared. It was and is hard to identify what and where the levers of change might be.

However, more recently, there have been whispers that, in the manner of other empires before it, globalisation may destroy itself. Or, at least, adapt dramatically in the quest to survive. Some of this has emanated from the international institutions charged with management of the global economy—murmurs about poverty reduction not economic growth, attempts to work with governments and civil organisations. Some has come in response to the fear that the dispossessed of the world cannot be contained indefinitely, and that somewhere, somehow, something has to give.

This volume has looked at forms of trade and global movement that have become a cause of international anxiety. This creeping underbelly has been taken to signify the dangers of unregulated global integration, a warning of what an uncontrolled globalisation could become. In fairness, such trades have been portrayed as aberrations, a distortion of the wholesome benefits of international trade. Yet there is always a lingering concern— what if this is a sign of things to come?

DIFFERENT ACCOUNTS OF THE END OF THE WORLD AS WE KNOW IT

The forms of transnational transaction and movement discussed in this work have been the cause of intense concern amongst the self-appointed leaders of the world. As a result, international institutions have developed policy documents and drafted agreements, all designed to contain the corrosive influence of such undisciplined forms of business. Drugs, guns, illegal immigrants and organised crime—these form a nightmare vision of how the poor world becomes integrated into the global economy, in ways that endanger individuals and disrupt societies. In these instances, the reckless pursuit of profit is seen to run counter to human well-being and steps must be taken to curb excessive entrepreneurial enthusiasm. There is nothing much new about this arbitrary division between respectable and illicit business, and every Robin Hood–style mythology about stealing from the rich to give to the poor confirms the popular belief that the respectable business of the very wealthy is far from honest. The small but significant shift in our time is that many are now suggesting that the conduct of legal transnational business creates social costs that are similar to criminal activity: "Financial instability alone is not always undesirable. Sometimes it is even a necessary indicator of changing market conditions. Rather I believe the current financial crisis that we so often speak about is actually a grave *social* calamity" (Kapstein, 2001, 352).

For all the whining about exchange rates and the uncertainties of a speculative market, these things matter only in the impact they have on everyday life. Fictional transactions are not a problem if their impact is fictional also. When a range of commentators seems to suggest that we stand at the brink of an abyss, what is suggested is not so much that the (also fictional) machine of the world economy will stop working somehow, but rather that the human costs of this endeavour are not sustainable. The small consolations that have encouraged ordinary people to tolerate the inequalities and exploitation of the capitalist economy in previous crises now no longer seem to be available. If the bargains that have secured a version of social stability—the compromise of Keynesian economic management, some guarantee of living standards, safeguarding of savings and pensions—disappear or become ineffective, how can the co-operation of ordinary people be bought?

In this vein, a number of commentators have argued that we are living through an unprecedented crisis, one which must lead to dramatic social change. Without recourse to the small social reforms and benefits that have characterised liberal democracies, with these including a moderate sense of security, what will bind together societies which are being split apart constantly by the processes of capital accumulation? Here I want to consider three influential and quite optimistic accounts of this potential crisis as a prelude to revisiting the larger argument about the place of illicit forms of trade in global integration and re-evaluating the multiple calls for effective regulation of the global economy.

Immanuel Wallerstein argues that the capitalist world-economy, which has been in existence since what he refers to as "the long sixteenth century" is at a moment of crisis. Wallerstein presents this as an inevitable systemic outcome, something that must have been coming all along:

> Like all systems, the linear projections of its trends reach certain limits, whereupon the system finds itself far from equilibrium and begins to bifurcate. At this point, we can say the system is in crisis and passes through a chaotic period in which it seeks to stabilize a new and different order, that is, make the transition from one system to another. What this new order is and when it will stabilize is impossible to predict, but the choices are strongly affected by the actions of all actors during the transition. And that is where we are today. (Wallerstein, 2003, 185)

To his credit, Wallerstein does not suggest that the outcome of this crisis is decided, only that systems reach such moments of crisis through the development of an internal logic. It is the processes of capital accumulation that spawn these tensions. Wallerstein identifies three key trends that indicate this crisis: deruralisation of the world; the externalisation of costs and the resulting ecological exhaustion; and the impact of democratisation. All three are a threat to the endless accumulation of capital, because they represent an unavoidable squeeze on profits.

By deruralisation, Wallerstein is referring to the escalating rate at which the rural population of the world is declining. This is important because wage levels have been kept down by exploiting workers who have relatively less bargaining power—most often by pulling rural residents into urban work. Over time, these workers change their economic expectations and come to demand higher wages, at which point a new rural enclave is sought. With fewer rural communities to exploit, the overall impact is that the average price of labour worldwide is increasing (Wallerstein, 1999, 80).

The externalisation of costs refers to the manner in which capitalists seek to avoid some of their costs by passing them on to someone else, most often the wider community. This can be done by dodging responsibility for disposing of their own waste; by paying the price for inputs but not enough to replenish these inputs; and by using infrastructure that has been built at a cost to wider society. The first two instances are understood increasingly to lead to unsustainable ecological costs—we are running out of places to dump dangerous waste and also of sources of raw materials. The third example of free-riding on social projects leads over time to an upward pressure on taxation, not least as the price of maintaining political stability, which adds to the squeeze on profits.

Democratisation is used here to mean that as more people all over the world are able to make demands on their governments, the demand has been for varieties of welfare and service from the state. Although people may not get the things they want, the pressure of their demands does increase state expenditure and, once again, this increases overall tax costs for everyone, including those chasing profits.

Wallerstein argues that this combined squeeze on profits is leading to a situation in which the accumulation of capital is under question. Each trend indicates that previous methods of ensuring the continuation of capital accumulation cannot be sustained—and without continual accumulation, capitalism cannot go on:

> We do indeed stand at a moment of transformation. But this is not that of an already established newly globalized world with clear rules. Rather we are located in an age of transition, transition not merely of a few backward countries who need to catch up with the spirit of globalization, but a transition in which the entire capitalist world-system will be transformed into something else. The future, far from being inevitable, one to which there is no alternative, is being determined in this transition, which has an extremely uncertain outcome. (Wallerstein, 2003, 45)

This is not an account of the inevitable and imminent triumph of the proletariat—although the pressure on profit is depicted as an outcome of the more mundane day-to-day forms of class struggle. Instead, the suggestion is that the world capitalist system is in crisis due to internal function failures, and that the powerful may find an alternative to this structure that enables them to maintain their position and privilege. This is not a crisis that proves that the underdog has won. What it is, in Wallerstein's account, is an opportunity to shape the future that emerges from these changes:

> We need to be debating the possible structures of the historical social system we want to construct as the present system collapses. And we ought to be trying to construct the

alternative structures now, and in the next half-century, during the period of transition. We need to pursue this issue forcefully, if not dogmatically. We need to try out alternatives, as mental experiments and as real experiments. What we cannot do is ignore this issue. For if we do, the world right will come up itself with new noncapitalist alternatives that will involve us in a *new,* hierarchical, inegalitarian world order. And then it will be too late, for a long while thereafter, to change things. (Wallerstein, 2003, 245)

In times of crisis, rulers of the world become willing to adapt the rules of the game, to give a little to maintain their power and privilege. The intense revolutionary potential of the earlier twentieth century led to the concessions of Keynesian economic management and state welfare provision. The crisis facing capitalism in the early twenty-first century may lead to calls for regulation, rethinking, and a curbing of the excesses of capitalist accumulation. Anything to buy a little time while a new inegalitarian order can be built. The task is to find some alternative, while the possibilities of transition are open. For Wallerstein, there does not seem to be a privileged subject whose historic destiny it is to carve this new world project—so perhaps that is a duty for all of us.

We have already discussed the impact of Michael Hardt and Antonio Negri's work, *Empire.* This is at the euphoric end of prophecies of global cataclysm—Hardt and Negri describe a reworking of the machinery of global power that gives rise to a newly reinvigorated revolutionary subject:

> Here is the strong novelty of militancy today: it repeats the virtues of insurrectional action of two hundred years of subversive experience, but at the same time it is linked to a *new* world, a world that knows no outside. It knows only an inside, a vital and ineluctable participation in the set of social structures, with no possibility of transcending them. This inside is the productive cooperation of mass intellectuality and affective networks, the productivity of postmodern biopolitics. This militancy makes resistance into counterpower and makes rebellion into a project of love. (Hardt and Negri, 2000, 413)

For Hardt and Negri, the expansionary tentacles of Empire have brought all resistance struggles into one—against the abstract power of Empire. Now the histories of all progressive movements have become folded into this new militancy, a militancy that does not privilege any one struggle or grant special agency to any one location, but which links them all. This vision of the new political activist is heavily influenced by the excitement of the early anti-globalisation movement and the energies that this new alliance unleashed, a movement that really believes that global capitalism can be dismantled through sheer force of will. However, there are few clues about how such leverage might be exercised—the new militant is not the proletariat formed as revolutionary agent through the contradictions of accumulation, and therefore has no particular structural advantage in campaigns for change. The fear is that, without this, we are hoping that protest alone will make a new and better world.

David Harvey, although also writing of the new imperialism and the fragility of US hegemony, is sceptical about the poetic vision of social change described by Hardt and Negri. Harvey is concerned that failing to differentiate between different struggles leaves us unable to identify potential progressive moments. Refusing globalisation, for example, can be a backward and reactionary business as well, and can spawn movements that are exclusionary and inegalitarian. Building a new world requires us to "recognize the positive gains to be had from the transfers of assets that can be achieved through limited forms of dispossession" (Harvey, 2003, 178). Sometimes capital accumulation through dispossession—what Wallerstein explains as the externalisation of costs—creates positive possibilities for social justice, not least because the periphery gains some negotiating leverage through this process.

Overall, Harvey also believes that there is some cataclysmic change on its way, due to the overstretch of the US economy: "if the US is no longer in itself sufficiently large and resourceful to manage the considerably expanded world economy of the twenty-first century, then what kind of accumulation of political power under what kind of political arrangement will be capable of taking its place, given that the world is heavily committed still to capital accumulation without limit?" (Harvey, 2003, 35).

Despite all the talk about a New American Century, the United States is a debtor nation that relies on large amounts of credit from the rest of the world. At the same time, the escalating costs of the war on terror bring new pressures to an already costly military machine. Even such famous celebrants of empire as Niall Ferguson have questioned the sustainability of an empire based on borrowed cash (Ferguson, 2004). Harvey suggests that the US has been in danger of imperial overstretch for some time: "Even before the events of 9/11, it was clear that neo-liberal imperialism was weakening on the inside, that even the asset values on Wall Street could not be protected, and that the days of neo-liberalism and its specific forms of imperialism were numbered" (Harvey, 2003, 190).

This sense that neo-liberalism, despite its not quite hidden encouragement of global inequalities, cannot safeguard the privileges of the developed world frames the discussion of this work. The instabilities unleashed by the emergence of a speculative financial market have come to be regarded as threats to the global economy as a whole—not only an opportunity for a few to make some quick money, but also something that endangers everyone's assets, whether they are rich or poor. Harvey argues that the only available alternative to global conflict over scarce resources, as rival powers seek to safeguard their ability to accumulate at each other's expense, is what he calls a "New Deal" imperialism. In an echo of the Keynesian interventions of the twentieth century, this international new deal would require greater intervention from states, or a coalition of states, into the workings of the global economy, primarily to curb the excesses of inequality, uncertainty and unaccountability that have plagued recent global experience. In fact, what is called for is a system of greater regulation—not unlike the calls we have heard from a variety of influential voices in world economic affairs.

ADAPT AND SURVIVE

This [reading] has sought to examine the fear that global integration may have given rise to an untameable underbelly, a kind of bastardised free trade that threatens to unravel the terms of respectable business. I have tried to explain that each new demon—gangsters, drugs, guns, migrants—establishes a global reach only by hitching a ride on the formal processes of globalisation. Illicit trade is enabled by some of the same structures as respectable trade; and while opening markets may encourage transnational transactions, it can also lock some regions into a dependency on such illicit trades. Economic liberalisation can allow organised crime to extend its ambition and reach—and the disarray after the demise of the Soviet Union has increased this opportunity. Drug economies have become embedded in certain regions as a direct outcome of the long and gruesome histories of neo-colonialism and global inequality. In the era of globalisation, the drug trade has also become a more powerful transnational player. Despite the hope that the end of the Cold War might end global arms build-up, new wars and battles over sovereignty and status fire new forms of arms race, now with far less predictable patterns. The movement of people has proved to be unstoppable, despite the harshest efforts of the developed world. Accepting and mobilising the benefits of migration may turn out to be the best option for rich and poor worlds.

Alongside all of this, the accusation that these dangers are harboured by failing states has accelerated the debate about the right to sovereignty. In response to all these real and imagined dangers, the international community has returned to the idea of regulation and global governance—some kind of institutional structure that can hold in all that free movement. Although little has been specified about what such a structure would be and how it might work, the multiple calls in relation to a variety of movements illustrate a shift in our way of life. No one believes that things can go on as they are. After all the painful and turbulent stories related in this book, in the end each one suggests that some kind of change is almost upon us. These seemingly solid structures are melting into air again. The only question is—what comes next?

2

Redefining Work, Gender, and Development

INTRODUCTION: REDEFINING WORK, GENDER, AND DEVELOPMENT, 1970 TO THE PRESENT

In the early 1970s, scholars and activists who participated in feminist movements that emerged in the United States and Western Europe asked why women were subordinated to men.

Initially, feminist scholars argued that men dominated women because they occupied "more important" positions in the economy and work. As we have seen, industrialization in the postwar period was seen by state officials as the key to economic development around the world. This made wage-earning men, who worked in industry, central players in the economic life of households and nation-states. But because most women were engaged in nonwage work and were not seen as playing important economic roles in the household or the economy, they could not lay claim to social equality.

Given these circumstances, feminist thinkers argued that if women wanted to obtain social equality, they would first have to change the work they performed. This could best be achieved if women left the home (and unpaid work) and found jobs in the paid labor force. By working for wages and making a more important contribution to the economy, women would be able to redefine gender politics, raise their social standing, and participate in economic development, as they had, for instance, in the United States during World War II.

Today, feminist scholars take a very different view. In recent years, as we have seen, wages have fallen and state benefits have been reduced in countries around the world, a product of debt crisis and globalization. Under these conditions, feminist scholars argue, the entry of women into the paid labor force may not substantially improve the economic conditions or social status of women around the world. So instead of just finding wage work, women should also rely on transforming the more "traditional" kinds of nonwage work and "subsistence" production to improve their economic circumstances, promote social equality, and contribute to genuine development. According to many contemporary feminist thinkers, this "alternative development" will be based primarily on the nonwage activities of people in households and communities, not on wage work in the labor force. So although feminists encouraged women to *join* the labor force in the 1970s, they now also encourage women to engage in work *outside* it.

Feminist thinking about work, gender relations, social equality, and development has changed dramatically since 1970. To appreciate how feminist scholars redefined work (paid and unpaid labor), gender (relations between women and men), and development (the direction that society is taking), it is important to review their ideas.

THE 1970s: HOUSEWORK, WAGE WORK, AND SOCIAL INEQUALITY

Margaret Benston, a political economist and professor at Berkeley, was one of the first scholars to redefine work and gender. In her work "The Political Economy of Women's Liberation" (1969), Benston argued that unpaid labor was a key reason why women were subordinated to men.[1] Because women were engaged in unpaid, subsistence work in the home, they produced goods and services with "use values," not commodities with "exchange values." For Marxists such as Benston, the distinction was important because it meant that women's domestic work did not contribute to the capitalist system of commodity production. By contrast, male wage workers, who produced commodities with "exchange values," contributed directly to the capitalist system. So long as women played a marginal economic role for capitalism, they would remain subordinated to men, who were seen as playing a central economic role. To improve the social standing of women, Benston argued, society needed to change the way women engaged in economic activity.

Ester Boserup, a non-Marxist development scholar whose book, *Women's Role in Economic Development* (1970), examined women's work around the world, agreed with Benston that women should change their economic roles to improve their social status.[2] To do this, Boserup argued that Third World governments should expand educational and employment opportunities for rural and professional women as a way to promote both gender equality and economic development. The work of Benston and Boserup initiated a wider discussion about the relation among work, gender equality, and development in different parts of the world, not just in the West but also in the postcolonial South,[3] what was then called the Third World.[4]

Benston and Boserup agreed that the unpaid work of women "subsidized" profit-oriented business by making it possible for them to pay male wage earners less than they would if women didn't help support them. As Benston put it, "The amount of unpaid labor performed by women is very large and very profitable to those who own the means of production. To pay women for their work, even at minimum wage scales, would imply a massive redistribution of wealth. At present, the support of the family is a hidden tax on the wage earner—his wage buys the labor power of two people."[5] Furthermore, Benston argued that "at present, our unpaid labor at home is necessary if the entire system is to function."[6]

Although Benston and Boserup agreed that women's work helped businesses get more for their money, they still regarded unpaid labor as marginal and relatively unimportant for capitalism, which reflected the dominant view during this period. But this view began to change with the publication of work by Mariarosa Dalla Costa in Italy and Selma James in the United Kingdom. In "Women and the Subversion of the Community" (1972), they questioned the assumption that unpaid labor was of marginal economic importance and argued that the family was "the very pillar of the capitalist organization of work."[7] They maintained that women's work in the home was central, not peripheral to capitalism.[8] Unpaid work, they argued, provided an invisible but *indispensable* "subsidy" to employers who hired and then underpaid male (and female) wage workers.

But even though women performed an indispensable economic role, they depended on the wages earned by men to survive, and this dependency kept them in a subordinate position. To remedy this, Dalla Costa and James demanded that the state pay women "wages" for housework, so they would not need to depend on male wages. They thought this would raise the status of women in the household and improve gender relations.

The "wages for housework" movement that emerged in association with Dalla Costa and James's analysis failed to persuade state officials to provide wages for women's work in the home. Of course, if governments had paid women wages for housework, they would, in effect, have provided an even greater "subsidy" to business, allowing employers to pay wage workers even less than they already did. From the perspective of households, wages for housework might have improved the social status of women in households, but they probably would have provided very little "net" economic gain (women would have been paid more, male wage workers less).

Brazilian sociologist Heleieth Saffioti contributed to this discussion by linking unpaid domestic work to the wider capitalist system in her book, *Women in Class Society*.[9] She argued that "invisible," unpaid housework not only subsidized employers but made an important contribution to total family income.[10] A woman's unpaid labor in the home "actually increases the family's real income since it adds to the husband's wages an amount of labor that can be transformed into wages."[11]

Saffioti's intervention, like those of her predecessors, contributed to a *revaluation* of women's domestic labor. Each of these theorists argued that women's work, which had been seen as marginal and unimportant, was *more* important, a more *valuable* economic activity than people had previously imagined.

Saffioti was also one of the first academic feminists to analyze the role of women on the global assembly line. Teaming up with Helen Safa, one of the first U.S. academics to study global feminism, Saffioti examined the global production and marketing of clothes.[12] They discovered that the system relied on the work of low-paid women workers in different settings. This discovery was important because the outsourcing of cotton apparel in the 1970s became a kind of model for globalization in the 1980s and 1990s, when corporations in the West outsourced male jobs in industry to women in low-wage countries as a way to cut costs (see Chapter 1).

Saffioti also argued that the basic unit of class was not the male wage worker but the whole working family, which included paid and unpaid workers, women and men, children and elders. This integrated approach suggested that unpaid women, not just wage-earning men, could play a key role in changing the system and reshaping development in more humane ways. Prior to this, Marxists had assigned a "revolutionary" role to wage-working men because their work at the "point of production" gave them a clear understanding of the nature of capitalist exploitation. But Saffioti's work persuaded many people that if women in households played key economic roles, they might also play an important role in radical social change. Writers such as Saffioti and Safa persuaded a generation of gender and development activists and scholars that unpaid labor should be reevaluated in economic, social, and political terms.

As part of this general revaluation of unpaid work, socialist feminists associated with *New Left Review,* a British journal, and the Union of Radical Political Economics, a group in the United States, debated whether unpaid domestic labor produced "use value" or "exchange value" (see Benston, above) and whether domestic labor was "productive" and contributed to the accumulation of capital or whether it was "unproductive" and did not lead to capital accumulation. This theoretical debate was important for some Marxists because if unpaid labor was "unproductive," then it would be difficult for them to make the case that women played important political or economic roles. But even though participants in the domestic labor debate contributed to the discussion about the exploitation experienced by working-class households, they became absorbed in a narrow, technical, theoretical debate. Eventually, they concluded that nonwage work supported productive labor and that feminists should examine the relations between different kinds of work, but this protracted debate sidetracked them at a time when feminists began to explore a wider set of problems relating to work, gender, and development around the world.

THE 1980s: WORLD-SYSTEM AND POSTMODERN CONTRIBUTIONS

Although feminist scholars had identified women's unpaid labor as an important economic activity, they had not examined how it developed historically, how it was organized in different settings, or how it was tied to the capitalist world-system. In the 1970s, Immanuel Wallerstein analyzed the structure of capitalism in *The Modern World-System* and traced its origins to Western Europe in the sixteenth century.[13] World-system scholars, Wallerstein among them, did not initially examine gender as a central relation in their analysis of global society. But in the late 1970s, Wallerstein, Joan Smith, and other scholars at the Fernand Braudel Center in Binghamton incorporated gender into the center of their analysis and began to study work and gender relations in households. They then joined with Hans-Dieter Evers, Claudia Von Werlhof, and others at the University of Bielefeld in West Germany to begin a systematic, historical analysis of households in different "zones" of the world-economy. They wanted to find out how women's unpaid work contributed to household income and how gendered work relations were structured in the "core" (rich countries in the West), in the "semiperiphery" (medium-income countries in the East and South), and in the "periphery" (poor countries in the South).

Using the "household," not the "family," as the unit of analysis and focus of their research, world-system and feminist scholars who participated in this and subject projects[14]—*Households in the World-Economy* (1984) and *Creating and Transforming Households: The Constraints of the World-Economy* (1992)—made a number of important findings that contributed to an empirical understanding of work, gender, and social inequality on a world scale.[15]

First, they found that "wages were not enough," that male wages did not provide enough income to support worker households *anywhere* in the world. The wages paid by employers covered only a portion of the cost of sustaining and reproducing households: a small fraction in the periphery (perhaps only one-tenth of a household's total income) and a larger fraction in the core (possibly three-quarters to four-fifths of a household's total income). Second, they found that households relied on different kinds of unpaid labor—market sales, rent, transfer payments, and subsistence or self-provisioning—to survive.[16] Third, they found that women and men in households relied on different combinations of paid and unpaid work to survive in different zones of the world-economy.

In the periphery, households relied chiefly on wages and market sales, or "petty marketing," in so-called informal markets. The scholars in the project insisted that informal markets were not "new" institutions and were not "outside" the system, as some economists believed. Instead, world-system scholars maintained, informal, "gray," or "black markets" were created by the world-economy and were integral to it.

In the core, households relied on different kinds of strategies. Before World War II, poor people in the core relied chiefly on wages and petty marketing to survive, much like households in the periphery. But after the war, they came to rely primarily on wages and a variety of state transfer payments, or "welfare" in its many forms. In the United States, welfare or transfer payments from the state included aid to families with dependent children but also farm subsidies to rural families, pension and health benefits, and tax deductions for interest payments on home loans. (The value of the mortgage interest deduction for homeowners, for example, is five times greater than all farm subsidies or all welfare payments to poor people.)[17] States provided welfare to poor households to discourage them from engaging in petty marketing activities, which were regarded as unsavory or illegal, and compensated them for the loss of income-generating opportunities in informal and black markets, which were closed down in this period.[18] So, for example, street lotteries or "numbers" rackets, which were operated by people in poor communities, were closed down and replaced with state-run lotteries.

By contrast, better-off households in the core relied on wage income from male (and female) household members and used their wages to purchase cars, refrigerators, washer-dryers, and other "means of production" appliances. They then used these durable goods to transport themselves, make dinner, and do laundry so they wouldn't have to purchase these goods or services from the market. Of course, these "self-provisioning" or subsistence activities required women and men in households to devote considerable amounts of unpaid labor to these tasks. Capitalist firms promoted self-provisioning in the core because it required workers to become consumers of cars and appliances, which expanded the market for these goods and increased the demand for the (mostly) male wage workers who manufactured them.

In general terms, the research on households by world-system scholars documented the work women did to maintain households *and* demonstrated the importance of unpaid forms of labor for the capitalist world-economy. This research showed how the system created gender, class, and ethnic divisions and hierarchies in different settings around the world. What's more, the research helped specify the different kinds of unpaid work done by women in households and demonstrated that "in the capitalist system, wages can never be the sole or principal mode of payment for the vast majority of the world's workforce. Wages must be combined with other forms of income. These other forms of income are never negligible."[19]

The insights provided by world-system scholars deepened feminist understanding of how the global system structured work, gender relations, and social inequality. But although world-system scholars explored the material world in detail, they neglected to examine cultural relations, media, religion, and ideologies.

During the 1980s, a diverse group of feminist scholars began examining cultural worlds. These "postmodern" scholars contributed to the development of "cultural studies" programs and redefined women's studies programs to include subjects not previously explored by "materialist" scholars.

The ideas of postmodern scholars were influenced by several political and intellectual traditions. First, postmodern scholars drew their ideas from some of the social movements that had emerged in the West during the 1960s. In the late 1960s, some social movements abandoned efforts to unite diverse groups in broad-spectrum coalitions to push for radical change and instead organized political groups with separate or singular identities. So, for example, advocates of Black Power abandoned work in the multiracial civil rights movement and organized groups based on African American identities. In a similar fashion, many women broke from the male-dominated New Left and antiwar movements and developed a women's movement based on raising the self-consciousness and political activity of women in women-only groups. Other groups—gays and lesbians, Native Americans, Latino/as—adopted similar political strategies. From these experiences, postmodern scholars developed the idea that political actors should refrain from coalition politics, largely because they inhibited or "silenced" the political expression of culturally subordinate, hybrid, and newly evolving identities. This led to the creation of an "identity politics" that encouraged the formation of new, nonbinary identities, which were seen as providing new sources of cultural and societal change.

Second, postmodern scholars also drew from an intellectual tradition called "structuralism," which emerged in France during the 1960s and 1970s. Structuralist scholars were primarily, but not exclusively, Marxists who were frustrated by the failure of wage workers to participate in the protests of the 1960s.

Structuralist scholars offered two explanations for the failure of the working class to assume the revolutionary role assigned to them by traditional Marxist theory. First, they argued that capitalism had created new kinds of work that led to the formation of new and different classes—composed of "intellectuals," "professional managers," and entrepreneurs or the "new petite bourgeoisie"—that occupied "contradictory" locations in the class structure.[20] These new classes divided the working class and prevented the formation of a revolutionary working-class consciousness. Second, structuralists argued that capitalism had created a powerful cultural-ideological superstructure or "civil society" outside the state. This civil society generated ideas and cultural practices, such as "consumerism," that inhibited the development of a radical consciousness or a counterculture that could compete effectively for control of civil society or mount a challenge to the capitalist state.

From the structuralists, postmodern scholars took two ideas. The first idea was that it was important to *differentiate* carefully between groups of people, because their interests often conflicted, rather than try to *abstract* or identify what different groups of people shared in common. Postmodern scholars, like structuralists, rejected the idea of engaging in a politics based on abstract, shared, common, or multidimensional characteristics. Instead, they insisted on a politics based on *difference*. Second, postmodern scholars embraced the structuralist idea that the study of culture or superstructure or civil society was important in its own right and went on to develop cultural studies as a field largely independent of economic-materialist studies. Unlike the structuralists, however, postmodern scholars emphasized the study of gender and sexuality and the body, which had been neglected in most structuralist work.

Postmodern scholars also drew on the postcolonial experience of people in or from India. Like the structuralists before them, Marxist scholars in India or in diaspora communities were frustrated by the inability of the communist party in India to play an important political role and by the failure of the huge, poor, rural peasantry to play a revolutionary role, as it had throughout Southeast Asia and China. Postmodern Indian scholars offered several explanations as to why a radical politics rooted in rural experiences failed to make headway in India. First, they argued that India's experience with British colonial rule made it difficult to develop a radical politics, of the kind expressed elsewhere, in postcolonial India. Second, they argued that Marxist political parties failed because they were too "universalistic," that is, they believed that Marxist "laws of motion" applied with equal force everywhere. Postmodern scholars argued that this insistence on universalism made Marxists unable to appreciate the specific conditions and particular circumstances of people in postcolonial India.

And then postmodernists argued that Marxism failed because it was too "essentialist." Marxists believed that *class* was the only essential or salient or significant social identity. But postmodern scholars in India argued that *caste* and other social identities were significant and that the Marxist insistence on a class-based politics prevented them from appreciating or mobilizing people based on other or hybrid identities. And last, postmodern scholars argued that Marxism failed because it was too "materialist," focused too much on economic conditions. Postmodern scholars, by contrast, argued that important political struggles were waged on cultural and ideological issues, in civil society, and that people engaged in forms of "resistance" that took on hidden or nonovertly political forms.

Colonial and postcolonial experiences in places such as India encouraged postmodern scholars to reject "universalist," "essentialist," and "materialist" approaches to political change, and this approach has been extremely influential among postmodern scholars elsewhere.

Postmodern scholars have made an important contribution by developing explanations for political failures of the left and drawing attention to the political importance of culture and identity. But their approach has not been unproblematic. Their insistence on "difference" and identity politics has made it difficult for people to make common cause or develop an effective politics in the South or West.[21] The grassroots identity-based politics celebrated by postmodern scholars in India failed to stop the rise to power of a right-wing, patriarchal, fundamentalist Hindu political party in India, which cut back funding for welfare and introduced market reforms that have opened the door to globalization in India. Much the same has occurred in the West, where identity and cultural-based political movements failed to stem the rise of right-wing, patriarchal, fundamentalist Christian political parties in the United States and parts of Western Europe.[22] Recall that structuralist and postmodern thinking grew up, in part, as a response to the perceived failure of left politics in the 1960s. But postmodern politics have not enjoyed appreciable success either. And after years of trying, a post-postmodern politics needs to be articulated.

Although the postmodern emphasis on culture highlighted issues that had been long neglected by materialist scholars, the emphasis on culture to the exclusion of economics was also problematic. To paraphrase Madonna, "We live in a material world." The reluctance of postmodern scholars to examine the material world made it difficult to analyze how identities and hierarchies were created, structured, and altered by the system. The postmodern rejection of universalism persuaded many people to reject the study of the global world-system because it was seen as universalistic. But this has made it difficult for postmodern scholars to appreciate the driving forces behind colonization, democratization, globalization, global warming, or any other macrolevel economic, social, political, or environmental development. Postmodern scholars celebrated isolated rebellions and moments of resistance but did not examine or explain their underlying, historical connections. Because they failed to research the history of global capitalism and its relations to the particular, postmodernists could not explain how oppositional hierarchies originated.

THE 1990s AND 2000s: THE WORLD (AND DEVELOPMENT) TURNED UPSIDE DOWN

At the turn of the century, feminist scholars turned thinking about development upside down. During the 1980s, the debt crisis foreclosed on the postwar development project in the South and East. In the 1990s, the advent of globalization, which was designed chiefly to cut costs, resulted in falling wages, falling commodity prices, and reductions in state benefits for people around the world. Under these circumstances, it was increasingly difficult to imagine that wages alone could sustain households or that women's entry into the paid labor force could substantially improve household living standards, as early feminists such as Benston and Boserup had hoped. Instead, feminist scholars such as Maria Mies, Veronika Bennholdt-Thomsen, and Claudie Von Werlhof, who had earlier participated in households research projects, argued that the debt crisis and globalization had brought women into the labor force as lower-paid substitutes for men and had forced women to make up for lost wage income and declining state benefits by increasing their unpaid workload. In *Patriarchy and Accumulation on a World Scale, The Subsistence Perspective,* and *Women: The Last Colony,* these scholars argued that capitalism was now treating women as the world's "last colony."[23] By this they meant that capitalism had previously relied on the incorporation and exploitation of colonies to fuel its development. Now, in the postcolonial or neocolonial period, capitalism was incorporating and exploiting women to fuel continued growth. But women in the South recognized this and organized social movements to defend and reclaim the "commons," on which "subsistence" and other nonwage activities depend.

FEMINIST PERSPECTIVES ON SUBSISTENCE

Feminists engage in change and work for women's self-sufficiency in different ways. One strategy feminists have adopted is to pressure dominant institutions, such as business and the state, to distribute more wealth and social benefits to working people. Feminists in this tradition have worked to build women's power by pressuring for-profit firms and the state to end their perpetuation of gender inequality and other injustices. These feminists often work to increase women's wages, eliminate gender and racial occupational segregation, address global inequalities, and improve working conditions. Or they may increase women's power and self-sufficiency by fighting state cutbacks, seeking increased state benefits, improving education, and addressing state violence.

Another strategy feminists have used to promote change is to bypass the dominant institutions and instead promote women's self-sufficiency by building alternative work relations that help sustain families and communities. By creating worker-run cooperatives and microenterprise projects, some feminist groups have created new ways for women to gain power and become more self-sufficient. Rather than remaining dependent on firms and the state to provide family wages and good living conditions, some feminist groups seek self-sufficiency by creating new work options and by seeking greater independence from the dominant system.

Middle-class feminists in the global North and women dealing with large-scale industrial production may be more familiar with political struggles that place pressure on firms and the state. Feminists who come from economically disenfranchised and rural communities in the global South may also be familiar, however, with efforts to create their own work options, which is sometimes described as a feminist subsistence perspective. The following selection describes an interaction between women who work for change from these two complementary vantage points.

In April 1995, some months before the beginning of the U.N. World Women's Conference in Beijing, Hillary Clinton, the First Lady of the USA, visited Bangladesh. She had come to find out for herself what was true of the success stories of the Grameen Bank projects in Bangladeshi villages, of which she had heard so much. The microcredits of the Grameen Bank were said to have improved the situation of rural women in Bangladesh remarkably. Ms. Clinton wanted to find out whether the women had really been empowered by these microcredits. For the Grameen Bank and development agencies, "empowerment for women" means that a woman has income of her own and that she has some assets.

Hillary Clinton visited the women of Maishahati village and interviewed them about their situation. The women answered: Yes, they now had an income of their own. They also had some "assets": some cows, chickens, ducks. Their children went to schools. Ms. Clinton was satisfied. The women of Maishahati were obviously empowered. But she was not prepared for the next round of the interview, when the village women turned round and asked her the same question. Farida Akhter reported the following exchange of questions and answers between the women of Maishahati and Hillary Clinton:

"*Apa* [elder sister], do you have cows?"
"No, I have no cows."
"*Apa*, do you have your own income?"
"Well, formerly I used to have my own income. But since my husband became president and moved to the White House I have stopped earning my own money."
"How many children do you have?"
"One daughter."
"Would you like to have more children?"
"Yes, I would like to have one or two more children, but we are quite happy with our daughter Chelsea."

The women from Maishahati looked at each other and murmured, "Poor Hillary! She has no cow, no income of her own, she has only one daughter." In the eyes of the Maishahati women Hillary Clinton was not empowered. They felt sorry for her.

Source: Veronika Bennholdt-Thomsen and Maria Mies. *The Subsistence Perspective.* New York: Zed Press, 1999, 1–2.

❀   ❀   ❀

Mies, Bennholdt-Thomsen, and Von Werlhof observed that women's nonwage or subsistence work relied on the "commons"—land on which to grow food; clean water to use to bathe children, cook meals, and water livestock; timber to burn for fuel or fashion into shelter; oceans to fish; and public spaces (markets) and healthy communities free of violence or coercive taxation so that people could barter, share, and swap goods without fear of assault or expropriation. For proponents of the subsistence perspective, the health of the commons—of ecosystems and the environment, of communities and civil society—was crucial to the survival of households around the world. They argued that women have recognized this and have organized social movements to protect the commons and promote its sustainable use and development.[24]

This insight contributed to a new appreciation of grassroots and global environmental movements, which were seen as crucial to women's work and the economic survival of households. Work by Ann Leonard (*Seeds II*), Carolyn Sachs (*Gendered Fields*), and Richard Douthwaite (*Short Circuit*) showed how gender struggles, social movements, and the environment were related and how each relied on the other for success.[25]

These developments helped turn feminist development thinking upside down. In the 1970s, feminist scholars had argued that wage work was central to development and that women's unpaid work was of supplementary or marginal significance. But at the end of the century, feminist scholars argued that state subsidies and *wage* work now played an increasingly marginal and unstable economic role for most households and that various kinds of *nonwage* or *subsistence* work played an increasingly important role for households. What's more, scholars maintained, the defense and expansion of these "traditional" kinds of work helped lay the groundwork for genuine, sustainable, "alternative development." From this perspective, "development" begins at home, not in the market, and women, not men, play a central role in its realization. This view inverted postwar ideas about development.

REVERSING THE PRIORITIES OF DEVELOPMENT

Different feminist subsistence perspectives have emerged from feminists' examination of human needs and their reevaluation of social priorities, which became a necessity as indebtedness and impoverishment grew in the global South. Feminists and activists who analyzed the post-1975 situation argued that global capitalism had failed to provide living wages and good living conditions for most of the world's people. They then asked: what type of development do most people want? Feminist groups, especially those familiar with the independent-subsistence perspective, emphasized the need to place a priority on social reproduction, not production, as Dalla Costa explained in the following excerpt.

Along with environmental degradation, repression, economic violence, militarization, and ethnocide, . . . debt and what type of development have also become increasingly central themes in the debates of the various networks of women scholars who are active in studying the many aspects of human suffering, and militant in combating them. On one hand, there has been a growing worldwide awareness of how decisive these two factors are in determining the condition of women and their labor—and hence for social reproduction as a whole. On the other hand, in their historical role of responsibility for reproduction, in many situations, *women now represent the new outposts for interpretative insight, denunciation and initiative, in a reversal of priority from production to reproduction.* This was one of the results achieved in the early days of the feminist movement of the 1970s, whence it has come to represent the starting point for others, above all ecological and pacifist movements in the 1980s and early 1990s. In these movements, the women usually represent the driving force.

Source: Maria Rosa Dalla Costa. "Introduction." In Maria Rosa Dalla Costa and Giovanna Dalla Costa, eds. *Paying the Price: Women and the Politics of International Economic Strategy.* New York: Zed Books, 1995, 1–14, 11 [emphasis added].

At the same time, feminist scholars began to rethink relations between people in the West and people in the South. During most of the postwar period, government officials, business leaders, and representatives of international aid agencies and NGOs had thought that if poor people in the South followed instructions and changed their behavior, they would develop. But of course the debt crisis and globalization overturned this image. Some people in the South did what they were told by people in the North, and it ruined them. At the end of the century, feminists such as Mies were joined by a transnational group of scholars associated with Development Alternatives for Women Network (DAWN).[26] They argued that women in the South, not developmentalists in the North, had gained a critical perspective on social change that enabled them to develop strategies that could promote genuine development and that "individuals and grassroots groups in the North can use and develop DAWN's perspectives within their own contexts and share insights to enrich the DAWN process."[27]

Scholars associated with DAWN argued against advancing a singular "model" of development, as northern developmentalists had done, and insisted instead that there be a "diversity of feminisms, responsive to the different needs and concerns of different women, *and defined by them for themselves* [emphasis added]."[28] Further, they argued that diverse feminisms be *connected.* This view contrasted with the contention of postmodern scholars that efforts not be seen as connected because that led to "universalist" thinking.

For example, in *Feminism Without Borders,* Chandra Mohanty criticized the postmodern assertion that things should be seen as different and unconnected and insisted that connections between different groups be examined and located in a global, multicultural context.[29] Drawing on the work of Vandana Shiva and Grace Lee

Boggs, Mohanty argued that place-based civic activism leads to politics that connect marginalized communities to broad antiglobalization movements:

> This [civic to global activism] is evident in the example of women of color in the United States, as well as in Shiva's example of tribal women in the struggle against deforestation and for an intellectual commons. It is then the lives, experiences, and struggles of girls in the Two-Thirds World that demystify capitalism in its racial and sexual dimensions—and that provide productive and necessary avenues of theorizing and enacting anticapitalist resistance.[30]

Feminists need to examine changing relationships between women in the one-third and two-thirds worlds, or between world-minority women in the global North and the world-majority women in the global South. Feminist analysis reveals that globalization is reorganizing people's relationships through recolonization and that women's historically constructed understandings of global division contribute to new frameworks of international change.

> Globalization colonizes women's as well as men's lives around the world, and we need an anti-imperialist, anticapitalist, and contextualized feminist project to expose and make visible the various, overlapping forms of subjugation of women's lives. Activists and scholars must also identify and envision forms of collective resistance that women, especially in their different communities, enact in their everyday lives. It is their particular exploitation at this time, their particular epistemic privilege, as well as their particular forms of solidarity that can be the basis for reimagining a liberatory politics for the start of this century.[31]

This will require transnational feminist movements to address both capitalist profit making and social justice issues.

"Standpoint" feminists such as Patricia Hill Collins and Nancy Naples have urged activists to appreciate the collective strength that comes out of the experience with different standpoints, people who are located differently within hierarchical power relations.[32] Comprehensive standpoint feminists, such as Collins and Naples, include an examination of ongoing global and colonizing power relations as part of their analysis of intersecting gender, sexuality, racial, and class hierarchies.

In recent years, feminist scholars from the South and the North have argued that the success of each depends on the success of others. So, for example, a women's coffee cooperative in the South depends on the women's fair-trade NGO in the North; feminist environmentalists in the North who want to curb global warming depend on the efforts of grassroots groups to defend rain forest "commons" in the South.

More recently, proponents of the women, culture, and development (WCD) approach, which was first suggested by feminist scholars in 2003, have argued that critical development studies, feminist studies, and cultural studies be combined. Drawing on the work of Juliet Mitchell and Eli Zaretsky, WCD scholars have argued that "production and reproduction cannot be separated in the lives of most women."[33]

But although it is important to examine the entangled character of women's productive and reproductive lives, as WCD scholars do, men's gender relations must also be addressed. It is important to focus on gender transformations by and for women but also on transformations for men. Finally, it is important to examine community and global activism from a historical perspective that includes an appreciation of the environment, culture, and participatory activism.

READING

In *Feminism Without Borders,* Chandra Talpade Mohanty articulated a transnational, feminist intellectual and political framework that enables women and men in the one-third and two-thirds worlds to see how they are connected by local and global injustices and chains of economic exploitation. As she develops a critique of two common women's studies methodologies, she presents her approach to research and action, which she calls the Feminist Solidarity or Comparative Feminist Studies Model.[34]

NOTES

1. Margaret Benston, "The Political Economy of Women's Liberation," in Rosemark Hennessy and Chrys Ingraham, eds., *Materialist Feminism* (New York: Routledge, 1997), 17–23.

2. Ester Boserup, *Women's Role in Economic Development* (New York: St. Martin's Press, 1970).

3. The concept identified as "postcolonial" has been increasingly criticized because people continue to see evidence of ongoing coloniality and imperialism of various kinds. "Postcolonial," a concept that developed from postmodern analysis, emphasizes the radical break between the historical period when countries in the global South were formally colonized and the historical period when countries had become politically independent from European and other colonial powers. Scholars such as Andrea Smith have questioned the use of "postcolonial" because it fails to see diverse and ongoing forms of colonization. See Andrea Smith, *Conquest: Sexual Violence and American Indian Genocide* (Cambridge, MA: South End Press, 2005). We agree that imperialism and coloniality are ongoing and that the concept "postcolonial" has introduced confusion. World-systems scholars have stressed ongoing processes of imperialism or coloniality.

4. The term *Third World* was originally used during the Cold War to describe countries that were "nonaligned" politically and wanted to develop their own political and economic strategies for development, without being told what to do by the "First" capitalist world and the "Second" communist world. The political meaning of what it was to be a Third World country was slowly lost, and eventually it came to mean countries that were "poor." With the end of the Cold War, and the disappearance of much of the Second, communist world, the term has been abandoned.

5. Benston, "The Political Economy of Women's Liberation," 22.

6. Ibid., 23.

7. Mariarosa Dalla Costa and Selma James, "Women and the Subversion of the Community," in Hennessy and Ingraham, *Materialist Feminism,* 40.

8. Ibid., 41, 49–50.

9. Helen Saffioti, *Women in Class Society* (New York: Monthly Review Press, 1978).

10. Ibid., 4, 281–283.

11. Ibid., 282.

12. Helen I. Safa, *The Myth of the Male Breadwinner: Women and Industrialization in the Caribbean* (Boulder, CO: Westview Press, 1995).

13. Immanuel Wallerstein, *The Modern World-System: Capitalist Agriculture and the Origins of the European World-Economy in the Sixteenth Century* (New York: Academic Press, 1974).

14. As a graduate student in 1977, Dickinson was a founding member of the Households Research Group at the Fernand Braudel Center at Binghamton University.

15. Joan Smith, Immanuel Wallerstein, and Hans-Dieter Evers, *Households in the World-Economy* (Beverly Hills, CA: SAGE, 1984); Joan Smith and Immanuel Wallerstein, *Creating and Transforming Households: The Constraints of the World-Economy* (Cambridge: Cambridge University Press and La Maison des Sciences de l'Homme, 1992).

16. Smith and Wallerstein, *Creating and Transforming Households,* 7–9.

17. Torry D. Dickinson and Robert K. Schaeffer, *Fast Forward: Work, Gender, and Protest in a Changing World* (Lanham, MD: Rowman and Littlefield, 2001), 141.

18. Torry D. Dickinson, *Commonwealth: Self-Sufficiency and Work in American Communities, 1830 to 1993* (Lanham, MD: University Press of America, 1995); Torry Dickinson, "Gender Division Within the U.S. Working Class: Households in the Philadelphia Area, 1870–1945," in Smith, Wallerstein, and Evers, *Households in the World-Economy.*

19. Smith and Wallerstein, *Creating and Transforming Households,* 254.

20. Robert Schaeffer, "A Critique of 'New Class' Theorists: Towards a Theory of the Working Class in America," *Social Praxis* 4, nos. 1 and 2 (1977): 75–99.

21. Sidonie Smith and Julia Watson, eds., *De/colonizing the Subject: The Politics of Gender in Women's Autobiography* (Minneapolis: University of Minnesota Press, 1992); Naila Kabeer, *Reversed Realities: Gender Hierarchies in Development Thought* (New York: Verso, 1994); Inderpal Grewal and Caren Kaplan, eds., *Scattered Hegemonies: Postmodernity and Transnational Feminist Practice* (Minneapolis: University of Minnesota Press, 1994).

22. In the United States, fundamentalist Christians tend to be Protestant, though they have been joined in recent years by conservative Catholics and Jews, whereas in Western Europe, fundamentalist Christians tend to be conservative Catholics, as in France, Italy, and Poland.

23. Maria Mies, *Patriarchy and Accumulation on a World Scale: Women in the International Division of Labor* (London: Zed, 1984/1986); Veronika Bennholdt-Thomsen and Maria Mies, *The Subsistence Perspective: Beyond the Globalized Economy* (London: Zed, 1999); Maria Mies, Veronika Bennholdt-Thomsen, and Claudia Von Werlhof, *Women: The Last Colony* (London: Zed, 1998).

24. Von Werlhof later broke with Mies and Bennholdt-Thomsen, arguing that cooperatives did not assist women but instead increased women's workloads.

25. Ann Leonard, ed., *Seeds II: Supporting Women's Work Around the World* (New York: Feminist Press, 1995); Carolyn Sachs, *Gendered Fields: Rural Women, Agriculture, and the Environment* (Boulder, CO: Westview Press, 1996); Richard Douthwaite, *Short*

Circuit: Strengthening Local Economies in an Unstable World (Devon, England: Green Books, 1996).

26. See for example, Gita Sen and Caren Grown, *Development, Crises, and Alternative Visions: Third World Perspectives* (New York: Monthly Review Press, 1987).

27. Ibid., 12.

28. Ibid., 18–19.

29. Chandra Mohanty, *Feminism Without Borders: Decolonizing Theory, Practicing Solidarity* (Durham, NC: Duke University Press, 2003).

30. Ibid., 235.

31. Ibid., 236.

32. Nancy Naples, *Feminism and Methods* (New York: Routledge, 2004).

33. Kum-Kum Bhavnani, John Foran, and Priya Kurian, *Feminist Futures: Re-imagining Women, Culture, and Development* (London: Zed, 2003), 7. See Juliet Mitchell, *Women's Estate* (New York: Pantheon Books, 1971), and Eli Zaretsky, *Capitalism, the Family, and Personal Life* (New York: Harper and Row, 1976).

34. Chandra Talpade Mohanty, "Antiglobalization Pedagogies" from "'Under Western Eyes Revisited': Feminist Solidarity Through Anticapitalist Struggles," in Mohanty, *Feminism Without Borders*, 238–245.

ANTIGLOBALIZATION PEDAGOGIES

Chandra Talpade Mohanty

Let me turn to the struggles over the dissemination of a feminist cross-cultural knowledge base through pedagogical strategies "internationalizing" the women's studies curriculum. The problem of "the (gendered) color line" remains, but is more easily seen today as developments of transnational and global capital. While I choose to focus on women's studies curricula, my arguments hold for curricula in any discipline or academic field that seeks to internationalize or globalize its curriculum. I argue that the challenge for "internationalizing" women's studies is no different from the one involved in "racializing" women's studies in the 1980s, for very similar politics of knowledge come into play here.[1]

So the question I want to foreground is the politics of knowledge in bridging the "local" and the "global" in women's studies. How we teach the "new" scholarship in women's studies is at least as important as the scholarship itself in the struggles over knowledge and citizenship in the U.S. academy. After all, the way we construct curricula and the pedagogies we use to put such curricula into practice tell a story—or tell many stories. It is the way we position historical narratives of experience in relation to each other, the way we theorize relationality as both historical and simultaneously singular and collective that determines how and what we learn when we cross cultural and experiential borders.

Drawing on my own work with U.S. feminist academic communities,[2] I describe three pedagogical models used in "internationalizing" the women's studies curriculum and analyze the politics of knowledge at work. Each of these perspectives is grounded in particular conceptions of the local and the global, of women's agency, and of national identity, and each curricular model presents different stories and ways of crossing borders and building bridges. I suggest that a "comparative feminist studies" or "feminist solidarity" model is the most useful and productive pedagogical strategy for feminist cross-cultural work. It is this particular model that provides a way to theorize a complex relational understanding of experience, location, and history such that feminist cross-cultural work moves through the specific context to construct a real notion of universal and of democratization rather than colonization. It is through this model that we can put into practice the idea of "common differences" as the basis for deeper solidarity across differences and unequal power relations.

FEMINIST-AS-TOURIST MODEL

This curricular perspective could also be called the "feminist as international consumer" or, in less charitable terms, the "white women's burden or colonial discourse" model.[3] It involves a pedagogical strategy in which brief forays are made into non-Euro-American cultures, and particular sexist cultural practices addressed from an otherwise Eurocentric women's studies gaze. In other words, the "add women as global victims or powerful women and stir" perspective. This is a perspective in which the primary Euro-American narrative of the syllabus remains untouched, and examples from non-Western or Third World/South cultures are used to supplement and "add" to this narrative. The story here is quite old. The effects of this strategy are that students and teachers are left with a clear sense of the difference and distance between the local (defined as self, nation, and Western) and the global (defined as other, non-Western, and transnational). Thus the local is always grounded in nationalist assumptions—the United States or Western European nation-state provides a normative context. This strategy leaves power relations and hierarchies untouched since ideas about center and margin are reproduced along Eurocentric lines.

For example, in an introductory feminist studies course, one could include the obligatory day or week on dowry deaths in India, women workers in Nike factories in Indonesia, or precolonial matriarchies in West Africa, while leaving the fundamental identity of the Euro-American feminist on her way to liberation untouched. Thus Indonesian workers in Nike factories or dowry deaths in India stand in for the totality of women in these cultures. These women are not seen in their everyday lives (as Euro-American women are)—just in these stereotypical terms. Difference in the case of non-Euro-American women is thus congealed, not seen contextually with all of its contradictions. This pedagogical strategy for crossing cultural and geographical borders is based on a modernist paradigm, and the bridge between the local and the global becomes in fact a predominantly self-interested chasm. This perspective confirms the sense of the "evolved U.S./Euro feminist." While there is now more consciousness about not using an "add and stir" method in teaching about race and U.S. women of color, this does not appear to be the case in "internationalizing" women's studies. Experience in this context is assumed to be static and frozen into U.S.- or Euro-centered categories. Since in this paradigm feminism is always/already constructed as Euro-American in origin and development, women's lives and struggles outside this geographical context only serve to confirm or contradict this originary feminist (master) narrative. This model is the pedagogical counterpart of the orientalizing and colonizing Western feminist scholarship of the past decades. In fact it may remain the predominant model at this time. Thus implicit in this pedagogical strategy is the crafting of the "Third World difference," the creation of monolithic images of Third World/South women. This contrasts with images of Euro-American women who are vital, changing, complex, and central subjects within such a curricular perspective.

FEMINIST-AS-EXPLORER MODEL

This particular pedagogical perspective originates in area studies, where the "foreign" woman is the object and subject of knowledge and the larger intellectual project is entirely about countries other than the United States. Thus, here the local and the global are both defined as non-Euro-American. The focus on the international implies that it exists outside the U.S. nation-state. Women's, gender, and feminist issues are based on spatial/ geographical and temporal/historical categories located *elsewhere.* Distance from "home" is fundamental to the definition of international in this framework. This strategy can result in students and teachers being left with a notion of difference and separateness, a sort of "us and them" attitude, but unlike the tourist model, the explorer perspective can provide a deeper, more contextual understanding of feminist issues in discretely defined geographical and cultural spaces. However, unless these discrete spaces are taught in relation to one another, the story told is usually a cultural relativist one, meaning that differences between cultures are discrete and relative with no real connection or common basis for evaluation. The local and the global are here collapsed into the international that by definition excludes the United States. If the dominant discourse is the discourse of cultural *relativism,* questions of power, agency, justice, and common criteria for critique and evaluation are silenced.[4]

In women's studies curricula this pedagogical strategy is often seen as the most culturally sensitive way to "internationalize" the curriculum. For instance, entire courses on "Women in Latin America" or "Third World Women's Literature" or "Postcolonial Feminism" are added on to the predominantly U.S.-based curriculum as a way to "global-ize" the feminist knowledge base. These courses can be quite sophisticated and complex studies, but they are viewed as entirely separate from the intellectual project of U.S. race and ethnic studies.[5] The United States is not seen as part of "area studies," as white is not a color when one speaks of people of color. This is probably related to the particular history of institutionalization of area studies in the U.S. academy and its ties to U.S. imperialism. Thus areas to be studied/conquered are "out there," never within the United States. The fact that area studies in U.S. academic settings were federally funded and conceived as having a political project in the service of U.S. geopolitical interests suggests the need to examine the contemporary interests of these fields, especially as they relate to the logic of global capitalism. In addition, as Ella Shohat argues, it is time to "reimagine the study of regions and cultures in a way that transcends the conceptual borders inherent in the global cartography of the cold war" (2001, 1271). The field of American studies is an interesting location to examine here, especially since its more recent focus on U.S. imperialism. However, American studies rarely falls under the purview of "area studies."

The problem with the feminist-as-explorer strategy is that globalization is an economic, political, and ideological phenomenon that actively brings the world and its various communities under connected and interdependent discursive and material regimes. The lives of women are connected and interdependent, albeit not the same, no matter which geographical area we happen to live in.

Separating area studies from race and ethnic studies thus leads to understanding or teaching about the global as a way of not addressing internal racism, capitalist hegemony, colonialism, *and* heterosexualization as *central* to processes of global domination, exploitation, and resistance. Global or international is thus understood apart from racism as if racism were not central to processes of globalization and relations of rule at this time. An example of this pedagogical strategy in the context of the larger curriculum is the usual separation of "world cultures" courses from race and ethnic studies courses. Thus identifying the kinds of representations of (non-Euro-American) women mobilized by this pedagogical strategy, and the relation of these representations to implicit images of First World/North women are important foci for analysis. What kind of power is being exercised in this strategy? What kinds of ideas of agency and struggle are being consolidated? What are the potential effects of a kind of cultural relativism on our understandings of the differences and commonalities among communities of women around the world? Thus the feminist-as-explorer model has its own problems, and I believe this is an inadequate way of building a feminist cross-cultural knowledge base because in the context of an interwoven world with clear directionalities of power and domination, cultural relativism serves as an apology for the exercise of power.

THE FEMINIST SOLIDARITY OR COMPARATIVE FEMINIST STUDIES MODEL

This curricular strategy is based on the premise that the local and the global are not defined in terms of physical geography or territory but exist simultaneously and constitute each other. It is then the links, the relationships, between the local and the global that are foregrounded, and these links are conceptual, material, temporal, contextual, and so on. This framework assumes a comparative focus and analysis of the directionality of power no matter what the subject of the women's studies course is—and it assumes both distance and proximity (specific/universal) as its analytic strategy.

Differences and commonalities thus exist in relation and tension with each other in all contexts. What is emphasized are relations of mutuality, co-responsibility, and common interests, anchoring the idea of feminist solidarity. For example, within this model, one would not teach a U.S. women of color course with additions on Third World/South or white women, but a comparative course that shows the interconnectedness of the histories, experiences, and struggles of U.S. women of color, white women, and women from the Third World/South. By doing this kind of comparative teaching that is attentive to power, each historical experience illuminates the experiences of the others. Thus, the focus is not just on the intersections of race, class, gender, nation, and sexuality in different communities of women but on mutuality and coimplication, which suggests attentiveness to the interweaving of the histories of these communities. In addition the focus is simultaneously on individual and collective experiences of oppression and exploitation and of struggle and resistance.

Students potentially move away from the "add and stir" and the relativist "separate but equal" (or different) perspective to the coimplication/solidarity one. This solidarity perspective requires understanding the historical and experiential specificities and differences of women's lives as well as the historical and experiential connections between women from different national, racial, and cultural communities. Thus it suggests organizing syllabi around social and economic processes and histories of various communities of women in particular substantive areas like sex work, militarization, environmental justice, the prison/industrial complex, and human rights, and looking for points of contact and connection as well as disjunctures. It is important to always foreground not just the connections of domination but those of struggle and resistance as well.

In the feminist solidarity model the One-Third/Two-Thirds paradigm makes sense. Rather than Western/Third World, or North/South, or local/ global seen as oppositional and incommensurate categories, the One-Third/Two-Thirds differentiation allows for teaching and learning about points of connection and distance among and between communities of women marginalized and privileged along numerous local and global dimensions. Thus the very notion of inside/outside necessary to the distance between local/global is transformed through the use of a One-Third/Two-Thirds paradigm, as both categories must be understood as containing difference/similarities, inside/outside, and distance/proximity. Thus sex work, militarization, human rights, and so on can be framed in their multiple local and global dimensions using the One-Third/Two-Thirds, social minority/social majority paradigm. I am suggesting then that we look at the women's studies curriculum in its entirety and that we attempt to use a comparative feminist studies model wherever possible.[6]

I refer to this model as the feminist solidarity model because, besides its focus on mutuality and common interests, it requires one to formulate questions about connection and disconnection between activist women's movements around the world. Rather than formulating activism and agency in terms of discrete and disconnected cultures and nations, it allows us to frame agency and resistance across the borders of nation and culture. I think feminist pedagogy should not simply expose students to a particularized academic scholarship but that it should also envision the possibility of activism and struggle outside the academy. Political education through feminist pedagogy should teach active citizenship in such struggles for justice.

My recurring question is how pedagogies can supplement, consolidate, or resist the dominant logic of globalization. How do students learn about the inequities among women and men around the world? For instance, traditional liberal and liberal feminist pedagogies disallow historical and comparative thinking, radical feminist pedagogies often singularize gender, and Marxist pedagogy silences race and gender in its focus on capitalism. I look to create pedagogies that allow students to see the complexities, singularities, and interconnections between communities of women such that power, privilege, agency, and dissent can be made visible and engaged with.

In an instructive critique of postcolonial studies and its institutional location, Arif Dirlik argues that the particular institutional history of postcolonial studies, as well as its conceptual emphases on the historical and local as against the systemic and the global, permit its assimilation into the logic of globalism.[7] While Dirlik somewhat overstates his argument, deradicalization and assimilation should concern those of us involved in the feminist project. Feminist pedagogies of internationalization need an adequate response to globalization. Both Eurocentric and cultural relativist (postmodernist) models of scholarship and teaching are easily assimilated within the logic of late capitalism because this is fundamentally a logic of seeming decentralization and accumulation of differences. What I call the comparative feminist studies/feminist solidarity model on the other hand potentially counters this logic by setting up a paradigm of historically and culturally specific "common differences" as the basis for analysis and solidarity. Feminist pedagogies of antiglobalization can tell alternate stories of difference, culture, power, and agency. They can begin to theorize experience, agency, and justice from a more cross-cultural lens.[8]

After almost two decades of teaching feminist studies in U.S. classrooms, it is clear to me that the way we theorize experience, culture, and subjectivity in relation to histories, institutional practice, and collective struggles determines the kind of stories we tell in the classroom. If these varied stories are to be taught such that students learn to democratize rather than colonize the experiences of different spatially and temporally located communities of women, neither a Eurocentric nor a cultural pluralist curricular practice will do. In fact narratives of historical experience are crucial to political thinking not because they present an unmediated version of the "truth" but because they can destabilize received truths and locate debate in the complexities and contradictions of historical life. It is in this context that postpositivist realist theorizations of experience, identity, and culture become useful in constructing curricular and pedagogical narratives that address as well as combat globalization.[9] These realist theorizations explicitly link a historical materialist understanding of social location to the theorization of epistemic privilege and the construction of social identity, thus suggesting the complexities of the narratives of marginalized peoples in terms of relationality rather than separation. These are the kinds of stories we need to weave into a feminist solidarity pedagogical model.

NOTES

1. While the initial push for "internationalization" of the curriculum in U.S. higher education came from the federal government's funding of area studies programs during the cold war, In the post–cold war period it is private foundations like the MacArthur, Rockefeller, and Ford foundations that have been instrumental in this endeavor—especially in relation to the women's studies curriculum.

2. This work consists of participating in a number of reviews of women's studies programs, reviewing essays, syllabi, and manuscripts on feminist pedagogy and curricula, and topical workshops and conversations with feminist scholars and teachers over the last ten years.

3. Ella Shohat refers to this as the "sponge/additive" approach that extends centered paradigms to "others" and produces a "homogeneous feminist master narrative." See Shohat 2001, 1269–72.

4. For an incisive critique of cultural relativism and its epistemological underpinnings see Mohanty 1997, chapter 5.

5. It is also important to examine and be cautious about the latent nationalism of race and ethnic studies and of women's and gay and lesbian studies in the United States.

6. A new anthology contains some good examples of what I am referring to as a feminist solidarity or comparative feminist studies model. See Lay, Monk, and Rosenfelt 2002.

7. See Dirlik, "Borderlands Radicalism," in Dirlik 1994. See the distinction between "postcolonial studies" and "postcolonial thought": while postcolonial thought has much to say about questions of local and global economies, postcolonial studies has not always taken these questions on board (Loomba 1998–99). I am using Ania Loomba's formulation

here, but many progressive critics of postcolonial studies have made this basic point. It is an important distinction, and I think it can be argued in the case of feminist thought and feminist studies (women's studies) as well.

8. While I know no other work that conceptualizes this pedagogical strategy in the ways I am doing here, my work is very similar to that of scholars like Ella Shohat, Jacqui Alexander, Susan Sanchez-Casal, and Amie Macdonald.

9. See especially the work of Satya Mohanty, Paula Moya, Linda Alcoff, and Shari Stone-Mediatore.

3

Feminist Pathways to Democracy and Equality

INTRODUCTION: FEMINIST PATHWAYS TO DEMOCRACY AND EQUALITY, 1990 TO THE PRESENT

Around the world, women engage in unpaid subsistence work to survive. But the cooperative and reciprocal relations associated with these activities are important not only for the economic survival of households; they are important politically for the creation of participatory democracy. People can use their experience with economic forms of collaboration to develop a participatory, democratic politics in local groups and communities. Shared economic experiences can be a model for shared political practice. Feminist-led groups practice social change by redefining democracy and equality from the ground up, by connecting with other movements, and by helping to lead environmental, peace, and other movements. Activists with Development Alternatives for Women Network (DAWN) have noted that "increasing intersections of analysis and actual interconnections and collaboration [have taken] place between the movements for economic justice and people-centered social development" and with movements for peace, civil liberties, and democracy.[1] Local and global groups that engaged in "participatory action," which consists of knowledge-seeking "research," education, planning, and action, can contribute to democracy and equality.

When members of participatory action groups decide by themselves how to identify problems, devise solutions, and carry out change, they challenge traditional notions of democracy and the public good. Feminists who connect social change in the home with change in the community, at work, and in civic politics challenge the idea that private lives and public politics should be separated. Taking Chantal Mouffe's critique of liberal democracy as a starting place, Robin Truth Goodman argued that people can reverse the historical separation between private and public spheres.[2] Goodman argued that civic education can help people overcome the separation between private lives and the public good and learn how to change the system. When inclusive movements use participatory action as a way to understand and change society, they can reintegrate private and public spheres, define democracy from the ground up, create a powerful form of direct civic engagement, and establish a civic egalitarianism.

In recent years, participatory change has been carried out by diverse kinds of research-based, grassroots, and global groups. These groups practice a face-to-face form of democracy that asks participants both to explain what is bothering them and to listen to what is said in a "deep" way. As Sally Hacker learned in her ethnographic research, "deep listening" can reveal how these groups can move forward, how the problem can be introduced to wider audiences, and what they might do to bring about change.[3]

Participatory action groups consist of people with different and multiple identities. Their political practices are informed by the reciprocal and redistributive economic relations that sustain households. The collaborative unpaid work done by women in households (see Chapter 2) provides a kind of economic model for democratic political practices, which are also based on shared experience and collaboration.

Janet Conway argued that every agent occupies multiple subject positions, a point made by Chantal Mouffe.[4] Because participatory action groups typically consist of people with multiple subject positions, they can have multiple impacts on society. If these multilayered groups engage in multiple, simultaneous rebellions against dominant, intersecting hierarchies, they can redefine democracy and take steps that complement the actions taken by other groups and promote change in new areas. Movements grow out of dynamically emerging collective identities, as Sonia Alvarez has shown.[5] And these multi-identity movements express both the full array of intersecting inequalities and an integrated combination of movements and participatory actions *against* hierarchy and *for* new ways of governing, working, and living together.

In the past, projects initiated by "outsiders" or "invaders"—terms the educator Paulo Freire used to describe well-meaning but exogenous efforts to promote social change—typically failed to promote long-term, democratic change.[6] But sustained partnerships among grassroots groups, civic organizations, and feminist NGOs can promote economic literacy, facilitate the exchange of knowledge about political-economic change, and enable women to "link their everyday struggles for survival with the need for macro policy changes."[7] When feminist groups create fair global production and marketing networks, they simultaneously lay the groundwork for regional sustainability and self-sufficiency.[8] If grassroots groups, interregional networks, and global organizations cooperate, they can promote long-term, inclusive, alternative development that meets people's needs.

Feminist-led projects can also advance social justice by "slowly and painfully reempowering forms of social accountability that escape the market," Sandra Harding has argued.[9] But for this to happen, it will be necessary for feminists involved in gender, environment, and sustainable development (GESD) to combine indigenous knowledge from the South with technological knowledge bases in the North.[10] Sustainable development will require a "world of sciences," she argued, one that feminist and related social justice movements around the world will need to construct and redeploy.[11]

THE RE-CREATION OF DEMOCRACY AND EQUALITY

There are many useful ways to start social change research. Some groups start with a grounded analysis of what is going on in their everyday lives. Others begin by examining and interpreting local-to-global histories and see how they have shaped people, constrained them, generated intersectional social action knowledge, provided skills and resources, and made it possible for people to envision a better future. To understand social change, Dorothy Smith has written, it is important that people see themselves as part of their social reality, not external to it. According to Smith, the past social construction of society "shapes the direction and framework for the future."[12] She said, "[W]hat we build interlocks with what others build; we build what we know how to build with the materials that come to hand. None the less, we move into the future as into a building, the walls, floors, and roof of which we put together with one another as we go into it. It is an ongoing creation of and in *action*."[13]

The process of building a new society is a global one, given the fact that global society created the architecture of the society we inhabit. For activists, building a new society requires moving between thought and action, learning how to use their ideas and their own experiences to build feminist, democratic, and egalitarian social relations at grassroots, regional, and global levels. Dorothy Smith has argued that this reconstruction process is facilitated by "our [radical] experience in learning with each other how to speak together as women."[14]

FEMINIST APPROACHES TO RESEARCH

Feminist research reflects the two intellectual traditions that have shaped women's studies: academic studies and democratic social action studies. Feminist social change always contains some intellectual work, but academic work is often done without any engagement in the intellectual work of activism. Both types of intellectual work inform each other, and academic and social action research can be strengthened by linking these two traditions together. In both the university and the wider community (of which the university is just one part), doing good feminist research means joining together academic research, which examines social change related to gender and other intersecting hierarchies, and activist research, which facilitates and carries out social change. Feminist research examines both epistemology (or the study of knowledge) and ontology (or the study of material life and grounded "beingness" in daily life). The following selection provides an introductory overview to how feminist · research might be taught in the classroom.

With the development, growth and transformations in feminist epistemologies, feminist researchers draw on a wide range of research methods to conduct their work. From narrative analyses to in-depth interviews, ethnographies and content analyses, oral histories and discourse analyses, surveys and experiments, feminists apply a particular methodology when conducting their research that reflects their unique vision. They view research holistically—as a process, and thus pay attention to the synergy between the context of discovery and the context of justification. Feminists have changed conceptions of what truth is, who can be a knower, what can be known. By creating situated and partial knowledges, by attending to the intersection of gender and other categories of difference such as race, class and sexual preference in its analysis of social reality, feminist research is open to new knowledge—asking new questions.... This is accomplished in many ways. There are multiple feminisms, not simply one.

Mostly, feminists conduct research for women. Whether it be by seeking knowledge from and about women in order to record their valuable life experiences, or to change women's lives through social policy, a feminist methodology aims at creating knowledge that is beneficial to women and other minorities.... In this vein many feminists are social activists seeking to use their research to better the social position of women. While feminist scholarship varies in epistemological position and research, a feminist approach to research helps give voice to the experiences, concerns, attitudes, and needs of women. Feminists working in and developing emergent traditions seek to go farther than giving voice to Others and actually aim at disrupting social systems of oppression by utilizing the complex standpoints cultivated by such systems.

Source: Sharlene Nagy Hesse-Biber, Patricia Leavy, and Michelle L. Yaiser. "Feminist Approaches to Research as *Process*: Reconceptualizing Epistemology, Methodology, Method." In Sharlene Nagy Hesse-Biber, Patricia Leavy, and Michelle L. Yaiser, eds. *Feminist Perspectives on Social Research.* New York: Oxford University Press, 2004, 3–26, 22.

But women-to-women communication is just one aspect that needs to be developed. The expression of the imperialized/colonized, racialized, cross-gendered, and sexualized parts of ourselves must also be encouraged. Part of this process involves seeing and redefining who we are as individuals and how we define ourselves as social beings. Social change is a radical, personal-to-global process. Nancy Fraser offered this insight about pragmatic theories that can contribute to change: "[P]ragmatic theories insist on the social context and social practice of communication, and they study a plurality of historically changing discursive sites and practices. As a result, these theories offer us the possibility of thinking of social identities as complex, changing, and discursively constructed."[15]

Democratic and egalitarian organizing across intersecting social groups has been an effective way to fight global racism. Women's informal networks and kin-ship groups have helped build grassroots democracy. As the antiapartheid struggles in South Africa and the civil rights movement in the U.S. South demonstrated, women used new definitions of democracy and equality to tackle oppression. They made their own "freedomways" by joining cross-gender organizations, forming autonomous women's groups, and articulating their new citizenship as individuals within families, neighborhoods, mutual aid organizations (such as churches and savings groups), and antiracist groups (such as the National Association for the Advancement of Colored People [NAACP], the African National Congress [ANC], and black consciousness groups). In South African townships, informal women's networks coalesced into pro-woman, antiracist, Manyano collectives. These grassroots groups led campaigns against the "24–7" (twenty-four hours a day, seven days a week) pass system that white rulers imposed on black women and men to control their movements. They struggled against the expropriation of land and the forced removals of black residents and against apartheid laws that provided a good formal education for white children and consigned black children to inferior schools.[16] In South Africa, black women redefined democratic political power by connecting informal household and community groups with new organizations.

Much the same occurred in the United States. The 1955–1956 Montgomery bus boycott, a boycott modeled in part on South African bus boycotts in the late 1940s, relied on the informal networks created by women church members who had long organized meals, carpools, and services for people in the community. These informal networks and church-based social clubs were run in a democratic fashion that relied on a consensus approach to decisionmaking. The infrastructure of the boycott was rooted in the unpaid subsistence work that women in the church had long done for people in the community. They were joined, during the boycott, by educational and legal nongovernmental organizations such as the Highlander Center, a labor education school in Tennessee where Rosa Parks was trained, and where the NAACP provided legal advice. The formal political organization that ran the bus boycott grew out of informal women's networks and diverse political organizations that already existed, and the democratic politics they practiced was informed by long-standing, consensus-based democracy.[17] In both the U.S. South and South Africa, women's groups used their own experiences and practices to challenge the system and to advance equality through grassroots democracy.

In both the South and the North, inclusive feminist groups have changed individual lives, social networks, and global relations in ways that establish demo-cratic decisionmaking and social equality. One way that women-led groups have accomplished this has been by using democratic decisionmaking and working toward inclusiveness, a process that has taken many forms. Sonia Alvarez has argued that the transnationalization of feminisms since 1975 has meant that many grassroots movements have built "transborder connections from the bottom up."[18] Feminisms are diverse. They reflect not only the relational context in which they have emerged but also the influence of transnational movements. In Latin America, Alvarez has argued, "an internationalist identity-solidarity prevailed in the 'encuentro-like' intraregional feminist activism of the 1980s and 1990s."[19]

Feminist and other new social movements have reinvented revolution, according to Gail Omvedt and a group of feminist researchers.[20] This powerful force for change emerged from urban, autonomous movements that addressed the neglect of gender inequality and sexual violence in anticaste and anticlass movements. Women's autonomous movements have tried to address women's concerns in farmer and environmental groups outside of political parties and leftist organizations. These intersectional feminist groups are "antisystemic" because they are opposed to caste and patriarchy and committed to building a "nonlooting, sustainable society."[21] This new feminist approach challenges not just one but all of the intersecting relations of exploitation. "It redefines exploitation to include issues of caste, gender, rural livelihoods, and the environment; it develops new participatory and nonhierarchical organizations; and it articulates new understandings of development that question the industrial/capitalist international model and provide community-based alternatives based on equality and justice."[22]

Many women's movements in India draw on women's experiences and skills to end their oppression. They move between integrated, holistic social change theories about production, reproduction, material life, and spiritual life and the implementation of new forms of activism.[23] The mutual development of social change theories that are informed by social action projects is referred to as "movement-driven analysis." Movement-driven analysis is a critical part of participatory action research, as it has been defined by Paulo Freire and process-oriented feminists who have engaged in ongoing learning about effective social change strategies.

Movement-driven analysis can be used, for example, to develop strategies for delinking from imperialist global structures and creating new networks that promote greater regional self-sufficiency. "To be effective, the delinking process must begin at the grassroots level of the local communities," argued D. L. Sheth.[24] According to Sheth, nonviolence and noncooperation were used by Mahatma Gandhi as a means of undermining the legitimacy of colonial power. This noncooperation and delinking process takes movements through a "series of dualisms" that allows a new set of social relations to grow outside of the imperial realm.[25] An analogy can be made between delinking from colonial rule and delinking from neocolonial relations that tie North and South together. For feminist alternative development to become established over the long run, it would be critical for inclusive feminist groups in the North and South to delink from relations that historically have bound together areas on an unequal basis and to build sustainable, egalitarian relations. Caribbean feminist groups that have engaged in multilayered, dualistic politics to promote social transformation have learned that it is critical to "continuously devise political strategies informed by a commitment to gender justice."[26]

Rather than waiting for governments to promote democracy and equality, social change makers have redefined democracy by networking with other groups in the

South and North and taking local and global actions that promote new ways of living. Local organizations should take the lead, now that human rights and "globalization from below" have been introduced by transnational movements and proponents of the global women's agenda established at the Beijing conference, Radhika Coomaraswamy has argued. "Individuals and groups at the local level have become an essential part of an international civil society," she maintained.[27]

BUILDING FEMINIST DEMOCRACY AND EQUALITY THROUGH PARTICIPATORY ACTION

Feminists have led a cultural and economic revolution against violent intersecting hierarchies by engaging in participatory actions that address the concerns of diverse social movements. Contemporary grassroots and global activists are nurturing new forms of local and global power as they redefine the scope of politics in broad, intersecting, democratic, and participatory ways. Participatory action groups, which in the past have imagined that gender doesn't matter, have been enhanced in recent years by the inclusion of people who address gender and sexuality. And feminist participatory action research has been enhanced by practices that have addressed male privilege, sexual privilege, and racial/colonial violence. Women's leadership in alternative development has bolstered efforts to challenge authorities, advance alternatives, and help people gain confidence in their ability to analyze, research, and build a more just society.

The refining of feminist participatory action methodologies can help activists build inclusive movements by defining alternative development as part of feminism and by embedding feminist actions within alternative development. This means linking democratic and inclusive needs assessments with women-inclusive program planning, gender-sensitive project implementation, and an ongoing feminist evaluation of alternative development strategies.

The parallel worlds of gender and development and participatory development need to be more tightly integrated, Andrea Cornwall has argued. Both aspects of change involve the expansion of democratic decisionmaking and the extension of people's ability to act. Cornwall argued that "participatory research is fundamentally about the right to speak."[28] To make a long-term difference, she maintained, alternative development needs to grow out of women's and other disenfranchised groups' engagement with change: "[P]articipatory development must engage with the questions of difference: to effectively tackle poverty, it must go beyond 'the poor' as a generic category, and to engage with the diversity of women's and men's experiences of poverty and powerlessness."[29] Women and men must see their concerns as being broader than gender. Social change practices are strongest when both gender groups claim an equal and broad interest in all areas of transformation.

Historically, it has been a challenge for grassroots groups to engage both gender groups on all issues. For example, in India's Joint Forest Management (JFM) program, where community participants gained access to the forest by serving on forest management committees, women faced cultural taboos about speaking out and were denied the right to collect firewood from a protected area of the forest. According to Bina Agarwal, a scholar who studied the project, women complained, "What forest? . . . Since the men have started protecting it, they don't even allow us to look at it!"[30] "[S]imply including women will not in itself enable them to exercise their agency in decision-making arenas. Strategies are instead needed to increase women's confidence and awareness of their rights, in order for them to be more assertive in joining such committees and to speak out."[31] For this, she suggested, the presence of a gender-progressive NGO, especially a women's organization, is a major factor: membership in such organizations, she argued, makes women more self-confident and assertive and more vocal in mixed gatherings. It may help to have the involvement of feminist NGOs that address both women's concerns *and* women's, men's, and children's concerns, which are related to multiple, simultaneous dimensions of difference.

Inclusive groups need to take on gender, sexuality, racial and ethnic, linguistic and religious, class, and global location privileges and disadvantages simultaneously. Advocacy and conflict resolution are critical parts of challenging privilege and ending exclusion. Even when gender and age have been addressed in successful ways, feminists have sometimes forgotten to address class differences. By specifically addressing male *heterosexual* privilege in households and in intimate heterosexual relationships (not just male privilege in society), one participatory women's project in South Africa became more effective at ending male violence and accessing male wages. Cornwall referred to Kabeer's conclusion that development organizations and feminist movements need to do more than just promote gender equity. Women and members of excluded groups need to benefit from a project's success and "do so on terms which respect and promote their ability to exercise choice."[32] Work and cultural relations need to be changed so that marginal people can speak, be heard, and participate in alternative development. If they are excluded, privileged and powerful people will direct the course of social change.

What lessons have been learned about women and participatory action, and how do these relate to alternative development? In some cases, alternative development has been advanced when women and marginal men gained new skills in advocacy, conflict resolution, and assertiveness training. It has not been enough to introduce new training programs and place women on key committees. Cornwall has argued that the capabilities of women and members of other marginal groups need to be strengthened so that these actors become "makers and shakers" and not just "users and choosers."[33] At a recent fair trade summit sponsored by Equal Exchange in 2006, small producers from Latin America described this as the difference between actively "driving" change with others and passively "riding" along, like passengers who watch an unfair world go by. As Cornwall said in her study of women and participatory development, ultimately equitable development is about changing *all* the relations of power. This means dismantling the hierarchical matrix of local and global power, practicing democratic engagement, and constructing new ways of living.

❀   ❀   ❀

USING PARTICIPATORY EDUCATION TO
ADDRESS POWER DIFFERENCES

Feminists and others engage in "participatory education" for change when they have identified shared reasons for working on common concerns and issues. In the following selection, Andrea Cornwall suggested that feminists and other activists get away from organizing as women (or as any group with a specific gender, racial, or other identity). To help people work together to end power imbalances, she suggested that people engage in participatory education because they all need empowerment. This empowerment focus encourages men along with women to fight sexism and racism, and it encourages women to work with men to help end social injustices, which leads to political crossovers.

It is important to recognize that people from diverse social backgrounds sometimes work together to address common concerns. Change makers may come from diverse gender, ethnic/racial, class, and global location groups. Although they may have grown up in different countries, neighborhoods, and school settings, they work together to end society's injustices, which touch them in different ways. Participatory activists usually reject many of the social categories that have been manufactured by global society. Getting people to build new relations together and to relink themselves through connections that humanize each other are essential parts of contemporary participatory education.

Shifting the focus from fixed identities to positions of power and powerlessness opens up new possibilities for addressing issues of equity. In practical development terms, this shift implies more of a role for participatory approaches to explore, analyze, and work with the differences that people identify with, rather than identifying the needs of predetermined categories of people. This approach calls for sensitivity to local dimensions of difference and works with these differences through building on identifications rather than superimposed identities.... In this way, concerns that are conventionally seen as gender issues—such as violence against women—can become points of identification that some women, and some men, can mobilize around as entry points for change....

This outlook would not preclude a direct focus on issues that women in general might commonly identify with, such as, for example, property rights. It would not require abandoning completely the important struggle for women's rights. But this approach would help move beyond the assumptions that all women identify with gender issues and that bringing about changes is a zero-sum game in which women in general are pitted against men in general. Doing so would also recognize that some men may be just as affronted by the exclusion of women and may be important allies in combating its effects; and that some men are themselves excluded from development initiatives that appear to benefit men in general. Equally, this change would serve to tackle some of the consequences of defining interventions in terms that fail to embrace the needs of women and men who fall outside the boundaries treated by assumptions about "women's needs," as is the case in domains like reproductive health....

Changing the frame to focus on relations of power and positions of power and powerlessness offers an entry point for rethinking approaches to gender and participation. While tensions ... continue to provide obstacles to making participation in development more sensitive to difference, they also offer opportunities for bridge-building that can make the most of points of connection between GAD [Gender and Development] and participatory development. The myths and assumptions that underlie approaches to gender and participation have served important purposes in putting these issues on the development agenda. The time has come, however, to move beyond imposing the straitjacket of the categories and concepts that comes with conventional approaches to gender, or superimposing myths of community on the contested terrain of participatory development. To realize the potential of shared commitment to voice and choice, new alliances are needed that can both acknowledge the diversity of relations, institutions, and interactions that sustain poverty and powerlessness and seek new ways to bring about change. The challenge ahead lies in how to refashion our tools and reformulate our strategies to capture these opportunities and to make more of a difference.

Source: Andrea Cornwall. "Making a Difference? Gender and Participatory Development." In Shara Razavi, ed. *Shifting Burdens: Gender and Agrarian Change Under Neoliberalism.* Bloomfield, CT: Kumarian Press, 2002, 197–231, 197.

By using participatory action processes, Peggy Antrobus has argued, feminists have "developed the capacity to take responsibility for work that [they could carry out] while holding the government accountable for those areas which were deemed to be the responsibility of the state."[34] As the state cuts back services to working people, feminist groups have used grassroots democracy to organize volunteer efforts to provide services, an effort that helps create new, noncapitalist governing practices.

According to feminist ethnographer Lourdes Arizpe, action research was a methodological innovation that provided a solution to the problem that researchers from the North experienced when they conducted ethnographic research on disenfranchised women in Latin America.[35] And the use and abuse of power needed to be addressed in any research project, participatory or otherwise. Diane Wolf made these observations about the abuse of power, which were minimized in participatory action research:

The most central dilemma for contemporary feminists in fieldwork, from which other contradictions are derived, is power and the unequal hierarchies or levels of control that are often maintained, perpetuated, created, and re-created during and after field research.... Power is discernible in three interrelated dimensions: (1) power differences stemming from different positionalities of the researcher and the researched (race, class, nationality, life chances, urban-rural backgrounds); (2) power exerted during the research process, such as defining the research relationship, unequal exchange, and exploitation; and (3) power exerted during the post-fieldwork period—writing and representing.[36]

One of the advantages of joining or starting a participatory action group is that the participant becomes a researcher from the inside. This eliminates some of the feminist research dilemmas that come with looking at the social change work of others. The learner-centered core of participatory research also invites members to question dominant theoretical approaches for dealing with intersecting forms of violence and exclusion.[37]

Alternative development practitioners have learned to avoid imperializing and to support or join movements in a variety of ways. Paulo Freire, who both facilitated and participated in social action work, developed educational processes in the 1970s and 1980s to cultivate theory-action-praxis movements.[38] Similarly, Colombia's Orlando Fals Borda simultaneously prepared groups to use action research to challenge repression and large landowners, leading to invasions of large estates and plantations and other grassroots actions directed at ending poverty.[39]

Although social action engagement had doubtless taken place in an underground way for centuries, social action research soon was conducted in an overt way by feminists who did ethnographic studies. In the 1980s, land-tenure researchers Carmen Deere Diana and Magdalena León made a commitment to do their participatory action research in ways that promoted women's consciousness raising. Every intervention strategy, wrote Deere and León, should help empower women so that they create new developmental solutions.[40]

One challenge for activist-thinkers is to determine how outside, sympathetic researchers should relate to feminist community action groups and how grassroots democratic groups should relate to outside researchers, writers, and activists. In general, it has been useful to engage with people in the places where they live and work and to link up with groups that do related work in another part of the region, the country, or the world. It has been helpful for researchers to join activists who have very different social identities, such as people who live in a different zone of the world-economy and who come from different racialized, sexualized, and class backgrounds. But in this situation, joining means learning from others, perhaps for years. Because class divides have widened in recent years, economically disadvantaged people have fewer options. For this reason and many others, it is rarely helpful to direct participatory action research from the outside, either as an activist or as a university employee. Whereas progressive academics used to emphasize bell hooks's idea that *teachers* were the key to change, activists now stress hooks's related idea that *participatory learners* are the key to change.[41]

In recent decades, feminist groups have designed various ways to engage local people in the exploration of power relations and social alternatives. Feminist groups have tried to track the impact of change by staging political plays and keeping social change diaries. Participatory learners have sometimes kept social change diaries: pictorial diaries (showing key local changes over a number of years), member-level diaries (showing how economic changes and movement initiatives impacted women), and self-help group-level diaries (where women shared their own learning diaries with group members, a process that was then recorded in a group diary).[42] By evaluating these diaries, groups have refined participatory action research and developed new ways to carry out social change. They have also helped feminist groups understand why local groups, not university researchers, should remain in charge of self-education and alternative development.

One challenge with community action research has been how to make sure that women's needs and social change visions are taken seriously. In order to minimize the rise of new forms of exclusion in grassroots groups, Uma Narayan argued that activists need to "make political and civic institutions as open as possible to everyone."[43] People who are socially marginalized and powerless need to be brought into new political processes "so that they may become active participants in articulating their interests, commitments and visions for justice."[44] To open up politics, Narayan argued, feminists need to go beyond gender and sexuality and to take on related issues, such as transnational economic structures, asymmetrical relations between states, racial inequalities, nationalistic practices, and the international effects of U.S. Christian fundamentalism.[45] These integral parts of movement development, which take place in face-to-face interactions but may also be initiated through cyberspace, can be seen as part of feminist local and global struggles to redefine democracy and equality through political engagement and participatory action.[46] To promote interrelated transformations like these, feminists and egalitarians need to see how technology and technological skills could be used to end gender and other inequalities and to promote "economic, political, and cultural citizenship."[47]

READING

"From Research to Action" demonstrated how Thailand's Research and Action Project on the Traffic in Women (RATW) employed feminist participatory action research to study the trafficking of women and girls and to address this problem on multiple levels. The general action processes developed by RATW relate to projects around the world. Key issues are North/South power relations, the lack of good jobs and good wages, gender discrimination in education and employment, the rapid development of the sex industry, and the challenges of developing nonwage employment.[48]

The selection from Paulo Freire's *Pedagogy of Indignation* identifies democratic, group-defined, educational processes that have been used by feminists to research society, promote democracy, and carry out social change. Throughout the world, feminist and other movements have promoted change through democratic, educational participatory engagement. This process-based educational methodology calls for activists to apply thought to action and for social change learning to occur from these direct experiences with praxis.[49]

NOTES

1. Josefa S. Francisco, "Paradoxes for Gender in Social Movements," *Development* 46, no. 2, Thematic Section (2003): 24–26, 25.

2. Robin Truth Goodman, *World, Class, Women: Global Literature, Education, and Feminism* (New York: Routledge, 2004), 29.

3. Dorothy E. Smith, "Editor's Introduction: On Sally Hacker's Method," in Sally Hacker, *"Doing It the Hard Way": Investigations of Gender and Technology* (Boston: Unwin Hyman, 1990), 4–5.

4. Janet M. Conway, *Praxis and Politics: Knowledge Production in Social Movements* (New York: Routledge, 2006), 8.

5. Sonia E. Alvarez, "Translating the Global: Effects of Transnational Organizing on Local Feminist Discourses and Practices in Latin America," *Meridians: Feminisms, Race, Transnationalism* 1, no. 1 (2000): 29–67.

6. Micere Githae Mugo, "Popular Paradigms and Conceptions: Orature-Based Community Theatre," in William G. Martin and Michael O. West, eds., *Out of One, Many Africas: Reconstructing the Study and Meaning of Africa* (Urbana: University of Illinois Press, 1999), 197–212, 202.

7. Viviene Taylor, "Europe and Africa: Gender Challenges for African Development," *Development* 41, no. 4 (1998): 41–45, 45.

8. Amrita Basu, "Globalization of the Local/Localization of the Global: Mapping Transnational Women's Movements," *Meridians: Feminism, Race, Transnationalism* 1, no. 1 (2000): 85–109. Reprinted in Carole R. McCann and Seung-Kyung Kim, eds., *Feminist Theory Reader: Local and Global Perspectives* (New York: Routledge, 2003), 68–77.

9. Sandra Harding, *Science and Social Inequality: Feminist and Postcolonial Issues* (Urbana: University of Illinois Press, 2006), 109.

10. Sustainable agriculture is a concept that can refer to a sustainable farm. It often doesn't refer to sustainable society or a sustainable world. Alternative agriculture often refers to a new way of living. This is one reason why we usually refer to alternative development.

11. Harding, *Science and Social Inequality*, 100–109, 156.

12. Dorothy E. Smith, *Texts, Facts, and Femininity: Exploring the Relations of Ruling* (New York: Routledge, 1990), 53.

13. Ibid.

14. Ibid., 5.

15. Nancy Fraser, "The Uses and Abuses of French Discourse Theory," in Nancy Fraser and Sandra Lee Bartky, eds., *Valuing French Feminism: Critical Essays on Difference, Agency, and Culture* (Bloomington: Indiana University Press, 1992), 177–194, 191.

16. A. Bahati Kuumba, "'You've Struck a Rock': Comparing Gender, Social Movements, and Transformation in the United States and South Africa," *Gender and Society* 16, no. 4 (August 2002): 504–523, 515.

17. Martin Luther King Jr., a young man who had just taken his first job, became the spokesman for the boycott, but it is clear from Taylor Branch's account that he generally followed the lead of the women who organized and sustained the yearlong boycott. Taylor Branch, *Parting the Waters: America in the King Years, 1954–63* (New York: Touchstone, 1989), 143–205.

18. Alvarez, "Translating the Global," 30.

19. Ibid., 31.

20. Gail Omvedt, *Reinventing Revolution: New Social Movements and the Socialist Revolution in India* (New York: M. E. Sharpe, 1993), 318.

21. Ibid., 513.

22. Ibid.

23. Ibid., 514.

24. D. L. Sheth, "Alternative Development as Political Practice," *Alternatives* 12 (1987): 155–171, 159.

25. Ibid., 159.

26. Violet Eudine Barriteau, "Confronting Power and Politics: A Feminist Theorizing of Gender in Caribbean Societies," *Meridians: Feminism, Race, Transnationalism* 3, no. 2 (2003): 57–93, 83.

27. Radhika Coomaraswamy, "Are Women's Rights Universal? Re-engaging the Local," *Meridians: Feminism, Race, Transnationalism* 3, no. 1 (2003): 1–18, 13.

28. Andrea Cornwall, "Making a Difference? Gender and Participatory Development," in Shahra Razavi, ed., *Shifting Burdens: Gender and Agrarian Change Under Neoliberalism* (Bloomfield, CT: Kumarian Press, 2002), 197–231, 198.

29. Ibid., 197.

30. Ibid., 205.

31. Ibid., 207.

32. Ibid., 219.

33. Ibid., 227.

34. Peggy Antrobus, "Women's Defense of Local Politics in the Face of Structural Adjustment and Globalization," *Development* 41, no. 3, Local/Global Encounters (1998): 72–76, 74.

35. There are serious political questions about whether outside researchers should even lead a group in community action research, including when the facilitator makes an effort to base the curriculum on material that relates to the context in which participatory activists and other learners explore social, economic, political, and cultural concerns. For an outsider's directing of women's action work, see Mary Morgan, "Working for Social Change: Learning from and Building upon Women's Knowledge to Develop Economic Literacy," in Parvin Ghorayshi and Claire Bélanger, eds., *Women, Work, and Gender Relations in Developing Countries: A Global Perspective* (Westport, CT: Greenwood Press, 1996), 195–208, 197.

36. Diane L. Wolf, *Feminist Dilemmas in Fieldwork* (Boulder, CO: Westview Press, 1996), 2.

37. Vijé Franchi and Tanya M. Stuart, "Rapid Assessment Procedures: A Participatory Action Research Approach to Field Training in Community Prevention and Intervention," in Vijé Franchi and Norman Duncan, eds., *Prevention and Intervention Practice in Post-Apartheid South Africa* (Binghamton, NY: Haworth Press, 2003), 99–115, 102.

38. Paulo Freire, *The Politics of Education: Culture, Power, and Liberation* (New York: Bergin and Garvey, 1985), 45–54.

39. Lourdes S. Arizpe, "Anthropology in Latin America: Old Boundaries, New Contexts," in Christopher Mitchell, ed., *Changing Perspectives in Latin American Studies: Insights from Six Disciplines* (Stanford, CA: Stanford University Press, 1988), 143–162, 146.

40. Lourdes Arizpe was one of the first feminists to research women in the informal sector. *The Marias,* Professor Arizpe's work on Mexico's women street vendors, appeared in bookstands throughout Mexico City by early 1974. See Carmen Deere Diana and Magdalena León, "Conclusion," in Carmen Deere Diana and Magdalena León, eds., *Rural Women and State Policy: Feminist Perspectives on Latin American Development* (Boulder, CO: Westview Press, 1987).

41. bell hooks, *Teaching to Transgress: Education as the Practice of Freedom* (New York: Routledge, 1994), 13.

42. Helzi Noponen, "Participatory Internal Learning for Grassroots NGOs in Micro-Credit, Livelihoods, and Environmental Regeneration," *Development* 42, no. 2 (1999): 27–34, 28–30.

43. Uma Narayan, *Dislocating Cultures/Identities, Traditions, and Third World Feminism* (New York: Routledge, 1997), 37.

44. Ibid.

45. Ibid., 38–39.

46. Leslie Regan Shade, "Whose Global Knowledge? Women Navigating the Net," *Development* 46, no. 1 (2003): 49–54, 53.

47. Gillian Youngs, "Closing the Gaps: Women, Communications, and Technology," *Development* 45, no. 4 (2002): 23–28, 27.

48. Siriporn Skrobanek, Nataya Boonpakdee, and Chutima Jantateero, "From Research to Action," in *The Traffic in Women: Human Realities of the International Sex Trade* (London: Zed, 1997), 80–97.

49. Paulo Freire, *Pedagogy of Indignation,* with a foreword by Donald Macedo (Boulder, CO: Paradigm Publishers, 2004), 15–21, 24–25.

❀

From Research to Action

Siriporn Skrobanek, Nataya Boonpakdee, and Chutima Jantateero

The second phase of the Research and Action project on Traffic in Women (RATW), from November 1993 to October 1994, focused on working cooperatively with women in their communities to address the issue of trafficking. The primary objective was to identify appropriate strategies, both at the village level and nationally, to combat the traffic in women. The approach was to be participatory, that is, led by the people most directly affected by trafficking. The role of the research team was to assist with devising and developing such strategies. This was to include spreading information, raising awareness, and organising groups to decide on and to implement the strategies. This [reading] details the results of this phase of the project.

Three villages were selected; the choice was based on the extent of trafficking and on the degree of interest shown by village women. Project activities were also pursued in the urban centres of Bangkok and Pattaya. In the north, the project team worked in Rim Mon village, which had a long history of migration for prostitution and a large number of returned sex workers. In the northeast, Ton Yang village was included, but Khon Na was replaced by a neighbouring village, "Isla Thong." Na Thong was the home of 15 young women trafficked to Japan between 1989 and 1991, and the mothers of these women had contacted the research team for assistance in bringing them home. This seemed a good starting point from which to develop strategies for resistance to trafficking. In Pattaya, the researchers worked with local sex workers; in Bangkok, mostly with agency personnel.

MOTHERS IN NA THONG VILLAGE

When the research team first visited Na Thong, ten mothers there had lost contact with daughters who had gone to Japan. They wanted help in bringing their daughters home. They had borrowed money, sold cattle or mortgaged land to pay the broker's fee of 25,000 baht (US$1,042). The broker, who lived locally and was a relative of one mother, had told them that their daughters would be working in a restaurant for 20,000 baht a month. The women now believed that they were working as prostitutes. The promised remittances had failed to arrive, and the debts incurred at home were still unpaid. The mothers did not dare ask for assistance from government officers, because they had been warned against sending their daughters away.

A public tribunal on traffic in women, organised by the Asian Women's Human Rights Council, was held in Tokyo in March 1994, and this provided an opportunity for the group to talk openly about its experiences. The research team had suggested that they send a representative to Tokyo, and Nee was elected as spokesperson.

Before she went, Nee met all the mothers to discuss their experiences. Some had already changed their minds about wanting their daughters to return, either because they had heard from them in the meantime or because they had received money from Japan. One daughter had written to her mother, warning her to trust nobody. This frightened others, who decided to leave things alone. During her visit to Japan, Nee met migrant workers, visited agencies which help migrants, and visited Thai women imprisoned for killing their moneylender. She came to understand more about the difficulties faced by illegal migrant workers, and about Thai women coerced into working as prostitutes in bars and clubs.

With assistance from a local agency, Mizura, and the Japanese police, Nee found her daughter. She had just finished paying off her debt and had become a sex worker in a restaurant. The local media covered the work of the tribunal and Nee's search for her daughter. When Nee returned with her daughter to Na Thong, she told others about the working conditions and the contracts which bound the workers. A public discussion was held in Na Thong, led by Nee, and attended by people from neighbouring villages. She inspired others to write to their daughters, asking for the truth about their work in Japan. Some were shocked to learn that their daughters were employed as sex workers, but others were more pragmatic about the need to earn fast money.

The 300 people who attended the first meeting saw a video and slides dealing with the circumstances in which migrant Thai women live in Japan. For a majority, this was the first they had heard or seen of the reality. Similar meetings were held in the district and provincial centres, where Nee was joined by a number of returned women migrants, who spoke of their experiences in Singapore and Japan. These meetings were well attended, and there were requests for Nee to visit other districts where the emigration rate was high. A returned migrant from Rim Mon in the north came to one meeting, and went back to her village to organise a women's group there.

COMMUNITY REACTION

Reactions to the meetings and the disclosure of the conditions in which women were living were not all positive or compassionate. One woman complained:

> Nee said too much. She should not say that our daughters are prostitutes and suffer misfortune. Some believe their daughters are doing the right thing. Nee talked too

much because she wanted others to believe her. Staying a few days there, how could she know the country thoroughly?

Others, who had received money from their daughters, were angry because they now knew how it had been earned. One suggested Nee should go and work in Japan herself. This anger reflected the strength of the social and moral divisions between "good girls" and "bad girls." The same attitude compels returned women to remain silent about their experiences. Many returnees do not stay in their home villages, but prefer to go and live elsewhere in Thailand.

Communities do not necessarily support those who have been forced into prostitution. Following Nee's personal disclosure about her daughter's experience, some villagers blamed the daughter. The researchers also became targets for anger. One government officer accused the research team of humiliating the young women for their own ends. The village head, who was related to Nee, told her to desist because it brought disgrace on the family, and hence upon him also. These reactions made the research team more cautious about using local women to recall their experiences in public. The presentation of such stories clearly runs the risk of exposing them to possible further abuse.

It is clear that much of the traffic in women remains in shadow, and that a collusive unknowing sometimes unites families with agents, traffickers and exploiters. While the whole nexus remains hidden, face may be saved; but the young women must suffer in secrecy and silence.

THE MIGRANT WOMEN'S NETWORK

Following the provincial meeting in Nong Khai, three women who had been abused by traffickers and employers worked with the research team to record their personal histories. All these women, Mali, Chantra and Duangta, also organised groups in their home villages to spread awareness of migration and trafficking. The telling of their stories gave them real comfort, because, in doing so, they came to perceive that what had happened to them was only part of wider social and economic processes, and was not a consequence of personal error or fault. They were able to understand the relationship between individual experience and the unbalanced social and economic conditions of men and women, rich and poor, both nationally and internationally.

Ton Yang Village Information Centre
Experience gained from activities in Na Thong village clarified the need to make known what life is really like for migrant women. Mali, who had worked in Singapore, started a group with the purpose of educating the people of Ton Yang, and a neighbouring village, "Kham Wan." This group was supported by the research project, especially with books and videos about migration, prostitution and the kind of life women can expect when they work in foreign countries. Members of the group started discussions after women had given testimony about their own experiences, the sufferings and sorrows they had endured.

The reaction from young people taking part was very powerful. Many said they would never go overseas in search of work now that they had some idea of what to expect. The women themselves, when they came to reflect on these sessions, struck up a strong rapport with their audiences.

The way Thai prostitutes in Japan are treated is depressing. People are not aware it is like this. You feel sad for the parents whose daughters have gone away to work. It would be all right if they knew the sacrifices their daughters are making, if they knew the real cost of the money they earn. It is very sad for the parents who do not know.

The ones who went abroad came back and built a big house; they have more money to spend. Some people still want to follow them. Migration brings problems to the community.

The women and young people in Ton Yang agreed to set up an information centre. To begin with, this was done in Mali's living room, but later, they extended her house to provide a space for reading matter and information relating to migration. Government officers have also contributed documentary material: Among visitors to the centre have been people from Na Thong, who are keen for something similar in their village.

More and more women and men approached Mali, seeking advice on migration or information about what they could do when employment contracts were not fulfilled. Mr. Kham and his friend sought her help following their deportation from New Zealand, when they had paid large fees to brokers on the promise of agricultural jobs. Mali suggested they sue the broker's company. In spite of this experience, they were still anxious to migrate far for work, because, they said, the wages in neighbouring countries were too low. Brokers are quick to promote new destinations with promises of even greater potential earnings.

The existence of the centre and the work of the group have made Mrs. Tan, who is the mother of Paeng and Peaun, unhappy. It has interfered with her work of recruitment for her daughters in Japan.... Her youngest daughter has even joined the group.

Returned Migrants Group in Rim Mon
While Ton Yang and Na Thong saw women leave for what turned out to be sex work abroad, the people of Rim Mon observed foreigners coming to their village for sex. Women with experience of sex work overseas were coming back to Rim Mon having amassed considerable wealth. Some were being supported by foreign men. It was assumed that those who had not yet returned had been less successful.

The researchers worked with some of these women in Rim Mon, particularly with those who had experienced discrimination when they came home, or who were still suffering from the trauma of working abroad.

Kham Por had been forced into prostitution by the Yakuza in Japan. She had tried to escape, but only when a Japanese customer paid her debt was she allowed to leave. She lived as the second wife of this man, but when her baby died, she came home. Her husband still visits her and gives financial support. Kham Por suffers from nightmares that the Yakuza are still after her. She has been in hospital several times. The villagers think she is neurotic. After revisiting Kham Por in 1996, the Foundation for Women learned that she had been forced to disown her baby, and to pass it over to the Japanese wife, so that the child should not end up as illegitimate under Japanese law.

Kham Por sought out the researchers, because she was sorely in need of friends. Later, she was elected president of the returned women's group. The village head could see the potential power of the group, if only because they were better off than most, but he would not offer his support. He was cynical about migrant women workers.

If they need money, they just go south, or send their daughters. It's more comfortable than bag-weaving until their backs ache.

Kham Por started to teach other returned women, and was involved in planning vocational training for young women villagers. This had to stop when she went back into hospital.

Kham Por had introduced the researchers to other returned women, who provided valuable information which would either validate or deny the evidence collected in the first phase of the project. Most of these women had been outside the mainstream of village life. In spite of the obvious benefit the village had received from remittances, the women who had been the instruments of making this money were sometimes rejected. They were asked to help out at Songkran (the traditional Thai new year festival), because they could afford the elaborate Thai costumes required for the ceremony. In talking with the researchers, these women were able to speak of their dissatisfactions with their life as returnees, and to identify a possible new role for themselves.

> We should work with the housewives' group, because there are no other appropriate groups or programmes for women in the village.

> I would like it if there were other work for the people in our community.

> I wish that women in the community could cook properly so that we could welcome visitors, and not feel inferior. And it's a pity they don't know better manners when it comes to eating.

The researcher contacted government agencies to arrange for instruction in cookery. Field visits to other women's groups were organised. In the [end], the members of the group decided that the high cost of investment in food production and the limited market were against them. They moved on to look at other ideas.

> Women need to learn and understand other people's skills and tricks of the trade, because women have to work also.

> If women are not developed, how can the country be developed?

> We are, the women of a new age, we can do what we want by ourselves. We don't have to wait for men. We can do it, but we have never been given the opportunity.

They learned that working together is effective, and earns respect. Even the village head changed his mind and lent his support to the group.

> When we worked together and showed how useful we are to the village, people appreciated us more. Women came to understand that responsibility has to be shared. Although each one had to help herself, she also needed to contribute to the wider group. In the meetings, everyone had the right to express her opinion. There was no need to whisper behind our hands.

Visits to other women's groups encouraged and strengthened their resolve. They named themselves the Women's Development Group, Rim Mon village. Following Duangta's visit to the north-east, they organised a seminar on migration and prostitution in cooperation with the local sub-district committee and the Community Development Division of the Ministry of the Interior. The seminar was titled "Unemployment after the Farming Season." Those who took part agreed that the main reason for migration was poverty, and lack of knowledge on how to make and market other produce. The success of the meeting led them on to other activities, and women from neighbouring villages began to talk about the way the traffic in women affected their own communities.

BENEFITS OF PARTICIPATION

The idea behind participatory research, and especially feminist research, is that through collective working, women will be able to articulate problems and work together on solutions. It was most clearly successful in Rim Mon, partly because the women there had not previously formed themselves into a collective entity. In Ton Yang and Na Thong, vocational groups had been established earlier. In Rim Mon, the practice of pooling and sharing ideas was new for some women. Most had had direct experience of prostitution, and this gave life and authenticity to the discussions. The researchers did not have to provide information on trafficking, as was the case with some other groups; and this left the women free to focus more on the process of working together in groups.

The group in Ton Yang consisted mainly of women who were anxious about the issue in relation to the fate of their children. The history of sex work migration in Ton Yang can be traced back to a single individual—a woman called Pang—returning from Japan, who set about recruiting others. The story runs that she brought home a million baht; and this is said to have convinced parents that big money was there for the making in Japan. More recently, two other women came back, also with considerable wealth. The members of the group felt that they had to make sure that people in the village received a more balanced picture than this rosy view of easy money. They arranged video and slide presentations on trafficking and migration, and these were followed by discussions.

These children face many difficulties; they have to endure a great deal.

The girls had to put up with whatever they found there but the parents at home thought they were having a good time. They believed what their children wrote and told them.

Stories from real life inspired those taking part to devise concrete solutions that could actually be put into practice in the village. In Na Thong, there had been many women's development activities, but none which concentrated on finding solutions through collective effort. The group started soon after the meetings which Nee had organised. One of the more popular seminars was about the law and legal procedures in foreign countries, and the kinds of help which migrant workers can draw on. This was also the first time that men had taken part in large numbers.

Spreading Information

The second phase of the research confirmed that many villages lacked accurate information on migration—how it came about, what would happen to those who left, the pitfalls as well as the advantages. This was, therefore, a major focus of the women's energies. Activities included:

- core group members who had been directly caught up in trafficking, and who spoke about their personal experiences;
- researchers and others who could give out accurate information on legal issues—labour regulations, immigration laws, marriage to foreigners and the support available to children;
- documentary videos on child labour, prostitution, migration and trafficking;
- printed material—books, posters, picture books;
- presentation of the real life stories of trafficked women.

Other events included debates between children on the issues, and role-play on the stories, in the books. Everything was designed to promote two-way communication, and to build understanding of all the implications of migrant sex work.

Changes in Attitude and Behaviour
The overwhelming impression people have of work in Japan is that it pays well. Women were sending home enough money to buy land and to renovate houses. Parents were unaware of the dangerous and damaging circumstances in which their daughters were working.

> I never thought it was cruel. I only knew that she sent a lot of money home. (Ton Yang)

> Seeing the video gave her sleepless nights. She was unhappy to see Thai girls being hit and even killed. She was afraid she would see her own daughter on the video. (Na Thong)

The reality of the conditions of work was shrouded in silence. Even returnees rarely spoke of their experiences, preferring to collude with the illusion that everything was fine. Families continued to borrow money and to mortgage their land to pay agents' fees. As they came to learn more about the life of migrant women workers, and the routine sexual exploitation they suffered, the enthusiasm of people became tempered; they showed more compassion.

> I feel sorry for those who went away to work, and who risked their lives, lost their virginity for money. If only I had known this before, I would not have let them go. (Na Thong)

During the course of the research, people came to talk about doing things differently. Young people said they would be more cautious in seeking work outside the village. Wealthier families spoke of furthering their children's education before they would permit them to look for work. In Na Thong, the youth leader reported that all the students who finished their six years of compulsory education that year went on to secondary school. The circumstances that led young people to want to leave still existed, but it was hoped that the new awareness that had come might make them more alert and think twice before leaving home. By the time the project was concluded in Na Thong, women were still leaving for work abroad, but it was found that they were now applying to travel legally, through the Department of Labour. The destination now was more likely to be Taiwan than Japan. The women most immediately involved with the project gained confidence from working with others, and were more ready to contact agencies for assistance. They became more hopeful that they would be instrumental in effecting change.

Vocational Activities
Apart from alerting people to the reality of migration for sex work, the women's groups saw the urgent need for wider local work opportunities for women and girls. In Na Thong, they gave this priority over everything else, and focused on the weaving group. In Ton Yang and Rim Mon, they combined vocational skills and the spread of information. They did not expect vocational projects to lead to a wider range of new work possibilities.

Weaving Group in Na Thong. Early in the Na Thong discussions, one woman community leader mentioned the availability of interest-free loans for income-generating projects from the Community Development Department of the Interior Ministry. The women thought that reviving traditional weaving skills, using the local designs of their area, might be a possible means of creating extra income. The researchers helped with the application for the loan, and arranged visits to existing weaving groups. When no response came from the Community Development Department, the researcher suggested taking a low-interest loan from elsewhere. But the group, fearful of further debt, became discouraged. They decided to disband the weaving group, at least until the harvest was over.

Sewing Group in Ton Tang. The women's group was attracted by sewing, and contacted the Non-Formal Education Department for training. They could use equipment they already owned, but needed a wider market for selling the garments. They pursued this for a time, but when demand dropped away, the sewing project was abandoned.

The experience of these two groups demonstrates the obstacles to local employment creation, including delays in obtaining loans, the lack of outlets for products, and the absence of organising skills for cooperative enterprises.

Bag-making in Rim Mon. Vocational training in Rim Mon served as a means of bringing women together to talk about migration. Income-generating work was used to get the group to work in harmony, although the income was not the main purpose of the group. The women worked well together, and there was talk of extending the idea to other groups within the village. The alternative emphasis in this group, whereby the dynamics of the group took precedence over income generation, is, in part, the key to its success. The Rim Mon women were, in general, better off than the other groups, so they could afford to adopt a more relaxed attitude towards additional earnings. For the others, improvement in finances was a major consideration, and the obstacles to this led to frustration and conflict.

Casework Assistance

Help and counselling with individual problems was part of the overall purpose of the project. The benefits extend beyond the particular family: the example helps to win credibility and support from other people in the village and community leaders.

Assistance with Documents. The difficulties over arranging documents for migrants were similar in all villages. These included government officers who demanded unofficial additional payments for preparing documents. People were often confused about which documents were required, and in what language they should be drawn up. The researchers were able to help with translations, and they accompanied villagers on their visits to government offices. The presence of researchers inhibited the officials from demanding extra fees. The confusion over official documents and correct government procedures leads to a situation which traffickers can easily exploit.

Locating Women Abroad. The researchers, in collaboration with staff from the Foundation for Women, helped parents trace daughters who had disappeared overseas. Some searches were happily concluded, others ended with the sad news that the women had died. There were many cases where parents had lost contact with their daughters.

Applications for Scholarships. One means of combating the traffic in women is by prolonging the education of girls. The advantages are twofold: they are kept busy with study, and at the same time they are enhancing their skills for when they enter the labour market. For poor families, keeping children at school beyond the compulsory limit is too costly. In the second phase of the research, 12 scholarships were provided from project funds, and these were offered to young girls thought to be vulnerable to recruiters.

Tuition. The researchers helped young women with literacy. They also ran typing classes in Na Thong, particularly Thai/English typing skills. The equipment for this was provided by the Foundation for Women. The enthusiasm for acquiring new skills and becoming literate, especially among young women, gives some indication of the reservoir of unmet need for further education and the desire to work outside traditional agricultural labour. Some women returning from abroad hesitated before joining classes run by the Non-Formal Education Division.

> I want to study, but I don't want to be in a large class. I am shy. If the government officer is the teacher, I won't study. (Rim Mon)

The officers were impatient with this.

> We don't understand why they are shy. They've worked in Bangkok and other places. They shouldn't be shy.

The researchers tried an approach that would put them at ease. Their teaching was based upon an exchange of ideas and feelings. Many young women acknowledged this.

> At first I was shy, but now if there is anything to learn, I will do it. Reading develops our minds.

OBSTACLES ENCOUNTERED

The project encountered some hostility, particularly from those families receiving money from daughters overseas.

> Why are you concerned with other people's business? If they want to go, what does it matter? It's better to go and earn money to spend than to stay home and starve. (Ton Yang)

The promotion of understanding had to be structured in such a way that it did not offend families whose daughters were abroad, and so that it did not add to the discrimination against returned sex workers.

One unanticipated outcome of the project was that recruitment agents and brokers were praised and congratulated by families who felt their daughters had been successful. This was the opposite of the response of those women whose stories were featured in the videos and books. In Rim Mon in particular, from where there is a well-beaten path to overseas prostitution, there were many wealthy returned women. Their very presence was an eloquent denial of the message which the project was seeking to convey.

> This job is not a mistake. Right now, money can save our lives, never mind our honour. Disparaging prostitution only makes villagers dissatisfied, especially the parents of the women in prostitution.

The researchers had to make clear the difference between trafficking and prostitution. Traffic, it was explained, was about coercing women into prostitution, or into any other work, denying them adequate wages and dignified working conditions.

PARTICIPATION OF EXTERNAL AGENCIES

Local Government Personnel

Officials cooperated with and, in some cases, took part in the activities surrounding the project. Local community development officers assisted by advertising the seminars. Senior officers chaired some meetings. They were clearly familiar with the problems of migration and trafficking, but, so far, no official programmes had been set up to deal with the issue. The work of the women's groups gave them a chance to become involved without waiting for official permission.

In Rim Mon, the local teachers had already been working against trafficking and child prostitution. They had set up a counselling project specifically for girls at risk, and had arranged exhibitions illustrating the dangers of child prostitution. They had also gone with students to Bangkok for college entrance exams, and helped with applications for scholarships designed to prevent poorer children from dropping out of school. They were supported in this by the District Education Office. They reported that a higher proportion of girls are now completing their six years of compulsory education and going on to further study.

The Community Development Department has also given practical help by offering interest-free loans for income-generating schemes. This worked well in Rim Mon, as reported above, but delays in approval in Udon Thani province prevented any benefit being derived from it in Na Thong. The need for loans in Rim Mon confirms the observation that remittances from women's work in urban centres or overseas were being used mainly for capital expenditure—repairing houses or buying white goods—and little of the money was saved. A few women had started a convenience store with their earnings, but, overall, the money was deployed on conspicuous consumption and the flaunting of wealth.

Central Government Activity

The beginning of the FFW project coincided in 1992 with a government crackdown on child prostitution. The Chuan Leekpai Government gave the primary responsibility for the fight against child prostitution to the Department of Public Welfare. The Department set up a committee to oversee the achievement of this objective. This committee distributed a manual to the agencies involved, with an outline of their campaign and ideas for cooperative efforts. The National Commission on Women's Affairs, part of the Office of the Prime Minister, also formed a committee to inquire into the sex entertainment business.

Social Programmes. The government established social programmes to focus on women who have worked in the sex industry. These include the "welfare home" of the Department of Public Welfare, for women released into their custody following conviction on criminal charges related to prostitution. Other aspects of the programme include vocational training, both for convicted women and for young people considered to be at risk.

Educational Programmes. The Education Department provided opportunities for further education for young people, through scholarship programmes and "welfare schools" for girls at risk. The scholarships were established in the northern provinces, from where many girls migrate for sex work, and where there are limited places in secondary schools.

Media Projects. The Department of Public Welfare published information for families on child prostitution and trafficking. The Ministry of Foreign Affairs also ran a media campaign on illegal migration to Japan, intended to inform and deter potential migrants.

Legal Programmes. The national strategy in terms of the law was to foster greater cooperation and coordination between government departments in implementing existing laws. These departments included Public Welfare, Provincial Administration, Foreign Affairs and the police.

Perhaps more significant was the drafting of a bill to reform the 1960 Abatement of Prostitution Act. Nongovernmental organisations lobbied vigorously in favour of the decriminalisation of prostitution, and harsher penalties against traffickers and the clients of child prostitutes. The bill did include more rigorous punishment for procurers and for the clients of under-age prostitutes, and a reduction in penalties for adult prostitutes. This bill was enacted in December 1996, and is now in force.

A second bill currently before Parliament seeks to replace the 1928 Anti-Trafficking Act, which would extend protection to boys, and provide for assistance rather than punishment for victims of trafficking. Penalties for trafficking would also be increased. This bill still awaits the final reading and approval by Parliament. (January 1997)

Health Programmes. The Ministry of Public Health screens prostitutes for sexually transmitted diseases, including HIV. There have been difficulties in offering this service to immigrant sex workers, mainly because of the lack of translation and interpretation facilities. The ministry has also surveyed the sex industry with a view to targeting its programmes more effectively.

Following an evaluation of these projects, a number of limitations were identified. Vocational and educational support programmes have been set up only in the northern provinces. This takes no account of the existence of child prostitution and trafficking in other regions, notably in the northeast. The vocational programme of the Public Welfare Department provided skills training to 2,000 young women a year. The average income generated by this amounted to between 60 and 150 baht per day (US$2.50–6.25), which was considered too low to sustain a commitment by the young women to the work. Participants complained that the skills they acquired were limited and not adapted to their needs. Many were not convinced that prostitution was a bad choice of occupation. The Department of Industry also ran a skills-training programme in an effort to resist child prostitution. It set up projects in 72 villages, but only 1,363 individuals completed the programme, and, of these, only 262 were girls between the ages of 13 and 18.

Nongovernmental Activity

There were not many nongovernmental organisations (NGOs) working directly on trafficking. However, the research team was able to collaborate with four organisations for the purpose of collecting data and in the analysis of service delivery to trafficked persons. The operations of NGOs can be divided into four main areas of work designed to resist trafficking and child prostitution.

Social Programmes. These include making available emergency shelter for victims of trafficking, counselling, health care education and some vocational training. Each NGO has a particular target group and a specific way of working: the Centre for the Protection of Children's Rights, for example, provides assistance, shelter and rehabilitation to abused children under 18. The religious-based groups focus on services to women who have been arrested or trafficked, but are rarely in a position to do much about the underlying factors which contribute towards trafficking.

Legal Programmes. Some agencies provided legal advice and assistance during court hearings and proceedings. The overall level of expertise was not high, and there was not a great deal of interest in using the law to combat trafficking or to seek compensation for its victims. The difficulties in this respect were exacerbated by the indifference of law enforcers, and inadequate protection of the privacy of witnesses and victims.

Disseminating Information. Part of each NGO's purpose was to bring home to the public the scale and extent of trafficking and prostitution. The most effective work through the media was accomplished in cooperative ventures between governmental and nongovernmental agencies. Great care had to be taken to ensure that the women involved were not placed in further jeopardy by publicising their real-life stories.

NGOs and the International Dimension. To dismantle international trafficking networks, cooperation between NGOs across national boundaries is required. Campaigns to change government policies and to provide effective help for trafficked persons must be coordinated by popular movements and NGOs in both sending and receiving countries. Such collaboration has worked well in tracing missing persons, in the joint provision of social and legal assistance in both the country of residence and the country of origin, and in media campaigns to inform the public. One good example of this has been the cooperation between NGOs in Japan and in Thailand to plead for leniency in the Shimodate case. The obstacles to such international efforts include language difficulties and cultural differences in ways of looking at and dealing with the issue. Some organisations underestimate the capacity of the women themselves to act on their own behalf.

Cooperation to Combat Trafficking
Powerful national and international strategies are needed to combat international trafficking. At present the level of cooperation between agencies within countries and between countries is inadequate.

Between Government Departments. The researchers found evidence of duplication between departments in their efforts to counter child prostitution. Cooperation between representatives of different departments was more effective in implementing the law which deals with the detention and "rehabilitation" of sex workers. This has little impact on the sex industry itself. When it came to the Department of Public Welfare and the Ministry of Foreign Affairs working together to check applications for passports, this proved to be an unsuccessful tactic to discover whether trafficking was involved. The Public Welfare Department had instructions to check the background of young Thai women who applied for passports, to ensure that traffickers were not involved. The Foreign Affairs Ministry, however, refused to pass on information about applicants, on the grounds that it might be accused of unnecessary interference and discrimination.

The best examples of cooperation between governments are to be found in the detention and repatriation of illegal immigrants. The police officer interviewed in Malaysia by the project researcher stressed the cooperation with the Thai branch of Interpol in providing interpreters for cases against migrant sex workers. The Thai government, however, exhibited little interest in the plight of Thai women forced into prostitution overseas. During one case in Germany, in which defendants were prosecuted for forced prostitution, requests to the Thai police for witnesses were refused (Rayanakorn 1995).

Between Government and NGOs. The response to the issue and to the women themselves is a source of conflict between government and nongovernmental agencies. During the second phase of the research, the team was supporting a witness for a prosecution in Germany. It sought the compliance of the Thai police department. The police later released the information, including the identity of the victim, to the local press. They continued to defend their action, even though this threatens further collaboration between them and the Foundation for Women.

There were, however, examples of effective cooperation. The Thai Embassy in Tokyo is responsive to Japanese NGOs in bringing assistance to Thai women in distress. The Thai Ministry of Labour and Social Welfare and the Ministry of Foreign Affairs have provided some financial support to these Japanese NGOs.

Between NGOs. Transnational cooperation between NGOs in providing material help to individual women is well established. This is impaired to some degree by agencies supplying inadequate background information to cases that they refer and failing to follow them up. Cooperation within the country is also limited. Where it occurs, it is mostly on the basis of individual cases, rather than in a concerted effort to lobby government on the particular legislative measures required to address the problems.

International Organisations. In October 1994, the Foundation for Women, together with the VENA Centre of the University of Leiden and the Women's Studies Centre of Chiang Mai University, organised an international workshop on migration and trafficking of women. Some 70 people from 22 countries took part. The event concluded with an action plan for international cooperation, and recommendations were drawn up for national and international policies.

The Global Alliance Against Traffic in Women (GAATW) was formed. Its function is to coordinate efforts across national boundaries to promote international law reform and the adoption and enforcement of laws to combat trafficking. Part of its mandate is also to spread information and to promote research. It has set up working groups in a number of countries, including a group for research and coordination at the Foundation for Women in Bangkok.

CONCLUSION

Evidence emerged from the second phase of the project of the ability of migrant women themselves, their families, and communities, to take on the issue of trafficking. Governmental and nongovernmental agencies can provide support and information to active groups rooted in village and community. Outside agencies can contribute by linking women's groups across the country, and by arranging fact-finding trips. The participation of women in discussions and decisions about trafficking and migration is vital at all levels, for it is their livelihood, their lives, and their freedom that are at stake.

The research also identified gaps in cooperation between agencies, many of which derive from conflicting views on prostitution and women migrants. Efforts to eradicate trafficking can be made more difficult by negative attitudes towards sex workers. This not only leads to gratuitous humiliation of the women, but also undermines cooperation on the prosecution of traffickers.

At present, prostitution represents the most hopeful option for some women. This, in turn, raises other vital questions. Is it more useful to apply the law to improve their working conditions, or to seek to eliminate the whole industry? The distinction must be maintained between issues of trafficking and of prostitution. Where prostitution is forced by coercion or violence, the law must be deployed against recruiters, brokers, agents and employers, and all those who collude with this damaging and degrading trade.

❀

First Letter: On the Spirit of this Book

Paulo Freire

I like to be human, quite contrarily, because changing the world is as hard as it is possible. It is the relationship between the difficulty and possibility of changing the world that poses the question of how important the role of awareness is in history; it poses the issues of decision, of option, of ethics, of education and its limits.

Education makes sense because the world is not necessarily this or that, because human beings are as much *projects* themselves as they may have projects, or a vision, for the world. Education makes sense because women and men learn that through learning they can make and remake themselves, because women and men are able to take responsibility for themselves as beings capable of knowing—of knowing that they know and of knowing that they don't. They are able to know what they already know better and to come to know what they do not yet know. Education makes sense because in order to be, women and men must keep on being. If women and men simply were, there would be no reason to speak of education.

Awareness of the world, which makes awareness of myself viable, makes unviable the immutability of the world. Awareness of the world and awareness of myself make me not only a being in the world, but one *with* the world and *with* others. It makes me a being capable of intervening in the world and not only of adapting to it. It is in this sense that women and men can interfere in the world while other animals can only *touch* it. That is why not only do we have a history, but we make our history, which equally makes us, and thus makes us historic.

However, if I refuse the fatalist's discourse, which immobilizes history, I also refuse the no less narrow-minded discourse of historic willfulness, according to which change will come because it is said that it will. Deep down, both of these discourses negate the dialectic contradiction all individuals experience within themselves, that of knowing oneself to be an object of history, while also becoming its subject.

It must be emphasized that the discourse on the impossibility of improving the world is not one that *verifies* impossibility; rather it is an ideological discourse intended to make possibility not viable. It is, for this very reason, a reactionary discourse; at best, it is a desperately fatalistic discourse.

The discourse on the impossibility of changing the world is the discourse of those who, for different reasons, have accepted settling for the status quo, either from despair or because they benefit from it. Settling for the status quo is the ultimate expression of quitting the struggle for change. The ability to *resist* is lacking or weak in those who settle for what is. It is easier for anyone who has given up on resisting, or for whom resisting wasn't ever possible, to cozy up to the tepidness of impossibility, rather than to embrace the permanent and almost always uneven struggle for justice and ethics.

It is important, however, to emphasize that there is a fundamental difference between those who settle into hopelessness, subjected as they have been to the asphyxia of *necessity* that precludes the adventure of *freedom* and the struggle for it, and those who find in the discourse of settling an effective instrument to block change. The former are the oppressed without horizons; the latter are the impenitent oppressors. That is one of the reasons why the progressive literacy educator must not be satisfied with the teaching of reading and writing that disdainfully turns its back on the reading of the world.

That is also the reason why progressive militants need, even quixotically so, to oppose the domesticating discourse which says the people want less and less politics, less talk, and more results. Those who emphasize the ideology of doing naturally believe, and would like to inculcate into the popular classes and others, that any reflection upon who will benefit from an action, or about how much a project has cost or could cost, constitutes unnecessary blah-blah-blah, for *doing* is what really matters. In reality, it is not so. No work is ever disassociated from whom it serves, how much it costs, or how much less it could cost without sacrificing its effectiveness.

Dealing with the city, with the polis, is not simply a technical matter; it is above all a political one. As a politician and progressive educator, I will continue in my struggle to bring clarity to public goings-on and to oppose the absurd view taken by many: "He steals, but gets things done. He has my vote."

I would like to underscore that, in line with the present considerations, the constant exercise of "reading the world," requiring as it does a critical understanding of reality, involves denouncing it and, at the same time, heralding that which does not yet exist. The experience of reading the world as a book to be read and rewritten is not in fact a waste of time, some ideological blah-blah-blah, a sacrifice of time that should be fervently spent in the transparence and transference of content—as the reactionary "pragmatics" among educators charge. Quite the contrary, when done with methodical rigor, a reading of the world founded in the possibility men and women have created along their long history to *comprehend* the concrete and to *communicate* what is apprehended undeniably constitutes a factor in the improvement of language. The exercises of apprehending, of finding the reason or reasons for what is apprehended, of denouncing apprehended reality and announcing its overcoming, all are part of the process of reading the world. They make way for the experience of *conjecture,* of supposition, of opinion still lacking precise foundation. Through methodical curiosity, the reading of the world can lead to moving beyond *conjecture* per se to a *vision for the world.* The greater presence of *innocence,* which characterizes curiosity at the moment of *conjecture,* starts to make more and more room for a disquieting but secure criticalness, which makes it possible to overcome pure opinion or conjecture toward a vision for the world. That vision is conjecture defined with clarity; it is the possible dream to be made possible through political action.

Critically reading the world is a political-pedagogical doing; it is inseparable from the pedagogical-political, that is, from political action that involves the organization of groups and of the popular classes in order to intervene in the reinventing of society.

Denouncing and announcing, when part of the process of critically reading the world, give birth to the dream for which one fights. This dream or vision, whose profile becomes clear in the process of critically analyzing the reality one denounces, is a practice that transforms society, just as the drawings of a unit a factory worker is to build, which he or she has in his or her head before making it, makes possible the actual manufacturing of the unit.

In keeping with my democratic position, I am convinced that discussion around the dream or vision of the society for which we struggle is not a privilege of the dominant elites or of progressive political leaderships. On the contrary, participating in the debates on a vision for a different world is a right of the popular classes, who must not be simply "guided" or pushed toward a dream by their leadership.

With the advent of the existence men and women created with the materials life provided them, it became impossible for them to be present in the world without reference to a tomorrow. The form which that tomorrow or future will take, however, is never inexorable. On the contrary, it is problematic. Tomorrow is not a tomorrow given ahead of time. I must fight to have it, but I must also have a drawing of it as I struggle to build it, just like the factory worker needs the drawings for a table in his head before building it. So it is with the vision and the dream for which I fight.

One of the foremost tasks for a radical and liberating critical pedagogy is to clarify the legitimacy of the ethical political dream of overcoming unjust reality. It must work through how genuine the struggle is and how possible change is. That is to say, it must work against the dominant fatalist ideology, its power to encourage immobility on the part of the oppressed and their adaptation to unjust reality, both of which are requirements for the dominant order. Radical and liberating critical pedagogy must defend an educational practice where the rigorous teaching of content is never done in a cold, mechanical, or untruthfully neutral manner.

It is in this sense, among others, that radical pedagogy must never make any concessions to the trickeries of neoliberal "pragmatism," which reduces the educational practice to the technical-scientific training of learners, *training* rather than *educating.* The necessary technical-scientific education of learners for which critical pedagogy struggles has nothing to do with the technicist and scientist narrowness that characterizes mere training. For this reason, the capable and serious progressive educator must not only teach his or her discipline well, but he or she must also challenge the learner to critically think through the social, political, and historic reality within which he or she is a presence. For this reason, as he or she teaches his or her discipline seriously and rigorously, the progressive educator must not settle or quit the struggle, defeated by the fatalist discourse which points to one single historic exit today—acceptance, taken to be an expression of modernity, rather than "backwardness" of the reality before us because what is is what must be.

Obviously, the freedom-loving, critical educator's role is not to impose on the learner her taste for freedom, her radical refusal of the dehumanizing order; it is not to say that there is only one way to read the world—hers. The teaching of her discipline alone, no matter how competent, does not subsume her role. As her actions become testament to the seriousness with which she works and to the ethical rigor with which she deals with people and facts, the progressive teacher must not be silenced before the statement that "the homeless are chiefly responsible for their life of destitution." She must not be silenced before the discourse that points to the impossibility of changing the world because reality is what it is.

The progressive teacher teaches the contents of her discipline with rigor, and demands, with rigor, that the learners produce, but she does not hide her political option in the impossible neutrality of her occupation.

The progressive educator does not allow herself any doubt with respect to the right boys and girls from the masses, *the people,* have to know the same mathematics, physics, or biology that boys and girls from the "happier parts" of town learn. At the same time, she never accepts that the teaching of any discipline whatsoever could take place divorced from a critical analysis of how society works.

As she underscores the fundamental importance of science, the progressive educator must also emphasize to poor boys and girls, as well as to the rich, the duty we all have to permanently question ourselves about in whose favor, or in favor of what, we make science.

The task of progressive men and women is helping the development of that dream of world change, as well as its realization, be it in a systematic or nonsystematic manner; be it at school, as a math, biology, history, philosophy, or language teacher; be it at home, as father or as mother dealing with sons and daughters; or be it in relationships with business associates. That is the task of men and women who not only speak of democracy but also live it, always seeking to make it better and better.

If we are progressives, and indeed open to the other, we must make an effort, humbly so, to narrow the distance between what we say and what we do as much as possible.

We cannot speak to our children, or in their presence, about a better world, one less unjust, more human, while we exploit those who work for us. At times, we may even pay better wages, but we can still fall for the old song of "reality is what it is, and I cannot save the world by myself."

It is important to give testimony to our children that it is possible to be consistent, and even more, that being consistent is the final stage of our being whole. After all, being consistent is not a favor we do others, but rather an ethical manner of behaving. Thus, we must not be consistent hoping to be compensated, praised, or applauded.

4

Humanizing Social Relations

INTRODUCTION: HUMANIZING SOCIAL RELATIONS, 1990 TO THE PRESENT

The exploitation and violence associated with the capitalist world-system tend to dehumanize women and men around the world. Feminist movements have demanded an end to exploitative, hierarchical, and violent social relations. Humanizing social relations, they have argued, will depend on an ethic that values redistribution and sharing and on practices that create egalitarian, not exploitative, social relations. As Lourdes Arizpe has argued, "People in every culture are highlighting their singularity *but are aware of the need to cooperate with their fellow cohabitants in the rest of the planet....* Slowly, through the same mediums that carry the voices of war, other voices are gradually creating networks in the search for a rational, sustainable way of dealing with the present global threats [emphasis added]."[1]

While people work to humanize relations around the world, it is important to identify the social forces (capitalists and state officials) that drive the capitalist world-system forward and the practices (direct exploitation, indirect exploitation, and unequal exchange) that have long *de*humanized women and men.

CAPITALISTS AND STATES

As the name indicates, the "capitalist" system is animated by capitalists who exploit people and nature in a relentless search for profit. They are the heart of the system.[2] Their energetic search for profit is the pump that drives the system forward. But they cannot do it alone, and never have. They need state officials to create conditions favorable to the search for profit, to act as the lungs, if you will, for the capitalist heart.

State officials have done two things that are essential if the heart is to function. First, they have provided subsidies (oxygen) to capitalist firms. They provided domestic territories and overseas colonies where capitalists could exploit people and resources. In the United States, for example, they provided land for railroads and farms (the Homestead Act), water for agriculture (the Reclamation Act), highways for transport, education and training for workers, immigrant workers for industry and agriculture (immigration laws and the Bracero Program), and a navy, army, and police to protect investment overseas and property at home.

Second, state officials have absorbed the costs or wastes (carbon dioxide) associated with capitalist development. They have replanted forests cut down by timber companies; treated water fouled by industrial and agricultural waste; taken care of workers laid off by private firms or injured on the job; provided relief for widows, children, single mothers, and the poor who are unable to survive on wages paid by private firms; and provided health care and pensions for retired workers. By absorbing part of the social and environmental costs associated with capitalism, state officials have made it possible for private firms to "externalize" many of the costs of doing business, which has enabled them to secure higher profits than they would otherwise.[3]

Of course, the relation between capitalists and state officials has varied considerably. In some countries, capitalist firms have dominated the relation and state officials have been very weak. Think of Elizabethan England, where the state was weak and officials allowed privateers (Sir Francis Drake) and monopolies (the Royal Africa Company) to conduct foreign policy, capture slaves, and wage war on their own account, or of contemporary Somalia, where the central government has ceased to function and capitalist warlords compete for power like freebooters of yore. In other cases, state officials have dominated the relation. Think of the Soviet Union, where state officials ran virtually every business but did so in order to generate a surplus that could be used to finance industrialization and economic development, or of Nazi Germany, where state officials enrolled capitalist firms in their program of military industrialization and genocide. But even though state officials in both countries dominated business, their goal was much the same: to exploit labor and natural resources and generate a surplus or profit that could be used to industrialize the economy and strengthen the military. Although capitalism was not supposed to exist in the Soviet Union after the communist revolution in 1917, economist Nikolai Kondratieff observed that the economy exhibited the regular "breathing" rhythms of expansion and contraction that were characteristic features of "capitalist" development.[4] (He was purged and executed for his observations.) In most countries, however, the relation between capitalists and state officials lies somewhere between the capitalist privateer model and the socialist entrepreneur model, and they collaborate to promote economic development and political power.

Of course, the capitalist world-system consists of more than 190 states and countless businesses and multinational corporations that compete with every other business. This means that capitalists/state officials in one polity compete with capitalists/state officials in all the other polities for profits and political power. Because there is no central "brain" or administrative government that regulates or imposes order on the system as a whole, the result is a systemic anarchy that expresses itself in competition, conflict, and war. If there were a global government, the world-system would be an "empire," not a capitalist world-system.[5] Because the system is based on anarchy (which means "without government"), it is regularly beset by economic boom and bust, political conflict and war. During its long history, a few states have managed to establish a political-economic "hegemony" and impose some "order" on the system—as Holland, Great Britain, and, recently, the United States have done. But these "great powers" did not eliminate economic or political anarchy from the system; they only attenuated it.

In their pursuit of profits and power, capitalists and state officials have long exploited women and men around the world. Historically, they have used "direct exploitation," "indirect exploitation," and "unequal exchange" to exploit and dehumanize people the world over.[6]

In *Capital*, Karl Marx accurately described the "direct exploitation" of wage workers in industry and agriculture.[7] But by focusing on the experience of male wage workers in industry, he neglected to examine and failed to appreciate the "indirect exploitation" of women who engaged in unpaid and subsistence work in households, fields, or the streets. And he did not understand how indirect exploitation made it possible for capitalists/state officials in some regions to practice "unequal exchange" with other regions, a practice that contributed to wealth in the North and led to poverty in the South. By analyzing direct and indirect exploitation and unequal exchange, feminist and other inclusive scholars are learning to show how all three kinds of exploitation are connected, how workers of the world are joined together in a global division of labor, and how movements are developing humanistic projects to benefit everyone around the world.

❀   ❀   ❀

WE ARE ALL CONNECTED: GLOBAL WORKERS, CONSUMERS, AND ACTIVISTS

People have lived in a world-system driven by the ceaseless accumulation of profits on a world scale.* This ties everyone together and shapes our multidimensional identities, placing us both inside and outside of gender/sexuality/age, ethnic, and other oppressed groups. The capitalist world-system constructed working women and other disenfranchised groups as the primary producers of value. But these workers were defined as the least valued workers who made the least valued products. Employers did not pay these workers for the value they created, or they paid very little for it, especially when compared to the wages distributed to the most advantaged, least hardworking laborers in the world: white, upper-middle-class, middle-years, heterosexual men in the global North. In order to feed members of their households and to help neighbors, most of the world's laboring people had to organize a large portion of their work, which generated important use values, in-kind, and other "income" supplements to their low wages.

The whole system has rested on the generation of this hidden, gendered, and racialized subsidy to capital and the state: a subsidy that has come from the unpaid and self-organized work by the world's disenfranchised. By creating households that generated this hidden subsidy for capital and the state, the accumulators found that their profits grew from sources that were largely hidden from view. Women and other working people saw their wages suppressed and their freedom curtailed.

But the system's dependency on women and unpaid work also provided a pathway for revolt. When women-centered groups defined people's self-organized work as a way to survive outside of the global system, the accumulators found that they had a challenge. At many moments throughout the world-system's history, politicized women have redefined household and community work to mean "a pathway to liberation" (and not subjugation).

The reclaiming and redefinition of work by disenfranchised people are happening more and more, especially as local groups organize to reclaim the civil commons and engage in collective production and democratic decisionmaking. More disenfranchised women and men are inverting the priorities from profit making to social reproduction, and they are using their self-organized work as the economic base for initiating new societies.

The question for most of us is: how do we recognize each other's humanity and how do we allow change, global production, and the global market to distance us from each other and make exploitation seem natural, normal, and totally expected?

Working people in this class-based global society are directly connected to each other, though many ignore, deny, or resist this mutual interdependency. Today the relationship between worker households in the well-off global North and those in the poorer global South is often indirect. Their connection can perhaps be illustrated by the kind of relations exhibited in restaurants. When worker households in the North dine out, they consume food and drink made by others far away. Farmers, vintners, brewers, ranchers, and fishers produce food for the table in different settings around the world and receive small (and shrinking) sums for the goods they make. Diners are served by a small army of cooks, busboys, waiters, and washers who labor for low wages, scramble for tips, and wait silently by. The meal on the table is also made possible by the work of people who keep food-industry and service workers fed, clothed, washed, and trained to work for others. The work that women, wives, children, and elders do is not paid, but without their labor, farmers could not harvest food and waiters could not lay the table. Diners, of course, ignore these servants and concentrate instead on the cuisine and conversation at their table. But every bite that diners enjoy, every sip that they take is made possible by the exploitation of paid and unpaid workers, near and far.

Yet although diners benefit from the exploitation (of all these workers), they do not themselves organize this work or profit from it. Capitalist firms—the restaurateurs but also the companies that purchase grain, process beef, ship produce, supply napkins, scrutinize accounts, and draw up ads—organize the people who work in the food-processing and food-service industries. It is they who profit from the exploitation of paid and unpaid workers, from the sale of food to worker-consumers. Everyone in the restaurant, diners and servants and their off-stage assistants scattered across the globe, was brought together by capital. It is capital's mediating presence that shapes the whole scene.

Working people from the South, who are hidden by global market operations, have been forced or persuaded to toil for corporations and banks in the North so that the relatively well-off minority can continue to dine well. When household members in the wealthy core countries close their eyes for a cozy eight hours of sleep, downy nighttime covers are pulled up by the hands of hardworking moms in the world-economy's impoverished periphery, or by bonded child laborers, by teenage girls who make sneakers, by migrating dads who send money home, and by grandparents and aunts who vend gum and cigarettes. After the global North goes to sleep, the global South can slumber; before the North awakes, the South rises. Although formal slavery on plantations has been outlawed, a freer form of economic subordination now allows core workers to forget that they have been holding hands with and standing on the backs of peripheral workers for 500 years. During this time, workers in the North and South have made few efforts to team up. They have not done so because the entire global system is set up to cultivate the demands of workers and consumers in the North, paying them the highest wages (though at unequal levels) and allowing them to imagine what college they should attend, what car they should buy, what house they should furnish, and what vacation they should take when they retire, even if these goods were secured through bank credit and consumer indebtedness.

At this conjuncture in history, we need to ask: Will laboring people in the North and South be able to work together for their own collective good?

NOTE

*Nobody has explained the global economic processes of exploitation more clearly than Immanuel Wallerstein and Terence K. Hopkins, a team of scholars who, for decades, attended classes together, conducted research in various countries, analyzed social change, started a historical sociology graduate program at Binghamton University, and established the Fernand Braudel Center at Binghamton University, which brought researchers together, from around the world, to study social change. Friendship can provide a strong base for changing the world.

Source: Torry Dickinson and Robert Schaeffer. *Fast Forward: Work, Gender, and Protest in a Changing World.* Lanham, MD: Rowman and Littlefield, 2001, 4–5.

DIRECT EXPLOITATION

In *Capital,* Marx explained how capitalists profited from the "direct exploitation" of workers in industry and agriculture. Exploitation occurred as workers agreed, for example, to labor ten hours a day, six days a week, in exchange for a cash wage. (In agriculture, wages were often paid in cash but also in kind, which might have included the provision of food and clothing or the use of land.) Marx argued that this basic deal was unfair and exploitative for two reasons. First, it was unfair because workers—who owned no property, had few opportunities to generate cash income, and had only their labor to sell—were in a weak bargaining position, so it was difficult for them to set terms or conditions on the use of their labor during working hours. Second, and more important, workers generated more value for the capitalist than the capitalist paid them in wages. During the first hour or so of the working day, workers produced value equal to their wage. But during the rest of the day, workers produced additional or "surplus" value, which was claimed by the capitalist. After deducting the cost of wages, tools, and raw materials, the capitalist could redeem the surplus value produced by workers as profit, which could be consumed by the capitalist or used to finance the expansion of production and the creation of even more surplus value. It was the direct exploitation of wage labor that made it possible for capitalists to generate profit and accumulate capital.

Because capitalists compete with other capitalists, it is in the interest of individual capitalists to maximize the surplus produced by wage workers. Historically, they have had two ways to increase the surplus. First, they could increase the number of hours that workers produce value, a process Marx described as increasing surplus value in "absolute" terms. Second, they could introduce machines to increase the productivity of workers, a process he described as increasing surplus value in "relative" terms.

Increasing Absolute Surplus Value

Capitalists have generated more value from the workers they employ by increasing the number of hours in the working day, days in the work week, and weeks in the work year. In the late nineteenth century, when Marx wrote *Capital,* it was common for capitalists in the United States to demand that workers labor 12 hours a day, 6 days a week, 52 weeks a year, with time off for just a couple of holidays: the Fourth of July, Thanksgiving, Christmas, and New Year's. During the twentieth century, workers tried with some success to limit this practice, fighting to achieve the 8-hour day, 5-day work week, and 2-week paid vacation every year. But in recent years, capitalists have evaded these restrictions and once again increased absolute surplus value production. They have demanded that industrial employees work overtime on a more or less permanent basis and required salaried workers to work overtime without additional pay. Sixty-hour work weeks are common for many office workers, and businesses now expect workers to conduct business by e-mail, phone, or fax even when they are not at work: at home in the evening and on weekends, in cars during the commute to and from work. These expectations have extended the work day and the work week. Capitalist firms have also extended the work year by curbing vacation time. In the United States, 25 percent of workers do not have *any* paid vacation time and another 33 percent get only five days of vacation a year, a significant decline from previous decades.[8] As a result of these developments, capitalist firms have succeeded in increasing absolute surplus value production in recent years, much as they did in the late nineteenth century.

Increasing Relative Surplus Value Production

Capitalist firms have also introduced machinery to increase the productivity or efficiency of workers and make them each produce more surplus value. For example, when capitalists replaced manual typewriters with IBM Selectrics in the 1960s, then replaced these with personal computers in the 1980s and e-mail in the 1990s, they were able to increase the productivity of office workers enormously. This enabled them to eliminate the "secretarial pool," where women used to type up letters dictated by managers, and required managers to type up and send their own letters and reports. Because capitalists did not increase wages as fast as the productivity of office workers rose, they were able to increase the production of surplus value.

Of course, wage workers recognized that the introduction of machines into the workplace—assembly lines in factories, mechanical harvesters in agriculture, electronic machines and computer technologies in offices—made it possible for capitalists to lay off unnecessary workers and increase the pace of work. So they organized sit-down strikes and joined trade unions to curb these practices. But even workers in unions found it difficult to slow the introduction of new technology, prevent layoffs, or control the pace of work. In the postwar period, they generally settled for higher wages as their productivity rose, though wage gains never kept pace with productivity increases. But in recent years, capitalists have refused to share productivity gains with workers. Instead, they have taken the profits derived from increased productivity and rewarded high-level managers and shareholders.[9] So even though workers are more productive (productivity in the United States has increased about 3 percent annually in recent years), wages have stagnated and capitalists have reaped the benefits of increasing surplus value production.[10]

But although Marx analyzed the "direct" exploitation of wage workers in industry and agriculture, he did not explore or analyze the "indirect" exploitation that made it possible. Marx failed to do so in part because he based his analysis on the treatment of individual, *male* wage workers (not on the women, children, and elders who pooled income in worker households),[11] in part because he assumed that wages, however low, would cover the cost of reproducing wage workers (rather than covering only a portion of the cost of reproducing worker households).

INDIRECT EXPLOITATION

Capitalist firms can increase the surplus that workers produce if they increase the amount of time that workers spend on the job (increase absolute surplus value production) or increase the amount of work they do on the job (increase relative surplus value production). Capitalists can also increase the surplus if they cut the wages that workers are paid. But if wages don't cover the cost of reproducing workers, as is the case for most workers around the world, capitalists can cut wages only if they can persuade women, children, and elders in worker households to do more nonwage subsistence work to cover the cost of reproduction. This is an "indirect" form of exploitation because capitalists do not themselves ask women to work harder so firms can cut male wages. Today firms benefit doubly from the exploitation of women because the unpaid work of women makes it possible to cut male wages, which increases the production of surplus for capitalists.

But how do capitalist firms persuade women to work harder so that business can pay male wage workers less? Historically, capitalist firms and state officials have assigned men a patriarchal role in worker households, designated women and children as their legal subordinates and, for a long time, as their property, and given men license to employ domestic and intimate forms of violence and rape to make sure women and children comply with male authority in the household and, indirectly, with capitalist patriarchy in society at large. The patriarchal, heterosexist, intimate violence in worker households, then, was central (not peripheral) to the ability of capitalist firms to maintain or increase high levels of indirect exploitation, which made it possible for them to cut wages and increase the production of surplus. Personal, intimate, domestic violence and sexual assault were not incidental to the system. It was not the residual expression of precapitalist social norms. Instead, it was part and parcel of a global strategy to cut the costs and increase the profits of capitalist firms. The capitalist world-system, then, has been characterized by violence at two levels: (1) the violence and war associated with the competition and conflict between groups of capitalists/state officials in different polities (states); and (2) the violence associated with the assertion of male authority in worker households, which helped manage the indirect exploitation of women and children.

Of course, women have long struggled against the assertion of male authority and the intensification of unpaid and subsistence work in households. They have struggled to undo their legal subordination to men and gain legal standing and political rights as women. As Martha Nussbaum has argued, "[L]iberty is not just a matter of having rights on paper, it requires being in a material position to exercise those rights."[12] Women have campaigned to end the legal license given men to practice domestic violence and sexual assault and have worked against systemic violence and war.

In recent decades, women have taken two steps that challenged the ability of capitalists and male wage workers to exercise patriarchal authority in households. First, an increasing number of women have chosen to break their legal relations with men, or, based on people's choices about how they respond to economic duress and global work options, they have established worker households ostensibly headed by women. The rise of divorce and the creation of households headed by women have been an important global development in this context, often bringing more independence and almost always higher levels of economic insecurity and longer hours of work. Second, women in worker households (headed by women or by men) have demanded greater access to reproductive technologies, control of their bodies, and reproductive rights, and they have decided, the world over, to bear fewer children. Fertility rates have declined in Protestant, Catholic, Jewish, Muslim, Buddhist, and pagan communities around the world.[13] Although women have taken these steps for a variety of reasons and at different rates, these two developments have had important consequences for the capitalist world-system and the indirect exploitation of women.

The rise of worker households headed by women has made it more difficult for capitalist firms to cut wages because divorce severs the link between wages and unpaid work. Capitalists cannot cut male wages—the general trend in the era of globalization—if they cannot expect women in households to pick up the slack. And declining fertility rates reduce the size of the available labor force. It is difficult for capitalists to cut wages where labor is in short supply. This is particularly true of the rich countries in the North, where fertility rates have declined most dramatically. To prevent labor "shortages" (which for capitalists means there is not a plentiful supply of cheap labor), capitalists and state officials in many countries (the United States among them) have encouraged or permitted large-scale immigration to help keep wages down.

The rise in divorce rates and the creation of households headed by women and the fact that women in households have demanded an end to domestic violence and sexual assault and greater control of their reproductive choices since the 1970s have threatened to undermine both capitalist firms, which rely on increasing indirect exploitation, and male authority in worker households, which makes indirect exploitation possible. These changes have also led to the intense overwork of greatly underremunerated women and girls, a situation that, given the rise of feminist movements and the instability of the global system, has opened up strong waves of resistance. These changes have also contributed to a reaction by fundamentalist religious groups—conservative Protestants and Catholics in the United States, Catholics in Western Europe, Orthodox Christians in Eastern Europe, conservative Muslims in countries from North Africa to the Philippines, conservative Buddhists in Sri Lanka, conservative Hindus in India, and conservative Jews in Israel and the Diaspora—who share a common desire in an era of global wage cuts for men to reassert male authority in households and restrict women's reproductive choices. This reassertion of religious fundamentalism is *not* at odds with contemporary globalization. It is *complementary* to it because, if successful, it would allow men to increase levels of indirect exploitation in the households. Ironically, this would permit capitalist firms to reduce the wages of men even more than they have, for fundamentalists and others.

Still, women's efforts to challenge male authority and violence have made it difficult for capitalist firms to practice indirect exploitation and treat women as the "last colony" (see Chapter 3) and have made it more difficult for men in households to direct this project.

UNEQUAL EXCHANGE

Capitalist firms rely on the direct exploitation of wage workers and the indirect exploitation of unpaid and subsistence workers. But capitalists in the northern "core" also rely on "unequal exchange" with workers in the southern "periphery" to generate surplus that can be used to fuel capital accumulation.[14]

In global terms, worker households in the northern "core" have a relatively *high* wage component and a relatively *low* nonwage component. That is, wages provide the bulk of the income they need to survive, whereas nonwage (unpaid and subsistence) work makes a small, but important, contribution to household income. By contrast, worker households in the southern "periphery" have a relatively *low* wage component and a relatively *high* nonwage component. This means they rely primarily on unpaid and subsistence work to survive and obtain a small, but important, share of their household income from wages. (See findings of household groups in Chapter 2.)

Because worker households in the periphery do not rely as heavily on wage income as their counterparts in the core, capitalist firms can pay them less than they would if wages covered a larger percentage of their household income. Essentially, capitalists can pay peripheral wage workers less because women and children work more (the indirect exploitation of nonwage workers is higher in the periphery). These unequal work relations and unequal exchange relations sustain each other, allowing employers to pay unequal wages and allowing the North's firms to pay unfair or "unequal" prices for goods made in the periphery.

There is another reason why capitalists in the core can underpay workers in the periphery. Capitalist firms have long monopolized the purchase of peripheral goods. They did so for a long time because state officials in the North gave them trade monopolies in their colonies. Because there were large numbers of sellers in the colonies, but only one buyer, companies in the core had a huge advantage when it came to setting prices or the terms of trade. (Monopsony—a monopoly of buyers—benefits buyers, not sellers.) In the postwar, postcolonial period, trade monopsonies gave way to trade oligopolies, where a handful of firms in the core dominated the purchase of goods from the periphery. Think of the three big chocolate companies—Mars, Nestlé, and Hershey—or the big oil companies before OPEC was established. To counter this, producers in the periphery organized producer "cartels" such as OPEC in the 1970s so they could bargain more effectively with monopsony buyers in the core. But the regional and global "free trade" agreements adopted during the 1990s made *producer* cartels in the periphery illegal while doing nothing to curb the power of *buyer* monopsonies in the core. Adam Smith long ago argued in *The Wealth of Nations* that free trade *cannot* coexist with monopoly. So the regional (North American Free Trade Agreement; NAFTA) and global (World Trade Organization; WTO) trade agreements cannot be said to promote "free trade." This is ideological language used to promote them, not an accurate description of what they do.[15]

Exchange between core and periphery has become even more "unequal" in recent years for a variety of reasons. First, the structural adjustment programs (SAPs) imposed on debtor states in the periphery required workers to produce more goods to earn the money to repay their debts. But increasing supplies have weakened their bargaining position and lowered the price of goods they make.[16] Second, many firms in the periphery have replaced male workers with female workers, which has enabled them to cut wages and increase levels of *direct exploitation*. Third, to cope with declining incomes and the rising costs associated with SAPs (which typically required states to stop subsidizing food, fuel, and transport; the end of subsidies raised the price of these essential goods), women have intensified their unpaid and subsistence work, which increased levels of *indirect exploitation*. And as workers relied more on nonwage income to survive, it became possible for capitalist firms to cut wages and increase the rate of *unequal exchange*.

Of course, workers in the periphery have struggled against the imposition of structural adjustment programs, the adoption of regional and global trade agreements, and the intensification of unpaid and subsistence work. But their historical disadvantages—colonialism—have made it difficult for them to fend off the multiple threats posed by contemporary globalization.

START THE HEALING

Women and men have struggled for centuries against different kinds of exploitation. This has been difficult to do, in part because people have often internalized their oppression. As Beverly Daniels Tatum has argued, everyone breathes in the toxic smog of racism,[17] capitalism, colonialism, violence, patriarchy, and oppression. People who breathe these poisons are sickened by them. When people internalize these toxins, they often come to view themselves as inferior, as passive victims, not active agents. In *The Wretched of the Earth,* Frantz Fanon described how exploitation and colonialism dehumanized people, sapped their energy and self-confidence, and undermined their capacity to act collaboratively for positive change.[18] Fanon argued that violence was one way to overcome this sense of inferiority and lethargy, expose the relations of power, and regain human agency. But although he helped diagnose the internalization of oppression, part of his solution—violence—was itself dehumanizing. To use Tatum's analogy, violence does not clear the air, it poisons the atmosphere.

Women's movements have had a different view of violence, in part because women have experienced firsthand the systemic violence associated with war—rape, forced prostitution—and intimate violence associated with the assertion of patriarchal authority in worker households. So feminists have used different, nonviolent strategies to overcome the internalization of oppression and have advocated nonviolent practices to humanize relations among oppressed people *and* between oppressors and oppressed. Oppressors are also dehumanized by the act of oppressing others. This last is important because egalitarian women and men recognize that people have multiple social identities and occupy different positions in oppressive hierarchies, so people are simultaneously oppressor and oppressed. Given this reality, it makes no sense to use violence against the "oppressor," because the oppressor, in some instances, is the self. Furthermore, the use of violence generates more violence against everyone, both in this generation and in the next.

Women and men have struggled against particular forms of exploitation and, in recent years, have begun developing a general or comprehensive approach to the dehumanization associated with them. In doing so, they have argued for an ethic of redistribution or sharing and fair play.

Direct Exploitation

Women and men have long struggled against the direct exploitation of wage workers. They formed trade unions and organized labor parties to shorten the work day, control the pace of work, slow the introduction of "labor-saving" technology, raise wages as their productivity increased, and address the problems associated with capitalists' efforts to increase exploitation in absolute and relative terms.[19] Civil rights and women's movements have campaigned against efforts to exclude them from the paid labor force and have challenged racial and gender discrimination at work.

Indirect Exploitation

Around the world, women in different settings have struggled against pressures to increase their work burdens and subordinate women to men in heterosexist households. Their struggles against domestic violence and campaigns for reproductive rights have been increasingly linked to struggles against systemic violence, war, rape, and militarized prostitution. As Kemala Kempadoo has written, it is critical to examine the "colonialisms, recolonizations, and cultural imperialisms, as well as specific local histories and traditions" that shape the agency of women and contribute to racialized sexual objectification.[20]

Unequal Exchange

For centuries, women and men in the periphery struggled against colonialism, which first created conditions that facilitated unequal exchange. During the mid-twentieth century, their collective efforts finally brought formal colonialism to an end.[21] In the postcolonial period, capitalists and state officials in the core have used global trade agreements and the World Trade Organization as a way to promote neocolonialism and unequal exchange. In response, activists in the core *and* in the periphery have combined in a global anti-WTO movement that has effectively wrecked efforts to consolidate and expand the power of the WTO and its efforts to increase levels of unequal exchange. Kempadoo has argued that if movements are going to promote change that will "benefit the majority of the world, not a select few," global institutions that are responsible for inhumanities and violence in the core—the International Monetary Fund, the World Bank, and the WTO—will have to be challenged.[22]

HUMANIZING SOCIAL RELATIONS

Women have struggled *against* different forms of exploitation and they have campaigned *for* humanizing social relations. Patricia Hill Collins has advocated engaging in a "process of self-conscious struggle that empowers women and men to actualize a *humanist* vision of community [emphasis added]."[23] This struggle would help people to redefine who they are and how they work, and it would be based on parity and inclusive participation, Nancy Fraser has argued.[24] According to Fraser, "participatory parity" would have three features for people participating in the struggle: it would (1) encourage the distribution of natural resources in a mutually interdependent way that would give all the participants a voice, (2) institutionalize common cultural values based on equal respect and equal opportunity for the participants, and (3) recognize individual group members as full partners in the process. Providing for families and communities would be valued instead of providing for the economic accumulation of a few.

@ @ @

FEMINIST POLITICAL ECONOMY AND THE GLOBAL REDISTRIBUTION OF WEALTH

If academic researchers and social activists want to support others who develop their "agency," their ability to act upon and shape the world, it is important to engage in change. Participatory action skills can best be developed through practice and engagement, not by thinking, reading, or discussing in the abstract. Taking action is one way to move beyond analyzing dominant ideologies and celebrating the formation of new cultural expressions that emerge from social fragmentations. As Lourdes Benería argued, one way scholars and social activists can address hunger and poverty is by facilitating changes that lead to the global redistribution of wealth. Because participatory engagement is a form of research, taking action may be the best way to understand the hidden gender, racial, class, and global dimensions of enrichment and impoverishment. It is critical to engage with the institutions in society that accumulate global wealth, misuse natural resources, and perpetuate inequalities. In addition, it is important to learn how people can create new social relations and new relations of self-sufficiency and subsistence. Carrying out these fundamental changes may be the best way to stop the reproduction of intersecting hierarchies.

As a result of the critiques of universalism, postmodern work emphasized issues of identity, difference, citizenship, and agency, resulting in the proliferation of what Nancy Fraser (1997) has called "fronts of struggle" having to do with the recognition of social groups or social expressions and assertions of difference and representation—including gender as well as subjectivity, race, ethnicity, sexuality, North-South diversity, and other forms of social differentiation. The effort has been a most dynamic source of analytical power, political struggles, and social change and we have learned a great deal from the interesting contributions resulting from these currents. New areas of academic inquiry have enriched our understanding, for example, of identity politics, sexuality and gender, symbolic representations/intersections of gender and race, the multiple levels of an analysis of the body, postcolonial realities and many others.

    Interestingly, these tendencies have run parallel, on the material side of everyday life, to the resurgence of neoliberalism across countries and to the globalization of markets and of social and cultural life—generating rapid changes that need to be understood and acted upon. Yet a good proportion of postmodern analyses has tended to neglect the dynamics of political economy, thus deemphasizing important areas of social concern having to do with the material and, more concretely, the economic. The result has been, in Nancy Fraser's terms, "a general decoupling of the cultural politics of recognition from the social politics of distribution." . . . This generated a growing imbalance between the urgent need to understand economic reality—since distribution is about the sharing of things material—and the more predominant focus on "words," including issues of difference, subjectivity, and representation.

These tendencies have been a matter of concern for a variety of authors as well. For example, in their book on land and property rights in Latin America, Carmen Diana Deere and Magdalena León, . . . also echoing Fraser's work, point out that "the theoretical energy of feminists in Latin America as well as internationally has centered on . . . issues of recognition rather than redistribution." . . . Thus, they insist that the relationship between fundamental factors affecting women's lives, such as gender and property, has not been sufficiently explored and that "attention to issues of redistribution, particularly of property, is fundamental for transforming gender relations and ending women's subordination."...

[T]he point here is not to say that the turn to culture and the emphasis on identity, representation, and agency are not important and useful, but to argue that something has been missing in the process: they need to be linked to other sources of empowerment having to do with the socioeconomic aspects of people's lives.

Source: Lourdes Benería. *Gender, Development, and Globalization.* New York: Routledge, 2003, 25–26.

It is not enough to end direct and indirect exploitation and unequal exchange. Humanizing social relations will require people in the North and South to develop new ways of interacting. As Jessica Horn has written, "The conversation must begin with a critical transformation of the culture of exclusion and arrogance that has come to dominate the 'globalized' world. . . . This process of recovery necessitates a deep reflection on the assumptions of the superiority of western technology and know-how and the imperative to 'develop' that are embedded in development discourse."[25]

In her article "Looking from the South," Horn agrees with the anticolonial insights of Samia Mehrez: bringing an end to colonization and unequal exchange requires an act of exorcism involving *both* the colonizer and the colonized.[26] This view draws on the observations of Albert Memmi (*The Colonizer and the Colonized*).[27] As Horn has argued, "The developers, and the 'developed' themselves need to engage in a very deep process of reflection over the beliefs that guide their actions and their relations of power that enable them."[28]

As part of a campaign to redistribute resources on a global scale, some inclusive movements have struggled to reactivate the kind of "traditional" redistributive relations that long existed in many societies. Indian scholars J. K. Bajaj and M. D. Srinivas have argued that many redistributive practices and traditions in India declined as a result of British colonialism and postcolonial capitalism: "Indians up to the present times seem to have always looked upon abundance of food as the primary condition of civilization, and *sharing* food was the primary discipline of civilized living."[29] But in this century, the redistributive ethic, which encouraged people with means to assist the poor, declined, and "scarcity and callousness have become the norm."[30]

A journey through any part of India, on the railway trains that cross the country, brings one in [close] contact with hunger and starvation. Young children sweep the floors of the trains to earn a bellyful of food, and fight with the waiters and each other for the right to the leftovers.... The scenes of hunger and starvation become even grimmer as one heads toward the great pilgrimage centres of India. The roads earlier used to be dotted with *chatrams,* the Indian institutions of hospitality, where bells were rung at midnight to invite the seeker to come and receive his food, and where orphaned children were provided shelter, food, education, and care till they were ready to face the world.[31]

For Bajaj and Srinivas, the problem now is to *recover* redistributive traditions and renew the kind of sharing that once bound people together in communities.

The new commitment to an ethic of redistribution and sharing will "require a fire burning from our deepest sources of spiritual strength and knowledge," Leela Fernandes has argued.[32] To redistribute wealth, the Sahiba Sisters Foundation, which works with women in Muslim societies, has turned from asset development to needs-based development.[33] This approach links professional urban women with poorer rural women and creates a new network of reciprocity that avoids notions of charity. Anne Hope and Sally Timmel describe Kenyan women in faith-based activist groups who have become more empowered when they realize, "We are not the problem. It is the structures or policies of the government, or the growing gap between rich and poor.... As people feel they are part of a current that is bringing about some real transformation, they grow in hope."[34] And David Korten has argued that the answer to the world's global crisis is not growth, but "a transformation of the values and institutions that define how we use the earth's bounty and distribute its benefits.... As we learn more about the nature of true movements we realize that they are characterized by values-driven, action-oriented flows of voluntary energy, given shape and direction by a shared vision."[35]

Women leaders have also engaged in participatory social justice projects that have grown out of institutionalized religion. Mexico's Christian Base Communities (CBCs), 70 percent of whose members are women, have argued that they are doing spiritual, activist work for social transformation. Women in participatory CBCs throughout Latin America have addressed health needs, worked for the liberation of the poor and oppressed, and served as leading educators in the University of the Poor, as CBCs are sometimes known.[36]

Household-organized work, even with all of the imposed constraints, has been used as an independent moment for women and men to begin restructuring everyday life from the ground up. When wages cover a small portion of the cost of a household's reproduction, households may share clothing and basic household items, or they may acquire them through bartering, which is a way of defining and exchanging equivalents at the grassroots level. And women have struggled with men for more egalitarian workloads. In Chiapas, Mexico, indigenous women in the Zapatista regional autonomy movement have demanded the right to rest and the right to "rescue their bodies from permanent exhaustion."[37]

According to Lorraine Code, feminists can learn to think globally by building on the work of theoreticians and methodologists such as Chandra Talpade Mohanty, who has examined global commodity chains to see how women are connected through unequal relations.[38] Alternative trade and work movements in different parts of the world have joined fair trade movements that challenge relations of unequal exchange and promote new kinds of *equal exchange*.[39] By removing midlevel retail capitalists in the global marketplace, the fair trade movement has worked to educate consumers in the North and make them more conscious of their connections to workers elsewhere and has helped meet the needs of producers and their families. By connecting workers' cooperatives with conscious consumers, fair traders have promoted redistribution and fair play and cultivated a new ethic of mutual responsibility and interdependence. The fair trade movement has interrupted capitalist global commodity chains, disrupted sexist and racialized structures of work, and strengthened the collective power of worker households in the South, beginning to reverse the terms of trade and work away from corporations in the North to collectively organized, direct producers in the South.[40] These diverse and multifaceted efforts have promoted an ethic that values redistribution and sharing and encourages practices that create egalitarian relations.

READING

The article "Playfulness, 'World'-Travelling, and Loving Perception" suggested that social relations would be more humanistic if we reached out to others, learned about diverse cultures as part of our own development, traveled to our friends' place that they call "home," and began seeing all of our relationships in a more humanitarian and loving way. For feminists and all social change makers, this is an important part of the process of connecting with people in their own countries and with people who are living in the global South and North. By engaging in cultural traveling as a part of friendship and family, we are learning to love others more deeply, and in doing so, we are learning to love ourselves.[41]

NOTES

1. Lourdes Arizpe, "No Alternatives Without Diversity," *Development* 45, no. 2 (2002): 21–24.

2. This analogy of the system's heart is drawn from Immanuel Wallerstein, *Historical Capitalism with Capitalist Civilization* (London: Verso, 1996). In dominant Western education, Herbert Spencer is referred to as the first sociologist to describe society as a system or as an organism. Emile Durkheim developed and enhanced this description by referring to mechanical and organic solidarity.

3. In the postwar period, taxpayers, labor, environmental, and consumer groups in the core asked state officials to prevent capitalists from externalizing costs by regulating business behavior or requiring business to pay for some of the social and environmental

costs of doing business. But since the 1980s, during the era of globalization, businesses have demanded an end to government "regulation" so they can once more externalize costs and increase profits. By and large, state officials have complied with these demands. See Immanuel Wallerstein, *World-System Analysis: An Introduction* (Durham, NC: Duke University Press, 2004), 47–48.

4. Andre Gunder Frank, "Long Live Transideological Enterprise! The Socialist Economies in the Capitalist International Division of Labor," *Review* 1, no. 1 (Summer 1977): 91–140.

5. Wallerstein, *World-System Analysis.*

6. "Direct" and "indirect" exploitation is a concept that grew out of a historical analysis of waged and nonwaged labor in the world-system. See Frances Moulder, "Global Women's Movements: A World-System Perspective," *Social Problems in the Modern World* (Belmont, CA: Thomson, 2000), 359–362.

7. Karl Marx, *Capital,* Volume 1 (New York: International Publishers, 1974).

8. Timothy Egan, "The Rise of Shrinking-Vacation Syndrome," *New York Times,* August 20, 2006.

9. Robert Schaeffer, *Understanding Globalization,* 3rd ed. (Lanham, MD: Rowman and Littlefield, 2005), 16.

10. "The median hourly wage for American workers has declined 2 percent since 2003.... The drop has been especially notable, economists say, because productivity—the amount that an average worker produces in an hour and the basic wellspring of a nation's living standards—has risen steadily over the same period. As a result, wages and salaries now make up the lowest share of the nation's gross domestic product since the government began recording the data in 1947, while corporate profits have climbed to their highest share since the 1960s. UBS, the investment bank, recently described the current period as 'the golden era of profitability.'" Steven Greenhouse and David Leonhardt, "Real Wages Fail to Match a Rise in Productivity," *New York Times,* August 28, 2006.

11. A household is an economic unit consisting of people who pool income. It is not necessarily a coresidential unit of people who live together in a "house."

12. Martha Nussbaum, "Women and Equality: The Capabilities Approach," *International Labor Review* 138, no. 3 (1999): 227–245, 231. A focus on obtaining political rights for women, in combination with reinterpreting and planting this change in a Thai context, is being tried by Buddhist feminists, Mae Chees, who are working for governmental and private organizational changes that will enable women to become ordained. Parichart Suwanbubbha, "Development and Buddhism Revisited: Arguing the Case for Thai Religious Nuns *(Mae Chees)," Development* 46, no. 4 (2003): 68–73.

13. Elisabeth Rosenthal, "European Union's Plunging Birthrates Spread Eastwards," *New York Times,* September 4, 2006.

14. Arghiri Emmanuel, *Unequal Exchange: A Study of the Imperialism of Trade* (New York: Monthly Review Press, 1972).

15. Robert K. Schaeffer, *Understanding Globalization: The Social Consequences of Political, Economic, and Environmental Change,* 2nd ed. (Lanham, MD: Rowman and Littlefield, 2003), 217–250.

16. Robert K. Schaeffer, *Understanding Globalization: The Social Consequences of Political, Economic, and Environmental Change,* 3rd ed. (Lanham, MD: Rowman and Littlefield, 2005), 95–152.

17. Beverly Daniel Tatum, "Defining Racism: Can We Talk?" in Amy Kesselman, Lilly D. McNair, and Nancy Schniedewind, eds., *Women: Images and Realities* (New York:

McGraw Hill, 2003), 360–364. Sociologist Allan Johnson used a different metaphor, suggesting we all live in a rainy society, which means we all get wet from the rain of racism and sexism.

18. Frantz Fanon, *The Wretched of the Earth* (New York: Grove Press, 1966).

19. Torry Dickinson and Robert Schaeffer, *Fast Forward: Work, Gender, and Protest in a Changing World* (Lanham, MD: Rowman and Littlefield, 2001), 205–223.

20. Kamala Kempadoo, "Women of Color and the Global Sex Trade," *Meridians* 1, no. 2 (2001): 28–51, 28. See also Shu-Ju Ada Cheng, "Rethinking the Globalization of Domestic Service: Foreign Domestics, State Control, and the Politics of Identity in Taiwan," *Gender and Society* 17, no. 2 (April 2003): 166–186, 179.

21. Robert Schaeffer, *Power to the People: Democratization Around the World* (Boulder, CO: Westview Press, 1997), 14–17.

22. Kempadoo, "Women of Color and the Global Sex Trade," 45.

23. Patricia Hill Collins, "Defining Black Feminist Thought," in D. Soyini Madison, ed., *The Woman That I Am: The Literature and Culture of Contemporary Women of Color* (New York: St. Martin's Griffin, 1994), 578–600, 598.

24. Nancy Fraser, "Institutionalizing Democratic Justice: Redistribution, Recognition, and Participation," in Seyla Benhabib and Nancy Fraser, eds., *Pragmatism, Critique, Judgment: Essays for Richard J. Bernstein* (Cambridge, MA: MIT Press, 2004), 126–147, 126–132.

25. Jessica Horn, "Looking from the South, Speaking from Home: African Women Confronting Development," *Development* 43, no. 4 (2000): 32–39, 38.

26. Ibid.

27. Albert Memmi, *The Colonizer and the Colonized* (Boston: Beacon, 1965), 8–17.

28. Horn, "Looking from the South, Speaking from Home," 38.

29. J. K. Bajaj and M. D. Srinivas, "*Annam Banu Kurvita:* The Indian Discipline of Growing and Sharing Food in Plenty," in Vandana Shiva and Gitanjali Bedi, eds., *Sustainable Agriculture and Food Security* (New Delhi: Sage Publications, 2002), 437–454, 441–442.

30. Ibid., 441–442.

31. Ibid., 442.

32. Leela Fernandes, *Transforming Feminist Practice: Non-Violence, Social Justice, and the Possibilities of a Spiritualized Feminism* (San Francisco: Aunt Lute Books, 2003), 22.

33. Salma Maoulidi, "The Sahiba Sisters Foundation in Tanzania: Meeting Organizational and Community Needs," *Development* 46, no. 4 (2003): 85–91, 98.

34. Anne Hope and Sally Timmel, "A Kenyan Experience for Faith-Based Transformative Action," *Development* 46, no. 4 (2003): 93–99, 94.

35. Ibid., 94. See also David C. Korten, *The Post-Corporate World: Life After Capitalism* (San Francisco: Berrett-Koehler, 1999).

36. Socorro M. Martinez, "Women's Leadership in Mexico: Education for Social Change at the Grassroots," *Development* 46, no. 4 (2000): 79–84, 80.

37. Marisa Belausteguigoitia, "The Right to Rest: Women's Struggle to Be Heard in the Zapatista Movement," *Development* 43, no. 3 (2000): 81–87, 82.

38. Lorraine Code, "How to Think Globally: Stretching the Limits of Imagination," in Uma Narayan and Sandra Harding, eds., *Decentering the Center: Philosophy for a Multicultural, Postcolonial, and Feminist World* (Bloomington: Indiana University Press, 2000), 67–79, 74–75.

39. Two fair trade organizations, one in the United Kingdom and the other in the United States, are named Equal Exchange. Both attempt to reverse what Arghiri Emmanuel named "unequal exchange," the systematic unfair trade advantages that have accrued to businesses and states in the North.

40. Rachel Lee wrote that "guerrilla action must begin to seize territory, or else dissolve." In "Notes from the (non)Field: Teaching and Theorizing Women of Color," *Meridians* 1, no. 1 (2000): 85–109, 102.

41. Maria Lugones, "Playfulness, 'World'-Travelling, and Loving Perception," in Gloria Anzaldua, ed., *Making Face, Making Soul: Creative and Critical Perspectives by Feminists of Color* (San Francisco: Aunt Lute Books, 1990), 390–402.

❀

Playfulness, "World"-Travelling, and Loving Perception

Maria Lugones

This [reading] weaves two aspects of life together. My coming to consciousness as a daughter and my coming to consciousness as a woman of color have made this weaving possible. The weaving reveals the possibility and complexity of a pluralistic feminism, a feminism that affirms the plurality in each of us and among us as richness and as central to feminist ontology and epistemology.

The [reading] describes the experience of "outsiders" to the mainstream White/ Anglo organization of life in the U.S., and stresses a particular feature of the outsider's existence: the acquired flexibility in shifting from the mainstream construction of life to other constructions of life where she is more or less "at home." This flexibility is necessary for the outsider but it can also be willfully exercised by those who are at ease in the mainstream. I recommend this willful exercise which I call "world"- travelling and I also recommend that the willful exercise be animated by a playful attitude.

As outsiders to the U.S. mainstream, women of color practice "world"-travelling, mostly out of necessity. I affirm this practice as a creative, rich, enriching and, given certain circumstances, as a loving way of being and living. I recognize that we do much of our travelling, in some sense against our wills, to hostile White/Anglo "worlds." The hostility of these "worlds" and the compulsory nature of the "travelling" have obscured for us the enormous value of this aspect of our living and its connection to *loving*. Racism has a vested interest in obscuring and devaluing the complex skills involved in this. I recommend that we affirm this travelling across "worlds" as partly constitutive of cross-cultural and cross-racial loving. Thus I recommend to women of color in the U.S. to learn to love each other by travelling to each other's "worlds."

On the other hand, the [reading] makes a connection between what Marilyn Frye has named "arrogant perception" and the failure to identify with persons that one views arrogantly or has come to see as the products of arrogant perception. A further connection is made between this failure of identification and a failure to love. Love is not used in the sense Frye has identified as consistent with arrogant perception and as promoting unconditional servitude. "We can be taken in by this equation of servitude with love," Frye says, "because we make two mistakes at once: we think of both servitude and love that they are selfless or unselfish."[1] Rather, the identification of which I speak is constituted by what I come to characterize as playful "world"-travelling. To the extent that we learn to perceive others arrogantly or come to see them only as products of arrogant perception and continue to perceive them that way, we fail to identify with them—fail to love them—in this particularly deep way.

IDENTIFICATION AND LOVE

As a child, I was taught to perceive arrogantly. I have also been the object of arrogant perception. Though I am not a White/Anglo woman, it is clear to me that I had early training in arrogant perception. I was brought up in Argentina watching men and women of moderate and of considerable means graft the substance[2] of their servants to themselves. I also learned to graft my mother's substance to my own. It was clear to me that both men and women were the victims of arrogant perception and that arrogant perception was systematically organized to break the spirit of all women and of most men. I valued my rural "gaucho" ancestry because its ethos has always been one of independence in poverty through enormous loneliness, courage and self-reliance. I found inspiration in this ethos and made a commitment not to be broken by arrogant perception. I can say this only because I have learned from Frye's "In and Out of Harm's Way: Arrogance and Love." She has given me a way of understanding and articulating something important in my own life.

Frye is not particularly concerned with women as arrogant perceivers but as the objects of arrogant perception. Her focus is, in part, on enhancing our understanding of women "untouched by phallocratic machinations."[3] She proposes an understanding of what it is to love women inspired by a vision of women unharmed by arrogant perception. To love women is, at least in part, to perceive them with loving eyes. "The loving eye is a contrary of the arrogant eye."[4]

I am concerned with women as arrogant perceivers because I want to explore further what it is to love women. I want to explore two failures of love: my failure to love my mother and White/Anglo women's failure to love women across racial and cultural boundaries in the U.S. As a consequence of exploring these failures I will offer a loving solution to them. My solution modifies Frye's account of loving perception by adding what I call playful "world"-travel.

It is clear to me that at least in the U.S. and Argentina women are taught to perceive many other women arrogantly. Being taught to perceive arrogantly is part of being taught to be a woman of a certain class in both countries. It is part of being taught to be a White/Anglo woman in the U.S. and it is part of being taught to be a woman in places: to be both the agent and the object of arrogant perception. My love for my mother seemed to me thoroughly imperfect as I was growing up because I was unwilling to become what I had been taught to see my mother as being. I thought that to love her was consistent with my abusing her (using, taking for granted, and demanding her services in a far-reaching way that, since four other people engaged in the same grafting of her substance onto themselves, left her little of herself for herself) and was to be in part constituted by my identifying with her, my seeing myself in her: to love her was supposed to be of a piece with both my abusing her and with my being open to being abused. It is clear to me that I was not supposed to love servants: I could abuse them without identifying with them, without seeing myself in them. When I came to the U.S. I learned that part of racism is the internalization of the propriety of abuse without identification: I learned that I could be seen as a being to be used by White/Anglo men and women without the possibility of identification, without their act of attempting to graft my substance onto theirs, rubbing off on them at all. They could remain untouched, without any sense of loss.

So, women who are perceived arrogantly can perceive other women arrogantly in their turn. To what extent those women are responsible for their arrogant perceptions of other women is certainly open to question, but I do not have any doubt that many women have been taught to abuse women in this particular way. I am not interested in assigning responsibility. I am interested in understanding the phenomenon so as to find a loving way out of it.

There is something obviously wrong with the way I was taught to love and something right with my failure to love my mother in this way. There is something wrong with my being taught to practice enslavement of my mother and to learn to become a slave through this practice. There is something wrong with my having been taught that love is consistent with abuse, consistent with arrogant perception. But I do not think that what is wrong is my profound desire to identify with her, to see myself in her.

The love I was taught is the love that Frye speaks of when she says "We can be taken in by this equation of servitude with love."[5] Even though I could both abuse and love my mother, I was not supposed to love servants: This is because in the case of servants one is and is supposed to be clear about their servitude and the "equation of servitude with love" is never to be thought clearly in those terms. But I could love my mother because deception is part of this "loving." Servitude is called abnegation and abnegation is not analyzed any further. Abnegation is not instilled in us through an analysis of its nature but rather through a heralding of it as beautiful and noble. We are coaxed, seduced into abnegation not through analysis but through emotive persuasion. When I say that there is something obviously wrong with the loving that I was taught, I do not mean to say that the connection between loving and abuse is obvious. Rather this connection has to be unveiled. Once it is unveiled, what is obvious is that there is something wrong with the loving.

I did not learn my lessons about loving well. This failure necessitated a separation from my mother: I saw us as beings of quite a different sort. I abandoned my mother while I longed to love her, though, given what I was taught, "love" could not be the right word for what I longed for.

I was disturbed by my not wanting to be what she was. I had a sense of not being quite integrated, my self was missing because I could not identify with her, I could not see myself in her, I could not welcome her world. I saw myself as separate from her, a different sort of being, not quite of the same species. This separation, this lack of love, I saw as a lack in myself, not a fault, but a lack. *Love has to be rethought, made anew.*

There is something similar between my relation to my mother as someone I was not able to love and the relation between women of color in the U.S. and White/Anglo women: there is a failure of love. I want to note here that Frye has helped me understand one of the aspects of this failure, the directly abusive aspect. I think part of the failure of love includes the failure to identify with another woman, the failure to see oneself in other women who are quite different from oneself.

Frye's emphasis on independence in her analysis of loving perception is not particularly helpful in explaining this failure of love. She says that in loving perception, "the object of the seeing is another being whose existence and character are logically independent of the seer and who may be practically or empirically independent in any particular respect at any particular time."[6] But this is not helpful, for example, in allowing me to understand how my failure of love toward my mother (when I ceased to be her parasite) left me not quite whole. It is not helpful since I saw her as logically independent from me. Neither does Frye's emphasis on independence help me understand why the racist or ethnocentric failure of love of White/Anglo women should leave me not quite real among them.

I am not particularly interested in cases of White/Anglo women's parasitism onto women of color but more pointedly in cases where the failure of identification is the central feature of the "relation." I am particularly interested in those cases in which White/Anglo women behave in one or more of the following ways towards women of color: they ignore, ostracize, stereotype, classify us as crazy and render us invisible. This behavior is exhibited *while we are in their midst.* Frye's emphasis on independence as key to loving is unhelpful because the more independent I am, the more independent I am left to be, the more alone I am left to be. Their world and their integrity have no use for me. Yet they rob me of my solidity through indifference, an indifference they can afford and which often seems studied. This points toward separatism in communities where our substance is seen and celebrated; where we become substantive, solid, real through this celebration. But many of us have to work among White/Anglos and our best shot at recognition has seemed to be among White/Anglo women because many of them have expressed a *general* sense of being pained at their failure of love.

Many times White/Anglo women seem to want women of color out of their field of vision. Their lack of concern is a harmful failure of love that leaves me independent from them in the same way that my mother became independent from me once I ceased to be her parasite. But of course, because my mother and I wanted to love each other well, we were not whole in this independence. White/Anglo women are independent from me, I am independent from them, I am independent from my mother, she is independent from me, and we cannot love each other in this independence.

I am incomplete and unreal without other women. I am profoundly dependent on others without having to be their subordinate, their slave, their servant.

Since I am emphasizing here that the failure of love lies in part in the failure to identify, and since I agree with Frye that in perceiving others lovingly one "must consult something other than one's own will and interests and fears and imagination,"[7] I will proceed to explain what I think needs to be consulted. Loving my mother was not possible for me so long as I retained a sense that it was fine to see her through arrogant eyes. Loving my mother also required that I see with her eyes, that I go into my mother's world, that I see both of us as we are constructed in her world, that I witness her own sense of herself from within her world. Only through this travelling to her "world" could I identify with her because only then could I cease to ignore her and to be excluded and separate from her. Only then could I see her as a subject even if one subjected and only then could I see how meaning could arise fully between us. We are fully dependent on each other for the possibility of being understood without which we are not intelligible, we do not make sense, we are not solid, visible, integrated; we are lacking. Travelling to each other's "worlds" enables us to *be* through *loving* each other.

I will lead you to see what I mean by a "world" in the way I proposed the concept to myself: through the kind of ontological confusion that we, women of color, refer to half-jokingly as "schizophrenia" and through my effort to make sense of this ontological confusion.

"WORLDS" AND "WORLD"-TRAVELLING

Some time ago I was in a state of profound confusion as I experienced myself as both having and not having a character trait: the trait is playfulness. I experienced myself both as a playful person and as a person who is not playful, a person who would be acting out of character if she were to express playfulness. At first I thought that the "multiple personality" problem could be explained away by lack of ease. Maybe my playfulness is very difficult to express or enact in certain worlds. So, it may be that in those worlds I lack the trait. But, of course, I need to explain what "world" means if that explanation is to be serviceable to me in my confusion as to who I am characterwise.

I can explain some of what I mean by a "world." I do not want the fixity of a definition because I think the term is suggestive and I do not want to lose this. A "world" has to be presently inhabited by flesh and blood people. That is why it cannot be a utopia. It may also be inhabited by some imaginary people. It may be inhabited by people who are dead or people that the inhabitants of this "world" met in some other "world" and now have in this "world" in imagination.

A "world" need not be a construction of a whole society. It may be a construction of a tiny portion of a particular society. It may be inhabited by just a few people. Some "worlds" are bigger than others.

A "world" may be incomplete in that things in it may not be altogether constructed or some things may be constructed negatively (they are not what "they" are in some other "world"). Or the "world" may be incomplete because it may have references to things that do not quite exist in it, references to things like Brazil. Given lesbian feminism, the construction of "lesbian" in "lesbian community" (a "world" in my sense) is purposefully and healthily still up in the air, in the process of becoming. To be Hispanic in this country is, in a dominant Anglo construction, purposefully incomplete. Thus one cannot really answer questions like "What is a Hispanic?" "Who counts as a Hispanic?" "Are Latinos, Chicanos, Hispanos, black Dominicans, white Cubans, Korean-Colombians, Italian-Argentineans Hispanic?" What it means to be a "Hispanic" in the varied so-called Hispanic communities in the U.S. is also up in the air. We have not yet decided whether there are any "Hispanics" in our varied "worlds."

So a "world" may be an incomplete visionary non-utopian construction of life or it may be a traditional construction of life. A traditional Hispano construction of Northern New Mexican life is a "world." Such a traditional construction, in the face of a racist, ethnocentric, money-centered Anglo construction of Northern New Mexican life, is highly unstable because Anglos have the means for imperialist destruction of traditional Hispano "worlds."

Some of the inhabitants of a "world" may not understand or accept the way in which they are constructed in it. So, for example, a recent Latin-American immigrant may not understand how she is constructed in White/Anglo "worlds." So, there may be "worlds" that construct me in ways that I do not even understand or I may not accept the construction as an account of myself, a construction of myself. And yet, I may be *animating* such a construction, even though I may not intend my moves, gestures, acts in that way.

One can "travel" between these "worlds" and one can inhabit more than one of these "worlds" at the very same time. I think that most of us who are outside the mainstream U.S. construction or organization of life are "world-travellers" as a matter of necessity and of survival. It seems to me that inhabiting more than one "world" at the same time and "travelling" between "worlds" is part and parcel of our experience and our situation. One can be at the same time in a "world" that constructs one as stereotypically Latin, for example, and in a "world" that constructs one as Latin. Being stereotypically Latin and being simply Latin are different simultaneous constructions of persons that are part of different "worlds." One animates one or the other or both at the same time without necessarily confusing them, though simultaneous enactment can be confusing to oneself.

In describing a "world" I mean to be offering a description of experience, something that is true to experience even if it is ontologically problematic. Though I would think that any account of identity that was not true to this experience of outsiders to the mainstream would be faulty even if ontologically unproblematic. Its ease would constrain, erase, or deem aberrant experience that has within it significant insights into non-imperialistic understanding between people.

Those of us who are "world"-travellers have the distinct experience of being different in different "worlds" and ourselves in them. We can say "That's me there, and I am happy in that 'world'." The experience is one of having memory of oneself as different without any underlying "I." So, I can say "That's me in there and I am so playful in that 'world'." I say that's *me* in that 'world' *not* because I recognize myself in that person. Rather that person may be very different from myself in this "world" and yet I can say *without inference* "That's me." I may well recognize that that person has abilities that I do not have and yet the having or not having of the abilities is always an "I have ..." and "I do not have ...," i.e., it is always experienced in the first person.

The shift from being one person to being a different person is what I call "travel." This shift may not be willful or even conscious, and one may be completely unaware of being different than one is in a different "world." Even though the shift can be done willfully, it is not a matter of acting. One does not pose as someone else; one does not pretend to be, for example, someone of a different personality or character or someone ... who uses space or language differently than the other person. Rather one *is* someone who has that personality or character or uses space and language in that particular way.

BEING AT EASE IN A "WORLD"

In investigating what I mean by "being at ease in a 'world,'" I will describe different ways of being at ease. One may be at ease in one or in all of these ways. A maximal way of being at ease, being at ease in all of these ways, is somewhat dangerous because people who are at ease in this way tend not to have any inclination to travel across "worlds" or tend not to have any experience of "world" travelling.

The first way of being at ease in a particular "world" is by being a fluent speaker in that "world." I know all the norms that there are to be followed, I know all the words that there are to be spoken. I know all the moves. I am confident.

Another way of being at ease is by being normatively happy. I agree with all the norms, I could not like any norms better. I am asked to do just what I want to do or what I think I should do. At ease.

Another way of being at ease in a "world" is by being humanly bonded. I am with those I love and they love me too. It should be noticed that I may be with those I love and be at ease because of them in a "world" that is otherwise as hostile to me as "worlds" can get.

Finally one may be at ease because one has a shared history that one sees exemplified by the response to the question "Do you remember poodle skirts?" There you are, with people you do not know at all. The question is posed and then they all begin talking about their poodle skirt stories. I have been in such situations without knowing what poodle skirts, for example, were and I felt so ill at ease because it was not *my* history. The other people did not particularly know each other. It is not that they were humanly bonded. Probably they did not have much politically in common either. But poodle skirts were in their shared history.

Given the clarification of what I mean by a "world," "world"-travel, and being at ease in a "world," we are in a position to return to my problematic attribute, playfulness. It may be that in this "world" in which I am so unplayful I am a different person than in the "world" in which I am playful. Or it may be that the "world" in which I am unplayful is constructed in such a way that I could be playful in it. I could practice, even though that "world" is constructed in such a way that my being playful in it is hard.

My description of what I mean by a "world" favors the first possibility as the one that is truest to the experience of "outsiders" to the mainstream. But that description also makes this possibility problematic because the "I" is identified in some sense as one and in some sense as plural (I am one and many at the same time). I identify myself as myself through memory and retain myself as different in memory. I can be in a particular "world" and have a double image of myself as, for example, playful and unplayful. This is a very familiar and recognizable phenomenon to the outsider to the mainstream in some *central* cases: when in one "world" I animate, for example, that "world's" caricature or stereotype of the person I am in the other "world." I can have both images of myself, and to the extent that I can materialize or animate both images at the same time, I become an ambiguous being. This is very much a part of trickery and foolery. It is worth remembering that the trickster and the fool are significant characters in many non-dominant or outsiders' cultures.

As one sees any particular "world" with these double edges and sees absurdity in them, one animates the person one is in that world differently. Given that Latins are constructed in Anglo "worlds" as stereotypically intense and given that many Latins, myself included, are genuinely intense, I can say to myself "I am intense" and take a hold of the double meaning. Furthermore, I can be stereotypically intense or be the real thing and, if you are Anglo, you do not know when I am which *because* I am Latin-American. As Latin-American I am an ambiguous being, a two-imaged self: I can see that gringos see me as stereotypically intense because I am, as a Latin-American, constructed that way in their "world." I may or may not *intentionally* animate the stereotype or the real thing knowing that you may not see it in anything other than in the stereotypical construction. This ambiguity is not just funny, it is survival-rich. We can also make a funny picture of those who dominate us precisely because we can see the double edges, we can see *them* doubly constructed, we can see the plurality in us and in them. So we know truths that only the fool can speak and only the trickster can play out without harm. We inhabit "worlds" and travel across them and keep all the memories.

Sometimes the "world"-traveller has a double image of herself and each self includes as important ingredients of itself one or more attributes of the other self: for example being playful and being unplayful. To the extent that an attribute is personality or character central, the "world" in which she has that attribute would have to be changed if she is to cease to have it. For example, the "world" in which I am unplayful would have to be changed for me to be playful in it. It is not as if, if I were to be at ease in that "world," I would be my own playful self. Because the attribute is personality central and there is such a good fit between the "world" in which I am unplayful and my being constructed unplayful in it, I cannot become playful, *I am unplayful* in that "world." To become playful would be for me to become a contradictory being. So, lack of ease cannot be a solution for my problematic case. My problem is not one of lack of ease.

I am suggesting that I can understand my confusion about whether I am or am not playful by saying that I am both and that I am different persons in different "worlds" and can remember myself in both as I am in the other. I am a plurality of selves. This is to understand my confusion because *it is to come to see it as of a piece* with much of the rest of my experience as an outsider in some of the "worlds" that I inhabit and of a piece with significant aspects of the experience of non-dominant people in the "worlds" of their dominators.

So, though I may not be at ease in the "worlds" in which I am not constructed playful, it is not that I am not playful *because* I am not at ease. The two are compatible. But lack of playfulness is not caused by lack of ease but lack of health. I am not a healthy being in the "worlds" that construct me as unplayful.

PLAYFULNESS

I had a very personal stake in investigating this topic. Playfulness is not only the attribute that was the source of my confusion and the attitude that I recommend as the loving attitude in travelling across "worlds" but also what I am scared to do without—ending up a serious human being, someone with no multi-dimensionality, with no fun in life, someone who has had the fun constructed out of her. I am seriously scared of getting stuck in a "world" that constructs me that way. A "world" that I have no escape from and in which I cannot be playful.

I thought about what it is to be playful and what it is to play and I did this thinking in a "world" in which I only remember myself as playful and in which all of those who know me as playful are imaginary beings. A "world" in which I am scared of losing my memories of myself as playful or have them erased from me. Because I live in such a "world," after I formulated my own sense of what it is to be playful and to play I decided that I needed to see what other people had said about play and playfulness. I read two classics on the subject: Johan Huizinga's *Homo Ludens*[8] and Hans-Georg Gadamer's chapter on the concept of play in his *Truth and Method*.[9] I discovered, to my amazement, that what I thought about play and playfulness was in contradiction with their accounts. Though I will not provide the arguments for this interpretation of Gadamer and Huizinga here, I understood that both of them have an agonistic sense of "play." Play and playfulness have, ultimately, to do with contest, with winning, losing, battling. The sense of playfulness that I have in mind has nothing to do with those things. So, I tried to elucidate both senses of play and playfulness by contrasting them to each other. The contrast helped me see the attitude that I have in mind as the loving attitude in travelling across "worlds" more clearly.

An agonistic sense of playfulness is one in which *competence* is supreme. You'd better know the rules of the game. In agonistic play, contest, competition, there is risk, there is *uncertainty*, but the uncertainty is about who is going to win and who is going to lose. There are rules that inspire hostility. The attitude of *playfulness is conceived as secondary to or derivative from play.* Since play is agon, contest, then the only conceivable playful attitude is an agonistic, combative, competitive one. One of the paradigmatic ways of playing for both Gadamer and Huizinga is role-playing. In role-playing, the person who is participating in the game has *a fixed conception of him- or herself.* I also think that the players are imbued with *self-importance* in agonistic play since they are so keen on winning given their own merits, their very own competence.

When considering the value of "world"-travelling and whether playfulness is the loving attitude to have while travelling, I recognized the agonistic attitude as inimical to travelling across "worlds." The agonistic traveller is a conqueror, an imperialist. Given the agonistic attitude one *cannot* travel across "worlds," though can kill other "worlds" with it. So for people who are interested in crossing racial and ethnic boundaries, an arrogant western man's construction of playfulness is deadly. One needs to give such an attitude up if one wants to travel. Huizinga, in his classic book on play, interprets Western civilization as play. That is an interesting thing for Third World people to think about. Western civilization has been interpreted by a white western man as play in the agonistic sense of play: he reviews western law, art, and many other aspects of western culture and sees agon, contest, in all of them.

So then, what is the loving playfulness that I have in mind? Let me begin with one example: We are by the river bank. The river is very, very low. Almost dry. Bits of water here and there. Little pools with a few trout hiding under the rocks. But mostly wet stones, grey on the outside. We walk on the stones for a while. You pick up a stone and crash it onto the others. As it breaks, it is quite wet inside and it is very colorful, very pretty. I pick up a stone and break it and run toward the pieces to see the colors. They are beautiful. I laugh and bring the pieces back to you and you are doing the same with your pieces. We keep on crashing stones for hours, anxious to see the beautiful new colors. We are playing. The playfulness of our activity does not presuppose that there is something like "crashing stones" that is a particular form of play with its own rules. Rather *the attitude that carries us through the activity, a playful attitude, turns the activity into play.* Our activity has no rules, though it is certainly intentional activity and we both understand what we are doing. The playfulness that gives meaning to our activity includes uncertainty, but in this case the uncertainty is an *openness to surprise.* This is a particular metaphysical attitude that does not expect the world to be neatly packaged, ruly. Rules may fail to explain what we are doing. We are not self-important, we are not fixed in particular constructions of ourselves, which is part of saying that we are *open to self-construction.* We may not have rules, and when we do have rules, *there are no rules that are to us sacred.* We are not worried about competence. We are not wedded to a particular way of doing things. While playful we have not abandoned ourselves to, nor are we stuck in, any particular "world." We are *there creatively.* We are not passive.

Playfulness is, in part, an openness to being a fool, which is a combination of not worrying about competence, not being self-important, not taking norms as sacred and finding ambiguity and double edges a source of wisdom and delight.

So, positively, the playful attitude involves openness to surprise, openness to being a fool, openness to self-construction or reconstruction and to construction or reconstruction of the "worlds" we inhabit playfully. Negatively, playfulness is characterized by uncertainty, lack of self-importance, absence of rules or a not taking rules as sacred, a not worrying about competence and a lack of abandonment or resignation to a particular construction of oneself, others, and one's relation to them. In attempting to take hold of oneself and of one's relation to others in a particular "world," one may study, examine and come to understand oneself. One may then see what the possibilities for play are for the being one is in that "world," one may study, examine and come to understand oneself. One may then see what the possibilities for play are for the being one is in that "world." One may even decide to inhabit that self fully in order to understand it better and find its creative possibilities. All of this is just self-reflection and it is quite different from resigning or abandoning oneself to the particular construction of oneself that one is attempting to take ahold of.

CONCLUSION

There are "worlds" we enter at our own risk, "worlds" that have agon, conquest, and arrogance as the main ingredients in their ethos. These are "worlds" that we enter out of necessity and which would be foolish to enter playfully.

But there are "worlds" that we can travel to lovingly and travelling to them is part of loving at least some of their inhabitants. The reason why I think that travelling to someone's "world" is a way of identifying with them is because by travelling to their "world" we can understand *what it is to be them and what it is to be ourselves in their eyes*. Only when we have travelled to each other's "worlds" are we fully subjects to each other.*

Knowing other women's "worlds" is part of knowing them and knowing them is part of loving them. The knowing can be done in greater or lesser depth, as can the loving. Travelling to another's "world" is not the same as becoming intimate with them. Intimacy is constituted in part by a very deep knowledge of the other self and "world"-travelling is only part of this knowledge. Some people, in particular those who are outsiders to the mainstream, can be known only to the extent that they are known in several "worlds" and as "world"-travellers.

NOTES

*I agree with Hegel that self-recognition requires other subjects, but I disagree with his claim that it requires tension or hostility.

1. Marilyn Frye, *The Politics of Reality: Essays in Feminist Theory* (Trumansburg, N.Y.: Crossing Press, 1983), 73.

2. Grafting the substance of another to oneself is partly constitutive of arrogant perception. See Frye, 66.

3. Frye, 53.
4. Frye, 75.
5. Frye, 73.
6. Frye, 77.
7. Frye, 75.
8. Johan Huizinga, *Homo Ludens* (Buenos Aires, Argentina: Emece Editores, 1968).
9. Hans-George Gadamer, *Truth and Method* (New York: Seabury Press, 1975).

5

Restructuring Gender to Promote Alternative Development

INTRODUCTION: RESTRUCTURING GENDER, SEXUALITY, AGE TO PROMOTE ALTERNATIVE DEVELOPMENT, 1990 TO THE PRESENT

During the 1970s, some feminist groups argued that "the personal is political." By this they meant that women's efforts to change intimate personal relations between women and men, challenge the domination of women by men in worker households, and redefine the personal and social meaning of "gender" were important political acts. Today, feminist scholars and activists argue that the transformation of intimate relations can contribute to the transformation of social relations generally and that efforts to link personal and social politics can contribute to alternative development.

Since the 1970s, feminist scholars and activists have also developed a broader understanding of "gender" as a social institution. Earlier, scholars viewed gender as an institution based on men's domination of women in society and personal life, which they characterized as "patriarchal." Because this institution was the product of historical developments and took particular forms in different settings, we argue that gender is an institutionalized, gendered, world-systemic hierarchy that is supplemented by family, local, ethnic, class, and patriarchal practices and ideologies. Like some feminist scholars, we also argue that gender patriarchy has other important dimensions. Kamala Kempadoo has argued that gender is defined not only by patriarchy (men's domination of women) but also by heterosexism (men's domination of women and of men with diverse sexualities), what she called "heteropatriarchy."[1] She has used

105

this term to emphasize how heterosexism and patriarchy have combined to help men exercise power in society.

> [H]eteropatriarchy signals a distinction and relatedness between the ways in which sexuality and gender are socially, legally, and politically organized. It is the combination that marginalized and criminalized gendered subjects who transgress established social boundaries. Heteropatriarchy ... denote[s] a structuring principle in Caribbean societies that privileges heterosexual, promiscuous masculinity and subordinates feminine sexuality, normalizing relations of power that are intolerant of and oppressive toward sexual desires and practices that are outside of or oppose the dominant sexual and gender regimes.[2]

This is an important contribution to the understanding of gender as a social institution. But we think that gender has a third important dimension: age. Heterosexist patriarchy is also dominated by *adult* men, not by elder men or by minors. We think it is important to conceptualize gender as a set of social relations defined by adults who dominate elders and youths (age), by heterosexuals who dominate nonheterosexuals (sexuality), and by men who dominate women (patriarchy). Following Kempadoo, we would characterize gender as a capitalist institution based on ageist, heterosexual patriarchy.

Although feminist scholars and activists have said a lot about the patriarchies, they have said less about the heterosexual character of patriarchies and even less about its ageist component. We think it's useful to see patriarchal capitalist society as being shaped in important ways by age and sexuality.

ADULT AGEISM

Colonizers, capitalists, state officials, and religious leaders have long insisted that sexuality and patriarchy in capitalist society be structured in relation to age, and they have assigned *adults* a preeminent place in the gender order. This is a departure from most precapitalist societies, which gave *elders* preeminent social authority. Colonizers and capitalists stripped elders of authority and assigned it to adult men because male workers who were still active as wage workers were seen as more "productive" and responsible than elders who no longer worked for a wage. Over time, "postwage" workers lost their social authority.

Much the same has been true for youths. In precapitalist societies, young people played important economic roles for households. They labored alongside adults and elders in the fields, in homes, on the streets, and in factories. But over time, these youths were stripped of these economic responsibilities and treated increasingly as "children," as "prewage" or "predomestic" workers. This was particularly true in the core, less in the periphery, where youths continued to work in different capacities.

To a large extent, capitalists and state officials have treated elders and youths in a similar fashion. They have restricted their ability to engage in economic activities or exercise social responsibilities or authority they once possessed and have reserved these activities and responsibilities for adults.

Adults exercise their dominion over elders and youths in a variety of ways. Adults use legal sanctions to prevent elders from keeping jobs in the labor force after they reach a certain age (retirement laws) or refuse to hire elder workers, even if they are more skilled and have more experience, because they are more costly than younger adult workers in terms of wages and benefits.[3] Adults pass laws to prevent youths from entering the labor force or engaging in work outside of the home or school. And adults adopt laws that deprive youths of the right to vote, drink, have sexual relations with their peers, obtain abortions, run away from home, drive cars, or sign contracts and conduct financial affairs on their own.

Increasingly, adults have exerted a growing power over elders, who had possessed rights as adults, by adopting laws that make it possible for adults to restrict or rescind elder rights on the basis of "competency," health, infirmity, or indigence. To some extent, adults discriminate against both elders and youths as "minors," whom adults regard as undeserving of the rights and responsibilities claimed by adults. Adult assumptions about what is appropriate or inappropriate for elders and youths, adults' use of laws to enforce the social-economic positions assigned elders and youths, and adults' determination to restrict or revoke the activities and responsibilities of elders and youths have shaped the meaning of sexuality and patriarchy in worker households and in society at large.

ELDERS

Although elder women and men have had their power diminished by adults, their opportunities restricted, and their social value demeaned, adult ageism has had different consequences for elder men and women. First, when elder men in the core exit the workforce or retire, they can lay claim to pensions, social security, and medical benefits as postwage workers. By contrast, elder women's claims on these resources are often derivative and depend on women's relations to elder men as wives or widows, particularly if they have labored as unpaid and subsistence workers during their adult years.

Second, elder men in the core can insist that they no longer *have* to work because they have "retired" from wage work. But elder women must *still* work because their relation to unpaid and subsistence work remains unchanged as they age. Women don't get to "retire" from domestic work but continue working until they are incapacitated or dead. Of course, in the periphery, elder men do not commonly "retire," either as wage or nonwage workers, and they cannot commonly claim benefits associated with wage work because businesses and states cannot provide them. In the periphery, the gender differences associated with age are *less* pronounced than they are in the core.

But in both the core and the periphery, elder women in many countries have had their domestic workloads *increase* in recent years because they have to care for grandchildren in skip-generation households. This is particularly true in Africa, where acquired immunodeficiency syndrome (AIDS) has killed many adult parents, and in poor communities in the United States, where drug use or incarceration has incapacitated adult parents and where elder women (grandmothers and aunts) have assumed responsibility for raising children.

Third, elder men can still lay claim to an active, sexual, reproductive role in society. That is, they can still father children with adult women. By contrast, elder women cannot play this role because they cannot bear children after menopause. Elder men use their ability to father children as another way to claim social status that is not available to elder women.

So although elder men and women are subject to domination by adults, elder men can in some circumstances use their status as "postwage" workers to claim financial resources, abstain from work, or father children and thereby dominate elder women in worker households. This illustrates the complex age dimension of patriarchies in capitalist society.

YOUTHS

In the core, adults gradually restricted the ability of youths to work at home, in the streets, in factories, or in fields and insisted youths work only in schools, which were designed to prepare them for work as adults. In the periphery, many youths still work in factories, fields, and the streets, largely because households depend on the income they generate, and fewer youths attend school, both because households need youths to work and because schools are often too expensive for poor households.

Generally speaking, adults discriminate against youths and treat them as minors who cannot claim adult rights and responsibilities until they mature. But adult ageism has different consequences for "boys" and "girls" (terms that denote their diminutive social status), just as it has for elder men and women.

Boys in the core and the periphery are seen as "prewage" workers and are prepared in school for their eventual entry into the labor force as wage workers. Girls, however, are treated as "prereproductive" workers and are prepared for school and at home for unpaid subsistence work and child rearing. In the periphery, adults are more likely to send boys to school and keep girls home, where they engage in unpaid and subsistence work *before* they become adults. In this context, the gender differences associated with age are *more* acute in the periphery than they are in the core (for elders, the opposite is true; see above).

Adults also encourage boys to prepare for adult lives as "fathers." Boys are encouraged to have voluntary and sometimes violent (rape) sexual relations with adolescent girls or prostitutes prior to marriage so they can fulfill their duties as adult fathers after marriage. As many feminist scholars have noted, military service and other collective male institutions (sports, fraternities) often initiate young men into "preparatory" and/or "predatory" heterosexual behavior.[4]

At the same time, adults actively *discourage* girls from "preparing" for their roles as mothers before they become adults. Adults warn girls that the kind of sexual activity endorsed for boys will threaten or ruin their prospects for marriage, particularly if they have children out of wedlock. Adults are generally less punitive toward girls in the core than they are in the periphery, but adults around the world treat girls differently than boys in this regard.

Again, although boys and girls are both subject to ageist domination by adults, boys can often engage in activities that girls cannot, and their relative privilege vis-à-vis adults helps boys dominate girls in the age-based hierarchy, just as elder men dominate elder women. In capitalist society, patriarchies are defined in part by adult ageism. They are also defined by heterosexist sexuality.

HETEROSEXIST SEXUALITY

In capitalist society, adult males insist that men and women and elders and youths adhere to a heterosexual standard of sexuality or intimate relations. They discourage, demean, and punish sexuality that does not conform to this standard, even though this insistence on heterosexuality as the only permissible form of intimacy is at odds with what is known about human sexuality.

In *Civilization and Its Discontents,* Sigmund Freud observed that people have diverse "polymorphous" sexual relations. But capitalist society, Freud argued, repressed multifaceted or pansexual relations and identities and insisted that women and men conform to a single, monogamous, heterosexual identity, which of course was restricted by age (see above). Anthropological scholars have generally agreed with Freud's assessment. In her book *Moon, Sun, and Witches,* for example, Irene Silverblatt found that people in precapitalist Peru had diverse sexual relations and identities, but that colonizers—capitalists, state officials, and church leaders—worked assiduously to repress them and forced people to adopt household-based, heterosexist, male-dominated standards of behavior.[5]

ON SEXUALITY: ANSWERING BASIC QUESTIONS

In the 1970s, some feminists and lesbian and gay activists began thinking of sexuality as variable and located on a continuum, both in terms of an individual's life span and in terms of the historical development of gender, sexuality, and age within different societies. Feminists began discussing the possibility that sexuality had a historically constructed, social component as well as an important biological component. Scholars and activists came to see identity as consisting of a multilayered continuum of identity that had the components of sex, gender, sexuality, and performance. In their definitions of sexuality, Michael Stevenson and Jeanine Cogin implicitly referred to the earlier debates that had led to a more general view that there is a fluid sexuality continuum. Their exploration of a sexuality continuum brought up feminist writings on some preclass societies, which, when compared to social relations in most places and times in the capitalist world, often displayed less rigid gender and sexual relations and allowed people to express more polymorphous characteristics in terms of sexual identity. When outside militaries and traders used their power to introduce class relations in these early societies, as global capitalist society expanded, the occupiers generally repressed polymorphous sexual practices and used the class-based state to impose different forms of heterosexist patriarchy. In the opening centuries of the capitalist world-system, as conquerors and traders brought new areas into the capitalist world, for-profit firms and states gradually broke up reproductive community structures and introduced heterosexist male–dominated households that relied heavily on the unpaid, low-paid, and microproducing and petty-marketing work largely done by women and girls. The social creation of gender, sexuality, and age divisions formed a key part of intersecting hierarchies. Heterosexism permitted global accumulation to rest on indirect, often nonmonetized, exploitation that occurred in households and neighborhoods and through the self-organized work of subordinated household members. These social divisions impact how we live and work for change today.

Among scholars, the term *sexual orientation* describes an enduring emotional, romantic, sexual, or affectional attraction to another person. Thanks in large part to the pioneering work of Alfred Kinsey, scientists often think of sexual orientation as the continuum that ranges from exclusive homosexuality to exclusive heterosexuality. Persons with a homosexual orientation are sometimes referred to as gay or lesbian. . . . Heterosexual persons are often referred to as straight. People with a bisexual orientation are found around the midpoint of the continuum. They may experience sexual, emotional, and affectional attraction to either sex.

Scientists as well as nonscientists . . . often confuse sexual behavior with sexual orientation. In the past, researchers have routinely assumed that individuals who have ever engaged in same-sex sexual behavior were by definition *homosexual*. To some degree, this continues in public discourse about sexuality. However, to equate behavior with identity is no longer considered scientifically rigorous. . . . Sexual orientation refers to feelings of emotional, romantic, and affectional attraction and sexual interest, not simply sexual behavior. Persons may or may not express their sexual orientation in their behaviors and their sexual behaviors may or may not reflect their sexual feelings and identity. . . . In other words, some heterosexual people have had same-sex experiences and many gay and lesbian people have had sexual experiences with the other sex.

Furthermore, contrary to assumptions made by the public and by antigay activists . . . engaging in same-sex behavior is not synonymous with the adoption of a gay identity (being gay or lesbian). *Sexual identity* refers to the extent to which people recognize their sexual attractions and incorporate those interests into their sense of who they are as sexual people. For some, it is a reflection of their sexual attractions and behavior; for others, it is not. In a survey of sexual behavior among U.S. adults, researchers . . . interviewed 3,432 people who were carefully selected to represent the U.S. adult population. Over 9 percent of the men in this study reported engaging in a same-sex sexual behavior at least once since puberty, while only 2.8 percent reported some level of gay identity. Among those interviewed, men who experienced both same-sex desire and same-sex behavior were very likely to identify as gay. However, some men with adult same-sex experience continued to engage in same-sex behavior without identifying as gay. Similarly, other men in the sample experienced same-sex desire without identifying themselves as gay. In other words, some men do not adopt a gay identity in spite of the fact that they engage in same-sex sexual behaviors or experience sexual desire for other men.... Clearly, equating same-sex sexual behavior with gay (or lesbian identity) seriously undermines the complexities of what it means to be gay (or lesbian or bisexual).

IMPORTANT DISTINCTIONS

Sexual orientation refers to an enduring emotional, romantic, sexual or affectional attraction to another person, which cannot be determined solely on the basis of sexual behavior.

Sexual identity refers to the extent to which people recognize their sexual attractions and incorporate those interests into their sense of who they are as sexual people.

Sexual behavior refers to erotic activity and is most broadly described in phrases like "Men who have sex with men" or "women who have sex with women"; sexual behavior is not always consistent with the labels (straight, gay, lesbian, or bisexual) people choose to describe their identities.

Source: Michael R. Stevenson. "Answering Basic Questions." In Michael R. Stevenson and Jeanine C. Cogin, eds. *Everyday Activism: A Handbook for Lesbian, Gay, and Bisexual People and Their Allies.* New York: Routledge, 2003, 39–55, 40–42.

But whereas Freud thought that capitalist society had more or less successfully repressed polymorphous sexual relations, Alfred Kinsey found that most people, even in the core, did not conform to the standard, heterosexual identity but instead had sexual relations with people that ranged along a continuum from heterosexual to homosexual.[6] Kinsey and others also argued that sexuality should be seen not only in physical terms but also in emotional-psychological terms. That is, Kinsey defined sexuality, or really intimacy, quite broadly and said that it had a physical dimension or axis but also an emotional-mental dimension. If sexuality is understood as physical-emotional intimacy, then most people have wide-ranging intimate relations with people of the same sex and people of the opposite sex. Many feminist scholars have endorsed this view, arguing that women and men have multiple and diverse sexualities. For example, Shulamith Firestone argued in "The Dialectic of Sex," which first appeared in 1970, that the seizure by women of means of reproduction and the use of new reproductive technologies would allow people to revert to pansexuality or polymorphous sexuality, which would end distinctions among heterosexuality, homosexuality, and bisexuality.[7]

❀ ❀ ❀

THE CONTINUUM OF SEXES

Middlebrook's feminist biography reconstructed the life of a U.S. woman musician who redefined herself as a man. As the reader joins this world, she/he learns about gender-change in the first half of the twentieth century, when sexual reassignment surgery was not a possibility. After meeting a woman who cross-dressed, Billy Tipton initially decided to pose as a male musician because it was almost impossible for women to find work as saxophone players, lead singers, band directors, and managers. Middlebrook documented how Billy Tipton made the social transition to a man, a "husband" to five women, and a father to adopted children. In this detailed biography, sexual identity was located within the context of gender redefinition. In this case, Billy Tipton redefined himself in the direction of patriarchal heterosexual power. Although the writer provided some critical examination of gendered power dynamics, Billy Tipton's life story is told in a respectful, empathetic way. Suits Me provides historical evidence that allows one to consider how class, patriarchy, gender/ sexuality, and white supremacy were defined in Billy Tipton's life.

The social conventions by which we recognize only two sexes and call them "opposite" conceal a number of biological actualities. Sex difference is defined at several bodily sites. Outside the genitals and, after puberty, the secondary sex characteristics: breasts and hips on a woman, Adam's apple and facial and body hair on a man. Inside lie the gonads (ovaries in the female, testes in the male), which direct sexual development through the production of estradiol for female development, testosterone for male. Yet male and female bodies synthesize variable amounts of both sex hormones, and the complexity of the interactions of the hormones results in so much variation that sex difference is best understood as a spectrum or continuum. One contemporary biologist has claimed that there are actually five discernibly different and biologically coherent human sexes. Female and male are two of the five. The others are mixtures. "Herms," or true hermaphrodites, possess one testis and one ovary; female pseudohermaphrodites, or "ferms" have ovaries and some aspects of the male genitalia but lack testes; male pseudohermaphrodites, or "merms," have testes and some aspects of the female genitalia but lack ovaries. "Each of these categories is in itself complex," the biologist Anne Fausto-Sterling observes. "The percentage of male and female characteristics, for instance, can vary enormously among members of the same subgroup." In the medical literature, the hermaphroditic types are classed together as "intersexes." The condition is thought to occur in possibly 4 percent of newborns.

    The external sex organs in human beings are visibly as different as a pair of gloves, one turned inside out: what is extended in one is concealed in the other. Yet in a newborn, the clitoris can be long, the penis abbreviated, the scrotum similar to labia. Such ambiguity is well known to pediatric endocrinologists, the usual referees when a baby's sex is not immediately obvious. Until very recently, medical treatment with hormones or surgery was often undertaken immediately, to insure that the external and internal sex organs matched up and gave one clear message at puberty. The treatment would be done early to help the child develop a secure psychological gender identity—the conviction, which is thought to form by age three, that one is a girl or a boy. Such medical intervention has grown controversial in the wake of recent reassessments of the notion that gender identity is an either-or proposition.

Source: Diane Wood Middlebrook. *Suits Me: The Double Life of Billy Tipton.* Boston: Houghton Mifflin, 1998, 136–137.

To some extent, capitalists and even state officials recognize the polymorphous character of sexuality-intimacy and work to promote the polymorphous sexual identities of women and men as *consumers,* not as workers or citizens who engage in democratic decisions about all aspects of society and culture. Capitalists appeal to the diverse emotional-physical sexualities of consumers and argue that sexual intimacy can be realized, sated, or enhanced if they purchase consumer goods: cigarettes, cars, sodas, clothes. Capitalist advertisers attempt to persuade consumers that their sexual appetites, their need for physical-emotional intimacy, can be met by inanimate objects—think of men's relations with cars, women's relations with shoes—or that consumer goods will enhance their intimate relations with other people, or both. To some extent, capitalists use sexuality the way food producers use sugar: it can be put into everything, where it both stimulates and satisfies the body's "natural" inclination for the "sweet," for the intimate. This process is most advanced in the core, and people in the periphery often remark with astonishment at the myriad and explicit ways that capitalists appeal to diverse consumer sexualities as an engine of economic development.

But although capitalists stimulate the polymorphous sexualities of women and men as *consumers,* capitalists and state officials restrict, regulate, discourage, and punish the polymorphous sexualities of women and men as *producers* and *reproducers.* They insist that adult women and men adopt a single, standard, sexual identity— monogamous heterosexuality—that is functional to the sexual division of labor in capitalist society. Nonstandard sexual relations and identities are seen as disruptive and transgressive. State officials treat people who engage in nonstandard expressions of sexuality not only as immoral but also, in many cases, as criminal or deny them civil rights available to heterosexuals by, for example, restricting their ability to marry. This makes it difficult for nonstandard partners to make the kind of legal contracts available to heterosexual couples, which in turn restricts their ability to purchase a home, adopt children, inherit property, delegate medical decisions, make durable wills, or share benefits associated with wage work (medical benefits, pensions, social security). State officials also permit heterosexuals to discriminate against nonheterosexual men and women in housing, employment, and military service, a situation that provides people with important claims on citizenship, economic benefits, and social status.

In recent years, capitalists, state officials, and religious leaders have been particularly upset by the rise of female-headed households and by households headed by same-sex partners. Both are seen as challenging the heterosexist standard and demonstrating the viability of nonstandard household relations and sexual identities.

UNDERSTANDING HETEROSEXISM

The link between patriarchy and heterosexism was first noted in 1970 by Radicalesbians, an activist group that focused on the importance of women's relating to other women:

> As long as women's liberation tries to free women without facing the basic heterosexual structure that binds us in one-to-one relationship with our oppressors, tremendous energies will continue to flow into trying to straighten up each particular relationship with a man, into finding how to get better sex, how to turn his head around—into trying to make the "new man" out of him, in the delusion that this will allow us to be the "new woman." This obviously splits our energies and commitments to the construction of the new patterns that will liberate us.[8]

To counter the dehumanization that came from living in a sexist society with rigid roles, in a society where lesbians and male homosexuals were classified and degraded as deviants, Radicalesbians argued that women needed to identify with other women, regardless of their sexuality, and become "women-identified women": "[W]hat is crucial is that women begin disengaging from male-identified response patterns. In the privacy of our own psyches, we must cut those cords to the core. For irrespective of where our love and sexual energies flow, if we are male-identified in our heads, we cannot realize our autonomy as human beings."[9]

Rather than primarily identifying with men and the male-dominated family, Radicalesbians argued that people needed to build a "society in which men do not oppress women and sexual expression is allowed to follow feelings."[10] Once women were able to reach out to each other, they could "begin a revolution to end the imposition of all coercive identifications, and to achieve maximum autonomy in human expression."[11]

In her feminist analysis that reinterpreted classic writings done by male scholars, Gayle Rubin, who first espoused this view in 1975, explored the connections among gender, sex (or sexuality), and society. Rubin introduced the idea that the gender order required female repression and the repression of all instinctual and nonheterosexual ways of relating. In all cultures, Rubin argued, "the social organization of sex rests upon gender, obligatory heterosexuality, and the constraint of female sexuality"[12] and the ability to "tame the wild profusion of infantile sexuality"[13] that is associated with polymorphous perversity,[14] a Freudian idea that Rubin appreciated. "Cultural evolution provides us with the opportunity to seize control of the means of sexuality, reproduction, and socialization, and to make the conscious decisions to liberate human sexual life from the archaic relationships which deform it. Ultimately, a thoroughgoing feminist revolution would liberate more than women. It would liberate forms of sexual expression, and it would liberate human personality from the straightjacket of gender."[15] For one of the first times, a large number of antisexists took notice of work that explored the historical repression of lesbian and gay desires and their relationship to mechanisms of male domination and patriarchy.

In the 1980s, the feminist scholar Adrienne Rich explored the historical roots of mandatory heterosexuality in "Compulsory Heterosexuality and Lesbian Existence," a work that relied heavily on anthropologist Kathleen Gough's analysis of the gender-control mechanisms invented by men. In "The Origin of the Family," Gough had argued that men used a variety of mechanisms to control women. They denied women their sexuality, forced male sexuality on women, controlled and exploited women's labor in production and reproduction, controlled or robbed women's children, confined women physically and prevented their movement, used women as objects in male transactions, restricted women's creativity, and withheld male-controlled economic, social, political, and cultural knowledge from women.[16] Rich subsequently wrote that Gough's analysis suggested "that *an enormous potential counterforce [—women and women's sexuality—was] having to be restrained* [emphasis added]."[17]

In her 1975 analysis of African American lesbians in literature, Rich examined how men restrained women's sexual feelings for each other. Rich argued that heterosexist men held women down because they were afraid of the power of the "lesbian continuum," which runs through each woman's life, and of the "feminism of action . . . which has constantly reemerged in every culture, and in every period."[18] According to Rich, the "lesbian continuum" includes all women who have experienced various forms of "primal intensity between and among women, including the sharing of a rich, inner life, the bonding against male tyranny, [and] the giving and receiving of practical support."[19] Rich subsequently related rebellions against global inequality to gender, sexuality, racial, and class inequality, which broadened the scope of "great movements for self-determination."[20]

❀ ❀ ❀

MALE AND HETEROSEXUAL DOMINATION IN AN UNEQUAL GLOBAL SOCIETY

There are so many hidden ways that heterosexual dominance is taken for granted. Many academics look at the oppression of the disadvantaged groups but do not challenge the privilege held by those in power. Many scholars question gender inequality and the social subordination of lesbians, gays, bisexuals, transgendered people, transsexuals, and queer people. But the ongoing social manufacturing of heterosexual power goes largely unnoticed and unquestioned by people who benefit from unearned heterosexist advantage.

Both heterosexual advantage and "homosexual" or queer disadvantage are directly aligned with dominant, patriarchal patterns of heterosexuality. They are an integral part of global sexism. "Thinking straight" refers to the ideological processes that reinforce heterosexual domination. These ways of thinking seem natural to most heterosexuals. Thinking straight is not any more natural, however, than sexist or racist ideology. Chrys Ingraham argued that the ideology of "thinking straight" serves to maintain, reproduce, and reinforce the sexuality hierarchy.

If we "do heterosexuality" and "do gender" in our everyday lives, to what extent can we "undo" them? . . .

If we can free ourselves from assuming the inevitability of some form of gender, then combinations of femininity and masculinity—and of same-gender or other-gender desire—do not represent the only human possibilities. If men and women are different products of a hierarchical relation, in the absence of that relation very different subjectivities and desires might emerge.

Much of what passes as radical in these "postmodern" times, then, does not envisage the end of gender hierarchy or the collapse of institutionalized heterosexuality, but simply a multiplying of genders and sexualities or movement between them. It might be argued that this would ultimately have the effect of rendering the difference between women and men as simply part of a fluid continuum of differences and of divesting heterosexuality of its privileged location. But seeking to undo binary divisions by rendering their boundaries more permeable and adding more categories to them ignores the hierarchical social relations on which the original binaries were founded. We cannot hope to abolish hierarchies by creating finer gradations or more movement within them. All this can achieve is a concealment and mystification of the material inequalities through which heterosexuality and gender are sustained at the macrolevel of structures and institutions as well as the microlevel of our everyday social practices.

Sexual lifestyles and practices are shaped by the commodification of sexuality . . . If our capacity to undo gender and heterosexuality is constrained by the structural inequalities that sustain them, then our ability to conceptualize their undoing is limited to the extent that our sense of ourselves has been constructed within a heterosexual, patriarchal, late capitalist social order. It may be that this accounts for . . . the failure to imagine a world without gender, without heterosexuality—and without other systemic inequalities deriving from the global reach of transnational capitalism. . . .

Radical intellectuals have abandoned those metanarratives, such as Marxism, which once promised a better future in favor of Foucault's view that power is inescapable. We can resist, subvert, and destabilize, but nothing much will change; or, if it does, there will be new deployments of power to be resisted, subverted, and destabilized. This is a politics of resistance and transgression, but not a politics of radical change.

Source: Stevi Jackson. "Sexuality, Heterosexuality, and Gender Hierarchy." In Chrys Ingraham, ed. *Thinking Straight.* New York: Routledge, 2005, 15–37, 32–33.

The heterosexist, male- and adult-dominated culture is opposed to "woman-identified womanness," "the lesbian continuum," and all other expressions of "queerness," Chrys Ingraham has written. She explored the social construction of institutionalized heterosexuality at length in her analysis of "white weddings" and her examination of heterosexual "straight culture."[21] Although a person's sexuality varies over his or her lifetime, institutionalized heterosexism encourages people to believe that sexuality is fixed and unchanging, she argued. People use socially constructed categories of sexuality to "situate ourselves within a value system that is patterned hierarchically."[22] In a society where heterosexuality is the standard, each kind of sexuality has different levels of cultural acceptability and provides individuals with different degrees of status and social legitimacy. Ingraham has argued that on the sexuality continuum, heterosexuality has been valued most, homosexuality least, and bisexuality has fallen somewhere in between. Moreover, some behavior is considered unacceptable, even for heterosexuals. Unemployed and fiscally "dependent" heterosexual husbands, promiscuous wives, and men and women who do not marry all face social sanctions because their behavior fails to meet heterosexual standards. Behaving in a "straight" heterosexual way means "comply[ing] with the prevailing meanings and ideological messages that organize heterosexuality."[23] Thinking and living "straight" involves failing to recognize that heterosexuality has been organized as the dominant construction in a power system. It also involves embracing entitlement and power that come with heterosexual behavior, without coming to terms with social and personal consequences of the hierarchical, systemic, and cultural roots of heterosexual domination, which shapes what some scholars refer to as *heteronormativity*.[24]

In this context, the social construction of performance needs to be added to the understanding of sexuality. For Judith Butler, performance can reinforce dominant relations, and it can subvert dominant culture by challenging, contesting, and overriding it. Gender attributes are performative, not expressive, Butler has written. Therein lies the revolutionary moment: gender is performed in discontinuous ways that break the rules and reshape gender in a restrictive culture based on masculine domination and compulsory heterosexuality.

> Gender ought not to be construed as a stable identity or locus of agency from which various acts follow; rather, gender is an identity tenuously constituted in time, instituted in an exterior space through a stylized repetition of acts.... If the ground of gender is the stylized repetition of acts through time and not a seamless identity, then the spatial meaning of "ground" will be displaced and revealed as a stylized configuration, indeed a gendered corporealization of time. The abiding gendered self will be shown to be structured by repeated acts that seek to approximate the ideal of a substantial ground of reality, but which, in their occasional *dis*continuity, reveal the temporal and contingent groundlessness of this "ground." The possibilities of gender transformation are to be found precisely in the arbitrary relation between such acts, in the possibility of a failure to repeat, a deformity, or a parodic repetition that exposes the phantasmatic effect of abiding identity as a politically tenuous construction.[25]

Although Butler has explored the performance of sex, gender, and sexuality more than anyone else, she has not yet explored how sex, gender, sexuality, and their socially constructed performance are related to other levels of social construction. The contestation of culture, gender, and heterosexuality and her mapping of the abstract body have not been placed within the historical processes of this particular society and its hierarchical structures and the global transformations that are taking place.

In this regard, it helps to be historically specific because, as Kempadoo has argued, race has a real power in the world.[26] Although some scholars have argued that race is a constructed or "invented" category and suggest that it doesn't or shouldn't really matter, Kempadoo argued that although it is "constructed," it assumes a real, material force in the world and should for that reason be taken seriously. In the same way, bodies are more than general fleshy abstractions that are induced to perform gender, which is what Butler has argued. In global society, bodies are shaped by local and global hierarchies and by long-standing movements that transform the real conditions of life. Gender and patriarchy may be social inventions, but they are also etched on bodies; they affect the corporeal world and the bodies in them. The capitalist world-system has created a highly unequal and divided world where some bodies are created as overfed and other bodies are created malnourished, where some gendered-racialized bodies are socially endowed with health and long life and others have been inscribed by violence and sped to early death.

PATRIARCHIES

In capitalist society, male and female biological identities are transformed or "constructed" into social identities with attributes that assign preeminence to men and establish relations that reinforce men's domination of women. Society shapes gender in ways that artificially manufacture the social categories of women and men, which are social identities, from the biological characteristics of females and males. Biological identities of just-born females and males are located in relationship to the gender order and are interpreted as having more or less social value depending on their biological sex. Institutions and people then shape their social identities from this interpretation of their biology.

It is also important to recognize that gender is more than "women." Every person has a gender, which is shaped by society and by individuals. Women-centered movements often challenge multiple oppressions because women are oppressed as women and also as members of other groups. Gender hierarchies are always tied to other intersecting hierarchies and cannot be separated from them, even when gender or race or class emerges as the primary challenge in certain situations. By dismantling the mechanisms that produce inequality and cultivating new ways of living and relating to each other, feminist activists can alter social relations from the most intimate to the most abstract.

Of course, feminist scholars and activists have written extensively about capitalist and precapitalist gender patriarchies, so we do not want to rehearse them all here. But in this context, it is important to recognize that a feminist appreciation of male domination around the world has helped women and also men to reconstruct the ways that women understand themselves, their relations with each other, their power in society, and their ability to change the way the world works.

Some feminist scholars have argued that male domination can only be challenged by women acting alone. Kirsten Campbell has argued that women should organize as *women* and that "feminist knowledges represent the possibility that discourses other than those of mastery can found intersubjective relations."[27] And Luce Irigaray has argued that women need to go on strike from men to preserve their autoeroticism and homosexuality, which suggests that women challenge patriarchies on their own.[28]

But we have found that although women can and do fight sexism on their own, they have also joined with men to articulate a social bond between subjects other than "mastery" in collective efforts to transform gender. Women fight male domination in different ways. They often use their social, gender identities as women to fight against racism and oppressive state policies or to promote peace and justice. Their experience with male domination gives them a position or standpoint from which to fight *other* hierarchies: heterosexist, ageist, racist, and so on. Feminism is not just about challenging male domination and all of its root causes but also about changing the meanings of race, class, sexuality, and age. Sometimes women do this in the company of men, in inclusive groups, and sometimes they do it in the company of women.

In recent years, for example, West African feminists in France, indigenous feminist women in Bolivia, and young feminist women in Iran have struggled simultaneously against indigenous patriarchies but also against racism and discrimination. Their efforts demonstrate that struggles over intimate relations between women and men can also challenge sociopolitical relations and promote new kinds of alternative development.

West African Women in France, Indigenous Women in Bolivia

Women have used feminist ideas to redirect alternative development, and they have planted themselves in the middle of labor migration movements, demanding that gender equality be addressed. When the French government refused to give official papers to new West African immigrants, women in the undocumented group, the *sanspapiers,* joined and led public protests. The group occupied a church in Paris, saw some of the male protesters deported to Mali, and then began a hunger strike to change their collective status as *clandestins.* According to Cathie Lloyd, women emerged as a powerful presence in this movement, first by confronting men's patriarchal behavior and attitudes in the group and then by using their own skills against French authorities.

> [W]omen kept the protest going despite the discouragement of the men who were prepared to disband the protest on several occasions.... [I]nitially the men did not allow women to attend the meetings to discuss tactics, but through their own organization women developed the resources to insist on such participation.... The women were in a stronger position than men to build networked support because they had more contact with neighborhood structures, such as schools, shops and local services, and their organizations reached across ethnic and national boundaries.

Above all, women as mothers effectively disabled the criminal stereotype of the "*clandestine*." They disrupted the "normal" public/domestic division, which underscores gender relations in political life to the detriment of women.[29]

Women in this movement challenged male dominance within the West African community, demanded the right to migrate from the South to the North and integrate into French society, and challenged the French state, forcing it to acknowledge that many households were not made up of nuclear families. By stressing individual rights, protesters challenged the family norms of the dominant group. In this movement, women gained power from their household and community networking, allowing them to keep the fight for an open frontier in a public context. As Lourdes Arizpe has argued, the struggles of migrants are a central force in "oppos[ing] the deepening of unequal access" and are working on "the means for the institutional redress of such unequal access."[30] Other political struggles are waged through the cooperation of women and men in households who "downshift" from extensive consumerism to socially responsible consumerism.[31]

In Bolivia, indigenous women leaders have organized around the idea that "in complementarity there is equality."[32] This allows them to oppose white and *mestizo* cultures and to receive support from men for their work in indigenous movements. It has been difficult for women to work for women-inclusive alternative development within male-run organizations, but they have decided that it is important for them to *keep* working in this environment. When indigenous women have worked in women-only groups, male-run organizations have incorporated them very slowly. As indigenous women worked for change, they addressed both practical gender issues (such as domestic violence) and development-related issues, such as women's access to land; patriarchal land-inheritance practices that privilege male sons; the need for voting and decision-making rights for all adult *comuneros*, not just adult men; increased access to education; and the need to provide technical training and credit for women.[33]

For some feminists and critical thinkers, finding an open space to discuss political and social issues has been a big challenge. Open conversations about political options often are held in mixed group settings that include men. In Iran, women activists have used the Internet as a meeting place where critical information can be exchanged. Like free-flowing conversations on a lively street corner, "Weblogestan" provides a safe, accessible place for activists and scholars to hold public dialogues. "By connecting local conditions to global forces by means of new media, young Iranians are challenging the authoritarian measures that limit individual rights and civil liberties. Concepts such as democracy, human rights, feminism and civil society are familiar to them, and they are open to debate and discussion through online journals and weblogs."[34]

Mixed-gender Internet dialogues have provided a way for college-age women in Iran, other Iranian women, and women in different countries to exchange ideas and movement strategies and to prepare for future actions. Once again, feminist organizing has taken forms that do not correspond to superficial and narrow understandings of gender and feminism. Feminists have forged ahead in many ways, and men have sometimes been their compatriots, co-organizers, and key partners in the struggle to discover real alternatives. When feminist-led groups carve pathways to the future, they work to replace ageist, heterosexual, patriarchal relations with ones that are more peaceful, accepting, and inclusive.

READING

Feminist change is carried out in diverse ways in Brazil and in other countries. And sometimes we may not even recognize this as feminist change, as demonstrated by Yvonne Corcoran-Nantes. Feminist consciousness can be overt, and feminists can focus on specific issues that only women face. And sometimes women's concerns and feminism become embedded within movements for a better quality of life. Both kinds of feminism are found in Brazil and around the world, and both kinds are making profound differences.[35]

In the second selection, June Jordan questioned what greater tyranny there is than to dictate to the human heart. In this writing, patriarchal heterosexuality was examined within a broad political framework.[36]

In the last selection, Jacqui Alexander introduced her framework that showed how contemporary transnational exploitation, state policies and repression, racism, and heteropatriarchy shape ideologies and everyday life for people in the Caribbean and in other areas.[37]

NOTES

1. Kamala Kempadoo, *Sexing the Caribbean: Gender, Race, and Sexual Labor* (New York: Routledge, 2004), 9.

2. Ibid.

3. Malcolm Gladwell, "The Risk Pool," *The New Yorker,* August 28, 2006, 34.

4. Cynthia H. Enloe, *Bananas, Beaches, and Bases: Making Feminist Sense of International Relations* (Berkeley: University of California Press, 1990); Cynthia H. Enloe, *Maneuvers: The International Politics of Militarizing Women's Lives* (Berkeley: University of California Press, 2000).

5. Irene Silverblatt, *Moon, Sun, and Witches: Gender Ideologies and Class in Inca and Colonial Peru* (Princeton, NJ: Princeton University Press, 1987).

6. Alfred C. Kinsey, *Sexual Behavior in the Human Female* (Philadelphia, PA: Saunders, 1953).

7. Shulamith Firestone, "The Dialectic of Sex," in Wendy K. Kolmar and Frances Bartkowski, eds., *Feminist Theory: A Reader,* 2nd ed. (Boston: McGraw-Hill, 2005), 273–288, 279.

8. Radicalesbians, "The Woman-Identified Woman," in Kolmar and Bartkowski, *Feminist Theory,* 242.

9. Ibid., 241.

10. Ibid., 240.

11. Ibid., 242.

12. Gayle Rubin, "The Traffic in Women: Notes on the 'Political Economy' of Sex," in Kolmar and Bartkowski, *Feminist Theory,* 273–288, 279.

13. Ibid., 285.

14. Firestone, "The Dialectic of Sex," 227.

15. Rubin, "The Traffic in Women," 285.

16. Kathleen Gough, "The Origin of the Family," in Rayna R. Reiter, ed., *Toward an Anthropology of Women* (New York: Monthly Review Press, 1975), 51–76.

17. Adrienne Rich, "Compulsory Heterosexuality and Lesbian Existence," in Kolmar and Bartkowski, *Feminist Theory,* 349.

18. Ibid., 351.

19. Ibid., 349.

20. Adrienne Rich, "Notes Towards a Politics of Location," in Carole McCann and Seung-Kyung Kim, eds., *Feminist Theory Reader* (New York: Routledge, 2003), 447–459, 458.

21. Chrys Ingraham, *Thinking Straight: The Power, the Promise, and the Paradox of Heterosexuality* (New York: Routledge, 2005).

22. Ibid., 2.

23. Ibid., 3.

24. Ibid., 3–4.

25. Judith Butler, "Gender Trouble: The Subversion of Identity," in Kolmar and Bartkowksi, *Feminist Theory,* 503.

26. Kempadoo, *Sexing the Caribbean,* 9.

27. Kirsten Campbell, *Jacques Lacan and Feminist Epistemology* (New York: Routledge, 2006), 179.

28. Luce Irigaray, "This Sex Which Is Not One," in Linda Nicholson, ed., *The Second Wave* (New York: Routledge, 1997), 323–329.

29. Cathie Lloyd, "Partnerships in the Struggles of Civil Society: African Women and the 'Sanspapiers' Movement in France," *Development* 41, no. 2 (1998): 58–61, 60.

30. Lourdes Arizpe, "Transitions in Development: Sustainability, Equity, and Conviviability," *Development* 43, no. 4 (2000): 15–16, 16.

31. Simon Zadek and Franck Amalric, "Consumer Works!" *Development* 41, no. 3 (1998): 7–14.

32. Carmen Deere Diana and Magdalena Leon, "Institutional Reform of Agriculture Under Neoliberalism: The Impact of the Women's and Indigenous Movements," *Latin American Research Review* 36, no. 2 (Spring 2001): 31.

33. Ibid., 15.

34. Fereshteh Nouraie-Simone, "Wings of Freedom: Iranian Women, Identity, and Cyberspace," in F. Nouraie-Simone, ed., *On Shifting Ground: Muslim Women in the Global Era* (New York: The Feminist Press, 2005), 61–79, 75.

35. Yvonne Corcoran-Nantes, "Female Consciousness or Feminist Consciousness? Women's Consciousness Raising in Community-Based Struggles in Brazil," in Carole R. McCann and Seung-Kyung Kim, eds., *Feminist Theory Reader: Local and Global Perspectives* (New York: Routledge, 2003), 126–137.

36. June Jordan, "A New Politics of Sexuality," in June Jordan, *Technical Difficulties: African-American Notes on the State of the Union* (New York: Pantheon, 1992), 187–193.

37. M. Jacqui Alexander, "On Living the Privileges of Empire" and "Why Pedagogies and Why Pedagogies of Crossing," in *Pedagogies of Crossing: Meditations on Feminism, Sexual Politics, Memory, and the Sacred* (Durham, NC: Duke University Press, 2005), 1–9.

FEMALE CONSCIOUSNESS OR FEMINIST CONSCIOUSNESS? WOMEN'S CONSCIOUSNESS RAISING IN COMMUNITY-BASED STRUGGLES IN BRAZIL

Yvonne Corcoran-Nantes

... My own research in Brazil, from which the empirical data in this chapter originates, was designed specifically to look at aspects of women's political participation in popular urban social movements in order to provide explanations for women's high profile in non-institutional politics.[1] It was clear that by the 1980s women participated in and led popular protest around a wide variety of issues related to urbanization, employment and the provision of basic services, which suggests that this political arena represents something of fundamental importance to women (see Safa 1990; Corcoran-Nantes 1990; Moser 1987). Moreover, the issues that interest women represent the major social and economic problems in developing countries and are also becoming key issues in the advanced industrial nations.

Women of the working poor in Brazil have, over the past two decades, strengthened their presence in non-institutional politics by protesting about the lack of basic services, health provision, transport, housing and unemployment. The methods of organization and political practice of popular urban social movements demonstrate the influence of women in them and similar practices can be found in many developing countries both in grassroots protest politics and women's organizations (see, for example, Mies 1988; Mattelart 1980; Cutrufelli 1983). I have argued elsewhere that these movements were not specifically created *for* women. It is women who form the majority within a social group whose socioeconomic experience in Brazilian society is neither reflected nor represented in other forms of political organization (see Corcoran-Nantes 1990). Consequently, women have played a major role in the formation and development of popular movements. Through their participation they have discovered a new public identity in a political sphere which, in many ways, they have made their own. Many women, through their political development in non-institutional politics, have gone on to extend their participation to political parties and trade unions as well as strategic gender protests along with women's organizations and feminist groups around issues such as birth control, rape, and domestic violence.

What seems to have developed is a bifurcated political sphere: male/institutional politics and female/non-institutional politics, which are identifiable by the nature of political/gender organization and action. The political practice in either sphere bears little resemblance to the other as in one the majority of political actors are male and in the other female. What I wish to consider here is the gender specificity of political practices in non-institutional politics and their implications for the relationship between politically reproduced gender spheres.

This [reading] will look at the development of political consciousness and solidarity among women of the popular urban movements in São Paulo. It is through these practices and women's influence on them that we can analyse the motivation behind their participation in this political sphere, how women view their role in society and what this represents for them. By looking at the various processes involved in conscientization and politicization such as forms of consciousness raising, self-help groups, oral history, and the struggle for literacy, I will argue that the development of women's political consciousness is far more complex than present analyses demonstrate. In Brazil, as in many other Latin American countries, women have created a political role for themselves based on their social status as wives and mothers but through which they have struggled for recognition of their roles and rights as workers, residents, and citizens.

GENDER: THE MISSING LINK IN ANALYSES OF POPULAR SOCIAL MOVEMENTS

Despite evidence to show the predominance of women in non-institutional politics, those who have attempted to analyse popular social movements have tended to ignore the question of gender. Those who have acknowledged or tried to give some explanation for women's participation and political consciousness tend to fall into two different camps. First, there are those like Jaquette (1989) who subsume female participation under the auspices of feminism or women's movements, thereby removing the question of gender from their analysis of popular protest in Latin America. Second, there are those like Chaney (1979) who prefer to confine themselves to a matrifocal analysis where the traditional role of women as wives and mothers and their relation to the reproduction of the labour force becomes the universal explanation, the *sine qua non*, for women's political practice and participation. The role of women in Latin American society is far too multifaceted for us to be satisfied with unitary explanations of their participation in the political sphere.

Political division of labour exists in political parties and trade unions in Latin America and many other parts of the world. Within institutional politics women's groups and women's departments are formed to present programmes and drafts of new laws or to develop a strategy to place women's issues on the political agenda. What this actually does is to take strategic gender issues and other issues that are of importance to women out of the mainstream politics within these organizations. In short, it removes them from the political agenda. Tying women's political participation exclusively to the question of feminism and women's movements is a wholly inaccurate picture of the extent of women's political participation and the motives and interests behind it. The majority of women who participate in the popular social movements are not motivated by a feminist consciousness; feminism for them has very little to do with the reality of their lives. In Latin American society, the marked inequality in the distribution of wealth and resources has further reinforced the idea, among the women of the urban poor, that feminism is a middle-class ideology for women who have all the social and economic advantages. Moreover, the institutionalization of domestic service on the continent has sustained the antagonism between classes whereby "fortunate" women exploit "less fortunate" women. The patron/client relationship which has evolved is a major barrier to any longstanding political association between them, and there have been occasions when this relationship has been politically exploited (Corcoran-Nantes 1988; Filet Abreu de Souza 1980; Chuchryk 1989). Consequently, there are considerable class differences in relation to how and in what forms of political organizations women participate.

Writers who do analyse women's participation in popular social movements tend to consider only one aspect (that of the sexual division of labour) as an explanation for their participation, either relating this exclusively to women's domestic role, or this, together with women's relationship to collective consumption (see Cardoso 1984; Safa 1990; Moser 1987; Evers et al. 1982). I have argued elsewhere that women's participation in social movements is also linked to their role in production and that most of the issues around which these movements are organized also affect men (Corcoran-Nantes 1990). Without doubt, women do legitimate their entry into the political spheres as wives and mothers but there are tangible reasons why women do so. In Latin American society *marianismo,* or the cult of Mary, still exists whereby women's status comes from their reproductive role, and this has often been a source of power for women (Stevens 1973). By utilizing this image, women can strengthen and legitimate their political involvement in the eyes of the state. Conversely, the state has also exploited the cultural identity of women, *os supermadres,* to secure their political support (Chuchryk 1989). The *supermadre* approach to politics is legitimated by women, men, and the state. Up to the present time no one has considered, for example, how far men take their role in the family into the political sphere.

Maxine Molyneux in her own work on women in post-revolutionary societies, has presented an excellent working hypothesis for considering the motivations and achievements of women's participation in political struggles. She divides gender interests into two broad categories. One is strategic gender interests which are directly related to women's subordination in a given society and the demands around which women's struggles are based on a strategy to overcome all forms of gender inequality. The other is practical gender interests which derive from women's ascribed role in the sexual division of labour, a response to their immediate practical needs and formulated by women themselves. These are shaped by class and ethnicity and are not necessarily part of a long-term strategy to achieve gender equality. She goes on to argue that in the formulation of strategic gender interests, practical gender interests have to be taken into account and it is "the politicisation of these practical interests and their transformation into strategic interests which constitutes a central aspect of feminist practice" (Molyneux 1985: 236–7).

It is practical gender interests which are the basis of women's political participation in popular social movements. The transformation of practical gender interests into strategic gender interests requires not only women's recognition of their power to represent their own interests but also that space exists within the prevailing political system to pressure the state into recognizing those interests. This is part of a complex political development process whereby women not only recognize gender interests but do so in relation to and in conjunction with other women, across class and ethnic boundaries.

POLITICAL PRACTICE: THE DEVELOPMENT OF POLITICAL CONSCIOUSNESS AND SOLIDARITY

... It is on the urban periphery of São Paulo that the fieldwork on which this chapter is based was carried out and concentrated on three popular movements: O Movimento de Favela (the Favela Movement—founded in 1976 to secure land title and to improve services and infrastructure in the settlements), O Movimento de Saude (the Health Movement—formed originally in 1973 with the aim of improving medical services at both the local and regional level), and O Movimento dos Desempregados (the Unemployed Movement—formed in 1983 to solve the immediate problems of unemployment through demands for unemployment benefit, funding to set up worker cooperatives and so on).[2] These popular movements are representative of the wide range of movements which existed, and continue to exist, in the urban periphery of São Paulo. One common feature is that participants in these movements are either exclusively or predominantly women.

Health, housing, and unemployment are typical of the kind of social questions that have attracted the interest of low-income women, and movements formed around these issues developed characteristics which reflect their involvement in them. The key factor to take into account here is that while the sexual division of labour tends in general terms to confine women for a large amount of their time to their homes and immediate neighbourhoods, low-income women are often involved in a wide range of activities which span the rather arbitrary divide between production and reproduction, with many having various modes of generating income (see Brydon and Chant 1989: 10–12). Women thus tend to be more responsive than men to issues that relate to socio-economic activities in both the public *and* private sphere. The political participation of women arises from the social bonds which are created via these activities in the community, through which they organize themselves and from which the political contexts of urban social movements are developed.

Moreover, the social, economic and even moral issues which have formed the basis of this type of political protest are directly associated with the nature of dependent capitalist development. They are issues which cannot be solved in the short term and are precisely those which have remained on the periphery of "mainstream" politics or have been given little or no priority in the programmes of parties and successive governments. It is hardly surprising, therefore, that some social movements have been in existence for over two decades and have only gradually gained improvements in the conditions of life for the urban poor. Various forms of consciousness raising were used by the popular movements, and the ways in which they were implemented differed from one movement to another. First, there was instruction in socialist theories to explain the socio-economic conditions of the urban poor and the importance of the popular movements to the struggle for political change in Brazilian society. This almost always involved the help of supporters of the movements such as the Church or political parties who had political material designed for the conscientization of the urban poor. Second, there was a form of consciousness raising which was a means of self-education and collective counselling, and dealt with issues and problems arising from, and related to, their struggles. This was a method of consciousness raising which women preferred to use in which self-help and the dissemination of information was a part of the process of political participation. The question of self-help also led to the formation of cooperative schemes in low-income neighbourhoods to provide practical solutions to the immediate needs of the local community. Third was the use of oral history, which was probably the most important and effective way of creating political consciousness and solidarity. All the popular movements had some means of recording and registering their political history but it was only in those movements in which women had organizational control that a strong emphasis was placed on the use of oral history as a means of conscientization.

CLASS CONSCIOUSNESS VIS-À-VIS FEMALE CONSCIOUSNESS

Consciousness raising based on the propagation of socialist theory was undertaken in various ways. In many cases it was an integral part of the political meetings of the movement itself during which an individual or group, usually with experience in political parties or left-wing Church groups, discussed current political issues relating to the problems of the urban poor. Sometimes it was little more than speech making, but on other occasions simple visual aids such as diagrams or cartoon pictures were used to show the participants how and why they suffered in Brazilian society. Women were quick to point out that in much of this material they were underrepresented and *their* experience in Brazilian society was rarely discussed at all. More sophisticated material was sometimes used, such as films or slides borrowed from the Catholic Church which has produced entire courses for the politicization of the popular classes.

These forms of consciousness raising stimulated interest and discussion both inside and outside the meetings but this was difficult to sustain over a long period of time. Women, in particular, lost interest fairly quickly because their political concerns centred on practical difficulties rather than theorizing struggles. It was, however, a successful way of selecting potential political activists. Experienced activists from political parties or left-wing ecclesiastical groups who participated in the popular movements would often utilize this form of consciousness raising to "recruit" new activists by inviting those people who demonstrated some "political aptitude" to attend their meetings. A significant number of women entered local party politics in this way....

In the Unemployed Movement the formation of women's groups spread swiftly from one region to another and the numbers of women committee members rose to 70 percent. In some regions, women's groups were formed as a result of initiatives by women themselves. In others, however, their formation was encouraged by men, who had organizational control of the Unemployed Movement, as a means of removing "women's issues" out of the general political demands of the movement. Wherever they emerged, they became a forum for the discussion of a wide range of issues such as women's political participation, male domestic violence, and women's role in society. Through the exchange of experiences, particularly those related to their own participation in the popular movements, many women were better able to face the problems arising from their political activities with the support of these groups which served to reinforce their commitment to the movement.[3]

Many women enjoyed the opportunity of talking about themselves and their lives, as well as finding out more about themselves and other women. These groups often developed into a mutual support collective wherein *companheiras* in the struggle became true friends who gave each other help in their personal, working and political lives. Some of these groups were little more than small women's meetings but others went on to join up with other women's groups and organize talks to which feminist speakers were invited to discuss topics such as "the history of women's political participation in Brazil" and "female sexuality: my body, my choice." Many of these groups joined with women's organizations and feminist groups on demonstrations and political protests about issues such as abortion, violence against women, and family planning. Consequently, these groups, although initially formed as a means of politicizing women within the popular movements through consciousness raising undertaken by women for women, sometimes became a vehicle for contacts with other women's groups or other women in a wide range of political organizations. Irrespective of how these groups developed, they gave women greater confidence in themselves, and many of the women who organized or participated in these groups went on to be elected local and regional coordinators of Committees of the Unemployed.

The Health Movement actually evolved from issues concerning women's health and that of their children. The use of self-education as a form of consciousness raising about these issues was a natural progression from the movement's initial aims and objectives. Their struggle to improve an inadequate and underfunded health service made women conscious of the need to take action themselves in the area of preventive medicine in an attempt to reduce the risk of health problems for themselves and their children. Women of the movement were principally interested in two main topics: first, ways in which they could prevent or reduce the risk of their children suffering from some of the more common childhood diseases in Brazil; second, access to information on contraception so that women could make an informed choice as to what methods were available and most suitable for them to use. In both cases, women turned to local doctors and nurses to help them produce booklets which they could use in their self-education groups....

The leaflets produced by the Health Movement on family planning were also an invaluable source of information for women. In Brazil there were no official family planning schemes or health advice services for women and the public health service offered little orientation for women who wished to use contraceptives, apart from advice on "natural" methods of birth control supported by the Catholic Church. In practice, while there was no official line taken by the government on the question of family planning, women of the working poor were often pressured into using sterilization as a permanent solution to their "problems" without being advised on alternative forms of contraception available to them.[4] The self-education groups and pamphlets were a means of informing women about the different methods of contraception available in Brazil, showing the advantages and disadvantages of each one to help women make an informed choice on what method was best for them. Women who did not participate in the Health Movement attended these informal groups on family planning and some of them went on to participate in the movement itself.

Meetings held by the Health Movement about the issues of family health and family planning were invariably held in people's houses, often as "street meetings" to which women from the movement would invite their friends and neighbours. Working from the pamphlets, women would discuss the questions raised and any practical difficulties which arose. No professional people participated in the groups: they were run by ordinary women who sought practical solutions to health problems which were not resolved within the public health service. The existence of the groups demonstrated the importance of the Health Movement in the struggle for a better health service and they reinforced or developed women's commitment to the movement.

This type of consciousness raising developed for women by women raised female consciousness in relation to strategic gender interests. It stimulated and developed a complex matrix of inter- and intra-class alliances between women around gender-specific issues. As women acquired a greater sense of themselves and gender inequality through their political practices in popular struggles, women's organizations in the low-income neighbourhoods emerged and grew in strength. By developing a political identity as women of the working poor, they were able to define their relationships clearly with other organizations, both inside and outside institutional politics. Consequently, when they entered political protests in association with political parties and trade unions on the one hand, or feminist groups and women's organizations on the other, in general or gender-specific political struggles, such as the Campaign for Direct Elections or Women against Violence Campaign, they were able to defend this identity and their practical gender interests from a position of greater political strength.

THE DEMAND FOR LITERACY AND POLITICIZATION

Adult literacy courses based on the methods of Paulo Freire, which use short literacy courses as a means of politicization, were also a popular and constructive form of conscientization.[5] Many of the urban poor who participate in the popular movements are illiterate. Women in particular have had few chances to educate themselves, and when they begin to undertake organizational roles in the movement there is tremendous pressure on them to obtain basic literacy skills. Dealing with members of the government, participating in negotiations and the need to take notes at meetings present difficulties to those who are unable to read or write.

Women often bypass these difficulties by using tape-recorders or by taking their children along to the regional or state meetings to take notes, so that they are able to recall the main points of discussion or proposals to report back to members of their group or the movement. However, the high rate of illiteracy amongst those who participate in the popular movements often gives a privileged position to people who can read or write. There are women with valuable political skills who have been elected as representatives or coordinators in the movements who hide the fact that they are illiterate. Whether it is from a feeling of inadequacy or as a result of internal or external pressure, it is invariably the leaders or representatives of the movements who instigate literacy courses as a means of educating both themselves and others in the popular movements.

Literacy courses are always undertaken with the help of activists from either the Church or the political parties who have experience in this field. These activists are invited by the movements initially to teach the literacy course, but eventually one or two members of the movement are shown how to deliver the course and this eliminates the need for outside help. The courses are nearly always oversubscribed and it is frequently women who are the most interested in becoming literate. This interest derives, primarily, from the desire to enhance and expand their new-found political skills; to be able to make notes, to vote in government elections, to read political material, or even to write their own placards were all skills that these women wanted to acquire. Thus, it was these factors which made this type of literacy course based on politicization ideal for the popular movements.

COMMUNITY ACTION AS POLITICAL ACTION

Cooperative work and mutualist schemes were two other activities which developed and strengthened the solidarity between those who participated in the popular movements. Amongst the urban poor they were a means of resolving immediate and socio-economic problems and could be of a short- or long-term nature. Cooperative work schemes usually entailed the sale of goods or commodities and only benefited those who participated in them. Mutualist schemes, on the other hand, involved the provision of services and frequently benefited those who did not participate in them as well as those who did. Irrespective of the schemes' beneficiaries, they arose from the political practice of the popular movements. These schemes became an integral part of their political organization and extended the members' political commitment to the idea of collectivism into the local community.

It was the Unemployed Movement that used cooperative work schemes as an immediate solution to the subsistence problems of its members and in the period 1983–85 they became popular amongst the unemployed throughout Brazil. Some state governments financed projects submitted by the unemployed, but in São Paulo the majority of financing came from the Paulista Association of Solidarity in Unemployment (APSD) and was only given to groups registered with the Association.[6] Once again it was women who were most interested in the schemes which covered a wide range of petty commodity production such as bread making, confectionary, tailoring, and craft production.[7] These schemes were "tailor-made" for women: they were located near the home, they used flexible work rota[tion] systems and initially there were few expectations that the financial remuneration would do more than help to sustain the family unit during periods of unemployment. However, some of these cooperatives became extremely successful and the share of the profits was comparable to women's wages in the formal sector. Some cooperatives were more successful than others, in financial terms, but most of them managed to provide subsistence wages for the unemployed who participated in them. Furthermore, some of the cooperatives gave a small percentage of their profits to the funds of the Unemployed Movement to help finance political action. . . .

ORAL HISTORY: THE STORY TOLD AND RETOLD

The use of oral history as a form of politicization was fundamental to the creation of a political identity for the movements themselves and for those who participated in them. Many of the popular movements do write down the history of their organization and struggles and use this material for the conscientization of new members. But the use of oral history is a rich and personalized tribute to past events and the contribution of each of the participants to the movement's "success." An oral history is developed from individual and collective experiences of those who participate in the movements. It is a vivid, living testimony of their political defeats and victories which are recalled at any and every opportunity to demonstrate the courage, tenacity, and commitment of those who participate in them. Women, without a doubt, are the most avid subscribers to this form of politicization. They take great pride in their ability to recall events and even conversations in the minutest detail, often dramatizing the conflicts and confrontations with government or the police during their struggles. It is the way in which they reaffirm the importance of their participation in this form of political organization and the viability of the popular movements as an instrument for political change and social change.

In the meetings held after a political protest has been carried out, those who participated recall their personal experiences of the struggle and how they felt about it. Not everyone who participates in the popular movements can or will participate in their protests and demonstrations. The practice of using individual accounts of events informs those who were not present, but it is also a means of encouraging far more people to participate. Everyone is given a chance to speak or ask questions; the emphasis is on the individual contribution to the collective; the relaxed, enthusiastic atmosphere of these meetings alleviates the inevitable anticlimax which follows the intense period of political activity leading up to collective action. For those who participate in the popular movement, *every* struggle is a success which is counted not only by the concrete victories obtained through the struggle in relation to the demands of the movement but also by its impact on both the government *and* the participants....

The oral history of the popular movements catalogues both the triumphs and tribulations of their political practice, and those who participate in the movements are the ones who make and develop this history. The past successes of a movement are often what sustains its organization and the political commitment of those who participate in the movements in some of the more difficult and less successful periods of its political action. Women in particular are eager to record their political experiences, to create for themselves and reaffirm a specific political identity, one in which women are not inconsequential but successful political actors. In this way, oral history is not merely an adjunct to the political action of the popular movements but one of the key elements of their political practice.

THE TRANSFORMATION OF GENDER INTERESTS

The many forms of political action employed by the popular urban social movements, as we can see here, have many different functions. The need for conscientization or the creation of solidarity within the movements themselves was not always the initial purpose of these practices but often became the reason for continuing or developing them. Some practices arose from a simple need or idea expressed by those who participate in the movements whilst others were a direct attempt to conscientize the popular classes. Irrespective of the impetus for or the development of such forms of political practice used by the popular movements, in most cases they reflected the desires and needs of the women who dominated this form of political organization. In doing so, it gave many women the chance to "improve" themselves and develop both socially and politically by utilizing a wide range of skills to enhance and expand their new-found political ones.

The political mobilization of low-income women arose from their practical gender interests as well as structural class differences in Brazilian society. Their daily battles for economic survival prioritized political action around issues related to the access of the popular classes to the benefits of economic development. The provision of urban infrastructure, adequate healthcare and transport not only affect women's activities in the reproductive sphere but also have limiting effects on their access to employment and income-generating activities. Nevertheless, as opposed to gender "neutral" analyses (Slater 1985), it would be wrong to describe urban social movements as women's social movements (Safa 1990); this would fail to acknowledge not only the participation of men in these movements but also the effects of gender relations within and between these movements and institutional politics.

In the popular movements men can account for up to 40 percent of the participants. Gender relations in this context are different from those in institutional politics. Women acquire political experience in association with men, but in a sphere where they predominate it is frequently on their own terms. As we have seen here, the political practices of the movements are strongly influenced by women and as such their political development is directly related to their gender subordination in society. They are able to strengthen and legitimate their political role and become experienced political actors. Those who go on to enter institutional politics are able to do so from a much stronger position and with greater confidence in their political abilities (Corcoran-Nantes 1988; Moser 1987).

Through their struggles around practical gender interests, women who have a similar socio-economic experience in Brazilian society develop greater solidarity and awareness in relation to strategic gender interests. Opposition to women's political participation at a personal political level reinforces their experience of gender inequality in other spheres. Through their contact with political parties and trade unions they develop cross-class links with other women from feminist groups and women's organizations. These links have been strengthened by their association in struggles around strategic gender interests. By developing a political practice which emphasizes not only class inequality but also gender inequality, these women began to construct a gender identity around strategic interests based on their socio-economic experience. Consequently, low-income women were able to articulate their priorities and interests in relation to other class-based feminist groups and organizations and to pursue strategic gender interests through their political action.

Nevertheless, for low-income women practical gender interests take priority in their political struggles and it is here that they have built the necessary basis for unity and solidarity. Class oppression, to which their gender subordination is directly related, has forced women to organize around issues related to their very survival and that of their families. These issues comprise the major social and economic problems in developing countries, and in this context, strategic gender issues take a secondary role or may not be considered at all. In Brazil, however, amongst women of the urban poor, female consciousness has developed around strategic gender interests, and whether they choose to describe these as feminist or not is irrelevañt. What is important for women of the popular classes is that their concerns are firmly on the political agenda.

NOTES

This reading was adapted from the author's keynote address to the Bisexual, Gay, and Lesbian Student Association at Stanford University on April 29, 1991. It was published in the *Progressive*, July 1991.

1. This [reading] is dedicated to Elisabeth Souza-Lobo.

2. The material on which this [reading] is based arises out of a wider research project conducted on the role of women in the organization and formation of popular urban social movements in Brazil during the period 1983–85. The research was funded by a postgraduate award from the Economic and Social Research Council. Fieldwork was carried out in nine low-income neighbourhoods from three different regions of the Greater São Paulo metropolitan area: Embu and Sta Emilia in the Southern Zone; Vila Rica, Vila Antonieta, Vila Sezamo, and São Matheus in the Eastern Zone; and Diadema, São Caetano do Sul and Maua in the "ABC" region to the far east of the metropolitan area. Interviews were held with over 200 women who were active participants in popular movements. All material and quotations used in this chapter are from the author's primary data, unless otherwise stated.

3. Many women faced strong opposition to their political involvement from their partners. In many regions, women's self-help groups gave practical help and support to those who were victims of domestic violence or who wished to separate from their partners.

4. The Health Movement in conjunction with feminist groups and women's organizations had strongly opposed all family planning proposals by the government for being far too authoritarian. For example, in 1985 the Head of the Armed Forces insisted that the question of family planning should come under their jurisdiction because it was a matter of National Security!

5. Paulo Freire created a literacy course which utilized political material as subject matter to teach adults, in the space of forty lessons, the basic skills of reading and writing while at the same time developing a political consciousness in the student. In recent years the Brazilian

Catholic Church has adapted this method for the conscientization of the popular classes, and many political militants attend weekend courses, held by the Church, to learn how to deliver this course.

6. The APSD was one of the successful outcomes of political action by the Unemployed Movement. This Association was sponsored by various ecumenical bodies and Churches in São Paulo to give financial support to cooperatives and employment schemes initiated by the unemployed themselves.

7. In all the Brazilian states where help was offered by the government, the majority of projects were either submitted by women or were to be carried out by them.

A New Politics of Sexuality

June Jordan

As a young mother, I remember turning to Dr. Benjamin Spock's *Common Sense Book of Baby and Child Care* just about as often as I'd pick up the telephone. He was God. I was ignorant but striving to be good: a good Mother. And so it was there, in that best-seller pocketbook of do's and don't's, that I came upon this doozie of a guideline: Do not wear miniskirts or other provocative clothing because that will upset your child, especially if your child happens to be a boy. If you give your offspring "cause" to think of you as a sexual being, he will, at the least, become disturbed; you will derail the equilibrium of his notions about your possible identity and meaning in the world.

It had never occurred to me that anyone, especially my son, might look upon me as an asexual being. I had never supposed that "asexual" was some kind of positive designation I should, so to speak, lust after. I was pretty surprised by Dr. Spock. However, I was also, by habit, a creature of obedience. For a couple of weeks I actually experimented with lusterless colors and dowdy tops and bottoms, self-consciously hoping thereby to prove myself as a lusterless and dowdy and, therefore, excellent female parent.

Years would have to pass before I could recognize the familiar, by then, absurdity of a man setting himself up as the expert on a subject that presupposed women as the primary objects for his patriarchal discourse—on motherhood, no less! Years passed before I came to perceive the perversity of dominant power assumed by men, and the perversity of self-determining power ceded to men by women.

A lot of years went by before I understood the dynamics of what anyone could summarize as the Politics of Sexuality.

I believe the Politics of Sexuality is the most ancient and probably the most profound arena for human conflict. Increasingly, it seems clear to me that deeper and more pervasive than any other oppression, than any other bitterly contested human domain, is the oppression of sexuality, the exploitation of the human domain of sexuality for power.

When I say sexuality, I mean gender: I mean male subjugation of human beings because they are female. When I say sexuality, I mean heterosexual institutionalization of rights and privileges denied to homosexual men and women. When I say sexuality I mean gay or lesbian contempt for bisexual modes of human relationship.

The Politics of Sexuality therefore subsumes all of the different ways in which some of us seek to dictate to others of us what we should do, what we should desire, what we should dream about, and how we should behave ourselves, generally. From China to Iran, from Nigeria to Czechoslovakia, from Chile to California, the politics of sexuality—enforced by traditions of state-sanctioned violence plus religion and the law—reduces to male domination of women, heterosexist tyranny, and, among those of us who are in any case deemed despicable or deviant by the powerful, we find intolerance for those who choose a different, a more complicated—for example, an interracial or bisexual—mode of rebellion and freedom.

We must move out from the shadows of our collective subjugation—as people of color/as women/as gay/as lesbian/as bisexual human beings.

I can voice my ideas without hesitation or fear because I am speaking, finally, about myself. I am Black and I am female and I am a mother and I am bisexual and I am a nationalist and I am an antinationalist. And I mean to be fully and freely all that I am!

Conversely, I do not accept that any white or Black or Chinese man—I do not accept that, for instance, Dr. Spock should presume to tell me, or any other woman, how to mother a child. He has no right. He is not a mother. My child is not his child. And, likewise, I do not accept that anyone—any woman or any man who is not inextricably part of the subject he or she dares to address—should attempt to tell any of us, the objects of her or his presumptuous discourse, what we should do or what we should not do.

Recently, I have come upon gratuitous and appalling pseudoliberal pronouncements on sexuality. Too often, these utterances fall out of the mouths of men and women who first disclaim any sentiment remotely related to homophobia, but who then proceed to issue outrageous opinions like the following:

- That it is blasphemous to compare the oppression of gay, lesbian, or bisexual people to the oppression, say, of black people, or of the Palestinians.
- That the bottom line about gay or lesbian or bisexual identity is that you can conceal it whenever necessary and, so, therefore, why don't you do just that? Why don't you keep your deviant sexuality in the closet and let the rest of us—we who suffer oppression for reasons of our ineradicable and always visible components of our personhood such as race or gender—get on with our more necessary, our more beleaguered struggle to survive?

Well, number one: I believe I have worked as hard as I could, and then harder than that, on behalf of equality and justice—for African-Americans, for the Palestinian people, and for people of color everywhere.

And no, I do not believe it is blasphemous to compare oppressions of sexuality to oppressions of race and ethnicity: Freedom is indivisible or it is nothing at all besides sloganeering and temporary, short-sighted, and short-lived advancement for a few. Freedom is indivisible, and either we are working for freedom or you are working for the sake of your self-interests and I am working for mine.

If you can finally go to the bathroom wherever you find one, if you can finally order a cup of coffee and drink it wherever coffee is available, but you cannot follow your heart—you cannot respect the response of your own honest body in the world—then how much of what kind of freedom does any one of us possess?

Or, conversely, if your heart and your honest body can be controlled by the state, or controlled by community taboo, are you not then, and in that case, no more than a slave ruled by outside force?

What tyranny could exceed a tyranny that dictates to the human heart, and that attempts to dictate the public career of an honest human body?

Freedom is indivisible; the Politics of Sexuality is not some optional "special-interest" concern for serious, progressive folk.

And, on another level, let me assure you: if every single gay or lesbian or bisexual man or woman active on the Left of American politics decided to stay home, there would be *no* Left left.

One of the things I want to propose is that we act on that reality: that we insistently demand reciprocal respect and concern from those who cheerfully depend upon our brains and our energies for their, and our, effective impact on the political landscape.

Last spring, at Berkeley, some students asked me to speak at a rally against racism. And I did. There were four or five hundred people massed on Sproul Plaza, standing together against that evil. And, on the next day, on that same plaza, there was a rally for bisexual and gay and lesbian rights, and students asked me to speak at that rally. And I did. There were fewer than seventy-five people stranded, pitiful, on that public space. And I said then what I say today: That was disgraceful! There should have been just one rally. One rally: freedom is indivisible.

As for the second, nefarious pronouncement on sexuality that now enjoys mass-media currency: the idiot notion of keeping yourself in the closet—that is very much the same thing as the suggestion that black folks and Asian-Americans and Mexican-Americans should assimilate and become as "white" as possible—in our walk/talk/music/food/values—or else. Or else? Or else we should, deservedly, perish.

Sure enough, we have plenty of exposure to white everything so why would we opt to remain our African/Asian/Mexican selves? The answer is that suicide is absolute, and if you think you will survive by hiding who you really are, you are sadly misled: there is no such thing as partial or intermittent suicide. You can only survive if you—who you really are—do survive.

Likewise, we who are not men and we who are not heterosexist—we, sure enough, have plenty of exposure to male-dominated/heterosexist this and that.

But a struggle to survive cannot lead to suicide: suicide is the opposite of survival. And so we must not conceal/assimilate/integrate into the would-be dominant culture and political system that despises us. Our survival requires that we alter our environment so that we can live and so that we can hold each other's hands and so that we can kiss each other on the streets, and in the daylight of our existence, without terror and without violent and sometimes fatal reactions from the busybodies of America.

Finally, I need to speak on bisexuality. I do believe that the analogy is interracial or multiracial identity. I do believe that the analogy for bisexuality is a multicultural, multi-ethnic, multiracial world view. Bisexuality follows from such a perspective and leads to it, as well.

Just as there are many men and women in the United States whose parents have given them more than one racial, more than one ethnic identity and cultural heritage to honor; and just as these men and women must deny no given part of themselves except at the risk of self-deception and the insanities that must issue from that; and just as these men and women embody the principle of equality among races and ethnic communities;

and just as these men and women falter and anguish and choose and then falter again and then anguish and then choose yet again how they will honor the irreducible complexity of their God-given human being—even so, there are many men and women, especially young men and women who seek to embrace the complexity of their total, always-changing social and political circumstance.

They seek to embrace our increasing global complexity on the basis of the heart and on the basis of an honest human body. Not according to ideology. Not according to group pressure. Not according to anybody's concept of "correct."

This is a New Politics of Sexuality. And even as I despair of identity politics—because identity is given and principles of justice/equality/freedom cut across given gender and given racial definitions of being, and because I will call you my brother, I will call you my sister, on the basis of what you *do* for justice, what you *do* for equality, what you *do* for freedom and *not* on the basis of who you are, even so I look with admiration and respect upon the new, bisexual politics of sexuality.

This emerging movement politicizes the so-called middle ground: Bisexuality invalidates either/or formulation, either/or analysis. Bisexuality means I am free and I am as likely to want and to love a woman as I am likely to want and to love a man, and what about that? Isn't that what freedom implies?

If you are free, you are not predictable and you are not controllable. To my mind, that is the keenly positive, politicizing significance of bisexual affirmation:

To insist upon complexity, to insist upon the validity of all of the components of social/sexual complexity, to insist upon the equal validity of all of the components of social/sexual complexity.

This seems to me a unifying, 1990s mandate for revolutionary Americans planning to make it into the twenty-first century on the basis of the heart, on the basis of an honest human body, consecrated to every struggle for justice, every struggle for equality, every struggle for freedom.

PEDAGOGIES OF CROSSING

M. Jacqui Alexander

ON LIVING THE PRIVILEGES OF EMPIRE

I did not awake this morning to the deafening noise of sirens or the rocketing sound of nonstop bombs. I did not awake to the missiles that fall like rain from the sky, exploding on contact with land, staking out huge craters within the earth, collapsing people into buildings, trees into rubble, men into women, hands into feet, children into dust.[1] Two thousand tons of ammunition in three hours. Forty-two air raids in one day. Twenty-seven thousand air raids in a decade.[2] I did not awake this morning to the taste of desolation, nor to the crusts of anger piled high from decades of neglect. I did not awake to the familiar smell of charred flesh, which sand storms use to announce the morning raid. I did not awaken in Basra to the familiar smell of hunger, or of grief for that matter, residual grief from the last twelve years that now has settled as a thick band of air everywhere. Breathing grief for a lifetime can be toxic. Breathing only grief simply kills. I did not awake in Falluja, symbol of the post-election settlement wager: votes in exchange for bombs. I awoke this morning from a comfortable bed, avoiding the interminable queues for rations of fuel or food, because I have the privilege to choose to live, unlike many who have lost their lives in the insatiable service of imperialism.

What do lives of privilege look like in the midst of war and the inevitable violence that accompanies the building of empire? We live the privilege of believing the official story that the state owns and can therefore dispense security, that war is over, that silence is a legitimate trade for consent in the dangerous rhetoric of wartime economy; the mistaken belief that we can be against the war yet continue to brand this earth with a set of ecological footprints so large and out of proportion with the rest of life on the planet that war is needed to underwrite our distorted needs;[3] to consume an education that sanctions the academy's complicity in the exercise and normativization of state terror; to continue to believe in American democracy in the midst of an entanglement of state and corporate power that more resembles the practices of fascism than the practices of democracy; to believe that no matter how bad things are here they are worse elsewhere, so much so that undermining the promises of American democracy is an eminently more noble and therefore legitimate undertaking, more so than the undermining of democracy in any other place in the world; to assume that the machineries of enemy production pertain to an elsewhere, not operating within the geographic borders of the United States of North America. One of the habits of privilege is that it spawns superiority, beckoning its owners to don a veil of false protection so that they never see themselves, the devastation they wreak or their accountability to it. Privilege and superiority blunt the loss that issues from enforced alienation and segregations of different kinds.

Pedagogies' central metaphor is drawn from the enforced Atlantic Crossing of the millions of Africans that serviced from the fifteenth century through the twentieth the consolidation of British, French, Spanish, and Dutch empires. At the time I conceived of the book in 2000, the world had not yet witnessed the seismic imperial shifts that characterize this moment. In one sense, then, *Pedagogies* functions as an archive of empire's twenty-first-century counterpart, of oppositions to it, of the knowledges and ideologies it summons, and of the ghosts that haunt it. The book has assumed such a consciousness, and necessarily so since we are living witnesses or casualties of empire's egregious practices. None of us now alive lived that first round, at least not in a direct way, but we can fill in the outlines provided by these contemporary excesses: in the return to a Republican-led militarized Reconstruction that polices the national body as it amplifies its global reach;[4] by the U.S. state's cynical deployment of tradition in a way that upholds the heterosexualization of family and of morality so as to eclipse any apprehension of the immorality of empire; in the recirculation and rearticulation of myths of (American) origin and destined might through an ideological force-field that manufactures and feeds an enemy made increasingly by the day more grotesque, while purveying a faith-based politics tied to the oxymoronic "armies of compassion";[5] in the disappearance of immigrants and the increased incarceration of women and people of color, drawing sharp fault lines that continue to make of citizenship a more fragile, highly contingent enterprise—the requirements of citizenship for empire are disturbingly antithetical to those requirements of citizenship for collective self-determination;[6] by the way this moment presses up against what democracy has been made to mean, since empire requires sacrifice—the sacrifice of consent—unable to function, as William Pitt suggests, within the slow, cumbersome machine of constitutional democracy on its back;[7] by the fact that this moment not only challenges but also undermines epistemic frameworks that are simply inadequate to the task of delineating these itineraries of violence that are given other names such as democracy and civilization; by probing our function and location as radical intellectuals (and I intend the term intellectual in the broadest sense of a commitment to a life of the mind whether or not one is linked to the academy) along the lines that Stuart Hall suggests—that is, our ethical commitments, the contours and character of our class affiliations and loyalties, and the interpretive frameworks we bring to bear on the histories to which we choose to be aligned; and, importantly, how we assess the size and scope of the wager involved in displacing collective self-determination with corporate institutional allegiances. We can fill in the outlines of empire since its multiple contradictions are everywhere seen in the hydra-headed quality of violence that constitutes modernity's political itinerary as its ideological cognates, militarization and heterosexualization, are exposed. We can fill in the outlines of empire since we have seen the ways in which freedom has been turned into an evil experiment—that is, in George Lammings's words, "the freedom to betray freedom through gratuitous exploitation."[8] We can fill in the outlines when we see how empire's ruthless triumph demystifies the corruptibility of the self, without respect for those who believed themselves incorruptible. Perhaps empire never ended, that psychic and material will to conquer and appropriate, twentieth-century movements for decolonization notwithstanding. What we can say for sure is that empire makes all innocence impossible.[9]

WHY PEDAGOGIES, AND WHY PEDAGOGIES OF CROSSING?

This [reading] spans what feels like a lifetime compressed into a decade. It is an inventory of sorts of my multifaceted journey with(in) feminism, an inventory that is necessarily pluralized by virtue of my own migrations and the confluence of different geographies of feminism. In this volume I am concerned with the multiple operations of power, of gendered and sexualized power that is simultaneously raced and classed yet not practiced within hermetically sealed or epistemically partial borders of the nation-state. I am also concerned with the unequal diffusion of globalized power variously called postmodernism or late capitalism, yet understood in these pages as the practice of imperialism and its multiple effects. Put differently, one of my major preoccupations is the production and maintenance of (sexualized) hegemony understood, in the Gramscian sense, as a map of the various ways that practices of dominance are simultaneously knitted into the interstices of multiple institutions as well as into everyday life. To understand the operation of these practices I traveled to various sites of crisis and instability, focusing to a large extent on the state, whose institutions, knowledges, and practices stand at the intersection of global capital flows, militarization, nationalisms, and oppositional mobilization. While differently located, both neo-imperial state formations (those advanced capitalist states that are the dominant partners in the global "order") and neo-colonial state formations (those that emerged from the colonial "order" as the forfeiters to nationalist claims to sovereignty and autonomy) are central to our understandings of the production of hegemony.[10] The nodes of instability include heterosexuality's multiple anxieties manifested in the heterosexualization of welfare and the defense of marriage in the United States and the criminalization of lesbian and gay sex in Trinidad and Tobago and in the Bahamas; the consolidation of the military-industrial-prison complex that both promotes the militarization of daily life and the most contemporaneous round of military aggression and war; the ideological production of various hegemonic identities: the soldier, the citizen patriot, the tourist, and the enemy on the part of state institutions and corporate capital; the integration of the corporate academy into the practices and institutions of the state at this moment of empire and therefore made integral to the machineries of war; knowledge frameworks, particularly those that bolster and scaffold modernity's practices of violence that signify as democracy, such as cultural relativism; the global factory and its naturalization of immigrant women's labor; and the moments and places where apparently oppositional social locations and practices become rearticulated and appropriated in the interests of global capital, as is the case of white gay tourism. These nodes of instability form, as well, the base for the thematic organization of the seven chapters in this volume.

In this [reading] I am disturbed by these products of domination and hierarchy, particularly the psychic products that fossilize deep in the interior, forcing us to genuflect at the altar of alterity and separation, the altar of the secular gods of postmodernity, experienced as hypernationalism and empire. Physical geographic segregation is a potent metaphor for the multiple sites of separation and oppositions generated by the state, but which are also sustained in the very knowledge frameworks we deploy and in the contradictory practices of living the oppositions we enforce: the morally consuming citizen versus the morally bankrupt welfare recipient; the patriot versus the enemy; the loyal citizen versus the disloyal immigrant; "us" versus "them"; the global versus the local; theory versus practice; tradition versus modernity; the secular versus the sacred; the embodied versus the disembodied. And disturbance works as a provocation to move past the boundaries of alienation, which explains why *Pedagogies* is centrally concerned with the promise that oppositional knowledges and political mobilizations hold and with the crafting of moral agency.

If hegemony works as spectacle, but more importantly as a set of practices that come to assume meaning in people's everyday lives (that is, the ways in which ordinary people do the work of the state and the work of war), then all spaces carry the potential for corruptibility. Lesbian, gay, bisexual, transgendered and two spirit-communities, transnational feminist constituencies, women of color political mobilizations, and subordinated knowledges within the academy that have traded radicalism for institutionalization all carry these reciprocal antagonisms and contradictions. Thus, for this reason, but not for this reason alone, the stakes are quite high. Building oppositional practices within and across multiple simultaneous sites is imperative in political struggle as is the cultivation of the discipline of freedom and collective self-determination in terms that supercede those of free-market democracy. Yet, oppositional consciousness is a process rather than a given before the fact of political practice. And further, we cannot afford to be continually, one-sidedly oppositional.

Pedagogies is intended to intervene in the multiple spaces where knowledge is produced. I have deliberately chosen to interrupt inherited boundaries of geography, nation, episteme, and identity that distort vision so that they can be replaced with frameworks and modes of being that enable an understanding of the dialectics of history, enough to assist in navigating the terms of learning and the fundamentally pedagogic imperative at its heart: the imperative of making the world in which we live intelligible to ourselves and to each other—in other words, teaching ourselves. Because within the archaeologies of dominance resides the will to divide and separate, *Pedagogies* points to the reciprocal investments we must make to cross over into a metaphysics of interdependence. In the same way in which Paulo Freire narrated our ontological vocation to become more fully human, these pedagogies assemble a similar ontological imperative, which pertains to learning and teaching.[11] And since there is no crossing that is ever undertaken once and for all, this ontological imperative of making the world intelligible to ourselves is, of necessity, an enterprise that is ongoing.

Since the central metaphor of this book rests in the tidal currents of the Middle Passage, we should want to know why and how this passage—The Crossing—emerged as signifier. If here I am concerned with embodied power, with the power derived from the will to domination, I am simultaneously concerned with the power of the disembodied and the stories that those who forcibly undertook the Middle Passage are still yearning to tell, five centuries later. One such story is that of Kitsimba, who numbered among those who through the door of no return were shuttled from the old Kôngo kingdom to the Caribbean, circa 1780. Kitsimba unexpectedly showed up in this collection, so unabashedly bound up with materialism, that my aim is not so much to tell the story of her capture but to convey a particular meaning of pedagogy. Indeed, her emergence is pedagogy in its own right: to instruct us on the perilous boundary-keeping between the Sacred and secular, between dispossession and possession, between materialism and materiality—the former having to do with the logics of accumulation, the latter with the energy and the composition of matter. She has traveled to the heart of feminism's orthodoxies to illustrate that the personal is not only political but spiritual, to borrow Lata Mani's felicitous formulation.[12] She is here to meditate on the limits of secular power and the fact that power is not owned by corporate time keepers or by the logics of hegemonic materialism. As I show in chapter 7, within Kitsimba's universe reside the very categories that constitute the social, the most crucial of which is Time. Yet in the world she inhabits, dominant corporate, linear time becomes existentially irrelevant. Indeed it ceases to have any currency at all.

Put differently, pedagogies that are derived from the Crossing fit neither easily nor neatly into those domains that have been imprisoned within modernity's secularized episteme. Thus, they disturb and reassemble the inherited divides of Sacred and secular, the embodied and disembodied, for instance, pushing us to take seriously the dimensions of spiritual labor that make the sacred and the disembodied palpably tangible and, therefore, constitutive of the lived experience of millions of women and men in different parts of the world. Once Kitsimba appeared to claim the book's closing chapter, the title of this entire collection surfaced. Thus, I came to understand pedagogies in multiple ways: as something given, as in handed, revealed; as in breaking through, transgressing, disrupting, displacing, inverting inherited concepts and practices, those psychic, analytic and organizational methodologies we deploy to know what we believe we know so as to make different conversations and solidarities possible; as both epistemic and ontological project bound to our beingness and, therefore, akin to Freire's formulation of pedagogy as indispensable methodology. In this respect, *Pedagogies* summons subordinated knowledges that are produced in the context of the practices of marginalization in order that we might destabilize existing practices of knowing and thus cross the fictive boundaries of exclusion and marginalization. This, then, is the existential message[13] of the Crossing—to apprehend how it might instruct us in the urgent task of configuring new ways of being and knowing and to plot the different metaphysics that are needed to move away from living alterity premised in difference to living intersubjectivity premised in relationality and solidarity.

Pedagogies cannot be adequately assembled, however, without attention to the social relations of teaching in the multiple makeshift classrooms we inhabit, and so it is no accident that the gestation period for this collection coincides with much of my life as a teacher. *Pedagogies* thus pertains to what we are prepared to teach, the methodologies of our instruction and the particular challenges that arise in the task of demystifying domination. Still, the classroom is Sacred space. In any given semester a number of Souls are entrusted into our care, and they come as openly and as transparently as they can for this appointment.[14] To be sure, resistances develop as serious engagement morphs into confrontation with inherited nationalisms and their conceptual and identity structures. But outside of courses for which there is mandatory matriculation, the desire to show up stems from our curriculum that brings a promise to satisfy some yearning, as faint or as well-formed as it might be, to imagine collectivities that can thrive outside of hegemony's death-grip. I have not always been successful in simply teaching in order to teach, to teach that which I most needed to learn. More often I intended my teaching to serve as a conduit to radicalization, which I now understand to mean a certain imprisonment that conflates the terms of domination with the essence of life. Similar to the ways in which domination always already confounds our sex with all of who we are, the focus on radicalization always already turns our attention to domination. The point is not to supplant a radical curriculum. The question is whether we can simply teach in order to teach.

The Crossing is also meant to evoke/invoke the crossroads, the space of convergence and endless possibility; the place where we put down and discard the unnecessary in order to pick up that which is necessary. It is that imaginary from which we dream the craft of a new compass. A set of conflictual convergences of my own migrancy, rendered more fragile under empire, and the genealogies of feminist, neocolonial, and "queer" politics that are simultaneously transnational, all reside here. It is a place from which I navigate life, using the foot I keep in the Caribbean, the one I have had in the United States since 1971, the arithmetic of which continually escapes me, and yet a third foot, desirous of rooting itself deep in the forest of Mayombe in the Kôngo. Living and thinking this dialectic means refusing to insist on two feet, which would be the recipe for sheer imbalance. It means turning my three legs into the legs of the deep, round cooking pot used to prepare medicine on the open fire. Three feet make the stretch more necessary, more livable, more viable. Yet none of the preoccupations of these pedagogies could have surfaced in the absence of these very genealogies: a regional feminist movement in the Caribbean, which by the mid-1980s had begun to chart the failures of anticolonial nationalism, implicating capitalism and colonialism in the unequal organization of gender, and by definition, charting the terms of how feminism would be understood and practiced; a movement of black women in Britain whose political consciousness as excolonial subjects produced a series of political campaigns that implicated the British state in colonialism at home (practices around immigration and racism in housing and hiring) and colonialism abroad ("we are here because you were there"); and the political movement and theory of collections such as *This Bridge Called My Back, Home Girls,* and *Sister Outsider,* which squarely brought dominant U.S.-based feminism to its own crossroads, challenging it to a personal and epistemic self-reflection out of which feminism has never been the same.[15] These same texts provided some of the context in which I came to lesbian feminist consciousness as a woman of color in the mid-1980s. As Chandra Talpade Mohanty and I wrote in *Feminist Genealogies,* we were not born women of color but rather *became* women of color in the context of grappling with indigenous racisms within the United States and the insidious patterns of being differently positioned as black and brown women.[16] Thus, the analytical elements that comprise this volume intimate my own intellectual and political history, marking its convergence with cross-currents of different feminisms and belatedly with "queer" theorizing both inside and outside the academy, both elsewhere and here.

NOTES

1. See al-Radi, *Baghdad Diaries,* 125, for the environmental effects of the war.
2. Ibid., 21.
3. Wackernagel and Rees, *Our Ecological Footprint.*
4. I am referring here to the Reconstruction Act of March 2, 1867, in which the U.S. Congress stipulated that the former confederate states would be divided into five military districts, each headed by a general.
5. Stout, "Bush Pushes Faith-Based Agenda," www.nytimes.com/2003/02/10.
6. See Silliman and Bhattacharjee, *Policing the National Body;* Davis, *Are Prisons Obsolete?;* and Sudbury, ed., *Global Lockdown.*
7. Pitt, "Blood Money."
8. Lamming, *The Pleasures of Exile,* 158.
9. Ibid.
10. Lewis, correspondence with author, 2004
11. Freire, *Pedagogies of the Oppressed.*
12. Mani, *Interleaves.*
13. Allen, *Off the Reservation.*
14. I am borrowing here from Thích Nhât H'ahn, *Our Appointment with Life.*
15. Moraga and Anzaldúa, eds., *This Bridge Called My Back;* Lorde, *Sister Outsider,* Smith, ed., *Home Girls.*
16. Alexander and Mohanty, eds., *Feminist Genealogies,* xiv.

6

Feminists Reconstitute Work and Market

INTRODUCTION: FEMINISTS' RECONSTITUTION OF WORK AND MARKET, 1990 TO THE PRESENT

In recent years, women-inclusive movements have worked to promote alternative production and trade relations to assist producers in the South and link them with consumers in the North. Women's movements have redistributed assets and resources to improve the ability of worker households to generate the income they need to survive, and they have established institutions that promote development alternatives for workers, producers, and households around the world. These participatory movements have helped redefine gender, work, and the market and have created skeletal, prefigurative institutions that might, in the long term, challenge the global domination of capitalist institutions.

These movements have not tried to create a homogeneous, universal alternative to globalization. Instead, they have worked to establish diverse, heterogeneous alternatives to globalization. These alternatives retain the unique characteristics and strengths of people in different "places" and establish egalitarian relations with people in other places, what Wendy Harcourt and Arturo Escobar have called a "place-based globalism."[1] Diversity, they argued, is an essential part of "imagining a noncapitalist politics of place."[2]

> This combination of features [transnationalism and local] suggests a certain feminist understanding of being, doing, politics, and globality. The sense of globality one sees emerging out of many of the so-called global movements is one that does

not search for universal validity or an all-embracing global reality, no matter how alternative; but one that seeks to preserve heterogeneity and diversity, even as, and precisely through, new kinds of alliances and networking that we refer to as a self-organizing, decentralized, and nonhierarchical "meshworking." In short, these movements want to be practicing, already, the kinds of worlds they would like to bring into being.[3]

The idea is to create new global relations that reach around the world but also preserve heterogeneity and diversity. This approach contrasts sharply with the capitalist model of globalization, which promotes homogeneity and heterogeneity to sustain the global hierarchy. As an alternative to the "unequal homogeneity-heterogeneity" of capitalism, scholars and activists have proposed the development of local and global relations based on what might be called "egalitarian heterogeneity," which is rooted in various levels of democracy and resource sharing.

One way to distinguish between them is to think about coffee and the difference between Nestlé's instant coffee and fair trade coffee from cooperatives in Central America. Nestlé and other large monopoly firms purchase coffee from producers all over the world at prices that keep them impoverished; brew it into an indistinguishable, homogeneous, "instant" coffee; and sell it to consumers around the world at high prices. Nestlé helps to fragment workers by paying unequal wages to its coffee growers in the South and its manufacturing workers in the North. Transnational coffee companies push this homogeneous product because it enables them to maximize their control over prices and producers and facilitate the capture of markets and consumers around the world. In this case, global systemic homogeneity and heterogeneity help reinforce *un*equal global relations. By contrast, fair trade companies pay above-market prices to producers and make a wide variety of distinctive, specialty coffees available to consumers, a practice that promotes "egalitarian heterogeneity" because it promotes more egalitarian relations for producers in cooperatives, creates more egalitarian relations between producers in the South and consumers in the North, and delivers more heterogeneous products to the market and consumers around the world.

Although women-inclusive, place-based movements have been working to promote alternative development for the past twenty years or so, they are still in their infancy. It will take another twenty years or more to establish the local roots and make the global connections that will enable them to flourish and, eventually, provide a viable alternative to the capitalist model of globalization.

To survive and eventually challenge and replace capitalism, producers and workers in the South will need to establish new relations with worker-consumers in the North. Some of these relations have already been formed, but they need to be made wider and deeper. Movements have also introduced new tools—resources, information, meshworks, and social relations—that can help producer-worker households in the South generate income and improve their lives.

We will look first at women-inclusive consumer movements that promote alternative production and trade relations between North and South. Then we will examine movements that redistribute assets and resources so that households can improve their self-reliance. Finally, we will look at efforts to reorganize formal and informal relations and create institutions that provide the basis for inclusive development.

CONSUMER MOVEMENTS AND THE CREATION OF ALTERNATIVE PRODUCTION AND TRADE RELATIONS

Consumers have the ability to challenge the class structure and, at the same time, support social relations that sustain equality and democracy. Maria Mies was one of the first feminists in the North to appreciate the power of women consumers.[4] She argued that women could use their power as consumer "housewives" to change the direction of the world-economy. "A feminist consumer boycott would be *one* step in the direction of our liberation," she argued.[5]

> [I]f women are *ready to transcend* the boundaries set by the international and sexual division of labour, and by commodity production and marketing, *both* in the overdeveloped and underdeveloped worlds; if they accept the principles of a self-sufficient, more or less autarkic, economy; if they are ready, in Third World countries, to replace export-oriented production by production for the needs of people, then it will be possible to combine women's struggles at both ends of the globe in such a way that the victory of one group of women will not be the defeat of another group of women. This could happen, for instance, if the struggle of Third World women for the control of their own land and their subsistence production—often fought against the combined interests of international or national corporations and of their own men—was supported by a consumer boycott in the overdeveloped countries. [emphasis added][6]

Mies's work marked the beginning of a feminist commodity chain analysis, which suggested how women and other working people in the North and the South might be reconnected.[7]

Wendy Gordon agreed, arguing that "[w]omen are transformative agents in an emerging civil social movement" that seeks to change social relations through consumer organizing. This approach was adopted by Mothers and Others for a Liveable Planet, a women's organization based in the United States.[8]

> "Motivated by desire," in the words of Wendell Berry, "to making ourselves responsibly at home in this world," we are focusing on the choices and decisions we make in our daily lives, directing the power we wield in these actions toward the most beneficial ends within our particular means, and learning about ourselves and our partners in the world in which we live. In so doing, we hope to affect the consumer and corporate behavior and directly enhance environmental sustainability.[9]

Radical consumer activists such as Simon Zadek and Frank Amalric agreed with Gordon that "the *structural* driver of our current economic system is capital accumulation and profit," but they argued that "the *transforming* driver may well lie elsewhere, namely in the sphere of consumption" [emphasis added].[10] They saw alternative consumption as an important way to promote alternative development.

Fair trade in cocoa production and other agricultural products provides a good example of how global citizens can promote changes in unfair trade relationships by opening new markets for small producers in Latin America. Patricia Camacho has argued that the marginality of small producers prevents them from controlling their working conditions or the price of their goods. But fair trade can change conditions and prices and contribute to sustainable development. "[C]ooperation should promote trade programmes both in the North [alternative trade] and in the South [small producer organizations]. It should promote trade concessions and credit facilities in order to foster the initiatives of small producers and enable them to have sustained access to the market and the opportunity to improve the quality of their life."[11] Fair trade groups have also pressured the state to improve market access for small producers, which helps small producers shape their economic and political lives. In these developments, Camacho has argued, "we find the seeds of hope for democratization and development."[12]

Although some fair trade groups have assisted small farmers in agriculture, others have worked to assist wage workers in industry and promote fair wages. The Clean Clothes Campaign, which was started in the Netherlands in 1990, has worked to end exploitation in garment shops, supported the development of cooperative and fair wage workshops, and created a large and growing market for fairly traded clothes. Most Clean Clothes activists have demanded that garment factory owners and clothing retailers adopt an international code of conduct and agree to let independent monitors certify their compliance. Clean Clothes activists have encouraged unions in the North to fight for fair trade, educate consumers about global exploitation, and to seek out alternative sources and markets for clothes.[13]

Fair trade and fair wage activists have also asked consumers to scrutinize corporations that claim to practice "fair trade." Some corporations have introduced some certified fair trade products as a way to become socially responsible actors. This also enables corporations to compete with small-scale fair traders and persuade consumers that they are doing the right thing, even though the bulk of the products they offer are *not* fairly traded. Corporations will sometimes engage in a narrow range of fair trade activities if it is profitable and if they are pressured to do so by alternative trade organizations and consumers. Alternative trade organizations have worked to change the way corporations do business and to step outside of the global market that values profit making above the human needs of small producers. Fair trade organizations have worked to persuade corporations to adopt global fair trade and fair wage standards for all the products they sell, not just a few. And consumers have played an important role in demanding corporate change.

In the global South and North, fair trade groups have worked to connect small farmers, cooperatives, and collectively governed plantations with refiners and roasters, educators and marketers, investors and retailers, certifiers and monitors, and advertisers and consumers. These connections have resulted in the creation of a transnational, democratic movement for change. Consumers who buy food and agricultural products with fair trade labeling know that certified fair trade organizations (producer groups, importers and wholesalers, and retailers) have gone through a three-tiered monitoring process that has demonstrated they follow at least eight basic principles. According to the Fair Trade Resources Network, these minimal fair trade standards are (1) including disadvantaged groups that have been marginalized in the trading system, reducing poverty, and creating sustainable development; (2) building gender equity; (3) having transparent management processes and verifiable or accountable commercial transactions; (4) establishing long-term partnerships and building the capacity of producer groups; (5) paying a fair price, which includes a family living wage; (6) guaranteeing that working conditions will be healthy and safe; (7) promoting ecological practices that preserve the environment; and (8) educating the public about the importance of fair trade principles and practices. All fair trade organizations, such as Equal Exchange, go far beyond these practices by creating twenty-year linkages between democratic cooperatives in the South and cooperatives and nonprofits in the North, supporting producers that grow organic and bird-friendly products, returning a portion of the annual returns to producer cooperatives, and providing preharvest financing, and sharing ownership with growers.

The fair trade movement in Western Europe and, to a lesser extent, in the United States has survived for twenty difficult years. The next twenty years will test the ability of producer cooperatives in the South to survive and to expand. Their survival will depend on the creation of strong local networks that link fair trade cooperatives within particular countries and across the South and on strong connections between local producers in the South and consumers in the North. Fair trade organizations in the North will need to strengthen their ability to work with specific groups of producers in the South and in the North and find ways to establish cooperative networks around the world. As they work together through South-North and regional networks, fair trade groups will need to find ways to rebuff corporate efforts to co-opt or marginalize them. Fair trade and fair wage groups will also have to expand the range of goods they provide consumers around the world. To reach fair trade's overall goal of establishing long-term partnerships for alternative development, women and feminist-oriented organizations will need to shape all parts of the transnational fair trade movement. And movement organizations will have to find ways to address the problems created by drugs lords, arms dealers, human traffickers, sex traders, organ dealers, and violent guerrilla groups that can wreck democratic and cooperative efforts in places where states are weak (see Chapter 8).

REDISTRIBUTING ASSETS AND RESOURCES

Women who have transformed work and markets have also worked to improve access to land, water, and other resources. Women's power in households and in society is greatly affected by their access to resources and materials that can be used to produce and subsist. As alternative development scholars such as Shelley Feldman have noted, Bina Agarwal has made the argument that "the greater the ability of a person to draw on extrafamilial resources, the greater a person's bargaining position within the household."[14]

Today, the growing interest in "real development for all" has contributed to a new appreciation of the importance of "social wealth" and the value of "altruism, volunteering, cooperation, sharing and caring."[15] Social wealth, which takes the form of access to land, productive assets, and social networks, is key if women are going to obtain the food and income they need to ensure the survival of worker households. As Amartya Sen has written, access to social wealth and these "entitlements" can mean the difference between life and death for poor worker households.[16]

In Nicaragua, fair trade cooperatives such as Union de Cooperativas Agropecuarias-Miraflor (Union of Agricultural Producer Coopoeratives), which is located in the northeastern city of Estelí, have redistributed land as a way to assist women producers and their families. The Chamorro administration recently adopted a policy in 1995 that limited men's automatic claims to landownership and intervened to change the general patriarchal practice of men passing land only to male heirs. The government did so by insisting that land being redistributed under the state's agrarian reform program be given to partners who held *joint* title to the land. Nicaraguan president Violeta Chamorro instructed officials in charge of agrarian reform to give female heads of household title to land, an almost unheard-of practice. The benefits of reform are evident in democratic cooperatives such as UCA-Miraflor, where the 5,000-member cooperative voted to give twelve sweat-equity land grants to single, female heads of household and decided that land titled to women could only be passed on to *other* women. This type of grassroots governing, especially if practiced on a large scale, would reverse long-standing patriarchal inheritance practices and ensure that single women's land could not be seized by sons or husbands in the future.[17]

Having wealth enables female-headed and other households to get through hard times. For this reason, feminists have emphasized the importance of providing legally held assets to women, such as housing, small-business ownership, and cooperatively governed and owned land. The provision of basic stability, either through land or housing or other types of individual or collective ownership, has been especially important since the 1980s as families have faced growing pressures to migrate. More individual workers and families have migrated as work is reorganized globally, poverty increases, starvation becomes widespread in certain areas, gender violence grows, various wars and conflicts develop, drinking water becomes more scarce and other water is privatized, and private landowners, plantations, and the state seize land that had, by custom, been allocated to laboring households for growing food and raising animals. Migration has been just one of the ways the people respond to crisis. Other common responses have been for laboring women and men to reorganize production, to rebel against authorities, and to claim land and resources in nonviolent or violent ways.[18]

As mentioned by Avtar Brah, the International Organization for Migration indicated that by 1992 more than 100 million people, from all social classes, were migrating in the world, searching for employment-related opportunities, political freedom and human rights, and food and security. Twenty million of these people were refugees and seekers of asylum. Because of the demand for low-cost female labor, manufacturers and other companies have been seeking women workers for electronics factories, garment and textile factories, and putting-out production; this demand has triggered a feminization of migration, which has corresponded to the exploitation of women in low-paid production. Women now make up a growing segment of migrants in all parts of the world and in all groups of migrants. Women and their children now constitute one-half of the domestic and cross-border migrant population.[19] They need secure land tenure, income, and assets, and these assets need to be held, at least in part, in their own names. In her analysis of women's empowerment and the joint titling of land held on an informal basis, Namita Datta has noted that 40 percent of the world's people now live in informal, usually illegal, settlements in cities. Some cities in Asia, Africa, and Latin America now have 70 percent of their urban residents living in illegal, low-income, "squatter" neighborhoods.[20] To address housing needs in low-income neighborhoods, Mercedes González de le Rocha argued in *The Resources of Poverty* that Mexico's employers need to increase wages to cover the cost of market housing and that the state must build more lower-cost, subsidized housing.[21]

Although some governments in the North and South bulldoze illegal neighborhoods, many states have been persuaded by economists and activists to abandon these eviction policies and instead adopt limited land-tenure regularization policies, which have provided joint titles to married women and men.[22] This policy has simultaneously promoted gender equity, provided important legal assets to worker households, and provided basic government services to urban residents. In India, the government has provided some joint titles to poor people who had moved onto empty land, built their homes, and claimed the land and neighborhood as their own. The provision of joint land titles to people living in these informal Indian neighborhoods provided greater long-term asset security to some women, in much the same way that the Nicaraguan programs provided greater security to some women. In her study of state-regularized settlements in India, Namila Datta found that joint land titling provided significant benefits for women and improved their social status in the household:

> Holding relative education, income, and facilities of a regularized settlement constant, a joint title increases the probability of a woman [asserting] herself by 13 percent. Being in a regularized settlement with necessary civic services and tenure security increases by 20 percent the likelihood that a woman will report that she would protest the sale of her house. A woman earning some income makes her 11 percent more likely to report that she would resist her husband's unilateral decisions.[23]

Moreover, when women and men obtain joint title to land, they can apply for small loans. This can help them change work relationships and generate more income.[24] The point is that obtaining assets, such as land, is more important for women than securing cash or other forms of income.

Land reform can also provide a foundation for redefining agricultural develop-ment in an inclusive way. The postapartheid South African government has written gender and sexuality equity into its new constitution and provided for women in land reform projects. The state has introduced several important land reforms. First, it cautiously redistributed some of the land held by whites to the black majority. Second, the state returned land to black households that had been seized by white households during apartheid. Both steps helped women, particularly those who head households on their own, obtain land, which is an important asset that they can borrow against.[25]

GENDER-INCLUSIVE EFFORTS TO REORGANIZE WOMEN'S WORK

The Grameen Bank in Bangladesh and the Self-Employed Women's Association in India (SEWA) are two of the best-known projects that reduce poverty by taking steps to assist women. These programs demonstrate that by restructuring women's work and income-generating activities and by providing ways that women can help each other, women's poverty and inequality can be reduced. The Grameen (or "country-side") microcredit project was started in 1976 by Mohammed Yunus, an economics teacher. Yunus noticed that poor, landless, and self-employed women in Bangladesh only needed very small loans to go from earning a couple of pennies (U.S.) per day to making a living wage that could sustain their households. The Grameen Bank was set up in 1982 to provide small loans to really poor women who did informal work, allowing them to expand production in their microproducing and marketing businesses. Women went through common training and were placed in microloan groups that provided mutual support and encouraged quick and successful repay-ment of their loans. Once a woman paid back her loan, the money could be loaned to another member of the group. Success for one led to success for others, so women learned to help each other as a way to achieve individual goals.

Bangladesh's Grameen Bank model inspired activists to develop similar microcredit programs for women. For example, women in Chicago responded to women's disenfranchisement by adapting the Grameen Bank model and creating the Women's Self-Employment Project (WSEP).[26] This urban project helped women generate income, create jobs, and develop assets in a time of declining real wages and cutbacks in social services and education. WSEP staff and participants began carrying out some of the very activities that business and the state should have been doing: creating jobs, providing supportive services to women, providing training that led to self-sufficiency, and helping women develop assets. The Grameen Bank demonstrated that microcredit programs could help reduce poverty and place women at the center of microbusiness networks.[27]

The Grameen Bank and similar programs changed women's work by rupturing historical ties that led women to depend on dominant institutions: the state, business and the market, and patriarchal heterosexism. Given that the global system is unravel-ing and going through a crisis, the partial "liberation" of women from institutional dependence reduces some of the control that dominant institutions have over women and over labor as a whole. This opens a door to new kinds of self-sufficiency. Some political economists have criticized the Grameen Bank model because it means that women do more low-paid work that sustains a pool of potential household laborers. When seen at this level alone, the women's income from microcredit work is pooled with other household income, supplements grossly inadequate wages, provides an indirect subsidy to capitalist firms, and helps sustain the unequal global system.

Less obvious and perhaps more substantive change also results from Grameen Bank–type programs, however, and this relates to the goals of many alternative development programs. Microenterprise programs help groups of women become less dependent on the state and larger businesses, as they also learn to be less dependent on household patriarchs. Simultaneously, they learn to rely on each other and to organize their work together. As women turn away from a reliance on firms and the state, they develop the potential to take charge of organizing new social relations, outside of the global corporate domain. These liberating aspects of the Grameen Bank model include women's growing independence from the system, the development of organizing and community development skills, and women's increasing independence from adult heterosexual men who serve as the system's micromanagers.

In summary, transnational and state agencies and alternative development organizations employed the Grameen Bank's small-lending group model in rural and urban areas throughout the world, but they did so for very different reasons, and sometimes with unexpected results. Both institutional and alternative approaches shared a gendered dimension, as organizers reached out to increase women's income-generating capacities through microentrepreneurial activities. Transnational and national agencies used women as income-generators who offset real general declines in household income, which came from a combination of decreases in nonwage income and in real wages (in cash and in-kind), the erosion of the civil commons, structural adjustment policies in the South, and welfare and service cutbacks in the North. Women's microcredit formed part of a global strategy that sought to transfer growing costs of labor's reproduction onto the backs of women and girls. But even as this policy was working at the level of hidden subsidies to firms, it was backfiring at another. Rather than just reinforcing the system, institution-driven, gendered microenterprise programs had the unintended result of providing women with means to be more independent from corporations, the state, and heterosexist households. Alternative microenterprise programs had this goal all along: to provide women and their families with tools to pull away from the invisible profit-generating webs and to prepare women to redefine economy and society. From what Mohammed Yunus has said, this change to greater self-sufficiency and less entanglement with global institutions is positive, and more than he could have hoped for, but in the coming decades, global managers may work to undermine local autonomy that has come from independent microbusiness and cooperative organizations.

Also emerging from the Indian subcontinent was a second powerful model that altered women's relationships to each other, and to society. In 1972, low-income women in India organized the SEWA to address the problems they faced. SEWA was organized as a trade union for self-employed workers, as a bank for members, and as a women's organization that could increase women's self-sufficiency and political power.[28] This organization grew out of the Textile Labour Association (TLA), which was started in 1917 by Mahatma Gandhi and Ansuyabehn Sarabhai, the sister of a textile mill owner. Ela Bhatt, SEWA's eventual leader, was a lawyer for TLA, where she worked for the textile workers' labor union. When she left TLA, Ela Bhatt joined forces with self-employed women who were organizing in the west Indian state of Gujarat, and together they created SEWA. These self-employed women wanted to increase their bargaining power by organizing collectively and establishing an organization to support them. Eventually, the women's labor union created income-generating democratic cooperatives in agriculture, livestock, and handicrafts; provided nursery and childcare services; offered credit and savings plans and started a mobile bank; organized health cooperatives; developed marketing plans for members that bypassed predatory middlemen; taught members how to read, write, and do mathematics; and provided legal services.[29]

The spread of women's microenterprise programs around the world has removed some of the barriers that obstructed low-income women and men. These programs have improved women's access to credit, provided flexible schedules for the repayment of loans, used peer group solidarity as a substitute for collateral, provided simple loans that could be used to build assets and financial power, and helped women acquire business management skills. In addition to these economic benefits, many programs have gone on to provide important supportive services: job training, education, health and child care, and housing.[30]

In cooperative and microenterprise movements, participatory activists and supporting NGOs have learned to think about long-term institution building. In the United States, programs generated by the displaced homemaker movement demonstrated that comprehensive supportive services can help women overcome individual and social barriers to self-sufficiency. In a similar fashion, Euro-Action's small-enterprise program in Sudan, which assisted Muslim and Christian immigrants and refugees in primarily "slum areas" (or *diems*), used supportive services and microloans to help women and men become more successful petty traders, food makers and vendors, tea sellers, domestic workers, water carriers, mattress makers, carpenters, bicycle repairers, and tailors.[31]

A study of fifteen NGO-supported women's projects in India found that present-focused program managers, who only considered short-term issues, inhibited women's long-term self-sufficiency. Some microenterprise and microcredit programs have made short-term gains, but several long-term issues have emerged.

> [O]veremphasis on short-term financial sustainability can actually create conditions that make long-term financial sustainability unlikely, and that lack of explicit attention to developing mechanisms for developing participation and institutional sustainability will hinder progress toward poverty reduction and empowerment. Participatory self-help groups with multiple objectives, member self-management, and explicit support for capacity building for empowerment performed much better than the more narrowly focused credit unions and loan programs.[32]

If they are to succeed in the long term, microfinance programs need to do more than alleviate poverty; they must also empower women, D. Rajasekhar has argued.[33] Democratic, grassroots self-help groups need to be established where members formulate, implement, and monitor programs that empower members and meet their own needs. Successful self-help groups engage in self-management, self-reliance, and self-sustainability. And they should stay small in size, consisting of between nine and twenty-five women. Rajasekhar found that successful self-help groups provided accessible credit that took care of "consumption credit needs at the village level," made consumption loans at weekly meetings and provided the loans right away, and voted to grant loans even when little loan money was available, allowing even the poorest participants to get loans they needed to buy grain.[34] The more innovative groups have called for activists to reorganize work and market relations.

❀   ❀   ❀

UPAVIM: UNIDAS PARA VIVIR MEJOR/ UNITED FOR A BETTER LIFE: A GUATEMALAN WOMEN'S FAIR TRADE COOPERATIVE

Researchers Mary Littrell and Marsha Dickson introduced readers to Angela Bailon, who lives on a hillside in the outskirts of Guatemala City, where residents build their own homes with concrete blocks, which are often placed around steel girders made by contractors. Other residents make their homes with scrap wood, cardboard, and sheets of plastic. Unemployment is high, child care is scarce, and violence against women is prevalent. When her children entered preschool, Angela Bailon began working as the comanager of the craft cooperative United for a Better Life (Unidas Para Vivir Mejor; UPAVIM). Like many women in her neighborhood, Angela has done factory work, where she says that people were not treated as equals. The UPAVIM craft cooperative, in contrast, is built on the idea that the workers are equal. UPAVIM emerged after a U.S. nurse, who worked at one of Guatemala's growth monitoring clinics to prevent children's malnutrition, established a dental clinic in La Esperanza. The dental project evolved into a cooperative as seventy women joined together to make improvements in their lives and those of their children. This is how writers Littrell and Dickson described the daily activities of Angela Bailon, a handicraft producer for the fair trade cooperative known as UPAVIM.

As she begins her day at 5:00 a.m., Angela Bailon, a 39-year-old mother of three young children—ages 11, 9, and 3—rises, bathes, washes clothes, makes coffee, and heats the beans in her small home in Esperanza. At 6:30, she awakens her children for breakfast together. By 7:00, Angela and her younger son leave for UPAVIM, where Angela works as a comanager of the 50-member craft project. Angela's son plays in the nearby UPAVIM day care, where Angela visits him during the day for breastfeeding. Although Angela had childhood dreams of becoming a teacher, she left school at age 17 to help support her family of eight brothers and sisters. Angela's husband, whom she describes as *"el triste de mi vida"* (the sadness of my life) abuses drugs and alcohol and rarely contributes to household income.

Until she found work at UPAVIM 8 years ago, Angela took any job she could to support her family. These included washing clothes and hauling water containers for people when the water truck delivered the daily supply for the neighborhood in the middle of the night. For hauling 55 gallons of water, Angela received one quetzal or approximately U.S. $.17 (17 cents). At UPAVIM, Angela's daily schedule allows her to return home at noon to eat lunch with her older children and see them off to school. The whole family is reunited when Angela leaves work at 6:00 p.m. and meets her children returning from school. After supper together, the family is in bed by 9 p.m.

The poverty and responsibilities for raising young children so salient in Angela's life strike at the core of the alternative trade mission—working with deeply impoverished artisans who have marketable skills but little recourse to commence outside their communities. (Here) we profile three Guatemalan artisan organizations formed in La Esperanza, Chontalá, and San Apolonia during the late 1980s and early 1990s. All groups are committed to … fair trade guidelines … Particularly salient are paying a fair wage in the Guatemalan context [Angela Bailon earned Q14,000 per year ($2,333) or $871 over the 1997 per capita income of $1,462 for Guatemala]; offering equitable employment opportunities; providing safe, healthy workplaces; honoring cultural identity; and encouraging worker advancement. Partnership with North American Alternative Trade Organizations (ATOs) nourished every group at various points in their evolution. ATO partnerships assisted artisans in acting on their belief that "our hands are our future."

Source: Mary Littrell and Marsha Dickson. "Artisan Producer Groups: Our Hands Are Our Future," in Littrell and Dickson, *Social Responsibility in the Global Market: Fair Trade of Cultural Products.* Thousand Oaks, CA: SAGE Publications, 1999, 199–200, 206.

Along with women-inclusive place-based ecological development, inclusive and cooperative fair trade projects, women's asset development, and women's microcredit and microentrepreneur programs, at least two other development models have emerged that empower women. Remember that many projects combine a number of approaches in innovative ways. That is what Marketplace India and the Women's Sewing Cooperative in Nicaragua have done. Both projects use women's democratic producer cooperatives and fair trade market exchanges to redefine work and transnational trade linkages. Based in Chicago and Mumbai, Marketplace India is organized as a women-run, fair trade nonprofit in Chicago and as a coordinated group of women-owned cooperatives centered in the Mumbai region. The women's cooperatives in India engage in garment design and garment production, household ware production, and jewelry- and craft-making. These Indian-made, handwork and handicraft products are sold to U.S. and other consumers through a catalog, an online store, and retail outlets. Nonprofit and religious groups also hold local sales. Marketplace India has worked to place productive resources in the hands of women-owned cooperatives, to develop a model for reducing poverty in India, to preserve the environment, and to create a commodity chain of small producers that has equal exchange, fair trade, and fair pay and is locally run throughout. This has enabled producers to earn enough over subsistence level to send their girl and boy children to school and to buy materials for production.[35]

The second major feminist model for transnational change also has been provided by a fair trade, women-owned and -run cooperative that produces clothes in a small neighborhood outside of Managua, Nicaragua. The Jubilee Community House's Women's Sewing Cooperative was organized by female heads of household who had not been sewers. By entered the expanding field of fair trade garment work, these single heads of household (which now include a few single male heads) faced many barriers, including the fact that they were competing with Managua's transnational corporations that used free trade zone subsidies. The Women's Sewing Cooperative decided to apply for free trade zone status, too, which they were granted after they made a few adjustments in the worksite and their marketing commitments. This women's group became the first nonprofit, the first cooperative, and the first fair trade group to be granted the international benefits of free trade zone status.[36]

Another key model has been changing women's wage work by pushing for changes in industry and through the state. This has been a primary focus of feminist analyses of wage employment and of the global assembly line, in particular. Feminists have addressed the decline of unions in the global North and the South's political and workplace barriers that have prevented the development of unions in many countries. Transnational corporations have sought out new manufacturing homes in repressive regimes that have been characterized by dictatorship and not by democratic government and participation. It has been easy to predict where corporations would move next to take advantage of low-paid teen girls and women workers. Just as states and companies have dumped toxic wastes in places where people of color live, transnational corporations have sought out countries with authoritarian rulers or dictatorships, which private industry has relied upon to prevent unionization and curb political protest. As part of a tried-and-true strategy to keep the wage to an individual level (which creates near-starvation conditions for families), corporations have counted on repressive regimes, such as pre-1994 apartheid South Africa and today's China, to control the flow of women and men from rural to urban areas.[37] By forcing people to live in certain areas to have passes, the government can separate family members by gender and age and reduce families' ability to fight for food and better living conditions. In addition to the control of women's and men's movements within a country, China (like South Africa) has utilized a strict, top-down population control policy that regulates women. These are some of the conditions that have caused Chinese women to speak out and to resist.[38]

Organizing around women's wage work issues complements the organizing that takes place in informal and alternative work relations. According to Carmen Diana Deere, part of sustainable development is "the planned and effective implementation of the right to employment."[39] By a right to employment, Deere meant the right to work without coercion, have collective bargaining and effective representation, and participate in the organization of work. To achieve these rights, labor organizations have organized transnational movements and worked to persuade companies to recognize workers' rights and the right to fair wages and decent working conditions.[40] But because these organizations often focus on the formal sector and wage employment, they often ignore issues surrounding informal work, issues of critical importance to petty producers, vendors, and subsistence workers around the world. Naila Kabeer has argued that movements must stand up for everyone, wage and nonwage worker alike.

> If the struggle for better working conditions has become interdependent at the global level, it is certainly interdependent at the local. The struggle for labor standards needs to be broadened and made more inclusive through the institution of a universal "social floor" ... so that all workers, men as well as women, urban as well as rural, formal as well as informal, are able to organize around their rights without having to jeopardize their basic livelihoods.[41]

Kabeer argued that creating a "social floor" for the rights of wage and nonwage workers would contribute to "an upward harmonization of wages and working conditions, but based on push factors from below rather than pull factors from above."[42]

Having looked at ways that women-centered movements have addressed work and trade inequities, we will now turn to look at how feminist groups have addressed environmental issues as a way to promote alternative development.

READING

In "The Invisible Women," Sharon Navarro showed how women on the U.S. side of the Rio Grande developed their knowledge and skills to address exploitation, industrial displacement, and sexist and racial inequalities by joining hands with workers on the Mexican side of the border. Through numerous government-funded programs, La Mujer Obrera (The Working Class Woman) creates employment opportunities and provides job training and language classes to women who live in El Paso, Texas. Providing a powerful program model to others, this group has developed innovative, cross-cultural, and cross-border ways to address women's and job displacement issues.[43]

The next selection explains why it is important for governments to give joint home and property titles to women and men. Joint ownership marks a turn from prominent patriarchal patterns of home and landownership, where the adult man controls family resources. Namita Datta explored joint titling as an equitable asset development strategy in India. Looking at three informal neighborhoods in India, she examined women's home ownership in areas that became redeveloped when working families occupied land and constructed their own housing. Providing joint property titles to women and men is a critical way to increase women's assets in urban informal settlements and in other urban and rural areas. This gender-equity approach could be used in many countries to provide property for women, create more stable neighborhoods, and promote democratic decisionmaking. The importance of women's land- and home ownership needs to be recognized as an important empowerment and poverty alleviation strategy, as this short review of literature indicates.[44]

NOTES

1. Wendy Harcourt and Arturo Escobar, *Women and the Politics of Place* (Bloomfield, CT: Kumarian Press, 2005), 13–14.

2. Ibid., 11.

3. Ibid., 14.

4. Maria Mies, *Patriarchy and Accumulation on a World Scale* (London: Zed, 1986).

5. Ibid., 228–229.

6. Ibid., 232–233.

7. Priti Ramamurthy, "Why Is Buying a 'Madras' Cotton Shirt a Political Act? A Feminist Commodity Chain Analysis," *Feminist Studies* 30, no. 3 (Fall 2004): 734–769, 764.

8. Wendy Gordon, "Mothers and Others for a Liveable Planet: Women Promoting Civil Action in the Consumption Realm," *Development* 41, no. 3 (1998): 70–73, 73.

9. Ibid., 73.

10. Simon Zadek and Franck Amalric, "Consumer Works!" *Development* 41, no. 1 (1998): 7–13, 7.

11. Patricia Camacho, "The Building of Community-based Trade Systems: The Case of Cocoa in Ecuador," *Development* 41, no. 1 (1998): 94–95, 95.

12. Ibid., 95.

13. Janneke Van Eijk, "The Clean Clothes Campaign in Europe," *Development* 41, no. 1 (1998): 90–93.

14. Shelley Feldman, "Crises, Poverty, and Gender Inequality: Current Themes and Issues," in Lourdes Benería and Shelley Feldman, eds., *Unequal Burden: Economic Crises, Persistent Poverty, and Women's Work* (Boulder, CO: Westview Press, 1992), 1–26, 19.

15. Hazel Henderson, "The Politics of Aid: Moving Towards an Attention Economy," *Development* 42, no. 3 (1999): 64–70, 70.

16. Amartya Sen, *Poverty and Famines: An Essay on Entitlement and Deprivation* (Oxford: Clarendon, 1981).

17. In 2003, when Torry Dickinson joined Equal Exchange's fair trade educational trip to Miraflor in Nicaragua's cloud forest northeast of Estelí, she met some of the women who were given land grants.

18. Terisa Turner and Leigh S. Brownhill, "African Jubilee: Mau Mau Resurgence and the Fight for Fertility in Kenya, 1986–2002," special issue, *Canadian Journal of Development Studies* 22 (2001): 1069–1088.

19. Avtar Brah, "Diaspora, Border, and Transnational Identities," in *Cartographies of Diaspora* (London: Taylor and Francis, 1996), 178–210.

20. Namita Datta, "Joint Titling—A Win-Win Policy? Gender and Property Rights in Urban Informal Settlements in Chandigarh, India," *Feminist Economics* 12, nos. 1–2 (January/April 2006): 271–298, 271.

21. Mercedes González de la Rocha, *The Resources of Poverty: Women and Survival in a Mexican City* (Cambridge, MA: Blackwell, 1994), 262.

22. Hernando De Soto, *The Mystery of Capital: Why Capitalism Triumphs in the West and Fails Everywhere Else* (New York: Basic Books, 2000).

23. Datta, "Joint Titling—A Win-Win Policy," 291.

24. Ibid., 271–298.

25. Cherryl Walker, "Land Reform and the Empowerment of Rural Women in Post-apartheid Africa," in Shahra Razavi, ed., *Shifting Burdens: Gender and Agrarian Change Under Neoliberalism* (Bloomfield, CT: Kumarian Press, 2002), 67–92.

26. Richard Douthwaite, *Short Circuit: Strengthening Local Economies for Security in an Unstable World* (Devon, UK: Green Books; Dublin, Ireland: Lilliput Press, 1996), 133–135.

27. San Francisco's and Oakland's Women's Initiative for Self-Employment was one of the U.S. microlending programs that applied knowledge gained from the Grameen Bank's lending circles. See Lisa J. Servon, *Bootstrap Capital: Microenterprises and the American Poor* (Washington, DC: Brookings Institution Press, 1999).

28. Renana Jhabvala, "Self-Employed Women's Association: Organizing Women by Struggle and Development," in Sheila Rowbotham and Swasti Mitter, eds., *Dignity and Daily Bread: New Forms of Economic Organising Among Poor Women in the Third World and the First* (New York: Routledge, 1994), 114–138. Also go to the SEWA Web site.

29. Rekha Datta, "On Their Own: Development Strategies of the Self-Employed Women's Association (SEWA) in India," *Development* 43, no. 4 (2000): 51–55.

30. Nancy S. McDonnell, Tsitsi V. Himunyanga-Phiri, and Annie Tembo, "Widening Economic Opportunities for Women: Removing Barriers One Brick at a Time," in Gay Young, Vidyamali Samarasinghe, and Ken Kusterer, eds., *Women at the Center: Development Issues and Practices for the 1990s* (West Hartford, CT: Kumarian Press, 1993), 17–29.

31. Eve Hall, "The Port Sudan Small-Scale Enterprise Program," in Ann Leonard, ed., *Seeds 2: Supporting Women's Work Around the World* (New York: Feminist Press, 1995), 64–88.

32. D. Rajasekhar, "Impact of Microfinance Programs on Poverty and Gender Equality: Some Evidence from Indian NGOs," in Shara Razavi, ed., *Shifting Burdens: Gender and Agrarian Change Under Neo-Liberalism* (Bloomfield, CT: Kumarian Press, 2002), 151–196, 151.

33. Ibid., 187.

34. Ibid.

35. Mary Littrell and Marsha Dickson, "Marketplace India: Handwork of India," in *Social Responsibility in the Global Market: Fair Trade of Cultural Products* (Thousand Oaks, CA: SAGE, 1999). Also go to Marketplace India Web site.

36. Go to Web sites related to the Women's Sewing Cooperative, Jubilee House, Center for Development in Central America, Nueva Vida, Nicaragua (east of Managua). The Jubilee Community House's Women Sewing Cooperative sells its products (often made with organic yarn) to Maggie's Clean Clothes in Ann Arbor, Michigan, and to the Presbyterian Church of America's (PCUSA) sweat-free project that is run out of Louisville, Kentucky.

37. Eileen M. Otis, "Reinstating the Family: Gender and State-Formed Foundations of China's Flexible Labor Force," in *Families of a New World: Gender, Politics, and State Development in a Global Context* (New York: Routledge, 2003), 196–216.

38. Ibid., 207–215.

39. Carmen Deere et al., *In the Shadows of the Sun: Caribbean Development Alternatives and U.S. Policy* (Boulder, CO: Westview Press, 1990), 199.

40. Jane Collins, "Mapping a Global Labor Market: Gender and Skill in the Globalizing Garment Industry," *Gender and Society* 16, no. 6 (December 2002): 921–940, 937.

41. Naila Kabeer, "Labor Standards, Women's Rights, Basic Needs: Challenges to Collective Action in a Globalizing World," in Lourdes Benería and Savitri Bisnath, eds., *Global Tensions: Challenges and Opportunities in the World Economy* (New York: Routledge, 2004), 173–192, 188.

42. Ibid., 189.

43. Sharon Ann Navarro, "*Las Mujeres Invisibles*/The Invisible Women," in Nancy A. Naples and Manisha Desai, eds., *Women's Activism and Globalization: Linking Local Struggles and Transnational Politics* (New York: Routledge, 2002), 83–98.

44. Datta, "The Significance of the House as Property," in "Joint Titling—A Win-Win Policy?" 276–278.

LAS MUJERES INVISIBLES/ THE INVISIBLE WOMEN

Sharon Ann Navarro

NAFTA is a story of violence against women. It is a treaty that created violence against women and their families. There are tremendous implications, the economic implications and the whole impact it has had on women's health, their lives, their future, and their families. It is as violent as any beating, if not more destructive.

—La Mujer Obrera

El Paso, Texas, is a microcosm of the inherent contradictions created by the North American Free Trade Agreement (NAFTA) along the border. On the one hand, NAFTA profoundly shifted the focus of national and international commerce, moving it from an "East-West" emphasis to a "North-South" paradigm. In doing so, El Paso became the gateway to the tremendous economic opportunities available to Mexico and Latin America (Ortega 2000). At the same time, north of the U.S.-Mexican border, NAFTA acted as a catalyst, another force, or another trend, that is steadily squeezing Mexican-American women workers (in the garment industry) to the margins of the economic sector in El Paso. These Mexican-American garment workers are typically low-skilled and low-income women. As the garment industries close down their businesses and move across the border, the Mexican-American women that once worked in these businesses are being left out of the economic restructuring taking place under NAFTA. These women are being marginalized. The type of work that they have done—in some cases for more than twenty years—is now becoming obsolete and replaced by advanced technology.

Before this [reading] is presented to you, it is important to note that NAFTA is not characterized as *the main factor* for the displacement (or permanent layoffs) of female garment workers in El Paso. NAFTA is instead used by one grassroots nongovernmental women's organization, La Mujer Obrera (LMO), as a symbol of what they face as female workers in a border city, as a tool for political activism and mobilization. The women's organization examined in this study has succeeded in contextualizing NAFTA as a tangible culprit, the *primary cause* of their current struggle for a better quality of life for the displaced workers and their families.

LMO's direct response to globalization, as manifested in NAFTA, should not be interpreted to mean that one organization is simply bashing NAFTA only. Instead, because of the attention given to NAFTA by politicians, various interest groups, and scholars alike, NAFTA has simply become the topic of selection that organizations like LMO use as the source of their struggle. Similar agreements, such as the General Agreement on Tariffs and Trade, the Free Trade Area of the Americas, or the Multilateral Agreement on Investment, could just have easily been targeted.

For the Mexican-American garment workers in El Paso, an entire way of life and standard of living are fast disappearing. These Spanish-speaking women have worked all of their lives to provide for up to four generations of their families. Now they have lost their livelihood, their health-care insurance, their homes, and their futures. When NAFTA was first introduced in the late 1980s, various organizations with labor interests believed that NAFTA was going to be their opportunity to set labor standards for workers in the three participating countries. However, that was not at all what the crafters of NAFTA intended. Instead, labor interests were left out of NAFTA.

And so NAFTA became an incitement to discourse, an invitation to review the voices whose identities, as Spanish-speaking, female garment workers, are vehicles for political expression. This woman's nongovernmental organization mobilized to express their anxieties about the way NAFTA has affected their economic subsistence, their way of life. The struggle for this grassroots organization is not over the politics of influence, but to transform the terms and nature of the debate; it is a struggle to integrate previously excluded groups, voices, and issues into local and national politics.

Drawing on literature from political science, as well as from a wealth of new data obtained through fieldwork,[1] this study examines LMO's use of central icons, traditions, history, and customs from Mexican culture to mobilize constituents in appeals to U.S. local, state, and federal government institutions. More important, this study explores how one women's organization used the U.S.-Mexico border to highlight its struggle in the post-NAFTA era.

This [reading] is divided into three sections. The first focuses on the uniqueness of a border city in the post-NAFTA era. The second offers a gendered look at globalization as manifested in NAFTA. The last section looks at culture as a mobilizing tool for LMO, paying particular attention to the way in which LMO embraces Mexican culture to highlight the displaced workers' struggle.

EL PASO: A BORDER BETWEEN TWO WORLDS

The physical designation of a boundary may serve as an observable reminder that the politics, economics, and culture of countries and subnationalities differ (Agnew, Mercer, and Sopher 1984). The uniqueness of El Paso–Ciudad Juarez stems from the fact that a city from the First World shares a border with a developing city from the Third World. Boundaries create cultures and identities that impose order on cities, communities, and individuals by shaping them in a way that embodies the values and beliefs of a society or geographic location. The physical and cultural closeness of the United States and Mexico, as well as the political, social, and economic ties that connect them, creates an intriguing bicultural arrangement that provides a laboratory for studying identity formation and mobilization across borders.

In theory, a border is a line that separates one nation from another or, in the case of internal entities, one province or locality from another. The essential functions of a border are to keep people in their own space and to prevent, control, or regulate interactions among them. For the purposes of this study, the terms *border, borderland,* and *frontera* are used interchangeably. The terms are used to denote an area that is physically distant from the core of the nation; it is a zone of transition, a place where people and institutions are shaped by natural and human forces that are not felt in the core or heartland of the United States or Mexico.

For example, the U.S.-Mexico boundary is the busiest land border in the world, the longest and most dramatic meeting point between a rich and a poor country, and the site of the most intensive interaction between law enforcement and law evasion. Nowhere has the state more aggressively loosened and tightened its territorial border grip at the same time. Nowhere else do the contrasting state practices of market liberalization and criminalization more visibly overlap. The result has been the construction of both a borderless economy (via NAFTA) and a barricaded border. More concretely, the politics of opening the border to legal economic flows is closely connected to the politics of making it appear more closed to illegal flows: illegal drugs and migrant labor.

Oscar Martinez, one of the leading scholars on the U.S.-Mexico border, acknowledges the political, economic, and social cultural significance of the frontera. He proposes that the dynamics of the border create four models of borderland interaction: alienated borderlands, coexistent borderlands, interdependent borderlands, and integrated borderlands. Each model illustrates a different degree of cross-border interaction (Grimes 1998). For example, today interdependence is overwhelmingly dominant in the U.S.-Mexico borderlands, and therefore the most appropriate designation for that binational zone is the interdependent frontera. That is not to say, however, that elements of alienation, coexistence, and even integration are not part of the zone at a given time. Martinez's findings are nothing new for this border city and its border people. The influence of Ciudad Juarez on El Paso is a natural daily occurrence.

The uniqueness of the U.S.-Mexico border, specifically the border city in question, plays a critical role in the sociopolitical construction of identities. Kimberly Grimes, in her study of migration to the United States from Putla de Guerro, Oaxaca, Mexico, suggests that identities are rooted in geography. Grimes's claim holds the key to understanding the seemingly contradictory strategy of LMO, which on the one hand embraces the Mexican culture—which is suggestive of a "borderless cultural region"—to mobilize its members, but at the same time reemphasizes the U.S.-Mexico border to highlight the struggles of displaced workers. According to Grimes, borders play an important role in distinguishing "us" from "them." Moreover, people's sense of self includes identification with particular geographical spaces. People negotiate constructed political, economic, and social (cultural) borders of self-identification. Identities are grounded in space and time, and they transform as time passes, as people move across spaces, and as national policies and global conditions transform. People react to these changes and constructions by accommodating or challenging and/or resisting them.

MEXICAN-AMERICAN WOMEN WORKERS IN EL PASO:
A GENDERED LOOK AT GLOBALIZATION

For the close to 20,000 displaced workers, NAFTA and ongoing deep economic restructuring have not ushered in the new dawn of prosperity hailed by political leaders. The explosive growth of lower-paid export manufacturing jobs in the maquiladora sector in Mexico has been offset by the immense loss of jobs in the domestic manufacturing sector in the United States and Canada.

The globalization of capital necessary for economic restructuring is being deliberately hastened by most national governments, by international institutions like the International Monetary Fund and the World Bank, and by global corporations themselves. While international trade is nothing new, our system of nation-based economies is rapidly changing toward a "new world economy" (Takaki 1993). At the center of this change lies a sharp increase in capital mobility. Computer, communication, and transportation technologies continue to shorten geographical distances, making possible the coordination of production and commerce on a global scale. Lower tariffs have reduced national frontiers as barriers to commerce, thus encouraging transnational production and distribution. Corporations are becoming global not only to reduce production costs, but also to expand markets, elude taxes, acquire resources, and protect themselves against currency fluctuations and other risks, including the growth of organizations like LMO that would mobilize workers and demand that their interests and voices be heard in the new world economy (see also Brecher and Costello 1994).

Three hundred companies now own an estimated one-quarter of the productive assets of the world (Barnet and Cavanagh 1994, 15). Of the top 100 economies in the world, 47 are corporations—each with more wealth than 130 countries (Harison 1994). International trade and financial institutions like the International Monetary Fund, the World Bank, the European Union (EU), and the new World Trade Organization have cultivated powers formerly reserved for nation-states. Conversely, national governments have become less and less able to control their own economies. This new system, which is controlled by the so-called Corporate Agenda, is not based on the consent of the governed (Brecher, Childs, and Cutler 1993), and it has no institutional mechanism to hold it accountable to those whom its decisions affect.

In general, the effects of capital mobility, which is designed to increase economic efficiency, have been malignant for workers. An unregulated global economy forces workers, communities, and countries to compete with each other in an effort to attract corporate investment. Each tries to reduce labor, social, and environmental costs below the others.[2]

In the debates surrounding NAFTA, globalization and regionalization are often interpreted as homogenizing vehicles, without regard to the fact that women, and in particular women of color, are paying a disproportionate share of the costs of the processes of neoliberalism. Globalization hits especially hard racial/ethnic minorities in the United States and female factory workers in the U.S. (Larudee 1999, 123–63). It has profoundly changed the lives of women in El Paso, Texas, creating inequalities that interact with pre-existing class, ethnic, gender, and regional cleavages (Gabriel and Macdonald 1994, 535–62).

Job losses have been especially substantial in the apparel sector in El Paso and in some small communities that are heavily dependent on factories, which shut down and moved to Mexico. Since NAFTA took effect in 1994, El Paso has lost between 15,000

Table 6.1   NAFTA Job Losses in El Paso, January 1994–November 2000

YEAR	NUMBER OF DISPLACED WORKERS
1994	1,045
1995	2,193
1996	2,573
1997	3,435
1998	3,641
1999	2,125
2000	1,940
TOTAL	18,975

Source: Texas Workforce Commission.

and 20,000 jobs.[3] Table 6.1 shows the number of job losses from 1994 to 2000. Table 6.2 shows how Texas ranks in comparison to other states with respect to displaced workers. Free trade and the reduction of tariffs made it easier for companies to close plants and move to Mexico only to continue as maquiladoras (Myerson 1998, 1C, 22C).

In December 1998, El Paso's average unemployment rate was almost three times (11 percent) the state unemployment rate of 4.4 percent and the U.S. rate of 4 percent

Table 6.2   NAFTA-TAA Certified Workers, by State as of Mid-July 1997

State	Number	State	Number
Texas	*	Massachusetts	1,315
North Carolina	*	West Virginia	1,288
Pennsylvania	*	Kansas	1,184
New York	*	Kentucky	1,016
California	7,476	Alaska	780
Georgia	6,186	Louisiana	778
Indiana	5,811	Arizona	684
Tennessee	5,640	Connecticut	631
Arkansas	5,397	Montana	613
New Jersey	4,471	Maine	432
Ohio	4,413	Wyoming	392
Wisconsin	4,405	Vermont	361
Michigan	3,783	Minnesota	336
Washington	3,445	North Dakota	300
Missouri	3,329	Utah	292
Illinois	2,902	New Mexico	242
Florida	2,804	Oklahoma	230
Iowa	2,785	Nebraska	220
Oregon	2,550	New Hampshire	139
South Carolina	2,305	Maryland	86
Virginia	2,166	Idaho	83
Colorado	1,990	Nevada	76
Alabama	1,383	South Dakota	65

*The Department of Labor does not have the total number of displaced workers for the states of Texas, North Carolina, Pennsylvania, and New York, but claim they are the states with the highest numbers.
Note: Certifications are for January 1, 1994 to July 18, 1997.
Source: Department of Labor, NAFTA Trade Adjustment Assistance Office.

(Kolence 1999c, B10). The community of El Paso was for a very long time advertised as a low-wage, low-skill manufacturing paradise. A 1993–94 study conducted by the Greater El Paso Chamber of Commerce Foundation Inc. reported, "[I]f you want to be the low wage paying capital of the world, don't do anything, you're already there" (El Paso Greater Chamber of Commerce 1997, 10). Cheap Mexican labor, in particular, has always been El Paso's strongest selling point (also Garcia 1981). Roberto Franco, director of the City's Economic Development Agency, articulated this point best when he said, "El Paso was perceived as the jeans and slacks capital of the United States" (Kolence 1999a, 4).

Approximately 80 percent of the garment workers in El Paso's garment and other manufacturing industries were Mexican-American women. Their subordinate social status limits their employment opportunities and makes them vulnerable to exploitation. As a result of NAFTA, however, thousands of Mexican-American workers, many of whom had migrated from Mexico to El Paso in search of a better life, lost their jobs. A total of 97 percent of the displaced Mexican-American workers in El Paso are Hispanic, and 80 percent are women (Gilot 1999, 10B). One-third of these women head single households. Half are between the ages of 30 and 45, while the majority of the other half are older than 45. In addition, most of the affected workers are sustaining up to four generations of their families—themselves, their parents, their children and their grandchildren (La Mujer Obrera 1999a, 1). Using an average figure of four persons per household, the population affected by NAFTA in El Paso can be estimated at 40,000. When taking only into account the number of so-called certified NAFTA displaced workers,[4] the at-risk population is at least 80,000—13 percent of El Paso's population—and the potentially affected population is as large as 200,000. The women's job skills cannot easily be transferred from low-tech to the mid- to high-tech manufacturing jobs entering El Paso in record numbers (El Puente CDC/La Mujer Obrera 1999, 6). The testimonies of displaced Mexican-American women workers reveal their immense financial struggles. Typically over 45 years of age, with less than a fourth-grade education in Mexico, they have lost health insurance and other benefits because the businesses they worked for shut down production, and they are typically two to three months past due on rent and utilities.[5] The lead organizer of the Asociación de Trabajadores Fronterizos (Association of Borderland Workers), Guillermo Glenn (1999), describes the burden globalization has foisted on Mexican-American displaced woman workers:

> In El Paso, women suffer what is called a *'doble jornada"* (double day's work) because they have two jobs, one at home and one at the factory (or school since there are very few factories open). They suffer all the discrimination. Language discrimination, discrimination because they are Mexican, and discrimination because they are women.... There is still a lot of discrimination in terms of their role, in terms of their decision-making, in terms of how they are treated.

LMO has been working for nearly five years to make the conditions of Spanish-speaking, NAFTA-displaced women workers visible locally, regionally, and nationally. The seeds of LMO were planted in 1972, when a campaign to unionize workers in the Farah plant (the biggest jeans maker at the time) in El Paso intensified (see Coyle, Hershatter, and Honig 1980, 117–43). LMO was formed because women felt that the Amalgamated Clothing and Textile Workers of America, or for that matter, any union (such as the AFL-CIO), did nothing to address their needs, ignored their rights as *women* workers, and did not respect their membership as *women* members in the union (Flores

1998). This devaluation of women's work is deeply rooted in the history of U.S. labor unions. According to Glenn (1999), the old labor movement of the 1970s—including the one that organized Farah workers—"characterized itself as . . . [a] very macho kind of an organization. We (LMO) feel that the labor unions have not gotten away from that." For example, during the strike against Farah, male organizers in both the Amalgamated Clothing Workers of America and the AFL-CIO ignored women workers' concerns, such as sexual harassment, health care, child care, domestic violence, political education, and verbal abuse by their employers (Flores 1998). Moreover, employers often view the income of the female workers as "extra" or "supplemental" to their husband's income.

In 1981, following the Farah campaign, LMO was legally established as a nonprofit community-based organization of women workers in El Paso. LMO has defined itself, first and foremost, as a *woman's* organization (La Mujer Obrera 1993, 3). It combines community organizing, popular education, leadership development and advocacy into a comprehensive struggle for a better quality of life for the women and their families. Like other organizations operating in a resource-poor environment, the organization relies on outside funding (La Mujer Obrera 1999, 1 and 2). The organization turns to national churches, private foundations, the federal government, and local entities for financial support (Arnold 1999a). LMO initially had a yearly budget of $150,000, and in 1998–1999 its budget was between $500,000 and $750,000 (Arnold 1999b). The organization employs a total of six women as full-time organizers. The board of directors is made up of two men and five women, all of whom have been displaced by NAFTA. The support staff consists of a paid secretary and a grant writer as well as various interns and volunteers.

The organization struggles to achieve *siete necesidades basicas* (seven basic goals): decent, stable employment, housing, education, nutrition, health care, peace, and political liberty. One of LMO's principal objectives is to educate workers so that they are able to defend their rights and to take leadership positions in their own communities. Educational programs form the basis for organizing work and raise workers' awareness of their roles as *women* and as economic producers. Like other women's movements, LMO has struggled to integrate previously excluded issues into politics by pushing women's concerns (e.g., child care and health care) (Peterson 1992, 183–206). LMO also serves as a safe place where friendships develop, experiences are shared, and where women become educated not only about their rights as workers, but, perhaps most important, their rights as women, mothers, and spouses. To this end, LMO has established a child care center where displaced workers may leave their children while they attend school, look for work, or go to their jobs.[6]

To achieve institutional changes that will lead to the creation of genuine economic alternatives for workers in the midst of globalization, La Mujer Obrera has also recently reorganized and broadened its structure (La Mujer Obrera 1998, 4). The most critical developments have been the emergence of two new quasi-independent organizations under LMO's corporate umbrella. One is the Asociación de Trabajadores Fronterizos, which has taken on the worker and community organizing, direct action, and mass mobilization components of LMO's work (5). The association includes Spanish-speaking men and women workers who were employed and laid off from the manufacturing plants in El Paso. Launched during the summer of 1996 with the support of LMO, the association extends beyond LMO's traditional base of women garment workers and incorporates displaced men, workers from electronics, plastics, medical supply manufacturing, and other labor intensive industries. Growing from an initial membership of 20 workers to a current roster of more than 700 active members, the association has built a countywide network with representatives of LMO in seven factories and school committees throughout El Paso (6–7).

Through these networks, the association has the participation of more than 2,000 workers, the majority of whom are women, and a governing board of 14 displaced workers, two elected from and by each of the seven factory and school committees (26). At the same time, LMO began constructing its capacity to develop and operate community economic development programs on behalf of, and with, displaced workers. In December of 1997, LMO established El Puente Community Development Corporation as a vehicle for developing training and education, jobs, self-employment, housing, the development of microenterprises, access to credit and neighborhood revitalization strategies as a means to create jobs, income, and economic self-sufficiency for the workers and the organization. Moving into this arena has required that LMO negotiate and work with local, state, and federal agencies and officials for financial support (26–27).

By creating a space in the political and economic arena, LMO has already produced tangible results for the displaced workers. The organization succeeded in getting a $45 million grant—the largest grant ever given by the U.S. Department of Labor—to retrain displaced workers. To get this grant, LMO made its concerns known locally and nationally with one act that proved to be a turning point for LMO. On June 1997, several Mexican-American women (all from LMO) blocked the Zaragoza International Port of Entry, which is one of El Paso's busiest commercial bridges with Ciudad Juarez, Mexico, for one hour by stretching a rope across the port. The goal of the protest was to bring the plight of NAFTA-displaced workers to the attention of Secretary Robert Rubin of the Department of the Treasury, which is responsible for a variety of NAFTA programs. But instead of meeting with him, his representative, or other state or local authorities, protesters were arrested and charged with obstructing highway commerce.

The $45 million grant allows LMO to institute alternatives to existing federal and state retraining programs. These programs entitle displaced workers to benefits while attending English classes, courses for their general equivalency diploma (GED), and retraining within an 18-month period. Many of these programs, however, are plagued with a variety of problems, especially inadequate buildings and equipment, outdated curricula, incompetent or poorly trained teachers, and administrators who make racial/ethnic slurs and personal insults (Klapmeyer 1998).

In the summer of 1999, Margarita Calderon, a researcher at Johns Hopkins University, tested 60 displaced workers at 12 different schools to see what they had learned. The results were shocking. Only two of the 60 students, some of whom had spent up to five years in various federally subsidized training programs, had learned enough to handle an interview in English. Calderon, an expert in bilingual education, found that retraining schools set up for displaced workers had been using rigid teaching techniques long abandoned by better language schools, such as lectures and translation exercises (quoted in Templin 2000, B1 and B4). In addition, there is a perception among case managers, state and local agencies, school administrators, and teachers that "the displaced workers are just there to get paid and don't want to learn" (Klapmeyer 1998). Frustrated with many of the inept retraining schools, LMO opened up its own school for displaced workers on February 1, 1999. It hired a full-time teacher to teach English, the general equivalency examination and microenterprise training. LMO has also established a business incubator that will support the self-employment initiatives of displaced workers. Further, LMO is currently in the process of developing a bilingual adult education curriculum specifically designed for displaced workers in El

Paso. This curriculum will be the standard curriculum for every school in El Paso if they are to accept displaced workers in their schools. LMO has also played an instrumental role in helping El Paso win the Empowerment Zone designation that provides federal funds for economic development. As a result, the poorest area of the city—South Central—will receive much needed federal money for revitalization, which would create jobs. LMO plays a role in deciding how that money will be spent.

THE USES OF MEXICAN CULTURE FOR MOBILIZATION

For LMO, culture has become a unique dimension in women's activism. In her study of two Chicano struggles in the Southwest, Laura Pulido (1998, 31–60) points out that culture plays a key role in mobilization efforts both by "providing familiar and meaningful guideposts and by facilitating collective identity." The use of symbols, customs, traditions reminds people of who they are, of their share traditions past and present, and of what they can achieve by uniting and acting collectively.

In the 1960s and 1970s Latinos/Chicanos became aware of how their culture not only differed from, but was also maligned by, mainstream Anglo America. Once-shameful cultural icons were reappropriated and turned into symbols of resistance. In the course of building a movement, farmworkers and activists publicly displayed statues and posters of La Virgen de Guadalupe not only as a source of solace and inspiration, but also (and far more consciously at times) as an expression of pride in the Mexican culture and a tool of mobilization. By openly engaging in ritual prayer, they asserted their identity to the larger society (see Herrera-Sobek 1990; Rodriguez 1994). LMO similarly uses La Virgen de Guadalupe as an expression of inspiration and as a vehicle of mobilization and consciousness raising. For the women of LMO, La Virgen de Guadalupe thus not only represents strength, hope, and respect, but "she is also viewed as a woman and a mother who has suffered with the death of her son and, like her, we (displaced workers) are suffering for our families and our children" (Orquiz 1999).[7]

In a study of Mexican-American women in East Los Angeles, Mary Pardo examines how they transform "traditional" networks and resources based on family and culture into political assets to defend the quality of urban life. Here, the women's activism arises out of seemingly "traditional" roles, addresses wider social and political issues, and capitalizes on formal associations sanctioned by the community. Religion, commonly viewed as a conservative force, becomes intertwined with politics. Often, women speak of their communities and their activism as extensions of their family and household responsibility. Women's grassroots struggles center around quality of life and challenge conventional assumptions about the powerlessness of women as well as static definitions of culture and tradition (Pardo 1998).

LMO also identifies with the Mexican culture and its members through its landscape. Outside its building, LMO has corn (maize) stalks growing in place of an assortment of bushes or flowers. As Refugio Arrieta explains, "The maize is symbolic of our Mexican culture. It is a symbol of the resistance too.... It is more like the resistance that leads to maintaining the culture here and helping it live and grow here in the U.S. and not simply being forced to abandon the Mexican culture" (Arrieta 1998).

Moreover, LMO also tries to maintain and reinterpret its history and heritage with Mexico in symbolic remembrance of Emiliano Zapata and the Zapatista rebels. Hanging from some of the walls of LMO are portraits and pictures of Emilio Zapata and Zapatista *women* rebels. For LMO, Zapata and the Zapatista rebels represent the struggle of resistance against neoliberalism, specifically NAFTA. They represent in Mexico the voice of people who have been eliminated in Mexico by NAFTA. As one member stated, "We are kindred spirits because of what the U.S. economy is doing to Mexican-American factory workers and what the Mexican economy is doing to the indigenous people of Mexico" (Anonymous 1998). To some extent, LMO believes, like the Zapatistas in southern Mexico, that NAFTA will eliminate them from an economy that was built on their backs.

LMO further uses the Mexican *corrido* as a mobilizing mechanism that reflects their political situation.[8] For example, during Guillermo Glenn's trial on March 17, 1999, after he was arrested for his participation in the blocking of the Zaragoza Bridge, LMO members gathered outside the courthouse in protest. With the news stations there, LMO members began to sing the "Corrido de los Desplazados" (The ballad of the displaced), which they had written themselves:

Año de 94	In the year of '94
Comenzo la pesadilla	The nightmare started
Se robaron los trabajos,	They stole the jobs,
Nos dejaron en la orilla	They left us at the edge
Los obreros en El Paso,	The workers in El Paso,
Recuerdan bien ese día.	Remember well that day.

The "Corrido de los Desplazados" embraces all displaced workers, raises their level of consciousness, unites them, and inspires them to mobilize. This type of cultural practice also represents the organization's strategy of activism and mobilization. It adds to more conventional forms of political participation, such as voting, in an effort to stress demands for respect, dignity, and justice of the Mexican-American workers and their traditions. Cindy Arnold (1999b), coordinator of El Puente at LMO, summed up the organization's philosophy of political participation as follows: "For us, political involvement is not based on an electoral or party process, but [is seen] in terms of on-going dialogue with political leaders at all the different levels." As a political actor, LMO emphasizes that it has no political affiliation and does not endorse any particular political party or politician. Its legal charter as a community-based organization does not permit it to become involved in electoral politics. Now that half of its members are citizens and thus eligible to vote (a change that became evident in the last city election), it will also encourage its members to vote.

Yet the March 1999 protest in support of Guillermo Glenn also illustrated one of the obstacles to LMO organizing efforts, which stems from the roles typically ascribed to women in Mexican culture. These roles make Mexican women feel uneasy about their political activism—despite the fact that they do not see it as political. As local news cameras panned the crowd of LMO protesters, which included both men and women, some women hid their faces behind the protest signs because their husbands would be angry with them for appearing on television. One woman said, "My husband would be humiliated by his friends if they saw me on television" (Anonymous, 1999; my translation of the original Spanish).

In other instances, LMO activists have been accused by their spouses of neglecting their family obligations when they became involved with the organization (Olvera 1990, A12). Women in leadership roles often reveal that they have strained relationships with their husbands because they refused to adhere to the role of a traditional Mexican wife (I. Montoya 1999). Other women reported that it was okay for them to participate in LMO as long as they also did what was expected of them as mothers, housekeepers, and wives (Reyes 1999; see also Fernandez-Kelly 1990; Garcia 1981). Some women describe the difficulty of getting away from housework and their husbands. Maria Acosta describes the problem she has with her jealous husband: "Every time I get ready to come to the meetings, my husband gives me a hard time. He says that I come to [La] Mujer Obrera because I am either looking for a boyfriend or I come to meet my boyfriend."[9] According to Acosta's husband, there could be no other reason for her to come to LMO, despite the fact that it is helping her to get into a retraining program.

CONCLUSION

LMO's activism in response to global economic restructuring, as manifested in NAFTA, relies on contradictory yet successful mobilization strategy. On the one hand, LMO became visible when its members literally reemphasized the U.S.-Mexico border to highlight NAFTA's disastrous effects on Mexican-American women garment workers. On the other hand, LMO de-emphasized the U.S.-Mexico border culturally by embracing the Mexican culture. This is what makes the border city of El Paso unique. Displaced by NAFTA, the lives of the LMO women have been disrupted and forever changed by the corporate agenda driving NAFTA. Spanish-speaking women, who once migrated to El Paso in search of a better life, have received a rude awakening after dedicating their entire lives to building the city's economy. After having been subject to exploitation and limited employment in El Paso, these women are now being marginalized and slowly eliminated from an increasingly internationalized economy.

To mobilize these women, LMO has focused on Mexican culture as a vehicle that links individual members to the organization. The use of Mexican religious symbols, traditions, histories, and customs has served to reinforce a bond between the organization and its members, as well as to contextualize the plight of the NAFTA-displaced workers. At the same time, its creation of a transnationally shared space of Mexican culture has enabled LMO to become a legitimate economic actor in the city's economic restructuring. Symbols such as the *Virgen de Guadalupe,* the cultivation of corn stalks, pictures of the Zapatistas, and the use of the Mexican *corrido* have served as icons of political resistance against a transnational agreement that has affected their lives. The success of this strategy has manifested itself in the fact that no other organization in the U.S.-Mexico border region has achieved as much as has LMO. It has helped obtain El Paso's designation as an Empowerment Zone, won a $45 million grant for displaced workers, created two umbrella organizations—the Asociación de Trabajadores and El Puente, opened its own school for displaced workers, is currently developing the first bilingual adult curriculum for displaced workers, and has established a child-care center. All of its achievements serve as a testament to the power of a transnational culture in women's political activism. But, be that as it may, a much larger question looms: Although this essay is about one grassroots globalization movement at the U.S.-Mexico border, are there lessons to be learned from its experiences?

Certainly the first lesson points to the fact that any one specific identity—in this case the Mexican identity—may not necessarily be enough to forge a cross-border alliance. Other principal factors may come into play, such as shared gender, shared experiences, values, beliefs, ideology. For example, a much more useful and broader theme that workers could mobilize around could be the pursuit for social justice among all workers, specifically the push for "living wages." By mobilizing around the theme of social justice, LMO would broaden its support base by being inclusive of other grassroots organizations and perhaps catapult them into the international arena where their voices would be much more difficult to stifle. The most recent example of this was seen in the Summit of the Americas meeting on April 20–22, 2001, in Quebec City, where numerous grassroots movements gathered to protest the expansion of economic integration (free trade) at the expense of social justice.

In addition, what becomes evident in this essay is the importance of contextualizing the workers' situation under NAFTA. What this case study suggests is that mobilization depends upon the way in which an organization chooses to construct, define, identify, or contextualize itself given a certain set of circumstances. The way in which an organization chooses to identify itself and whether or not that particular identity resonates with its members has bearing on the organization's behavior and the perception external agencies, individuals, and institutions have of that organization. The perception of others outside of the organization may have significant political repercussions. For example, the identity of an organization can affect its access to resources made available only by governmental agencies.

Moreover, this essay also points to the growing participation of women in grassroots mobilization, specifically as leaders, against NAFTA, the Free Trade for the Americas Initiative scheduled for completion in 2005, as it is for the Multilateral Agreement on Investment and other similar agreements. Lisa Montoya and her colleagues correctly point out that political scientists have tended to neglect or discount Latina leadership and participation in electoral and community politics (Montoya, Hardy-Fanta, Garcia 2000, 555–61). A key issue within the debate about gender differences is whether there is an essential divide between the public and private dimensions of politics. For Latina women, much more than men, the boundary between these supposedly distinct spheres of life is blurred, indistinct. With their emphasis on grassroots politics, survival politics, and the politics of everyday life and through their emphasis on the development of political consciousness, Latina women see connections between the problems they face personally and community issues stemming from government policies.

NOTES

1. This study is based on 56 face-to-face interviews I conducted from August of 1998 through August 1999 in El Paso, Texas, with active women who have lost their jobs because of NAFTA—that is, businesses moving from El Paso to Mexico. I have defined as "active" those women who dedicate 20 hours to LMO by either attending weekly meetings, belonging to committees within the organization, volunteering their time, or attending and helping in organizing fiestas (parties), rallies, and protests. The interviews were conducted in Spanish (and on occasion in English) at LMO, protest and rally sites, and, when it was convenient for the person interviewed, over the phone. I have also included interviews with the lead organizers of LMO, a former bilingual teacher, who was employed to teach these women English at one of the many schools that offer English classes, a public relations spokesperson from one of the last mammoth garment industries (Levi Strauss) in El Paso, politicians, and various governmental/political officials. Depending on the individual, these interviews lasted between 15 and 75 minutes. In LMO, the women speak only Spanish, range in age from 35 to 72, and more than half have no more than a fourth-grade education in Mexico. At the

time of my interviews with the women of LMO, almost all of them were either in school learning English, studying for their high school equivalency diploma, or in some retraining program.

2. According to Brecher and Costello (1994), "race to the bottom" is the reduction in labor, social, and environmental conditions that results from global competition for jobs and investment.

3. This is the only credible number that I have seen reported.

4. In speaking with John Ownby of the Dislocated Worker Service Unit at the Texas Workforce Commission, I was told that being classified as "certified NAFTA displaced worker" might not reflect the true number of displaced workers. Businesses that close up shop because of NAFTA are supposed to certify their workers with the Texas Workforce Commission, which simply means that the workers were laid off because the business closed down due solely to NAFTA. Certification by the Texas Workforce Commission ensures that the displaced worker will be eligible for retraining programs. However, the Texas Workforce Commission does not have the manpower to see that businesses do in fact register their workers as certified NAFTA displaced workers. Thus, the number of certified displaced workers may not be a true account of displaced workers. Ownby believes the number to be much higher (Ownby 1999).

5. This information is based on face-to-face interviews and informal discussions with women.

6. The power of culture as a mobilizing force is not a new phenomenon. It has been instrumental in the civil rights movement, the Chicano movement, and the farmworkers' movement as well as many others.

7. In both my formal and informal conversations with LMO and staff members, this was the response given by all.

8. A *corrido* is a simple narrative ballad that relates an event of interest only to a small region; it may be a love song or a comment on a political situation.

9. This name has been altered to protect the identity of the woman. The information was revealed in a private informal conversation.

THE SIGNIFICANCE OF THE HOUSE AS PROPERTY

Namita Datta

Over the last few decades, the rapid rates of not only urbanization but the "urbanization of poverty" in most developing countries (Josef Gugler 1996; Martin Ravallion 2001) has brought the lives of urban poor, especially women, under extreme stress. Urban life, as differentiated from life in rural areas, is characterized by "commoditization, environmental hazard and social fragmentation" (Caroline O. N. Moser 1998: 4), all of which combine to increase urban women's vulnerability, especially in urban informal settlements. The "commoditized" nature of urban life refers to the way the urban poor have to pay for their food and shelter instead of relying on their own production as they do in rural areas (Moser 1998). The communal village land, which usually forms an important source of income for poor rural households (Narpat S. Jodha 1986), is replaced by urban land that is more steeped in concepts of individual landownership (Irene Tinker and Gale Summerfield 1999: 9).

In cities, money assumes a larger significance in determining one's ability to survive. With their limited income-generating capability, urban women are more dependent on their husbands for money, and hence for housing (Susanne Thorbek 1991), than their rural counterparts. Poor housing quality, inadequate sanitation and water supplies, and the lack of other basic services make urban life particularly prone to "environmental hazards" that place larger strains on women due to their domestic roles, including fetching water to cook, clean, and wash clothes and managing the house and children. "Social fragmentation" describes urban women's diminished access to traditional social support systems like the extended networks of family and friends common in rural areas; this social fragmentation is another reason poor, urban women are forced to be more dependent on their husbands. At the same time, this lack of strong kin networks in cities allows men to shirk responsibility for their children (Irene Tinker 1997) and fall into abusive practices.[1]

Even before considering these factors, women already tend to predominate the urban poor because of their marginalization within the labor market, their concentration in low-paid, insecure jobs in the informal sector, their unequal access to assets, and the inequality of resource distribution within households (OECD 1995: 26). Urbanization and gender interact in mutually reinforcing ways to make the urban woman more vulnerable than the urban man to the forces associated with poverty, thus worsening her relative bargaining power within the household.[2]

Home ownership not only reduces urban women's economic vulnerabilities, but it can also be a source of their empowerment for a number of reasons.[3] First, a house provides shelter and is therefore a valuable consumptive resource. Moreover, the quality of housing poor urban women obtain determines their level of access to water, toilets, and other civic amenities that come with regularization of squatter settlements. Women in informal settlements spend a substantial portion of their time and energy engaged in reproductive work due to the lack of these basic services (Moser and Peake 1987). Owning a secure house with basic services critically affects a woman's quality of life by lessening her burden of reproductive duties, and hence, allowing her more time for productive, income-earning opportunities.

Houses do not only function as consumptive resources for poor urban women—they also serve as productive resources (Kam Wah Chan 1997: 9), a fact that has been ignored by urban and housing studies that have largely conceptualized housing only in its consumptive form (Manuel Castells 1977; Peter Saunders 1986). Contrary to the popular myth that casts men as income-producing breadwinners and women as income-consuming homemakers, a large proportion of poor urban women produce household income from either at home or near their homes; housing is therefore a crucial determinant of women's income-generating capacities (Mallika Bose 1999).

Government policies seldom recognize the productive nature of housing, perhaps because women's productive work is still largely "invisible." Many women in Chandigarh's informal settlements, for example, supplement their incomes by running small, unlicensed enterprises from their homes—like cigarette and candy shops, telephone booths, tea shops, small informal crèches, beauty parlors, and even tailoring schools. These home-based enterprises are important for women for at least two reasons. First, they allow women to earn at least a modest amount of money while also tending to their housework and small children. And second, small enterprises remain one of the limited ways for economically disadvantaged women to earn a living in India, where a strong ideology of female seclusion makes any other work outside the home a sign of low social status, especially among low-income households.

Home ownership can play a productive, vital role in urban women's income earning and survival strategies via rental income as well. In times of distress, a homeowner can supplement her income by renting out a portion of her home. Several researchers have already established that rental income is a critical source of income for female-headed households, especially because of their limited access to other means of employment (Schlyter 1988; Kavita Datta 1995; Sunil K. Kumar 2001). Another way the house can act in a productive capacity is by providing collateral for credit in case the woman decides to set up an income-earning enterprise. In fact a home's credit-producing capacity could be beneficial to the woman in many other ways like sending her or her children to school or helping the family recover from an unexpected life event. Furthermore, a house is a valuable asset with a steady commercial value of its own—especially in cities where supply of low income housing in the formal sector almost always falls short of demand. As Jeremy Swift (1989) has argued, assets reduce vulnerability because they can be transformed either into production inputs, or directly into consumption in times of need. In the event that a woman homeowner has nothing else to fall back on in an emergency, she can always sell her house to raise resources for survival.

Vulnerability, according to Moser's (1998) definition, has two dimensions: sensitivity and resilience to changed circumstances. A house can reduce sensitivity and increase women's resilience if they are widowed, deserted, or if they decide to opt out of an exploitative marriage. Moreover, a house is important for one's health, one's sense of well-being, and one's self-esteem. Having control over one's environment, especially by having property rights on an equal basis, is one of the central human capabilities, essential for a life of dignity (Martha C. Nussbaum 2003: 42).

NOTES

1. In her study of five villages in Gujarat, Leela Visaria (2000) finds that domestic violence was higher in nuclear families than in joint families, showing that the joint family offered women some protection and acted as a deterrent to the husbands' use of physical force.

2. This is not to deny that urbanization can also have some positive effects on women (Graeme Hugo 2000). Cities can provide opportunities for women to participate in paid employment outside the home, escape traditions of rural life, learn new ideas, and get better health and education facilities. The argument here is that women in cities deserve special attention because urbanization places a stress on women that is different from both the stress on urban men and also that on women in rural areas.

3. While a house plays a significant role in a woman's life irrespective of whether she is a formal owner or not, the reasons cited make the point that formally owning an asset as significant as a house can be especially empowering for women as it increases their fall-back options and bargaining power.

REFERENCES

Bose, Mallika. 1999. "Women's Work and the Built Environment: Lessons from the Slums of Calcutta, India." *Habitat International* 23: 5–18.
Castells, Manuel. 1977. *The Urban Question.* London: Edward Arnold.

Chan, Kam Wah. 1997. *Social Construction of Gender Inequality in the Housing System: Housing Experience of Women in Hong Kong.* Aldershot: Ashgate.

Datta, Kavita. 1995. "Strategies for Urban Survival? Women Landlords in Gaborone, Botswana." *Habitat International* 19: 1–12.

Gilroy, Rose and Roberta Woods, eds. 1994. *Housing Women.* London: Routledge.

Gugler, Josef. 1996. "Regional Trajectories in the Urban Transformation: Convergences and Divergences," in Josef Gugler, ed. *The Urban Transformation of the Developing World,* pp. 1–14. Oxford: Oxford University Press.

Jodha, Narpat S. 1986. "Common Property Resources and Rural Poor." *Economic and Political Weekly* 21: 1169–81.

Kumar, Sunil K. 1978. "Role of the Household Economy in Child Nutrition." Occasional Paper 95. Ithaca, NY: Department of Agricultural Economics, Cornell University.

Moser, Caroline O. N. 1993. *Gender, Planning, and Development: Theory, Practice, and Training.* New York and London: Routledge.

Nussbaum, Martha C. 2003. "Capabilities as Fundamental Entitlements: Sen and Social Justice." *Feminist Economics* 9: 33–59.

OECD. 1995. "Women in the City: Housing, Services and the Urban Environment." Conference Proceedings, OECD Headquarters, Paris, 4–6 October 1994, Chapter 2, pp. 20–32. Paris: OECD.

Ravallion, Martin. 2001. "On the Urbanization of Poverty." Working Paper Series 2586. Washington, DC: World Bank.

Saunders, Peter. 1986. *Social Theory and the Urban Question.* London: Routledge.

Schlyter, Ann. 1988. "Women Householders and Housing Strategies: The Case of George, Zambia." Lund: National Swedish Institute for Building Research.

Swift, Jeremy. 1989. "Why Are Rural People Vulnerable to Famine?" *Institute of Development Studies Bulletin* 20: 49–57.

Thorbek, Susanne. 1991. "Gender in Two Slum Cultures." *Environment and Urbanization* 3(2): 71–81.

Tinker, Irene. 1997. "Family Survival in an Urbanizing World." *Review of Social Economy* LV: 251–60.

——— and Gale Summerfield, eds. 1999. *Women's Rights to House and Land: China, Laos, Vietnam.* London: Lynne Rienner.

7

Women and the Environment: Regenerative Development

During most of the postwar period, patriarchal capitalists and imperialist state officials in the North promoted the "development" of people and natural resources in the South. In capitalist society, men have treated both women and the environment as resources to control and plunder.[1] As a key part of a development strategy based on the plunder of women and the environment, policymakers, government aid officials, and NGO managers have advocated that international organizations advance population control as a way to curb rapid population growth. Population growth has been seen by these officials as the "cause" of poverty in the South, and gaining control of population growth has been seen as a way of controlling laboring people. Population control programs targeted women because state officials and NGO representatives did not think they could control the reproductive capacity or behavior of men, in large part because such efforts would undermine patriarchy and men's control of women. These officials also promoted the expansion of export agriculture and natural resource extraction, a development that effectively privatized environmental "commons," the oceans and fisheries, agricultural lands and tropical forests, water supplies and genetic resources upon which subsistence worker households depend. Capitalists and state officials argued that population control and resource extraction would deliver substantial economic benefits to poor and working households around the world. Of course, they also expected that these developments would increase the supply and lower the price of food and raw materials, which would assist development in the North.

But although these activities were supposed to promote development and "modernization," they had significant and important adverse consequences for people and environments, not just in the South but in the North as well. In recent years, women-centered movements and ecofeminists around the world have identified the social and environmental problems associated with "development" and have advanced strategies designed to reclaim global commons, practice effective stewardship, and promote sustainable and also *regenerative* social and environmental development.

We will first examine population control as a "development" strategy, describing the social and environmental problems associated with population control programs and efforts by women-centered movements to address these problems. Then we will look at the expansion of export agriculture and resource extraction in the South during the postwar period. We will assess its impact on people's livelihoods and on environmental commons and describe strategies being used in the South to reclaim these commons. Finally, we will look at ecofeminist movements in the North, which have developed collaborative approaches to regional and global environmental problems.

POPULATION CONTROL: COERCIVE MEASURES
AND VOLUNTARY EFFORTS

In the 1950s and 1960s, capitalists and state officials in the North became alarmed by the rapid rate of population growth, particularly in the South, and warned that rapid growth, if left unchecked, would detonate a "population bomb," with serious social and environmental consequences.[2] Proponents of this thesis argued that population growth would undermine social and economic development in the South because governments and economies could not provide the schools, health care, or jobs needed to meet the burgeoning supply of people. And they argued that population growth would harm the environment because the growing demand for food and natural resources would lead to the rapid depletion of the earth's resources and eventual scarcity. The rising price of energy and natural resources in the 1970s seemed to support these claims by providing evidence that these resources were growing "scarce."

In this context, population control was seen by government officials as a way to promote social and economic development *and* to protect the environment. In 1969, President Richard Nixon, who endorsed this perspective, announced that the United States would "give population [control] and family planning a high priority."[3] He subsequently promoted population control programs through U.S. and international aid agencies and in 1974 organized the first UN conference on population. But although U.S. officials increased aid for family planning programs, they also *cut* funding for overseas health care and food programs.[4] This practice was consistent with the view, held by population control advocates such as Ehrlich, that caring for and feeding people in the South would only encourage them to have more children. Proponents of tough-minded population control believed that governments in the

North should practice a kind of "triage," which meant "directing [food] aid to those countries with the greatest chance of survival while abandoning others to famine."[5] In a "food-short" world, feeding people who could not eventually feed themselves would be a waste of scarce resources.

Because proponents of population control believed that the threat from population growth was great, they supported strict and coercive measures to obtain results. And this approach was widely adopted by the international aid community in the North *and* by many governments in the South, first in India and then in China, the two most populous countries in the world. State officials in India and China (and elsewhere) adopted fairly coercive programs to cut birthrates. They introduced sterilization and other programs to monitor and control the reproductive lives of poor women, whom they viewed as being incapable of making the decisions necessary to cut birthrates. In China, the sterilization of women and the use of intrauterine device (IUD) implants are the main methods used to control reproduction. In the 1990s and early 2000s, more than 40 percent of couples relied on female sterilization to prevent pregnancy, and the government regularly forced women "to abort second pregnancies by threat of loss of jobs and benefits and by the imposition of heavy fines. . . . [Women's] use of contraception is highly monitored and aided by workplace birth cadres."[6] Male domination of the regime's policies has led to gender-selective abortion, female infanticide, and the widespread practice of putting girl babies up for adoption to childless couples in China and in other countries.

Of course, state officials have used coercive population control measures in other countries. In eastern and southern Africa, Akosua Adomako Ampofo found that authorities "adopted campaigns to contain the population growth of Black people through harmful injectibles and forced sterilization in Namibia and South Africa. . . . [T]he apartheid state urged white women to have babies while temporarily and permanently sterilizing Black women. Abortion was also used by the state, and by individual men, to control unwanted female fertility."[7]

But the coercive population control policies adopted by governments in India and China and elsewhere had a number of adverse consequences. First, where state programs were introduced in patriarchal settings, with little effort to alter patriarchal domination of women, they often proved harmful or fatal to women and girls. The determination of men to have male heirs in a restricted-birth policy environment led to the widespread use of amniocentesis to determine the sex of embryos. If the fetus was identified as female, men usually insisted that the fetus be aborted or the infant girl abandoned or put up for adoption. For example, at one well-known center in Mumbai, almost 100 percent of the 51,914 abortions performed in 1984–1985 were done to abort female fetuses.[8] These patriarchal practices resulted in skewed demographic profiles, where boys came to outnumber girls in some areas. Over time, the dearth of girls reduced marriage prospects for young men, a problem that proponents of patriarchy had not anticipated. In China, this has driven some men to desperate measures: kidnapping young girls and forcing them to marry.

A common misconception is that poverty is caused by poor women with too many children. As Sonia Correa, Adrienne Germain, and Rosalind P. Petchesky, feminists who worked on reproductive issues at the 1994 International Conference on Population and Development in Cairo, said:

> It's not easy to convince the public and opinion makers that average fertility [in Brazil] is already very low, and that the percentage of women who have more than three children is just 6 percent of women between 14 and 49. People see violence, they see beggars and homeless people living on the street and they connect that with women having too many children. The public does not yet fully understand the rights-based approach of Cairo. As an illustration, to address the "need for population control," some parliamentarians and policymakers are even urging a constitutional revision to authorize sterilization [for the poor]. It is very alarming.[9]

In their work on Latin America, Asia, and Africa, DAWN scholars such as Sonia Correa and Gita Sen found that poor people had very limited access to reproductive health services. In Mexico, where 80 percent of the people live in poverty and half of them in extreme poverty, women cannot afford to pay for reproductive technologies that would enable them to make reproductive choices and limit family size. It's not that people are poor because they have too many children; it's that poverty, in many areas, establishes conditions that make it difficult to prevent conception and to survive without children.

Second, coercive and involuntary population control programs actually *undermined* efforts to slow population growth. It turned out that noncoercive education and health care programs designed to empower women, increase their access to reproductive technologies, and improve their ability to make their own reproductive choices were *more* effective at lowing birthrates than coercive-involuntary and parrtiarchal programs. As one government scientist explained, "If we had concentrated more on the ... human resources element—female literacy, education—in the 1950s and '60s, [India] would have had a population of about 600 million [in 1989, instead of 800 million]."[10] And much the same is true in China. Amartya Sen has argued that "while China may get too much credit for its authoritarian measures, it gets far too little credit for the other, more collaborative and participatory policies it has followed, which have themselves helped to cut down the birth rate."[11]

Of course, women recognized this early on and took steps on their own to obtain access to reproductive technologies, take control of reproductive decisions in households, and downsize their families. Remarkably, women assisted by women-centered movements have asserted greater control over reproduction and reduced birthrates all over the world, *even* in states where patriarchal state officials, religious leaders, and men in households *oppose* the exercise of choice by women. In Brazil, for example, a country where the government has done nothing to promote birth control and where the Catholic Church adamantly opposes the use of reproductive technologies and the control of reproductive decisions by women, women have taken matters into their own hands and reduced birthrates dramatically. As one demographer explained, "Brazil has experienced the largest self-induced drop in human history ... compressing 100 years of fertility decline into 20 years."[12] Although women have not reduced birthrates quite as fast in other countries, the remarkable thing is that they have still done so in Catholic countries and in Muslim countries across the South, and they have done so despite the opposition of patriarchal state officials, religious leaders, and household members.

✦   ✦   ✦

ENGAGING ENVIRONMENTALISTS AND FEMINISTS IN COLLABORATIVE CHANGE

When feminist and environmentalist movements join, activists who work together can change the way that development is defined. Alternative development can be promoted when feminists, environmentalists, and participants in other movements engage in research and research-based social change. Democratic educational processes of learning together and developing new knowledge about ideas, social ways of living, and ways to make change lie at the heart of making alternative development. Women-inclusive social change that comes out of group-defined, participatory action research can be described as feminist community-development education. Although Gita Sen did not identify some of the important social change processes, she suggested that feminists' work on biological and social reproduction can be enhanced by promoting real development and environmental change.

[T]here is much in common between feminists and environmentalists in their visions of society and in the methods they use. Both groups ... have a healthy critical stance toward ecologically profligate and inequitable patterns of growth ... Both use methods that rely on grassroots mobilization and participation.... [B]elieve in the power of widespread knowledge and the rights of people to be informed and to participate in decisions affecting their lives and those of nations and the planet. Indeed, there are many feminists within environmental movements, North and South, and environmentalists within feminist movements.

Greater mutual understanding on the population question can result from a greater recognition that the core problem is that of development *within* which population is inextricably meshed....

[G]eneral and reproductive health improvements are mutually reinforcing....

Reproductive health is better viewed as a basic human right and thus *as an end in itself*, rather than as an instrument toward fulfilling demographic ends.

In the context of population and development, this means that the population issue must be defined as the right to determine and make reproductive decisions in the context of fulfilling *secure livelihoods, basic needs (including reproductive health), and political participation.* Although the reality in most countries in the world may be far removed from such an ideal, an affirmation of basic values would provide the needed underpinnings for policy and action.

Such values would imply, first of all, that economic growth and ecological sustainability must secure livelihoods, basic needs, political participation, and women's reproductive rights, not work against them. Thus, environmental sustainability must be conceptualized so as to support and sustain livelihoods and basic needs, and not in ways that automatically counterpose "nature" against the survival needs of the most vulnerable in the present. Where trade-offs among these different goals exist or are inevitable, the costs and burdens must not fall on the poorest and most vulnerable, and all people must have a voice in negotiating resolutions through open and genuinely participatory political processes. Furthermore, environmental strategies that enhance livelihoods and fulfill needs can probably help lay the basis for mortality and fertility reductions.

Second, population and family planning programs should be framed in the context of health and livelihood agendas, should give serious attention to women's health advocates, and be supportive of women's reproductive health and rights....

Third, reproductive health strategies are likely to succeed in improving women's health and make it possible for them to make socially viable fertility decisions if they are set in the context of a supportive health agenda overall....

Fourth, the mainstream Northern environmental movement needs to focus more particularly on gender relations and women's needs in framing its own strategies, as well as on issues raised by minority groups. These issues (such as raised by native peoples and African Americans in the U.S.) tend to link environmental issues with livelihoods and basic needs concerns in much the same way as do organizations in the South ([see the actions carried out by] West Harlem Environmental Action in New York).

Wide discussion and acknowledgement of these principles could help to bridge some of the current gaps between feminists and environmentalists, and make it possible to build coalitions that can move both agendas forward.

Source: Gita Sen. "Women, Poverty, and Population: Issues for the Concerned Environmentalist." In Lourdes Arizpe, M. Priscilla Stone, and David C. Major, eds. *Population and the Environment: Rethinking the Debate.* Boulder, CO: Westview Press, 1994, 67–86, 82–84.

By taking control of reproductive decisions, women around the world have demonstrated their ability to curb population growth, largely because they recognize that they will benefit from smaller families and that this will increase their educational and employment opportunities, raise incomes, and increase women's power in households. As Wendy Harcourt has argued, "poor women ... are the key to the good health for themselves and for their family and community livelihood."[13] It turns out that reproductive choice has enabled women to make decisions that curb population growth and facilitate alternative development at the same time.

In the 1970s and 1980s, women also discovered that poor, growing populations in the South were *not* responsible for resource depletion and the environmental problems associated with the expansion of export agriculture and resource extraction. It wasn't small fishers who were decimating wild fish populations, but industrial fishing fleets from the North. It wasn't small farmers and indigenous people who were laying waste to tropical forests, but giant cattle ranchers and transnational timber companies. And it wasn't large poor populations in the South who were depleting the world's energy supplies, but small, energy-intensive populations in the North. When people in the South realized they were not to blame for the world's environmental problems, as the proponents of population control had long argued, they began to examine how export agriculture and resource extraction contributed to social and environmental problems and began to take steps to reclaim environmental commons and practice regenerative development.

THE EXPANSION OF EXPORT AGRICULTURE AND NATURAL RESOURCE EXTRACTION

During the postwar period, capitalists and state officials in the North encouraged countries in the South to expand export agriculture and accelerate the extraction of natural resources. They did so between 1945 and 1980 because they saw it as a way to promote development. If countries in the South increased their production of food and raw materials, they could use the money they earned to finance their economic development. But as a result of the debt crisis in the early 1980s, capitalists and state officials in the North imposed SAPs on indebted countries in the South. They still encouraged them to expand the production of food and natural resources, much as they had in the earlier period, but instead of using the money they earned to finance *development* in the South, they were instructed to use the money they earned from the sale of food and natural resources to repay *debt*. This was a major change.

But although countries across the South increased their production of food and raw materials during both periods, the expansion of export agriculture and natural resource extraction contributed to a number of social and environmental problems. As the consequences of resource expansion became apparent, women-centered movements moved to address the social and environmental problems associated with development and debt. Let us first look at the expansion of export agriculture and then at the extraction of mineral and natural resources.

EXPORT AGRICULTURE

Capitalists and state officials encouraged the expansion of export agriculture first to finance development and then to repay debt. But this expansion contributed to a series of serious social and environmental problems. First, the expansion of "export" crops—foods such as coffee, tea, bananas, peanuts, cocoa, and oranges; feed grains such as soy and corn; and nonfood crops such as cotton and sisal—reduced the land devoted to indigenous "staple" crops—diverse varieties of rice, beans, wheat, corn, cassava, millet—that local people ate. As the supply of staple foods fell, their price increased, making it harder for poor and worker households to buy the food they needed to survive. It turned out that the growth of export agriculture contributed to growing hunger around the world, even though the total amount of food produced in the South increased.[14]

Second, the farmers who grew export crops used newly available green revolution technologies—hybrid seeds, chemical fertilizers, pesticides, and farm machinery—

to increase production. But the purchase of new technologies increased farm costs. And because farmers used the new technologies to grow more food, food supplies increased and prices fell. Rising costs and falling prices drove many farmers out of business or forced them to borrow heavily to stay in business. Many people migrated out of rural areas into cities, which could not provide adequate housing, sanitation, or employment for swelling migrant populations. Rural bankruptcy also led to the consolidation of land and to rising debt levels for the farmers who remained.

These negative *social* developments contributed to three important *environmental* problems. First, as export agriculture expanded, farmers moved into environmentally marginal areas—tropical rain forests, desert fringe areas—to produce export crops, and they were often joined by farmers trying to eke out a subsistence living in these environments. But the invasion of lands ill suited for long-term, intensive agriculture disrupted ecological systems and depleted fragile topsoils, which forced farmers to migrate through environmentally sensitive landscapes.

Second, the widespread use and misuse of chemical fertilizers and pesticides contaminated water supplies, resulted in species loss, and contributed to the deaths of hundreds of thousands of people from pesticide poisoning and related illnesses. In Asia, feminist researchers have found that transplanting rice and picking cotton exposes women to high levels of pesticides and contributes to gynecological ailments. "In China," Bina Agarwal discovered, "several times the acceptable levels of DDT and BHC residues have been found in the milk of nursing mothers, among women agricultural workers. In India, pesticides are associated with limb and visual disorders."[15] These developments sometimes join in perverse ways. In India, farmers who have tried to use costly technologies to increase production have borrowed heavily from usurious local moneylenders. But rising costs and falling prices have ruined many indebted farmers. To escape their debts and the shame associated with the loss of their farms and their livelihood, many farmers have swallowed pesticide to commit suicide. It is a terrible irony that a technology that contributed to farmer bankruptcy is used by farmers to escape bankruptcy. In 2003, the Indian government estimated that 17,101 farmers committed suicide in this fashion.[16]

Third, the construction of long-distance, energy-intensive commodity chains designed to deliver fresh flowers and vegetables from growers in the South to consumers in the North in the same day—roses and fresh-cut flowers have become a huge global industry, which leaders in China have announced they intend to capture—requires the massive application of pesticides and fumigants, continual refrigeration, and energy-intensive air freight and packaging systems.[17] The expansion of these extremely perishable goods has contributed to the rising use of energy and the global warming associated with it.

MINERALS, FORESTS, AND FISHERIES

The production of other raw materials has also accelerated across the South. The growing "harvest" of oil, minerals, timber, and fish differs from export agriculture in two ways. First, these activities are generally organized by large transnational corporations based in the North, not by indigenous, small-scale producers, as is the case with most export agriculture around the world. Second, to produce these goods, large corporations have to lay claim to the world's commons, to resources held in public trust by governments, or to resources shared by everyone on the planet.

So, for example, state officials in the South have permitted transnational corporations in the North to lay claim to their oil and mineral deposits, rain forests, and fisheries. In return, the corporations pay severance fees that governments can use to repay debt. As a result, natural resource commons, which had been typically held as a public trust by governments, are essentially privatized, sold to foreign companies, and used by consumers in the North. Of course, the world's oceans are not held in trust by any government. And in recent years these global commons have been plundered by private industrial fleets trawling for food and fish meal.

The expansion of natural resource extraction has had important social and environmental consequences. It has destroyed the livelihoods of indigenous peoples and worker households who have long engaged in subsistence activities in these commons. The production of oil in Nigeria has disrupted and destroyed the livelihoods of people living in the oil-producing delta. The destruction of rain forests has destroyed the livelihoods of indigenous peoples and subsistence producers in the Amazon, Indonesia, Malaysia, and Thailand. The destruction of fisheries by global factory trawlers has forced subsistence and local fisherpeople to hang up their nets. As wild fish stocks have declined, transnational corporations have established fish and shrimp farms in many places, which have contributed to the ruin of small-scale and coastal fisheries, species loss, and the contamination of marine environments.

The expansion of tourist industries in the South has also contributed to the privatization of commons, particularly in coastal areas, as fishing villages are cleared for beach resorts and agricultural lands are converted to golf courses. Both developments impose heavy social and environmental burdens on local people and landscapes, without providing many economic benefits in return. Tourism is a poor form of "development" because most of the money tourists spend on vacations in the South is captured by transnational airline and cruise companies based in the North, by multinational hotel chains, and by food-service companies from the North who import the wine and whiskey that tourists demand. All-inclusive resorts and cruise ships are designed *not* to let hard currency escape from tourist venues into local economies, where it might otherwise do some good.[18]

TOURISM FOR ACTIVISTS

In our previous anthology selection by Chandra Talpade Mohanty, the argument is made that superficial, voyeuristic feminist travel reinforces hegemonic thinking and ways of living, even if this travel and tourism are done via classwork, reading, or actual overseas travel. But when travel is done in ways that connect social change in different parts of the world, the journeys taken by visitors and the learning done by residents can lead to mutual education and international exchanges that promote long-term change in the global North and South. Global educational exchanges may be particularly fruitful in agri-ecotourism.

In contrast to ecotourism, where hotel-like businesses sell access to ecological presentations, agri-ecotourism takes place on sustainable and cooperative farms, where visitors learn how organic farming, the restoration of forests, the preservation of flora and fauna, and the development of solar, wind, and water power provide ways for communities to sustain themselves economically and ecologically. Some of these agri-eco sites may sell local products and services in the region, or they may be involved in fair trade relationships with the global North. Tourists and visitors stay in ecolodges or with local families in these communities, providing opportunities for residents and tourists to teach each other how to develop sustainable ways of producing and living.

The reclaiming of the civil commons lies at the heart of many women-centered, sustainable, alternative development efforts in the world today. Agri-ecotourism reintroduces visitors to the idea of the civil commons, which served as the reproductive center for communities before global capitalism. Imagine a vibrant commons with cows and horses grazing, with vegetables and grains bursting from the soil, and you may be seeing the commons of the past or the restored commons today. Of course, over the past 500 years, the continual reinvention of the civil commons continued to provide a key way for laboring households to generate cash and in-kind income that supplemented households' pooled wage income and state transfer payments. Alternative development has pushed the collective enhancement of the civil commons to a new level, one that revitalizes endangered ecosystems through people's engagement in ecofeminist, peace-oriented, and alternative trade networks. Participation in agri-ecotourism is one way for visitors and residents to benefit from local development initiatives that have global implications.

Agri-ecotourism allows for producers, workers, and consumers to discuss and share processes for reclaiming and collectively restoring the civil commons and to work together on the development of a network of civil commons. The "civil commons" refers to the local lands and resources that working people in one area have historically maintained to generate basic subsistence goods and to provide for their well-being. New communities emerge as local groups dedicate themselves to holistic environmentalism, interfamilial and intragroup reciprocity, and the democratic redistribution of collectively produced food and other resources. In collective situations, where newly invented communities begin reversing environmental damage to the civil commons, agri-ecotourism provides an important way for feminists, environmentalists, and networks of alternative producers and consumers to meet, establish short- and long-term exchanges of knowledge-based and material resources, and learn more about how to create a balanced and regenerative world. In her writing, Deborah McLaren introduced many readers in the global North to agri-ecotourism.

As tourists, we must make educated economic choices and support small-scale, locally owned and operated businesses. Get involved in your own community so that when you travel you will have a reason to be involved in other communities and will *stay involved....* Volunteer. Study. Learn about local currency programs and how you can start one in your community. Pressure large tourism companies to do more than greenwash. Organize a "reality tour" of your own community to examine environmental, economic, or social justice issues. Invite teachers, students, local community members, your family, city officials, religious leaders, local businesses (including those in tourism) and others to participate. Make activism a goal of the tour. Contribute funds to support more integrated, diverse critical tourism studies....

Creating links within communities is essential. Foreign-owned or foreign-operated tourism companies could help support local agriculture and more sustainable practices by buying local goods and services such as food and transportation. They could recognize the harm in building cluster sites and make sure that broad planning in the area included agricultural lands....

In rethinking tourism, we must analyze the role that tourists play in promoting current destructive practices. With pressure, the industry can be reshaped so that profits from tourism are redistributed more equitably. We must reduce consumption and respect natural limits rather than merely think "green." Technology is not neutral but interacts with society and nature. An essential step is replacing environmentally and socially obsolete high technology with more appropriate, less-consuming, and traditional technologies.

This task is enormous. The developed world is in a state of denial about such severe problems and voluntary change is unlikely. The developed world will have to be forced to change by community groups in the global South and by cross-border organizations everywhere. A more generous spirit and greater volunteerism with respect to tourism goes hand in hand with a condemnation of the elitist, materialist view that tourists are entitled to purchase other environments and cultures....

[B]ecause of global grassroots movements for change, developing a deeper understanding of the course we're on and the role of global tourism may be possible. Alternative strategies and movements are available, as are alternatives to tourism....

Throughout the world, among different cultures and classes, people are looking for self-determination. The world we are now born into and the society we know measures humans in terms of their economic worth [as it is socially defined]. Human potential is enormous and largely unrealized. Western-style capitalism and consumerism have undermined the possibility for people to make their own choices about their lives and to have opportunities for their futures. Tourism continues to play a tremendous role in spreading the corporate empire. However, this industry is different from many others. One of its primary functions is to develop human relationships, which I see as a chance to rethink and change our future.

Source: Deborah McLaren. *Rethinking Tourism and Eco-Travel.* 2nd ed. Bloomfield, CT: Kumarian Press, 2003, 141–142, 147, 151–152.

RECLAIMING THE COMMONS

Women-centered movements have responded to these social and environmental problems in a variety of ways. They have challenged global and local institutions that have promoted the expansion of export agriculture and natural resource extraction for the sake of debt repayment. Since the advent of the debt crisis in the early 1980s, movements across the South have protested the imposition of structural adjustment programs (SAPs) and the privatization and plunder of environmental commons. In Panama, "hundreds of Panamanian workers invaded the legislature chanting: 'I won't pay the debt! Let the ones who stole the money pay.'"[19] This kind of protest became so widespread across the South in subsequent years that sociologists have described them collectively as "austerity protests."[20]

In recent years, groups across the South have been joined by groups in the North, and they have demanded the outright cancellation of debt and forced the International Monetary Fund and the World Bank to consider debt relief, at least for the world's poorest countries in Africa and Asia.[21]

They have also been concerned about the adverse impact of SAPs on government health care spending. Vanitha Subramaniam has argued that reduced health care spending has had an adverse impact on women's health, including the failure to provide cancer screening or treat sexually transmitted diseases (STDs) and reproductive tract infections (RTIs).[22] As a result, the UN's Gender Working Group has argued that global institutions take a "human security approach," which means that governments and businesses must invest in poor women's health, create economic security, and use science and technology in a gender-equitable way.[23]

Women-centered movements have taken aim not only at global institutions that manage debt but also at local moneylenders, who lend money at extortionate rates and use contractual advantages to seize debtor lands and assets. As Turner and Brawnhill explain, Wangari Maathai, the Kenyan woman who won the Nobel Peace Prize, is an environmental activist who has worked to save forest and agricultural land and urban parks from destruction and to reclaim common lands from private, state, and other holdings. Maathai has also identified local male moneylenders as a problem because they are the local counterparts of global debt agencies insofar as they promote the destruction of the environment and undermine efforts by small farmers and foresters to engage in sustainable practices. "Now, it's time you stop sucking my people dry," she has argued.[24] In 2002, Maathai and land-reappropriation movements such as the Mungiki Kikuyu (the Congress) and the Organization of Villagers joined together to reclaim privatized lands and reestablish commons that could be used on a sustainable basis by local worker households in urban and rural areas.

In Kenya and India, activists have demanded that state officials introduce "fair lending" practices to reduce the stranglehold of local debt merchants, promote the viability of small farms, and reduce the epidemic of indebted farmer suicides in rural areas.

In India, women have led decades-long protests against the construction of large dams and campaigned to protect water supply "commons." Vandana Shiva has argued that water is a critical community resource:

> Since two-thirds of humanity depend directly on land, water and biodiversity for their livelihoods, the destruction—or privatization—of land, water and biodiversity creates poverty for the people who are left without food, water, and means of livelihood. However, in the commercial economy, this destruction registers as "growth."

Major dams, highways and ports are "development" projects in the commercial paradigm. These projects are, however, systematically resisted by local communities because they push people into underdevelopment. By destroying the ecosystems that support their livelihoods, this version of "development" robs them not only of their economic well-being but also of their homes and cultural security.[25]

Shiva and others have joined together in the World Social Forum to protect and reclaim genetic resources, which are being privatized and plundered by corporations and global progrowth institutions.[26] Women working in groups such as Social Action for Rural Tribal Inhabitants in India (SARTHII) have been actively engaged in antideforestation, antidam, and land reclamation efforts.[27]

At the Miraflor cooperative in Nicaragua, landholding women shape sustainable community development through solar-supported agri-ecotourism that features cloud forest restoration, cloud forest birds and animals, and cloud forest orchids. They cultivate organic and fair trade coffee, grow organic produce for local markets, raise horses and cows that are adapted to the cloud forest, and consult with other groups about cloud forest restoration.[28] In Venezuela, women have organized in ways designed to highlight the value of ecology in alternative development. There, women-led groups tend to be informal, ecological, democratic, participatory, stable, and relationship-based (making co-optation less likely). When mixed-gender organizations led by women address strategic issues that involve everyone (and not gender-specific or domestic concerns), they have received a lot of media attention in Venezuela.[29]

Women have taken an active role in these movements to prevent hunger and other social ills and to protect the environment, in particular environmental commons on which so much of life depends. Environmental commons—lands, forests, waters, fisheries—are crucial for women engaged in subsistence production. Women have sought to defend and reclaim the commons both so they can obtain the resources they need to survive—land for gardens to grow staple foods; timber for fuel wood; water for drinking, washing, and watering animals; marine environments for fisheries— and so they can act as "stewards" of these resources and, in that capacity, promote sustainable and *regenerative development.*

When resources are held in common by small, indigenous groups who can make collective, consensus, and/or democratic decisions about their use, they are used in a much more sustainable fashion than they are if they are divided, privatized, or used by outsiders who are not subject to local control. What's more, women must play a central role in decisions about the use of commons because they are typically the primary users and managers of common resources. Some government officials and aid agencies now recognize this and have taken steps to place important decisionmaking about common resources with local, women-centered groups—or to return it to them.

According to Wendy Harcourt and Arturo Escobar, the feminist politics of place has involved reconnecting the body with the environment, the economy, and political activity. The environment has to be reembedded with culture and the economy through women's conservation work, urban gardens, safe water, antimining, and forest preservation efforts.[30] Of course, women in the North and South need to work together to address the related problems of overconsumption and environmental degradation. Often choosing to circumvent the nation-state and to go under the radar of large-scale nongovernmental and international organizations, women-centered movements and environmental projects have started to address many interrelated environmental problems, especially through grassroots, cross-border, and transoceanic organizing.

DEVELOPMENT AND ENVIRONMENT IN THE NORTH

Back in the 1960s, state officials in the North worried that large and growing populations in the South would deplete natural resources and pollute or destroy natural environments. But it soon became evident that large populations in the South were not responsible for most environmental problems because they consumed few resources and little energy. Instead, environmentalists discovered that energy-intensive resource consumption by small populations in the North, particularly in the United States, were responsible for most of the planet's environmental ills. To some extent, capitalists and state officials in the North encouraged the expansion of agricultural and natural resource production in the South to generate income that could be used first to finance development and later to repay debt. But they also promoted this expansion because they knew (but didn't like to trumpet the fact) that rising supplies would drive down the price of these goods and that low prices would assist the "development" of users and consumers in the North. The profligate, intensive consumption of energy, food, and natural resources consumption in the North has been made possible or underwritten by the expansion of export agriculture and natural resource extraction in the South.

This profligate consumption has contributed not only to social and environmental problems in the South (see above) but also to social and environmental problems for people in the North and for the planet as a whole, global warming chief among them. But responsibility for these developments is not equally shared. In the United States, capitalist leaders and state officials have long supported policies designed to increase the supply of goods from the South and make them available to user-consumers in the United States at the lowest possible price, which in practice has also meant with the maximum amount of collateral social and environmental damage. Moreover, U.S. officials have tried to block efforts by government officials in Western Europe and Japan to curb energy use, as they did with regard to the Kyoto accords, which were designed to curb the production of the gases that contribute to global warming. In this context, U.S. officials have supported efforts by the Chinese regime to increase their energy consumption by burning high-sulfur coal, which contributes both to serious environmental pollution and to global warming.

These steps will likely cripple efforts to curb global warming because China is expected in the coming years to burn more coal and produce more global warming gases than the rest of the world combined.[31] U.S. officials have been willing to support the expansion of high energy consumption in China (to the detriment of the planet's environment) because this will help China keep down the cost of its manufactured goods and make it possible for users in the United States to continue consuming cheap Chinese goods. Cheap goods for Wal-Mart are evidently more important to U.S. policymakers than the health of the environment.

But capitalists and state officials in Western Europe and Japan have taken a different approach. They have taken steps to keep energy and resource costs fairly high to force businesses to adopt low-energy technologies and to persuade consumers to practice low-level energy use and resource consumption. For example, in Western Europe and Japan, businesses offer high-mileage microcars and governments provide low-cost public transportation to consumers, whereas Detroit struggles to sell low-mileage sports utility vehicles (SUVs), and the U.S. government lets public transportation systems wither. The approach taken in Western Europe and Japan is a sound economic strategy because energy-saving technologies lower costs for businesses and consumers *and* make them more competitive with U.S. firms as world energy prices rise.

ECOFEMINISM AND NORTH-SOUTH COLLABORATION

In the North, environmentalists and ecofeminists have emerged to challenge developments that have contributed to social and environmental problems in the North and in the South and have collaborated with women-centered groups in the South to promote alternative, regenerative development.

Ecofeminism is a broad term used to describe women and men who resist men's and society's domination over women and over nature. Carolyn Merchant has argued that ecofeminism is based on the idea of a new, inclusive partnership between people and nature:

> A partnership ethic is only one part of a new narrative or set of narratives about the human relationship with nature. And new narratives are only one part of what is needed for a sustainable world. The global ecological crisis and the decline of nature need to be reversed by new ways of producing, reproducing, and interpreting life on the planet. Poverty, hunger, and sickness need to be reversed by new forms of economics, politics, and science. Minorities and third world nations need to be full participants in global economy and ecology. Ecological economics, organic farms and gardens, sustainable livelihoods, green politics, wild places, ecological designs, human-scale cities, reverence for nature, chaos and complexity theories, and partnership ethics are among many new ways to achieve a sustainable relationship with nature. Nature's fate and humanity's fate are deeply intertwined. May both survive and fully live.[32]

Other ecofeminists such as Mary Mellor have argued that ecofeminists need to examine a host of problems associated with development because development has been "disproportionately inflicted on women, indigenous communities, marginalized and exploited peoples, and on the natural world and its nonhuman inhabitants."[33] Because development impacts women and "minorities," the ecofeminist movement has been able to connect protests against gender discrimination and racism with movements against environmental exploitation and degradation, Noel Sturgeon has argued.[34]

In the North, ecofeminists have organized to address problems related to (1) reproduction and population, (2) export agriculture and resource depletion, and (3) the destruction and reclamation of global commons.

Reproduction and Population

Ecofeminists around the world have joined efforts to end coercive reproductive policies—forced sterilization, the practice of female genital mutilation, restrictions on the availability of reproductive technologies and abortion—and to make reproductive technologies and abortion widely available and empower women to make decisions about sex, reproduction, and family size. At the 1995 UN Conference on Women in Beijing, delegates from around the world demanded progress on all these issues, which they saw as critical for women, economic development, population control, and the environment. And myriad women-centered groups have continued to advance the issues on this agenda.

Ecofeminists have also organized movements to protest toxic contamination of their communities, particularly because toxic chemicals contribute to reproductive health disorders that primarily affect women and children, a development described at length in Temma Kaplan's *Crazy for Democracy: Women in Grassroots Movements.*[35] One of the first of these was organized by Lois Gibbs to protest the dumping of toxic waste by Hooker Chemical in the Love Canal subdivision in Niagara, New York. The sludge laden with dioxins, pesticides, and polychlorinated biphenyl caused women to miscarry and their children to contract dangerous illnesses. Kaplan described how women used their identity as women and mothers to their political advantage. As Kaplan pointed out:

> [W]hat differentiated the women of the Love Canal Homeowners Association from other protesters was their self-presentation as traditional mothers trying to do their job. "Radicals and students carry signs, but not average housewives. Housewives have to care for their children and their homes," Lois Gibbs recalled later.... The homeowners learned to use the news media to project that image of themselves as they pursued a strategy for saving their families. Familiarity with television, especially with situation comedies like *I Love Lucy* and *The Carol Burnett Show,* provided models of strong women who retained typical feminine qualities.
>
> Portraying themselves as housewives helped otherwise ethnically and religiously disparate neighbors forge themselves into a community. In fact, a by-product of the homeowners' movement was the blending of two immediately recognized images of women. One melodramatically presented women, especially mothers, as innocent victims. From this vantage point, the homemakers were caught in a plot over which they had no control. But by virtuously resisting, standing up for their families, they gained license to act against the forces of evil. The other image developed in situation comedies. There, strong women such as Lucy, played by Lucille Ball, attempted to win their goals but always in a way that did not enhance their own power.[36]

This strategy of intentionally using stereotypical images of women and mothers to build a movement has been described by Gayatri Spivek as a kind of "strategic essentialism" that helps women organize politically in some situations.[37]

The Mothers of East Los Angeles organized as mothers, family members, and community members, linking public conceptions of mothering to environmentalism, quality schooling, and the development of healthy Chicano neighborhoods. When the Mothers of East Los Angeles first fought California's plans to build a state prison near Boyle Heights' schools, Father John Moretta of the Resurrection Catholic Parish reached out to the women. The name Mothers of East Los Angeles was coined by Father John, who had an interest in the film *The Official Story,* which personalized the history of women who marched for years in Buenos Aires' governmental plaza in opposition to the military dictatorship's torture and disappearance of women, children, and husbands. Like the women in Argentina, actions taken by the Mothers of East Los Angeles became associated with community nurturing and strong families. The Mothers of East Los Angeles also became identified as a powerful Chicana environmental and health group that fought the building of state prisons near schools and opposed the use of toxic incinerators in East Los Angeles (first conceived of as energy generators). Just as Argentina's Las Madres de la Plaza de Mayo raised global awareness about human rights, the Mothers of East Los Angeles extended human rights to include the struggle against the conscious placement of toxics in or near communities of color. The Mothers of East Los Angeles became seen as leaders in the struggle against environmental racism.[38]

Export Agriculture and Resource Depletion

Ecofeminists in the North have been concerned about the social and environmental problems associated with export agriculture in the South and with energy-intensive, pesticide-reliant agriculture in the North. They have joined efforts to secure debt relief and have challenged efforts by the World Bank and International Monetary Fund to promote development that has adverse social and environmental consequences.

Ever since the publication in the early 1960s of Rachel Carson's *Silent Spring,* environmentalists have worked to slow or halt the agricultural use of pesticides, which kill and injure people, contaminate water supplies, and destroy diverse, nontarget species. They have joined with small farmers around the world to promote sustainable and organic agriculture and to preserve the genetic diversity of plant and animal species; they have challenged "fast," high-energy, long-distance food systems and urged the development of local, seasonal, "slow" food systems in their place.

Because mineral and raw material extraction and use are typically destructive in social and environmental terms, ecofeminists have urged consumers to curb consumption and practice recycling. These practices have become widespread in the North for some products: paper products and some metals. For example, one-third of the copper used in the United States comes from recycled sources, a rather remarkable achievement.

Destruction and Reclamation of Global Commons

Of course, the biggest challenge is the ongoing destruction of global commons, particularly of the atmosphere by global warming gases. Ecofeminists have joined with other environmentalists and activists to curb energy use by energy-intensive users in the North. They achieved dramatic results after the first energy crisis of the 1970s–1980s and helped persuade users in the North to improve the energy efficiency of homes, businesses, and cars. Although Americans returned to profligate habits as oil prices fell in the late 1980s and 1990s, Western European and Japanese users continued to practice conservation and adopt energy-saving technologies and practices. And even though the Bush administration abandoned the Kyoto agreements designed to curb global warming, many U.S. businesses and states have taken steps on their own to comply. For example, California legislators concerned about global warming passed laws imposing strict requirements on energy providers, even on producers located outside the state.[39] State officials and businesses have done so both because it's the right thing to do and because it's a sound economic practice—it helps them stay competitive with energy-conserving firms in Western Europe and Japan.

Ecofeminist concern about protecting the global commons has not been limited to global warming. Ecofeminists have joined efforts to oppose tropical deforestation, the construction of large dams, the depredation of wild fish and aquatic mammal populations, and efforts to replace wild fisheries with energy-intensive farmed fisheries. They have opposed efforts by transnational firms to privatize water supplies in poor countries and efforts to privatize and patent genetic resources stolen from the world's genetic commons. They have joined growing and widespread protests against the World Trade Organization, which has promoted corporate efforts to privatize and patent genetic resources and to introduce genetically modified organisms into environments and food systems without assessing their social and environmental impacts. Anti-WTO protests have grown so strong that the WTO has been forced to delay work on its corporate agenda and hold meetings in dictatorships so they can avoid public protests by anti-WTO organizations.

Collectively, these movements, North and South, have led to a new understanding of the relations between people and the environment. As Bina Agarwal has argued, "women's and men's relationship with nature needs to be understood as rooted in their material reality, in their specific forms of interaction with their environment."[40] While women-centered movements work to address the social and environmental problems associated with "development" and "debt," they must also work to address the public and personal problems associated with social and domestic violence, which is the subject of the next chapter.

READING

The three selections on feminism and environmentalism all create holistic understandings of feminist activism, the development of social movements, and the regeneration of the environment. Although these writings explore how women took environmental action in the areas where they lived, all three selections provide a ground-up view of ecofeminist and other environmental actions on the civil commons. And in doing so by studying feminist and environmentalist thought and action, all three writings provide understanding of broader, global transformations. Marilou Awiakta's important writing on women, culture, and corn blended together feminist and scientific analysis of genetic and cultural diversity.[41] Farida Akhter explored how women have struggled to maintain genetic and cultural diversity by keeping native seeds in their own hands and by protecting indigenous people's civil commons from transnational expropriators.[42] And Terisa Turner and Leigh Brownhill provided a complex, feminist analysis of diverse struggles on civil commons in Kenya, including movements associated with Nobel Peace Prize winner Wangari Maathai. The writers analyzed different gendered, ethnic-racialized, and classed land occupation and civil commons movements within broader transformations in the world-system. By using historical, feminist, world-systems analysis to study the land occupations and civil commons movements, scholars Turner and Brownhill discovered that these movements promote alternative subsistence relations and reinvent the commons.[43]

NOTES

1. Maria Mies, Veronika Bennholdt-Thomsen, and Claudia Von Werlhof, *Women: The Last Colony* (Atlantic Heights, NJ: Zed, 1988); Maria Mies, *Patriarchy and Accumulation on a World Scale* (London: Zed Books, 1986, 1998).

2. T. O. Greissimer published the first book with this title—*The Population Bomb*—in 1954. Paul Ehrlich's more famous book of this name was published in 1968. It made many of the arguments advanced by Greissimer. See Paul Ehrlich, *The Population Bomb* (New York: Ballantine Books, 1968).

3. Quoted in Bonnie Mass, *Population Target: The Political Economy of Population Control in Latin America* (Toronto, ON: Women's Press, 1976), 63.

4. Ibid., 48, 50, 58.

5. Ehrlich, *The Population Bomb,* 160–161, 166.

6. Janet Momsen, *Gender and Development* (New York: Routledge, 2004), 55.

7. Akosua Adomako Ampofo, "Women's and Gender Studies in English-Speaking Sub-Saharan Africa: A Review of Research in the Social Sciences," *Gender and Society* 18, no. 6 (December 2004): 658–714, 690.

8. Maria Mies, "Sexist and Racist Implications of New Reproductive Technologies," *Alternatives* 12 (1987): 323–342, 339.

9. Sonia Correa, Adrienne Germain, and Rosalind P. Petchesky, "Thinking Beyond ICPD + 10: Where Should Our Movement Be Going?" *Reproductive Health Matters* 13, no. 25 (May 2005): 109.

10. Barbara Crossette, "Why India Is Still Failing to Stop Its Population Surge," *New York Times,* July 8, 1989.

11. Amartya Sen, "Population: Delusion and Reality," *New York Review of Books,* September 22, 1994, 70.

12. James Brooke, "Births in Brazil Are on Decline, Easing Worries," *New York Times,* August 8, 1989.

13. Wendy Harcourt, "Women's Health, Poverty, and Globalization," *Development* 44, no. 1 (2001): 84–90, 86.

14. For a detailed explanation, see Robert K. Schaeffer, *Understanding Globalization: The Social Consequences of Political, Economic, and Environmental Change* (Lanham, MD: Rowman and Littlefield, 1997), 143–182.

15. Bina Agarwal, "The Gender and Environment Debate: Lessons from India," in Lourdes Arizpe, M. Priscilla Stone, and David C. Major, eds., *Population and Environment: Rethinking the Debate* (Boulder, CO: Westview Press, 1994), 108–109.

16. Somini Sengupta, "On Despairing Farms, a Plague of Suicide," *New York Times,* September 19, 2006.

17. Keith Bradsher, "China Sets Goal of Selling Roses to All the World," *New York Times,* September 25, 2006. The expansion of the Chinese cut-flower industry will likely undermine this industry in other countries around the world.

18. Torry D. Dickinson and Robert K. Schaeffer, *Fast Forward: Work, Gender, and Protest in a Changing World* (Lanham, MD: Rowman and Littlefield, 2001), 97–98.

19. Susan George, *The Debt Boomerang: How Third World Debt Harms Us All* (Boulder, CO: Westview Press, 1992), 10–11.

20. John Walton, "Debt, Protest, and the State in Latin America," in Susan Eckstein, ed., *Power and Popular Protest: Latin American Social Movements* (Berkeley: University of California Press, 1989).

21. Catherine Caufield, *Masters of Illusion: The World Bank and the Poverty of Nations* (New York: Henry Holt, 1996); Bruce Rich, *Mortgaging the Earth: The World Bank, Environmental Impoverishment, and the Crisis of Development* (Boston: Beacon Press, 1994).

22. Vanitha Subramaniam, "The Impact of Globalization on Women's Reproductive Health and Rights: A Regional Perspective," *Development* 42, no. 4 (1999): 143–149, 148.

23. Gender Working Group, UN Commission on Science and Technology for Development, *Missing Links: Gender Equity in Science and Technology for Development* (Ottawa, ON: International Development Research Centre, 1995), 13.

24. Terisa E. Turner and Leigh S. Brownhill, "African Jubilee: Mau Mau Resurgence and the Fight for Fertility in Kenya, 1986–2002," special issue, *Canadian Journal of Development Studies* 22 (2001): 1037–1088, 1046.

25. Vandana Shiva, "Trade-Offs: Will the World Summit in Johannesburg Be a Global Party for Corporate Interests?" *Onearth* 24, no. 2 (Summer 2002): 2.

26. Vandana Shiva, "Community Rights, People's Sovereignty, and Treaties to Reclaim the Genetic and Water Commons," *Synthesis/Regeneration* 14 (Fall 2002): 47.

27. Madhu Sarin, "Wasteland Development and the Empowerment of Women: The SARTHII Experience," in Ann Leonard, ed., *Seeds 2: Supporting Women's Work around the World* (New York: Feminist Press, 1995), 110–136.

28. T. D. Dickinson, "Strengthening Women's Studies Through Applied Activism: Theoretical, Classroom, Regional, and Cross-border Strategies for Participating in Change," *Women's Studies International Forum* (Fall 2005). See also Miraflor Cooperative, UCA Miraflor, Nicaragua, www.arakis.es/~barneo.

29. María Pilar García-Guadilla, "Gender, Environment, and Empowerment in Venezuela," in Rae Lesser Blumberg et al., eds., *EnGENDERing Wealth and Well-Being: Empowerment for Global Change* (Boulder, CO: Westview Press, 1995), 213–237, 232–233.

30. Wendy Harcourt and Arturo Escobar, "Practices of Difference: Introducing Women and the Politics of Place," in Wendy Harcourt and Arturo Escobar, *Women and the Politics of Place* (Bloomfield, CT: Kumarian Press, 2005), 16.

31. Keith Bradsher and David Barboza, "Clouds from Chinese Coal Cast a Long Shadow," *New York Times,* June 11, 2006.

32. Carolyn Merchant, *Reinventing Eden: The Fate of Nature in Western Culture* (New York: Routledge, 2004), 246.

33. Mary Mellor, "Gender and the Environment," in Heather Eaton and Lois Ann Lorentzen, eds., *Ecofeminism and Globalization: Exploring Culture, Context, and Religion* (Lanham, MD: Rowman and Littlefield, 2003), 1–2.

34. Noel Sturgeon, *Ecofeminist Natures: Race, Gender, Feminist Theory, and Political Action* (New York: Routledge, 1997), 23.

35. Temma Kaplan, *Crazy for Democracy: Women in Grassroots Movements* (New York: Routledge, 1997).

36. Ibid., 22–23.

37. Gayatri Spivek with Ellen Rooney, "'In a Word': Interview," in Linda Nicholson, ed., *The Second Wave: A Reader in Feminist Theory* (New York: Routledge, 1997), 356–387.

38. Mary Pardo, "Mexican American Women Grassroots Community Activists: 'Mothers of East Los Angeles,'" in Gwyn Kirk and Margo Okazawa-Rey, eds., *Women's Lives: Multicultural Perspectives,* 2nd ed. (Boston: McGraw Hill, 2001), 504–511.

39. Felicity Barringer, "California, Taking Big Gamble, Tries to Curb Greenhouse Gases," *New York Times,* September 15, 2006.

40. Agarwal, "The Gender and Environment Debate," 93.

41. Marilou Awiakta, "How the Corn-Mother Became a Teacher of Wisdom," in Lorraine Anderson and Thomas S. Edwards, eds., *At Home on This Earth: Two Centuries of U.S. Women's Nature Writing* (Hanover: University Press of New Hampshire, 2002), 261–269. For the original version, see Marilou Awiakta, *Selu: Seeking the Corn-Mother's Wisdom* (Golden, CO: Fulcrum, 1994).

42. Farida Akhter, "Seeds in Women's Hands: A Symbol of Food Security and Solidarity," *Development* 44, no. 4 (2001): 52–55.

43. Leigh S. Brownhill and Terisa E. Turner, "Feminism in the Mau Mau Resurgence." *Journal of Asian and African Studies* 39 (1–2): 95–117. Thousand Oaks, CA: Sage, 2004.

HOW THE CORN-MOTHER BECAME A TEACHER OF WISDOM: A STORY IN COUNTERPOINT—TWO MIND-SETS, TWO LANGUAGES

Marilou Awiakta

Corn is often called "the supreme achievement in plant domestication of all time,"[1] and its diversity probably exceeds that of any other cultivated plant. Native peoples of the Americas are responsible for this achievement. But how did they do it? And how did the Corn-Mother become a teacher of wisdom—one who feeds the people in body and in spirit?

Two versions of the story, told from opposite mind-sets and in languages appropriate to them, deepen our understanding. Science describes the grain's development and history, which answers the objective, factual part of the question, How did they do it? Only Native people can interpret the spiritual component of the question—How were they enabled to cultivate corn? The response encompasses the Corn-Mother as a teacher of wisdom. The contemporary historian Antonia Frazer wisely points out that when studying a people whose land is occupied by others, "The memory of the people concerned is an important element . . . an element not always sufficiently regarded." Although science and the people's memory tell different versions, they are complementary and begin from the same point: The precise origin of corn remains a mystery.

I.

Science says that corn *(Zea mays)* originated from "a" wild grass, growing in a warm, wet place in the Western Hemisphere—"probably" in Mexico, "perhaps" as long as seven thousand years ago. Maize was the product of genetic mutation called "catastrophic sexual transmutation" (a term so momentous it makes me chuckle).[2] Studies indicate a spontaneous mutant of inedible teosinte, which would have remained inedible without human intervention. Indigenous peoples took the best seeds of one harvest and planted them for the next. Over time the seeds lost their wild covering and developed a husk. They could no longer drop to the ground and germinate on their own.

Through centuries of keen observation and experiments of trial and error, Indians became expert in cultivating corn. They learned principles of clearing fields, planting seed, companion planting (usually with beans and squash) and field rotation. Through cross-pollination, they created many varieties of corn. Inherent in the grain's genetic diversity was an equally diverse immune system, nature's survival strategy for the adaptation that is so crucial to survival. (Modern hybrids, which are specialized for uniformity, do not have this diverse immune system. In 1978 almost all corn planted in America was of one hybrid type. It was susceptible to a fungus disease that destroyed most of the year's crop.)

The original cultivators carefully maintained the hardiness of the grain. Innumerable varieties of corn seeds and pollens have been found in archeological excavations. Among the oldest findings are fossilized pollen grains in the ruins of the Aztec capital of Tenochitlan, more than two hundred feet beneath Mexico City; maize deposits near the old Inca capital of Cuzco in the Peruvian Andes; and, in the Bat Cave and Tularosa Cave in New Mexico, remains of maize estimated by radio carbon analysis to be forty-five hundred years old. Indeed, corn has been a staff of life for indigenous peoples for so long that science cannot reach back to their first meeting.

However, science does trace what happened afterward. Migrating peoples gradually spread maize over the Western Hemisphere, from 5 degrees north latitude in Canada to 40 degrees south latitude in South America. It grew long ago (as now) in jungles and deserts, in high mountains and on plains below sea level. Ears varied in size (as they still do) from smaller than a human thumb to two feet long. Colors have continued to range from white or yellow to maroon, blue or black. Although most contemporary Americans think of the "calico" or multicolored variety as "Indian corn," for centuries after European contact, all varieties were known generally as Indian corn or Indian maize (to distinguish it from the cereal grains, which the English generally referred to as "corn"). In terms of the original cultivators, these names are most accurate.

The five main types (not varieties) of corn are:

Dent: Usually white or yellow, it is called "dent" corn because as the seeds dry, a dent forms in them. The Indians of the southeastern states grew dent corn. Today most of the corn used in livestock feed is a dent crossed with a flint variety.

Flint: Extremely hard, like the rock for which it is named, this corn grows well in very cold or very hot climates and was the main crop of Indians in the northeastern states.

Flour: A soft corn that is easy to grind.

Sweet: A tender corn, high in sugar. Indians in many parts of the country have grown different kinds of sweet corn since long ago.

Popcorn: This variety is actually an extreme kind of flint corn. Its small, hard kernels contain no starch and explode when heated. This is the type of corn that was found in the caves of New Mexico. (It is said that it still popped!)

From these five basic types of corn, indigenous peoples of the Americas had developed innumerable varieties by the time traders from other continents began acquiring the grain, probably beginning in the 1100s.

They had also created an elaborate cultural complex, which included methods of cultivation, harvest and utilization. According to science, the early colonists in America took from the Indians not only the corn plant but also its "cultural complex," on which modern American corn growing is founded to a large extent. Corn today has three major uses: feed for livestock, food for humans, and use as a raw material for industry. The annual value of the world corn crop is about $200 billion.

So extraordinary is the power of corn that in recounting its history, even the scholarly and precise *Encyclopedia Britannica* is moved to poetic images, calling corn "the grain that built a hemisphere" and "the bridge" over which Europeans came to the New World. Corn also "traveled" so extensively in the other direction that today "a crop of corn matures somewhere in the world every month of the year."

This is as far as science's story can go. The words "cultural complex" mark its limitation. From the Indian perspective, this cultural complex is permeated with the sacred. Early settlers took the grain only—the physical aspects of its agriculture—and passed that knowledge to their descendants, most of whom still think of corn primarily as an it, an enabler in terms of nutrition and industry. For the story of the origin of the whole corn—the grain and its spiritual meaning—we must turn to descendants of those who lived the story, descendants who by ancient custom still refer to themselves metaphorically as "the People."

II.

How were their ancestors *enabled* to make this supreme achievement in plant domestication? And how did the Corn-Mother become a teacher of wisdom?

The essence of the answer lies in what Paul Encisco says about grinding corn, which applies to its cultivation as well: "What you're handling is very sacred ... and you've got to put yourself in tune with that spirit of what you're doing so it doesn't become a chore to you, but it becomes part of you. You're creating something, you're doing something. And what you must do is master it, so that as you begin and the rhythm begins to flow through you, you just begin with that feeling."

From time immemorial, the People have passed along this sacred mode, this unified way of thinking expressed in the language of connection and relationship—a synthesis of mind/heart/soul. Western thought is based on dichotomies, which separate spirit from matter, thought from feeling, and so on. Inherently, its language is detached, and that detachment has increased in a society now geared to technology and the domination of nature. Some readers may consider the language of relationship "romantic" and balk at the idea that "the supreme achievement in plant domestication of all time" was accomplished by using the sacred mode Enciso describes. But the People say it is true. Their traditions say it is true. And every month, somewhere in the world, a field of corn comes ripe.

Even in a high-tech society most of us have moments when we experience unified thinking. It becomes a magnifying lens—like the water of a deep, clear well-spring. Looking through the water, you see what is on the bottom as if it were within reach. Details are vivid—veins of leaves, color and texture of rock, slight stirrings of earth particles. The water draws your mind/spirit into the mystery of their meaning—in themselves, in their relationship to all of creation and to your own life. You become very still. Perceiving with your whole being, you feel part of all that is—a beautiful feeling.

We "just begin with that feeling" and go back about seven millennia to stand beside the People as they contemplate a certain wild grass. How do they know that among all the other grasses in that warm, wet place, this is the one to choose—the one that has had a "catastrophic sexual transmutation"?

They *think* about it. Thinking in unity of heart/mind/soul is the key to the phenomenon of corn's cultivation (as it will later prove to be the key to corn's role in the great genetic discovery made by a twentieth-century scientist).

The People feel the grass, smell it, taste it—and perceive a gift from the Creator. They begin to work with the gift. Putting themselves "in tune with the spirit of what they are doing," they select the best seeds from one crop of grass and plant them for the next. Remembering that what they "are handling is very sacred," they work patiently and with keen eyes season after season. Even before she makes herself fully known to them, the Corn-Mother ingrains a primary wisdom of the Creator: Abundance lies in the balance of taking and giving back with respect. As the People prove they have learned this lesson, the Corn-Mother gradually arrays her seeds in a sheath of leaves—a husk—and entrusts her life to their care.

In the rustle of her fields, she sings (as she still does) while she grows and ripens. The People sing back, planting with a good mind. The rhythm of her song flows through them as they touch her, breathe her sweet, fecund scent, enjoy the fruits of her labor (and their own). They think of what her ways mean for their lives. They see that the Corn-Mother thrives better in a field than in a single plant, as a person grows stronger among family and kin. They watch the almost invisible pollen drift from the tassels and stick to the corn silks that are part of the small bodies below. When a tube grows from the pollen into the silk, a kernel begins to form and swell with milk. As the plant grows, its long leaf cradles the ear, as a mother's arm cradles her child.

Contemplating this pattern of creation, the People see their own—the harmonic joining of the male and female to create new life. And the ear "walks from the stalk" in perfect balance, carrying within it a strong, singing energy. They celebrate this sacred generative power of the Corn-Mother—and of themselves—in ceremony, ritual and art (which usually also includes the deer, the Corn-Mother's counterpart). They create stories to reveal the mystery of her coming and the wisdom of her teaching, stories that embed the law of respect.

Wherever they go in their migrations or in their journeys along the great trade routes, the People take the whole corn with them—the grain and its spiritual meaning. They find the Corn-Mother "infinite in her variety," willing to adapt to their environment and sustain them according to their need. And she is very, very strong.

Over the centuries, the Corn-Mother *becomes part of them* and they *create something*—not only a food, a love of liberty and a philosophy of living, but also a way of governing their society. They learn to cooperate, balancing the rights of the individual with the common good. In their councils they develop the art of discussion and compromise. The Creator's wisdom of unity in diversity—from the many, one—is evident in the ear of corn, where each kernel remains individual, yet plays its part in the whole.

It takes centuries of thought for the People to apply this wisdom, because, like all humans, they are prone to quarrel and fight. ("When have seven Indians ever agreed on anything?") Gradually each tribe creates its own pattern of living in harmony with the creation and with each other. Some tribes extend the pattern to become nations or confederacies. In their relations with neighboring tribes or nations, many of the People learn to temper war from extermination to the reasonable redress of grievances, which involves protection of hunting grounds and food supplies as well as of trade routes, towns and villages. From time to time, there are eras of chaos and destruction, when the People forget the wisdom and have to learn the Creator's lessons over again.

Since they view the whole of creation through their sacred lens, the Corn-Mother is not their only teacher of wisdom. The deer, the buffalo, the caribou, the spider, the eagle, the salmon, water and plants—everything in nature speaks the cooperative laws of the Creator. In July 1992, at the Native American Writers Festival, one speaker said, "Nature teaches us democracy. For example, women, children and elders run the caribou into the trap-nets. We younger men take them down. Then everybody helps prepare the meat—there's plenty for everybody to eat. Nature teaches you democracy. Who can say which people or which jobs are more important?" Because corn is shared by most of the People in the Four Directions—-north, south, east and west—corn silk is a common thread that extends through time to the present. . . .

SELU SINGS FOR SURVIVAL

Wounds and shadows are still deep in America. The use and consume attitude is still strong, and many Americans feel that they are considered expendable by the society, the marketplace, the government. The things that divide us are many—race, religion, gender, sexual preference, education, on and on. But unity in diversity is the Corn-Mother's cardinal survival wisdom. In the grain, genetic diversity is the key to an immune system that enables adaptation and survival. Unity in diversity is also the basic principle of the Constitution, one that we should consider carefully as America becomes ever more culturally diverse. This issue is even more complex than it appears on the surface, because people "sow seeds" (sperms and eggs) wherever they go. From this perspective, the diversity in Americans may equal that of maize itself. If only Ginitsi Selu would speak directly to us on this issue. Maybe she already has. The story of a twentieth-century woman leads me to believe it. Through the work of her biographer, Evelyn Fox Keller, we are able to hear the story from the lips of the one who lived it.

We find her as a young woman, working hard in a cornfield in Ithaca, New York. The century is twenty-five years old, and she is two years younger. Petite, perky, sun-browned, she might be called pleasant looking—until we see the intense gleam in her eyes, the gleam of a "See-er," one who thinks purposefully, with unity of mind/heart/soul. What she is thinking about—and will continue to think about until the end of her days—is *Zea mays*. People say she sees things in corn that no one else can. Remarkable in one so young.

I sense a story, don't you? Maybe she will tell it. Her Celtic father comes from a storytelling tradition. The ancestors of both of her maternal grandparents were on the *Mayflower*. Intriguing to think that their descendant is working in a field of the same kind of corn they took from the beach near Provincetown three hundred years ago. There is a mystic quality in this connection—and in the See-er herself. But she is straightforward, too, and immediately answers our question, "Why can you see in corn what others can't?"

> You must have time to look, to hear what the material says . . . the patience to hear what the material has to say to you, the openness to let it come to you. You need to have a feeling for every individual plant. . . .
>
> No two plants are exactly alike. They're all different, and as a consequence, you have to know that difference. I start with the seedling and I don't want to leave it. I don't feel I really know the story if I don't watch the plant all the way along. So I know every plant in the field. I know them intimately. And I find it a great pleasure to know them.[3]

> Animals can walk around, but plants have to stay still to do the same things, with ingenious mechanisms. . . . Plants are extraordinary. For instance . . . if you pinch a leaf of a plant you set off an electric pulse. You can't touch a plant without setting off an electric pulse. There is no question that plants have all kinds of sensitivities. They do a lot of responding to their environment. They can do almost anything you can think of. But just because they sit there, anybody walking down the road considers them just a plastic area to look at as if they're not really alive.[4]

Obviously, the corn is not an "it" to the See-er. She feels the persona, the life within the grain. As she continues, we realize that she is studying maize as subject, not object. She touches the leaves and ears with great respect, explaining that "every component of the organism is as much of an organism as every other part"—including the gene. All of it is alive, active, responsive. Her eyes twinkle with merriment. All around us the corn "talks in the wind, in the language of movement," in harmony with what the See-er is telling us. Her credo is that nature is lawful. But to get to the laws, reason and experiment will not suffice. She agrees with Einstein that "only intuition, resting on sympathetic understanding, can lead to these laws . . . the daily effort comes not from deliberate intention or program, but straight from the heart.[5]

You and I smile at each other. It seems we've heard this story before. . . . It comes as no surprise when she says, "I have learned so much about the corn plant that when I see things, I can interpret them right away."

"In the beginning the Creator made our Mother Earth, then came Selu, Grandmother Corn." The Medicine Man and the See-er are singing the same song—in counterpoint.

In her early twenties at the time we encounter her, Barbara McClintock has already made her first major discovery in genetic research with maize, the initial step of a journey that will lead to the Nobel Prize in 1983. Perhaps it will also lead one day to a change of thinking in all of us about who we are.

In her first year as a graduate student at Cornell, McClintock was a paid assistant to another cytologist who had been working a long time at the problem of identifying maize chromosomes—of distinguishing the individual members of the sets of chromosomes within each cell. "Well, I discovered a way in which he could do it, and I had it done within two or three days—the whole thing done, clear, sharp, and nice," McClintock says. Her employer was not overjoyed with her success. "I never thought I was taking anything away from him; it didn't even occur to me. It was just exciting. Here we could do it—we could tell one chromosome from another, and so easily! He had just looked at the wrong place, and I looked at another place." Having found the right place to look, McClintock spent the following years doing just that.[6]

Readers of this book will understand that corn genetics is hard work, physically and mentally. The methods of growing the crop are the same ones Selu gave her grandsons. You have to clear a bright sunny place, plant, water, weed and "hoe and hoe and hoe." Mental hoeing is necessary, too, because compared to other plants and insects used in genetic research, corn is slow, slow, slow to grow. But it is sure, for the colors of kernels on a cob of maize are "a beautifully legible, almost diagrammatic expression of genetic traits."[7]

The central dogma of genetics had been—and would remain for many years— that once information gets into the cell it can't get out. When I was taking botany in the 1950s, genetics still was very boxed. If you crossed a purple bean with a white bean, for example, the subsequent colors could be precisely figured out through the principle of dominant and recessive genes. (Presumably, human genetics functioned the same way.) Life could be boxed, labeled, stacked in a very orderly manner. And scientists also anticipated discovering the atom's ultimate "bead." Just as we humans believed everything could be perfectly ordered and controlled, Mother Nature said, "Surprise!" The atom eased off into a thought. And the Corn-Mother gave the first intimation of what is now popularly called jumping genes.

In 1931, when she was twenty-nine years old, Barbara McClintock and her student, Harriet Creighton, published a paper in the *Proceedings of the National Academy of Science.* The paper was called "A Correlation of Cytological and Genetical Crossing-over in *Zea mays."* It demonstrated that the exchange of genetic information that occurs during the production of sex cells is accompanied by an exchange of chromosomal material. This work, which has been referred to as "one of the truly great experiments of modern biology," finally and incontrovertibly secured the chromosomal basis of genetics. In his *Classic Papers in Genetics,* James A. Peters introduces McClintock's work, "This paper has been called a landmark in experimental genetics. It is more than that—it is a cornerstone." Maize could now be used for detailed cytogenetic analysis of a kind that had never previously been possible with any organism.[8]

Continuing her researches, letting her material "guide and tell" her what to do, McClintock developed and conclusively proved that what she called "transposition" takes place in genetic material. That genes, in short, "jump." And genetic changes are *under the control of the organism itself.*

McClintock used a new kind of integrated language to present her theories. It was not the almost mathematical vocabulary scientists were used to hearing. Many stonewalled her. There were years when she couldn't communicate with the scientific community as a whole, years of lonely, solitary—and brilliant—work.

It is another of the mysterious circles that just as *Rising Fawn* was published in October 1983, and I was setting out with my deerskin pouches of corn seed, my mother sent a clipping that Barbara McClintock had won the Nobel Prize in Medicine. I had never heard of her. Mother wrote a note on the clipping, "Thought you'd be interested. Might come in handy one day."

Blessings on Mother!

McClintock said that Evelyn Witkin, a young geneticist who came to assist her at Cold Spring Harbor, New York, in 1944, was the "only one who had any understanding of what I was doing." Witkin said that what McClintock was finding was "completely unrelated to anything we knew. It was like looking into the twenty-first century."[9]

McClintock's discovery may well make as big a change in the Western mind as Einstein's theory of relativity has done. Through the atom we have learned that everything in the universe is connected, not just philosophically but concretely through energy. Now, through blood and markers in the chromosomes, we may come to see that we humans are truly sisters and brothers—one family in fact, as well as philosophy. All the boxes and labels society forces people into explode in a vision of a great, shining web of peace and creativity. The Corn-Mother engenders dreams.

Barbara McClintock says that science often misses understanding the whole picture because it focuses on an isolated part. She emphasizes over and over that one must have "a feeling for the organism." In fact, that is the title of Evelyn Fox Keller's biography of her. *Organism* is the name McClintock gives to the living, responsive sum and parts of *Zea mays,* the organism that in her own words "guided and directed her work, that spoke to her." It is interesting to think what name she would have given *Zea mays* if her ancestors at Plymouth had accepted the Indian's gift of whole corn: the grain and its story, its spiritual meaning. The important thing is that this great See-er communed with the mystery that is Ginitsi Selu. She made her first discovery on the ancestral lands of the Iroquois and continued her inquiry in the vicinity of where the Flemish missionaries centuries ago encountered a smell so sweet "that we stood still, because we did not know what we were meeting." What their hearts did tell them is that they were encountering a Presence. And if they had looked closely at the cornfield's edge, they might have seen a stag standing regal and staunch—maybe gleaming white—Awi Usdi himself.

As so many Americans do who have not been educated in Native American thought, Barbara McClintock connected her unified way of thinking only with the East (Tibet and China). In this aspect, her example underscores the importance of including indigenous history and culture in our national educational system. But McClintock's great work—her interpretation of what her "material told" her—and her integrated language have created a path for understanding among Americans of all races and have provided ways for us to make connections as human beings.

The Corn-Mother has been talking to us for a long time.

NOTES

1. Frank Waters, *The Book of the Hopi* (New York: Penguin Books, 1982), p. 134.

2. Arturo Warman, "Maize as Organizing Principle," in *Northeast Indian Quarterly* (now *Akwe:kon*): "Cultural Encounter II: Indian Corn of the Americas—A Gift to the World" (Ithaca, N.Y.: American Indian Studies at Cornell University, 1989), p. 21.

3. Evelyn Fox Keller, A *Feeling for the Organism: The Life and Work of Barbara McClintock* (New York: W. H. Freeman, 1983), p. 198.

4. Ibid., p. 199.

5. Ibid., p. 201.

6. Ibid., p. 40.

7. Ibid., p. 3.
8. Ibid., pp. 3, 4.
9. Ibid., p. 137.

SEEDS IN WOMEN'S HANDS: A SYMBOL OF FOOD SECURITY AND SOLIDARITY

Farida Akhter

FOOD SECURITY: NORTH AND SOUTH

Jahanara, a farmer woman in Pabna, stood up on the podium in front of 25,000 farmers to say, "Sisters, keep seeds in your hands." It was a biodiversity festival of farmers and weavers held in 1996 (UBINIG, 1996a). She was asked to speak on how she ensures food security in her household. The message she had for everyone was to keep seeds in their own hands. This is very symbolic. In the struggle of ensuring food security, women find this the most important strategy. The role that women play in preserving seeds is crucial for the enhancement of genetic resources and biodiversity. In rural households, the general practices of sharing seeds among sisters, neighbours and relatives is already helping enhance biodiversity and genetic resources, and therefore families have a wide variety of foods which are entirely outside the market.

In Bangladesh, women always preserve and conserve seeds. This is perhaps a general phenomenon for all agrarian communities. Despite all the technological interventions and efforts to accelerate a commercial seed sector in Bangladesh, seed preservation continues to be an important activity of rural women. Women keep seeds of cereals, vegetables, fruits, and many other crops.

Another prevalent notion of food security is to ensure local availability of food and the maintenance and accessibility of food sources in and around the immediate environment. It is very important to maintain and enhance biodiversity and "uncultivated" food sources rather than depending on food supply through state distribution systems. The farmers argue that it is not the cultivated food alone; rather, it is the availability and accessibility of the "uncultivated" food which can ensure food security for all, particularly for the poor. The uncultivated foods come from plants, aquatic species, fish, fruits which grow on their own in the common lands, water bodies and as partner crops in the cultivated fields. A majority of the poor survive on the availability of this uncultivated food (UBINIG, 2000).

The policy makers in the North do not understand these notions of food security. To the North, food security comes from the market and the state. Food is also a political weapon. Food security in concrete terms means to continue PL480 programmes of the USA or the Common Agricultural Policy of the European Union. Overall, "food security" is related to the question of war, militarization, profit and control. To the South, food security is an integral part of people's livelihood. It cannot be separated. "Food security" is associated with "famine," ensuring "natural" sources of food in the stressed conditions when agricultural production fails. Only by ensuring biodiversity and ecological richness can food sources from nature be secured.

In the South, we ask, can industrial agriculture, biotechnology and genetic engineering ensure food security? The answer is a clear "No." Why? First of all, it is common sense to understand that companies do not provide food for free. Food is a commodity to sell. For the communities, food is a gift and the locus of ethical relationships and community building processes. Communities can ensure food for their members if they control the production, distribution and exchange of food, not the corporations.

Second, food production is also the main livelihood activity for most of the rural communities. Therefore food security is also related to the livelihood security of the food producing communities. Dislocating this livelihood and making communities dependent on corporations is a disastrous path creating serious consequences. For example. destruction of food sources and dislocation of livelihood forces people to migrate. Women and children often become victims of trafficking for prostitution, organ trade, slave labour and other inhuman sufferings.

SOLIDARITY AMONG WOMEN AT THE WORLD FOOD SUMMIT (WFS)

"Food Security" is a catchword for UN bodies like the UN Food and Agricultural Organization (FAO), the World Food Programme (WFP), the national governments and even the big transnational corporations. The World Food Summit (WFS) held in 1996 intended to achieve "universal food security" by the year 2010, eradicating hunger and malnutrition. The Rome Declaration of the WFS in 1996 proclaimed that it is intolerable that more than 800 million people throughout the world, and particularly in developing countries, do not have enough food to meet their nutritional needs. But plans were made for the needs of only 400 million people to be dealt with by 2015. The Declaration of the WFS was nothing but to silence the critics of the North and South over the proposition of "free trade" and a biotechnology-based Super Green Revolution. Their concern for the hungry was to maintain that hunger will have to be solved by biotechnology and that genetic engineering is the answer to food security (Mazhar, 1998).

During the 1996 WFS in Rome, women from around the world got together to challenge the propositions of the FAO which were basically serving the interest of the transnational corporations. Based on the slogan of "Food Security Must Remain in the Hands of Women," the Women's Day on Food was organized on 15 November 1996 at the NGO Forum (Mies, 1996). In this forum, the concerns of women from North and South were similar. Food security was not seen only as a problem of the South but also a problem of the North. The strategy to solve the world food problem by genetic engineering and biotechnology—and generally by the industrialization of food—was criticized.

The Women's Day on Food was at the same time a celebration of the strength and capacity of women as food producers and food providers and their inventiveness with regard to better systems of food production, conservation and marketing. The day started by bringing fruits and bread into the conference hall, which was already a subversive action in such a mainstream meeting. Food, along with solidarity songs by women, made the day a very successful one, offering reassurance to the women of both North and South (UBINIG, 1996b).

Women in the North are the "consumers" of food produced by the MNCs. They are sufferers of gene-manipulated foods. Food production is no longer in the hands of women:

they are only the customers in the supermarket. "Knowledge" about food is disseminated by companies to the women through advertisements on television. The industrialized food, including many forms of genetically modified food, is thus in the regular menu, prepared very caringly by housewives. Cooking is nothing but the assembly of different pre-processed food items. On the other hand, women in the rural South are engaged in production, preservation and collection of food from cultivated and non-cultivated sources. Without women, agriculture is not complete. Women possess the knowledge about food and nutritional values of different plants, fruits, fish and animals and thereby decide on family consumption. They know medicinal values of food items which become an integral part of the family diet.

The Women's Day on Food was an extraordinary demonstration of solidarity among women of the North and South on the question of food security. Together they challenged the mainstream notions of food security and showed the realities in which women manage food security for their families as well as for their communities.

SHORTCOMINGS OF INTERNATIONAL AID

In 1998 the FAO theme for the World Food Day (celebrating its 53rd anniversary on 16 October) was "Women Feed the World." In the brochure made on the occasion of World Food Day, the FAO firmly acknowledged the fundamental contribution of women to household and national food security and the multiple roles rural women play throughout the entire food chain—from agricultural production to post-harvest processing and marketing as well as nutrition and food safety.

However, the FAO wanted women to have access to credit to expand and improve their farm activities, which included purchase of improved seeds, fertilizers, insecticides and herbicides etc. They maintained that rural women's limited access to financial resources thwarts their efforts to improve or expand their farm activities so as to earn cash income. The improvement in farm production is to be facilitated by improved seeds, pesticides, fertilizers etc. This is very much against the general perception of farm women about their own well-being as well as what is best for their farming activities. Women have been engaged in seed preservation for ages. Improved seeds from the market means taking away control of women over seeds. This is a direct attack on women's sovereignty in their own households.

The other UN agency working on food is the World Food Programme (WFP). which sees women as "vulnerable" and "distressed." WFP Vulnerable Groups Development (VGD) programmes aim to increase the earning power of the most disadvantaged rural women. Under this programme, wheat is provided as a grant "to give food insecure women a temporary break from the struggle to find food, and allow them to participate in NGO activities and attend courses which focus on market-based income generating activities and functional education (health, nutrition, literacy, numeracy etc.)" (WFP, 1997).

The experiences of the use of wheat by the WFP through the VGD programme have not been good. It has addressed the needs of the so-called distressed women in a disgraceful way. The distressed women are those who are widows, abandoned, divorced etc. The VGD wheat has been used by local elites for political reasons to get votes from the poor during elections. The coercive and target oriented population control programme relies on VGD wheat to get the young widows, divorced and abandoned women to be sterilized to fulfil the targets. The wheat is used for road construction under Food-for-

Work programmes. The additional amount of wheat is also used for getting poor people to work for re-construction projects on roads and culverts damaged by the flood. These roads are used to take the food from the villages to the cities, making the village people more food insecure.

Excessive dependence on food aid discourages production. The ability to pay for food is given more importance than production at the household level. The WFP is suggesting income-generating activities for the poor to be able to purchase food. Poverty, according to the multilateral development agencies, is the lack of purchasing power. Women are seen more as consumers of food rather than producers. In the rural areas, when poor women are given any support it is also for high-yield varieties and hybrid varieties of crops. and poultry. In all these cases, women's control over their production is losing out.

WOMEN WANT TO HAVE CONTROL OVER FOOD PRODUCTION

To move away from these distorted notions of "food security," women want to have control of food production, and that is done through control of seeds in women's hands. The battle of farmers for sustainable production of food is a continuing one. This battle is with companies trying to monopolize food production with unsustainable methods. The global trade in food is taking over the subsistence farmers and threatening their existence. We strongly believe that food security can only be ensured if it is in the hands of farmers.

The question of food security is intimately linked with the issue of biodiversity and enhancement of genetic resources. In agrarian cultures it is the women who conserve, preserve and germinate seeds. It is a highly detailed knowledge transmitted from mother to daughter, from sister to sister, from mother-in-law to daughter-in-law, or from a village sister to others.

The peasant women are engaged in keeping and preserving the seeds. Once modern agriculture was introduced, women faced the threat of losing the seeds. Farmers were asked to buy seeds from the market. Women became "powerless" in this process as they were "gradually being thrown out of their work in seed preservation. Women also observed that when the men bought the so-called improved seeds sold in packets, they also bought pesticides. The use of company seeds is associated with the use of chemicals, particularly pesticides. The pesticide companies are selling the seeds. Novartis, ACI, Monsanto are all pesticide and herbicide producing companies. When they sell seeds, it is bound to be poisonous.

Farmers are fighting against this and have come forward with a movement called Nayakrishi Andolon (NK, 1999). NK has primarily focused on seed preservation, conservation, sharing and exchange among the farmers. Hundreds of local varieties of rice, vegetables, fruit and timber crops, etc. have been reintroduced. Farmers are happily sharing and exchanging seeds among themselves and increasing the genetic resource base of their community.

REFERENCES

Mies, M. (1996) "The Women's Day on Food: Rome. 15 November 1996." Memo.
Nayakrishi Andolon (NK) (1999) *A Movement of Farmers for a Happy Life*. Dhaka: UBINIG.

UBINIG (1996a) "Report on Biodiversity Festival, 1996." Unpublished.

UBINIG (1996b) *The Women's Day on Food, World Food Summit, 13–17 November, 1996 Rome, Italy.* Dhaka: Narigrantha Prabartana.

UBINIG (2000) *Proceedings of South Asian Workshop on Uncultivated Food and Plants, Organized by Using Agricultural Diversity Research Award & South Asian Network on Food, Ecology & Culture.* Bangladesh: UBINIG.

WFP (1997) *Food Aid Reduces Poverty.* Dhaka: WFP Bangladesh.

FEMINISM IN THE MAU MAU RESURGENCE

Leigh S. Brownhill and Terisa E. Turner

A new series of battles is being fought at the Jubilee of the anti-colonial Mau Mau war in Kenya. In the period from 2000 to 2003, a new social movement has been involved in over 50 land occupations and instances of armed and unarmed defenses of land from enclosure. The struggle for land and freedom now involves the same social forces and some of the same individuals who were engaged in the war that brought Kenya's national independence in 1963.[1] At the fiftieth anniversary of Mau Mau, the "jubilation"[2] participates in the worldwide groundswell which is affirming a life-centered political economy against a profit-centered death economy. The front line protagonists of the new Mau Mau are peasant and landless women. They demand communal land titles; universal, free education and producer control of trade.

The Mau Mau of the 1950s was a composite of social forces including peasants, landless people, squatters, waged laborers, prostitutes, rural and urban women, hawkers, *ahoi* (tenants with customary land rights), those exiled from the Rift Valley, ex–WWII soldiers, and some ex-chiefs (Odhiambo, Atieno, and Lonsdale 2003; Robertson 1997; Rosberg and Nottingham 1966; wa Kinyatti 1986; wa Wanjau 1983). The multi-class features of the 1950s Mau Mau, along with regional distinctions in oaths and organization, indicate that there were, in fact, "many Mau Maus" with many origins and class aspirations. Similarly, there are many new Mau Maus. The new Mau Mau includes peasants, landless people, squatters, touts, *jua kali* (informal sector) artisans, waged laborers, prostitutes, rural and urban women, traders, refugees from the land clearances of the 1990s, students, retrenched workers, street children, hawkers, ex–Mau Mau elders, the unemployed, forest dwellers, pastoralists, revolutionary intellectuals, exiles, prisoners, settlement scheme tenants, professionals, human rights and faith-based activists, and members of nongovernmental organizations. This study focuses especially on the actions of landless women.

We examine resistance to enclosure in Africa using a theoretical framework called "gendered class analysis," which includes seven concepts: commodification, subsistence, globalization from above, globalization from below, fight for fertility, male deal, and gendered class alliance (Turner 1994).

This theory expands the definition of the working class to embrace both the *waged* and the *unwaged*. Capital encloses and commodifies nature, unwaged work, social services, and built space (Turner and Benjamin 1995). Women and other unwaged people rely upon these same "goods" for their daily production and reproduction. In their struggle with capital, the social power of the unwaged is precisely that they possess and stand on the very ground of subsistence which capital seeks to enclose, commodify, and destroy.

The life-centered or "subsistence" political economy is defined by Bennholdt-Thomsen and Mies (1999: 19) as:

> freedom, happiness, self-determination within the limits of necessity—not in some other world but here; furthermore persistence, stamina, willingness to resist, the view from below, a world of plenty. The concept of self-provisioning is, in our opinion, far too limiting because it refers only to the economical dimension. "Subsistence" encompasses concepts like "moral economy," a new way of life in all its dimensions: economy, culture, society, politics, language *etcetera,* dimensions which can no longer be separated from each other.

In the commodified or "death economy" of the "corporate male gang" (McMurtry 2001), profit is central and "life is, so to speak, only a coincidental side-effect. It is typical of the capitalist industrial system that it declares everything that it wants to exploit free of charge to be part of nature, a natural resource. To this belongs the housework of women as well as the work of peasants in the Third World, but also the productivity of all of nature" (Bennholdt-Thomsen and Mies 1999: 20–1).

"Globalization from below" is the process by which the capacities of local "civil commons"[3] are strengthened and linked to their counterparts elsewhere in the world. As corporate "globalization from above" proceeded in the 1990s, popular social forces united to resist. Marx tied the centralization of capital in ever fewer global corporations to the expansion and revolt of the global exploited class, members of which are "disciplined, united, organised by the very mechanism of the process of capitalist production itself" (Marx [1887] 1967: 763).

One way to conceptualize capital's attempt to assert a "new world order" and popular resistance to it is as a "fight for fertility." Fertility is the capacity to reproduce and sustain life in all its forms, principally people, their labor power, and their food. Land and labor, as well as the knowledge, bodies, and time of women, are major sources of fertility. Women therefore have a special stake in exercising control over their own fertility. They contend for control with their own menfolk and with capital, foreign and local. In the fight for control over fertility, capitalists make "male deals" with many men, and in particular kinsmen, who elicit, coerce, supervise, and regulate the exploitation of women's labor. "Male dealers" serve as intermediaries to channel resources and women's paid and unpaid labor into the commodified realm to make profits for capital and minor earnings for themselves. In contrast, some men break with the male deals and join women in gendered class alliances for the defense and elaboration of the subsistence political economy, against the incursion of capitalist commodified relations (Turner 1994: 20–1).

Three moments in the analysis of gendered class struggle are: (1) subsistence: the insurgents' program to foster a life-centered society for the well-being of all; (2) enclosure: the commodifying impacts on communities of neo-colonial development, of corporate globalization through structural adjustment programs, and, in the 2000s, of Empire; and (3) resistance: through a fight for fertility.

The study is presented in three parts. Part one examines precursors to the emergence of a new Mau Mau from the 1940s to the 1990s. Part two analyzes the resurgence of Mau

Mau in the period from 2000 to 2003. Part three addresses counterinsurgency against the new Mau Mau and concludes with a consideration of feminism in the movement.

PART ONE: SUBSISTENCE, ENCLOSURE, AND RESISTANCE: THE 1940s TO THE 1990s

Squatter women in the Rift Valley and small farming women in the reserves extended and defended the subsistence political economy during the 1940s (Brownhill 1994). The British responded with restrictions on the numbers of animals squatters could keep and the number of acres squatters could cultivate on the white settler farms (Throup 1987). In the Central Province reserves, the British demanded that women provide unwaged labor for soil conservation campaigns, which were designed to concentrate African settlement and "free" land for European appropriation (Mackenzie 1990; Mackenzie 1998).

The British were able to enforce the eviction of over 100,000 squatters from the Rift Valley and impose the privatization of clan land in the reserves during the 1950s. What African resistance had prevented the colonists from doing in the 1940s, they did at the point of a gun during the state of emergency from October 1952 to January 1960. They virtually obliterated women's customary entitlements to land by giving European title deeds to their African male "loyalist" allies (Tamarkin 1978). The British strengthened capitalist relations in the reserves while creating a largely female landless population that could provide cheap labor on the new African export-oriented farms and on the white settler plantations.

In the 1960s, the majority of women were landless because they were married to men who possessed no land or because they were widows, single mothers, abandoned wives, unmarried, or orphans. These women became plantation workers or moved to the forests, crown holdings, or cities to squat on public land. Some were able to join together with other women, pool resources, and buy exwhite settler land in the Rift Valley. Tens of thousands of families collectively purchased land in the highlands. By the 1970s, squatter women, "coffee wives,"[4] and Rift Valley collective landowners channeled much of their time and resources into strengthening the subsistence political economy in ways reminiscent of the 1940s. Coffee wives re-established women's work groups to expand their collective well-being. Some 23,000 women's groups raised money to put tin roofs on houses, bring piped water to villages, build schools and clinics, and send children abroad to university. Coffee wives established autonomous trade with urban and Rift Valley women. Squatter women were innovative, planting thousands of gardens in urban areas to feed their families, build trade networks, and sustain life through marketing their produce and prepared foods.

In the 1980s, the World Bank imposed structural adjustment, a new set of enclosures (Palast 2001). KANU politicians grabbed urban public land, and women who had squatted on public space found their gardens destroyed. The markets, kiosks, and residential sites of the landless were increasingly under attack as corrupt politicians sold off public spaces. In response, the landless organized to defend themselves. At the same time, rural coffee wives rejected the failing commodified economy, took back the resources that their husbands sought to direct into coffee, and focused on subsistence production of crops such as bananas, maize, and tomatoes (Brownhill, Kaara, and Turner 1997).

The World Bank policies of privatization, increased export crop production, and "user fees" were weapons against Africans' subsistence alternatives to low waged labor

(Federici 2001). The 1990s featured an intensification of the conflict between privatizers and the landless. In May 1990, Nairobi's Muruoto slum was the site of a pitched battle between landless residents and demolition crews sent to clear the land in preparation for its sale. Old Mau Mau women were crucial to the successful defense. The brutality of the state's armed forces in Muruoto engendered widespread resistance, which erupted on July 7, 1990 in the *Saba Saba* (in Kiswahili, this means "Seven Seven") general strike. Traders, subsistence farmers, and transport workers organized the strike by stopping traffic and closing markets throughout the country for three days. They demanded an end to police brutality, evictions, and slum demolitions. Structural adjustment policies had created conditions within which the dispossessed joined forces to resist the dictatorship and defend subsistence entitlements. The actions of coffee wives and landless urban slum-dwellers threatened debt repayment and the profits of investors in Kenya (Turner, Kaara, and Brownhill 1997). Their spokesmen in the Paris Club of Euro-American governments held up aid to pressure the Moi government to moderate dictatorship by re-introducing multiparty politics in 1991.

In the 1990s, state functionaries were increasingly violent in their attempts to enclose public land and to grab private land from rural subsistence producers and opponents of the dictatorship. By this time a low-intensity land war had emerged that directly pitted subsistence women against "male dealers" in league with government land grabbers. Elderly Mau Mau women were at the forefront of the direct action politics, which broke the land grabbers' single-party hold on the Kenyan state.

At Freedom Corner in February 1992, a hunger strike by mothers of political prisoners provided a platform for a cross section of Kenyans to speak out against the draconian policies of the Moi regime. Many of the mothers had fought in the Mau Mau war. A brutal police attack on the old women and thousands of supporters in March 1992 set the stage for a much wider, more militant coming together of disparate popular forces. One elderly Mau Mau fighter, Ruth Wangari wa Thungu threw off her clothes (in Gikuyu this is termed *"kutura nguo"),* thereby exercising a customary form of women's power to drive off police who were aiming to shoot at the protestors. In the pitched battle she stripped naked and cursed the police and the head of state by exposing her vagina.[5] The power of women over fertility was recalled in the most remote peasant households as major newspapers gave this deep customary curse front page coverage. After the police attack, the women occupied a nearby cathedral to carry on their hunger strike and vigil. The protestors remained there for one year and secured the release of 51 men from jail *(First Woman* 1994; 1997).

The actions of the Freedom Corner women crystallized into a new movement for the defence of the commons. Thousands joined *Mungiki* (in Gikuyu this means "Congress" or "the Multitudes"), *Muungano wa Wanavijiji* (in Kiswahili, "Organization of Villagers") and other organizations to resist rural and urban land clearances.[6] The rest of the 1990s was characterized by the explosion of popular forces who were increasingly bold in their confrontations with police and armed forces. The KANU regime was on the defensive but it continued massive land grabbing and violent enclosures, which it mislabeled as "ethnic clashes." By the end of the 1990s, KANU land-grabs were challenged by militant resistance from Muungano wa Wanavijiji, Mungiki, and a host of autonomous organizations of the dispossessed. Land defenses of the 1990s escalated into outright land occupations in 2000.

The new Mau Mau in Kenya has emerged in four organizational stages. The first period, 1975 to 1984, was characterized by the coalescence and dispersion of underground political organizing (MwaKenya 1987). This was followed by the democracy struggle of 1985 to 1992. By 1992, Mau Mau women elders and their allies had re-established open politics. This created the preconditions for stage three, 1993 to 1999, in which a proliferation of new organizations arose to both challenge corporate globalization and to institute a subsistence life economy. The land occupation movement of stage four, 2000 to 2003, ousted KANU from power, challenged corporate rule, expanded commoning and integrated Kenyan activists more closely into the global movement against capitalism and imperial war.

PART TWO: THE MAU MAU RESURGENCE, 2000 TO 2003

The land occupation movement reversed enclosures; stopped land grabbing; seized and repossessed land; changed the government; re-instituted free, universal primary education; and curtailed export production, which in significant measure, repudiated the debt. Transnational groups within the movement pursued reparations from the British for three types of alleged criminality: death and injury because of army land mines; soldiers' rapes of pastoralist women in the vicinity of Dol Dol between 1963 and 2004 (Walter 2003: 23); and atrocities during the 1950s Mau Mau war (McGhie 2003: 8; Mulama 2003).

As the numbers of activist organizations grew, so too did the range of actions they undertook. Organizations began to relate to one another in what became, by 2000, a multi-centered movement. It extended abroad through a network of refugees, exiles, and immigrants, such as Njoki Njoroge Njehu who headed the international *50 Years is Enough* campaign in Washington D.C. (Osoro 2001). Massive demonstrations against corporate globalization in the Americas, Europe, and worldwide, signaled to social movements in Kenya that they were not alone in their dispossession or in their resistance (Bassey 2002). Kenyans joined demonstrations in Seattle in 1999 against the World Trade Organization, in Genoa in 2001 against the Group of Eight, and in South Africa at the United Nations anti-racism and sustainability conferences in 2001 and 2002. "Land for the landless" was the theme that brought Kenyans together with international activists in these fora.

By 2000, it was apparent that the new Mau Mau was both national and international. This decentralized and global network of organizations pursued a new strategy as of January 2000. It moved from defense to re-appropriation of land. This shift accompanied a sharp increase in hunger and desperation between 2000 and 2003.[7]

Muungano wa Wanavijiji had been important to the shaping of these direct action strategies. In 2000, a diverse array of organizations occupied private land, defended public land from enclosure, and re-appropriated enclosed land in rural and urban areas. A few examples follow from the two years up to the December 2002 election (Turner and Brownhill 2001b: 1064–6). The movement began with pastoralists' successful occupation of private ranches in October 1999, when drought threatened their herds. By February 2000, when the Zimbabwe government initiated occupations of white settler farms, the anti-state Kenyan movement had already erupted (Brown 2000). In April 2000, workers and squatters autonomously organized themselves into the Taveta Welfare Society. They occupied a Greek-owned plantation seized from them by force during the colonial era. The Society's chairperson, Ruth Lelewu, said land theft was "a matter of life and death. Depriving thousands of people of their birth-right is not something to play with … The solution to the matter is for the government to buy the land and settle thousands of Taveta squatters. The community will not allow any other individual to buy the land" (Mutonya

2001). The British high commissioner in Nairobi, Jeffrey James, warned in May 2000 that foreign investors were being scared off by the calls to take over white-owned land (*Daily Nation* 2000).

Tenants of the state-run Mwea irrigated rice settlement scheme asserted control and succeeded in ousting one set of corrupt officials. In May 2000, Marakwet squatters occupied the 14,500-acre Cherangany state agricultural experiment station on learning that it had been grabbed by a senior government official. Ogiek traditional forest dwellers went to court to protect their forest land from enclosure and destruction. Squatters repeatedly attacked ex–Cabinet Minister Nicholas Biwott's farm and burned his crops after he "hived off" 1,000 acres of clan land from the Kaptagat Forest. In the fourth attack, in June 2003, nine people, including two elderly women, were arrested for pulling down a fence moments after it had been erected around the disputed land (*Daily Nation* 2003f).

By the December 2002 general election, the organizations involved in these actions had gained enough strength to remove the corrupt KANU government from power. In the new coalition government were champions of the resurgent Mau Mau, including Wangari Maathai as assistant minister for the environment. She had, since 1977, been organizing with rural women to assert women's customary claim to land through tree planting. Her participation in the 1992 Freedom Corner hunger strike was a lightning rod for the international media. Kiraitu Murungi was a lawyer for the political prisoners freed by the Freedom Corner Mau Mau women. He became minister of justice. The National Rainbow Coalition (NARC) of a dozen political parties won the 2002 election by promising justice; punishment of corruption; and the return of free, universal primary education. Land invasions escalated even more after NARC's leader Mwai Kibaki took office in 2003.

Kibaki's election was a major victory for the many organizations that had for decades challenged KANU and its policies. The landless had high expectations. It was a double victory for women who had fought for the re-institution of free universal primary education. In January 2003, on the first day of the new school year, thousands of mothers and grandmothers accompanied their children to primary schools and demanded that they too be enrolled. Access to schools was won by a gendered class alliance between women who have demanded education for girls since the 1930s and those men who worked to achieve this goal. Second, the school fees imposed by the World Bank were the equivalent of the colonial hut and poll taxes. School fees were women's largest cash expense and the major mechanism forcing them into the commodified market. The demand for free education was analogous to an anti-tax struggle. Women's double repudiation of coffee and school fees was a tremendous victory over the World Bank's subversion of subsistence.

The post-election period was dominated by labor rebellion, land takeovers and opposition to foreign corporate-military intervention. In the mobilization of the multitudes, all exploitations were excoriated. Land take-backs took precedence.

The year 2003 opened with an explicitly feminist uprising against sexual and economic exploitation. On January 20, 10,000 women workers in the Athi River Export Processing Zone destroyed 16 textile factories, raided Kitengela shopping center, looted shops, and battled contingents of anti-riot police. Teargas prevented them from trashing a second shopping center. The women strikers "broke gates and smashed windows at Alltex EPZ, Nodor and Tri Star EPZ to flush out the workers who had not joined the strike and moved from factory to factory in the expansive garments manufacturing zone to ensure all the [24 factories'] operations were paralysed" (Mulaa and Githaiga 2003). The strikers demanded an end to sexual exploitation and harassment, a medical scheme, transport at night, compensation for overwork, remittance of their statutory deductions to the National Social Security Fund and the National Hospital Insurance Fund, sick leave, and no termination for illness (Mulaa and Githaiga 2003).

All sectors experienced labor insurgency in the first six weeks of 2003. Trade union bureaucrats had lost control over waged workers and the press claimed that an incipient revolutionary situation was on hand.[8]

On February 3, 2003 in Thika, a stronghold of Mungiki, 2,000 oil workers staged a sit-in at Bidco, a refinery owned by ex-president Moi and his cabinet minister Nicholas Biwott. The strikers demanded permanent status after working for ten years as casual laborers in the strategic oil industry. They demanded an end to 13-hour shifts at U.S. $2.60 a day with no overtime pay and no medical coverage *(Daily Nation* 2003c).

The land occupation movement of 2003 was different from the preelection movement in two ways. First, the scale of occupations increased dramatically in 2003. While dozens of cases were recorded in the *Daily Nation* in the two years prior to the December 2002 election, in the post-election period there was a virtual "jubilation" of land reappropriations. There were vastly more territories, incidents, and people involved. Second, the new Mau Mau moved from defense to offense. There was a qualitative shift on the part of the movement to outright occupation of new terrain. This shift had two facets. From 2000 to 2002, some resisted eviction by land grabbers while others converted from export to subsistence crops. After 2003, the landless began a massive move to expand onto new ground. Complementing this facet was a deeper transformation. The 2000 to 2002 period involved women and their allies defending subsistence social relations in gardening, transport, marketing, collective work, and collective savings. The 2003 expansion of the movement impelled the parallel expansion of subsistence relations into larger territories, collectivities, and networks.

The quantitative and qualitative expansion of the land occupation movement was made possible by the increased control that workers and traders extended over transport and marketing between 2000 and 2003 *(East African Standard* 2001). The capacity to move produce from farm to market called for an increase in land under subsistence production. Urban and regional demand for low-priced, indigenous foods grew stronger as foreign corporate imports monopolized commodified markets, which were inaccessible to most of the population, especially the half that survived on less than one U.S. dollar a day (Inter-Church Coalition on Africa 2000).

By ousting KANU, militants put sections of the police on hold. Land claimants now moved forward in large numbers with great speed to refashion property relations. Some examples follow. On January 21, 2003, demonstrators invaded and repossessed a state-owned Kenya Agricultural Research Institute (KARI) farm in Kiambu said to have been grabbed by private developers in 1993, only to be foiled by police. Another KARI farm in Kitale was invaded on January 25, when 13 houses were burned and property destroyed on the public land that had been allocated to individuals *(Daily Nation* 2003b). On January 27, 1,700 students from Nakuru's Kenyatta Secondary School destroyed 60 mud-walled rental houses and a church under construction on land belonging to their school (Agutu 2003). On February 7, 300 squatters invaded 322 acres in Kilifi and sub-divided it among themselves. Police drove them away (Oketch and Ringa 2003). A month later, 5,000 squatters returned and occupied some 2,700 acres. A spokesperson said the take-over was autonomous, with "no politician behind it." The squatters denied having leaders. They "had a committee since July 2002 to coordinate the land occupation" (Kithi and Mwandoto 2003).

In February 10,500 traders stormed the Soko-Huru market in Nyeri and reconstructed their stalls on the spot where two people were shot dead in 2002 during a forced eviction: "the traders sub-divided the plots amongst themselves and prepared to start selling their wares" (Ogutu 2003). On the same day, the government repossessed the Kenyatta International Conference Centre (KICC) from KANU and de-privatized the Kenya Cooperative Creameries.

Between January 21 and July 2, 2003, Kenya's *Daily Nation* reported some 30 instances of land occupation and repossession of property from landgrabbers.[9] Occupiers were from many ethnic groups and were concerned with access to many different kinds of land. Seventeen of the 30 cases were organized by school children, parents and teachers, herders, squatters, neighborhood watch committees, traders, community groups, landless farmers, women and men, young and old. The remaining 13 cases involved the government revoking title deeds to irregularly allocated land, buildings, and houses.

The reported cases encompassed more than 50,000 acres of land. In a single action the government reclaimed 300 irregularly allocated plots. The cases have occurred throughout the country, from the coast to the borders with Uganda, Tanzania, Somalia, Ethiopia, and Sudan. By June 2003, the land occupation movement had re-appropriated the following types of property: playgrounds, settlement schemes, forests, stadiums, urban neighborhood land, a cemetery, public farm research centers, public utility plots, markets, private ranches, game reserves, dump grounds, bus terminals, and road reserves. Under re-appropriation were: school grounds, the National Cereals and Produce Board property, hospital compounds, parking areas, fire stations, council clinics, weather stations, loading zones, open air markets, public gardens, social halls, public toilets, housing estates, open spaces, parks, alms houses for the old and the poor, rivers, lakes, the grounds of courthouses, and government houses. The scope of the "liberation" was all-encompassing. It was as if the new Mau Mau was taking back the whole of the society, environment, and polity.

In March 2003, the lands and settlement minister Amos Kimunya announced that all land owners were to be issued with new title deeds. He was reported to have stated that "second-generation title deeds would be introduced to weed out those which were issued fraudulently. The move is aimed at undoing the damage of fake title deeds which have been blamed for double registration of land ... Well-connected people in the former government, assisted by professionals in the ministry, had also used the fake titles to grab public utility land. The current titles in use were misused by the former government to obtain land fraudulently and can no longer be considered sacrosanct" (Muriuki 2003).

In Kenya, multiple competing land tenure systems are in force (Okoth-Ogendo 1989). The land occupation movement justified takeovers with reference to at least three potentially contradictory and overlapping "bundles of land entitlements": British legal, customary, and moral claims (*Africa* 1989; Turner and Brownhill 2001b). A *Daily Nation* editorialist conceded a "fact" that landless Kenyans had long asserted: that the British colonial legal system was an inadequate tool for the resolution of conflict over land:

> What about the helter-skelter which our land ownership system has become? It is extraordinary that, legally, the colonial land tenure situation is what still obtains. The post-independence governments have merely misused an already unjust law to allocate land to suit their narrowest political interests. *Almost all public land and property have been grabbed* by undeserving individuals. The web is widespread and intricate. With a myriad of social, political, economic, legal and even cultural strands, how can it be

undone by an approach as legalistic as the Njonjo team took? [*Daily Nation* 2003g, emphasis added][10]

In July 2003, after six months in power, the new government made the remarkable revelation that "almost all public land and property have been grabbed by undeserving individuals" *(Daily Nation* 2003g). This grabbing of public property was life-threatening to landless women. By 1985, 100,000 people constituted an army of urban gardeners in Nairobi. Two thirds of them were women. Almost all occupied public, open spaces of the city (Freeman 1991: xiii, 82). This autonomous "army" cultivated thousands of gardens which fed families, supplied markets, and contributed to Nairobi's reputation as the "green city in the sun." When politicians and developers grabbed "almost all public land," they evicted the occupants and destroyed their subsistence livelihoods. The Nairobi pattern prevailed nationwide. This explains much of why women initiated and are the majority in the new Mau Mau.

The activism of a resurgent Mau Mau forced the government to disband corrupt land boards and land tribunals which for over 20 years had been instrumental in the misappropriation of land (Otieno 2003). Kibaki set up an official land theft inquiry on June 30, 2003 to ascertain "exactly who has what and where, how he/she acquired it, and whether it can be reclaimed justly" *(Daily Nation* 2003g). This inquiry cannot possibly resolve millions of individual counter-claims especially because it is limited to the British legal system, the very tool used by thieves to steal the commons. Nor is state ownership a solution. The new Mau Mau land occupiers have claimed state land and sought collective titles. Elderly Mau Mau women in Muungano wa Wanavijiji have long fought for specifically communal title deeds for residential and market sites, with equal access and tenure rights for women and men. In 1998, they asserted that any just resolution of the land crisis must take into account the principle that everyone has a right to land *(First Woman* 1998). The Lands Ministry countered the call for collective title deeds with a promise to develop a comprehensive slum land tenure policy *(Daily Nation* 2003e). Will the new policy build on Muungano members' initiatives at collectivity or will it entrench individualized private property relations?[11]

PART THREE: COUNTERINSURGENCY

Corporate globalizers, the imperial U.S. regime, and elements within the Kenyan state responded to the multitudes with counterinsurgency. A good cop/bad cop routine was played out in Kenya through the velvet glove of "poverty alleviation reforms" and the mailed fist of "anti-terrorist" repression. Factions of the coalition government and civil service in conjunction with corporate rulers scrambled to throw some palliative reforms at the insurgents and to co-opt the compliant.[12] In the meantime, they attempted to retool the relations of global commodification.

Forty years of KANU rule had come to an end, but many "homeguard-loyalists" were still in office. They and their class allies continued to own huge farms, plantations, ranches, and city properties. Class factionalism appeared early in the coalition government as male dealers worked to protect their ill-gotten wealth. While some members of parliament such as Murungi and Maathai sought social and environmental justice, others courted the World Bank and IMF as had KANU. These others introduced counter-insurgent strategies in the arenas of property rights, agricultural production, mining, and militarism.

As political space opened, elderly Mau Mau veterans called for substantive not symbolic recognition and justice. A faction in the government claimed that the demands of the Mau Mau had been met. Presidential aid Dzoro announced that no land will go to the 1950s freedom fighters *(Daily Nation* 2003d). Within three months of taking office, members of parliament and police warned the landless to halt the invasions and allow the government to repossess public land.

Kibaki reinstated subsidies and price supports for export agriculture. Export crops had been destroyed by many farmers and especially by women. The agriculture ministry's official emphasis on reviving exports was part of a reinstatement of the male deal in agriculture (Ronald 2003). The refusal by coffee wives to grow the crop was met by a new effort to re-impose commodified agricultural relations.

Despite opposition, Kibaki approved "foreign aid," titanium exploitation, and oil exploration (Makokha 2003). On February 15, 2003, Kenyans took part in the 50 million strong global demonstrations against the U.S. war on Iraq (Museka 2003). In mid 2003, the *Daily Nation* reported "rising public protests at what is seen as Washington's bullying tactics against Kenya" (Gatheru 2003).

On an international level, in the 2000 to 2003 period, dominant capital shifted its strategy from corporate globalization to imperialism. U.S. oil and military corporations funded a neo-conservative "coup" in Washington D.C. and the Bush regime launched a "world war without end" (White House 2002). Unipolar imperial militarism trumped multi-polar corporate globalization. U.S. military interventions are a response to failure and factionalism within the World Trade Organization and to the growing international coordination of popular struggles against corporate rule (Bichler and Nitzan forthcoming; Klein 2003: 7; Laxer 2003).

U.S. capital responded to challenges to its rule in Kenya with policies that reduce the country to the status of a province in the empire. First, a made-in-the-USA draft anti-terrorism bill, if passed, would allow the United States police full access to information, persons, and physical space in Kenya.[13] American agents could enter Kenya and arrest anyone at any time for actions as innocuous as using the Internet.[14] The anti-terrorism bill is an attempt to close the openings for direct action and was hotly contested.[15] Second, the U.S. government unsuccessfully pressured its Kenyan counterpart to pledge never to seek prosecution of United States military personnel before the International Criminal Court. Third, the United States announced plans to build at least seven military bases in Africa, including a "forward base" in Kenya.[16] In June 2003, one opponent commented in the *Nation* that "as the official corporate voice, the US government will try to twist our Cabinet's arm by tying the military pressure to 'aid' resumption by the IMF and the World Bank" (Ochieng 2003). U.S. militarization and a version of the U.S. Patriot Act are direct threats to the implementation of collective land entitlements. A central objective of imperial repression is to undermine and break up the world move towards commoning.

CONCLUSION: FEMINISM IN THE MAU MAU RESURGENCE

Each of the cycles of struggle in Kenya between 1940 and 2003 contain three approximately decade-long phases: (1) subsistence; (2) enclosure; and (3) resistance. The initial cycle examined here extended from the 1940s to the 1960s. First, in the 1940s women elaborated their subsistence activities and relations. Second, when the 1950s Mau Mau war is considered from the point of view of women's land rights, it can be seen as a period of enclosure (Kershaw 1997: 335). Third, during the 1960s women began a period of resistance expressed in at least three modes. Landless women squatted on all kinds of public land; those landless women who could, joined women's groups or "buying companies" to purchase farms; and, finally, coffee wives channeled resources into the community and the domestic economy.

By the 1970s, a subsequent cycle of struggle had begun, first with women's elaboration of an integrated subsistence political economy. Markets and transport systems united them and forged a closer union with pastoralists still established on the commons. Second, in the 1980s, with structural adjustment, the landless lost access to public space that was enclosed by corrupt politicians. Coffee wives found their food crops sacrificed by husbands who wanted to increase cash crop production. Third, in the 1990s, landless women's resistance erupted in the Muruoto, Saba Saba, and Freedom Corner insurgencies and continued in a multiplying array of community organizations and political associations.

In 2000, the multitudes moved to occupy land and defend public space from land grabbers. This third cycle began with their assertion of subsistence over the death economy of commodification.

In 2003, the Kenyan land occupation movement was nascent, especially compared to, for example, the landless workers' movement in Brazil (Veltmeyer and Petras 2002: 86–7). Thousands of organizations involving millions of Kenyans demonstrated their intention to re-establish a producer-controlled life-centered society. They wanted an end to the corporate theft of Kenya's fertile farmland. They did not want to be exploited on plantations or in factories. They wanted their own land for their own production. Their direct actions to take land constituted a radical step that went far beyond declarations and demonstrations with demands written on banners. Kenyans voted with their feet in a march back onto the land.

The commodification of Kenya's economy led to impoverishment, starvation, and environmental ruin. Millions of Kenyans made it known, through direct action, that their solution was the defense and revitalization of the commons. More commodified production and unfair "free trade" could not solve the crisis caused by those very capitalist relations. This applied equally to land redistribution. A refurbished private land tenure regime could not resolve the inequities caused by the expansion of the private tenure system imposed by the British. Kenyans were not driven to defying death because their subsistence political economy was incapable of sustaining them. They were defiant because the global corporate regime had for more than a century been parasitic upon the subsistence political economy. Solutions to Kenya's social, economic, and environmental crises were prefigured in the direct actions taken by the new, feminist Mau Mau in Nairobi, Dol Dol, and Kilifi. There, respectively, the multitudes made progress in realizing collective title deeds to common land, reparations for rape, and autonomous organization of the commons by villagers.

Feminism can be defined as the recognition that women are exploited and the fight against that exploitation. In this sense, the Mau Mau resurgence is feminist in at least five ways. First, since the 1940s and before, women have fought for control over fertility. The fight for fertility continued in the 2000 to 2003 period in an expanded set of struggles. Women and men in gendered class alliances counterattacked against those who had dispossessed them of almost all means of survival. Women's struggle in the new Mau Mau was a life and death struggle between, on the one hand, starvation, HIV/

AIDS, and illiteracy, and, on the other hand, good nutrition and health, literacy, and community well-being. Second, women neither surrendered in the Mau Mau war nor subsequently (Turner and Brownhill 2001a). Their demand for land has not yet been met (*Africa Watch* 1991; Walsh 2003). They were dispossessed of customary land rights in the 1950s. In the 1980s, their subsistence commoning on family land and in public spaces was curtailed by the new enclosures of structural adjustment. The new Mau Mau has arisen in particular to challenge these second enclosures.

Third, landless women's demands for land for all, education, and autonomous trade were taken up by the movement as a whole. The momentum of the land occupation movement has forced a recognition that any land redistribution must go beyond the narrow legalistic framework of British law. Any fundamental resolution of the struggle for "land and freedom" must take into account the moral and customary claims asserted by the subsistence forces within the new Mau Mau. Fourth, the Mau Mau resurgence actively engaged in repossessing "values" especially produced by women and on which they depend. These include the common life goods of nature, social services, built space, and time itself. Fifth, women resisted rape, beating, and genital mutilation not as individuals but in common, and in alliance with men. This resistance was inextricable from the struggle for land. Maasai women were able to begin the collective prosecution of British soldiers for rape because their communities were strengthened by the transnational organizing that won them compensation for the devastation caused by land mines. Women textile workers went on strike and rioted against sexual exploitation. Their capacity to confront their exploiters was enhanced by land occupations which opened alternatives to waged work.

The "fight for fertility" was earlier defined as a struggle in which women contend with their own menfolk and with foreign and local capital for control over land, labor, knowledge, time, and the use of their bodies. In this fight, capitalists make "male deals" with those men who regulate the exploitation of female labor necessary to realize all other aspects of fertility. The new Mau Mau is feminist in the degree to which these relations of exploitation were negated. Women's strike against cash crop production was the negation most costly to capital and its local allies. This, taken together with the five initiatives listed above, constitutes an immense gain for women in the three-way gendered class struggle to control fertility. The women and men of the Mau Mau resurgence broke the "male deals." Together, in gendered class alliances, they began to re-invent the commons and re-assert their autonomy from capital. This is the feminist content in the resurgence of Mau Mau.

NOTES

1. Padmore (1953: 254) described the Mau Mau war as: "a full-scale military operation—the biggest colonial war in Africa since the Boer war. Over thirty thousand British troops have been assembled to assist the local police force, the Kenya Regiment recruited exclusively from among the European male population, the Kikuyu Home Guards, and the King's African Rifles are in open warfare against what the Africans call the Kenya Land Liberation Army."

2. The biblical concept of jubilee contains six elements: "first, jubilee happened every fifty years. Second it restored land to its original owners. Third, it canceled debt. Fourth, it freed slaves and bond servants. Fifth, it was a year of fallow. Sixth, it was a year of no work" (Linebaugh and Redicker 2000: 290).

3. McMurtry (2001) defines civil commons as any social construct which enables universal access of members of a community to a life good. For a critique of globalization from below, see Laxer (2003).

4. We use the term "coffee wives" elsewhere to refer to all export crop–producing women.

5. Wangari Maathai offered her explanation of the meaning of the women's use of the curse of nakedness: "they were showing disgust and contempt for sons who had the nerve to come and beat their own mothers. In Kikuyu tradition, they were cursing the men, saying, 'I have no respect for you. I wish I had never given birth to you' " (cited in Zwartz 1992). See also Miring'uh and Masai (1992); Turner (1994: 140–1) and Turner et al. (2001) for analyses of West African women's use of this curse to confer "social death" on personnel of foreign oil companies and other "male dealers."

6. For a gendered critique and comparison of Mungiki and Muungano wa Wanavijiji, see Turner and Brownhill (2001). See also CESNUR (2001); Harris (2000); Wamue (2001); and World History Archives (2000). There were many Mau Maus and there are many Mungikis. In a 2001 article, we argued that Mungiki, like the Mau Mau of the 1950s, is a multi-faceted organization in which "divergent views contend." Moreover, we wrote that "Mungiki (Congress) is a multi-class, mass organization that claims 4.5 million members. These are drawn from a cross-section of society, and include dispossessed hawkers as well as members of the Kenyan Parliament and armed forces" (Turner and Brownhill 2001: 1079, 1043). In contrast, in a 2002 article, David Anderson (2002: 531, 534) paints Mungiki with a single stroke. For him it is a "marauding gang" that uses "strident, violent, criminal and increasingly intimidatory tactics." It is important to denounce anti-democratic and repressive politics by any faction. It is only open, democratic and popular politics that can advance the struggle for a life economy. However, Anderson's monolithic treatment silences that force within Mungiki which constitutes women's struggle for land and freedom. This struggle has expanded since the 1950s and has found fertile ground for development as one of the "many Mungikis" as well as in other organizations such as Muungano wa Wanavijiji. Anderson's totalizing judgement against Mungiki calls for repression against those "Mungikis" fighting for democracy and land. His blanket denunciation echoes the colonial propaganda of Ian Henderson (1958) and other counter-insurgency operatives. Their demonization of all Mau Mau as terrorist gangsters was used by the British to legitimize massacre and mass imprisonment of freedom fighters. Currently, the U.S. government's neo-con "war-without-end" is expanding its efforts to target "failed states" within which "terrorism" might emerge. In what approximates pre-emptive legitimization, Anderson's narrow characterization of Mungiki locates Kenya more prominently in the line-up for U.S. military intervention.

7. The economy was in a slump and the European Union banned agricultural imports from Kenya because test results showed that they contained higher than the acceptable quantity of toxic substances and hence violated consumer and labor safety standards (Njeru and Aduda 2003; Tomlinson 2003). Food and cash crop production fell significantly while child labor increased (Kimenyi 2002: 11, 22). Poor performance in tourism in 2000 worsened after the November 2002 attack on an Israeli hotel in Mombasa. When the new government refused to join Bush's "coalition of the willing" in its war on Iraq and pursued "anti-terrorism" with less than the requisite fervor, Britain and the United States announced travel bans in May and June 2003 (Nyagah 2000; Onyango-Obbo 2003).

8. One editorialist observed that the economy was "more and more vulnerable to wildcat stoppages and a climate of chaos and uncertainty in the industrial sector. In this climate of high expectation, the impoverished classes start demanding radical changes…. And, sooner or later, the narrow economic grievances by the protesting workers will transform into broad political demands" (Kisero 2003).

9. In the two-year period from 2000 to 2002, the *Daily Nation* reported some 20 land occupations and defenses. It is estimated that the *Daily Nation* documented, in the first six months of 2003, only from 1 percent to 25 percent of the total number of strikes, uprisings, land defenses, and invasions. There was a sixfold increase in reported cases from approximately one to six per month.

10. The Njonjo Commission on Land Law was set up in November 1999 by the Moi government to address matters related to land: registration, documentation, tenure, and legislation.

"How," the editorialist asked, "could that inquiry be trusted when it was beholden to a Government which had been the primary cause of the problem, one whose other commissions of inquiry have been but a cynical way of avoiding a solution?" *(Daily Nation* 2003g).

11. See Table: "Difference between World Bank corporate 'land reform' and popular redistributive land reform" in Turner and Brownhill (2001b: 1044). See also Rosset (2001).

12. The co-optation of sections of Mungiki began in 2000. Some "leaders" were reaping private profits from Mungiki's control over *matatu* (minibus) routes. Divisions between "leaders" and ordinary members signified the move of some men into male deals with local capitalists. The involvement in 2001 of several Mungiki in the killing of rivals on *matatu* routes and in the slum community of Kariobangi caused a further division in the organization. When, in 2002, Mungiki founders ran for political office on a KANU ticket, many members decamped. Part of the fallout of the co-optation of sections of Mungiki is the growing strength of other organizations to which people turned as an alternative to the discredited Mungiki.

13. The full text of the draft anti-terrorism bill introduced to Kenya's Parliament was reprinted in the *Daily Nation* on July 3, 2003 and is available in the *Nation*'s on-line edition (www.nationaudio.com/News/DailyNation).

14. "The Bill creates a general climate of fear and suspicion in which the State is invested with coercive, intrusive, and intimidating powers. No area of private activity is spared. The Bill makes it criminal, for example, to surf the Internet and collect or transmit by email information that is likely [in the judgement of the United States and Kenyan states] to be useful to a person committing or preparing an act of terrorism" (Mutua 2003).

15. In August 1998 there were attacks on the U.S. embassies in Nairobi and Dar es Salaam. In November 2002 there were two further incidents. One commentator opposed U.S. presence in Kenya on the grounds that it attracted terrorists and subjected Kenyans to U.S. pressure to curtail their civil liberties and national sovereignty (Mutua 2003).

16. As of mid-2003 U.S. military bases were planned for Kenya, Mali, Ghana, Senegal, Tunisia, Morocco, and Algeria (Mugonyi and Kelly 2003; *The Economist* 2003).

REFERENCES

Africa 1989. "Special Issue on Land Tenure in Africa." *Africa* 59(1).

Africa Watch 1991. *Kenya: Taking Liberties.* New York: Africa Watch.

Agutu, Mark 2003. "70 Families Made Homeless." *Daily Nation* (Nairobi), January 28.

Anderson, David M. 2002. "Vigilantes, Violence and the Politics of Public Order in Kenya." *African Affairs* 101: 531–55.

Bassey, Nnimmo 2002. "What Peace in the World Today?" International Day of Peace Solidarity, Kenule Saro-Wiwa Gallery, ERA Headquarters, Benin City, Nigeria, September 21.

Bennholdt-Thompsen, V. and Maria Mies 1999. *The Subsistence Perspective: Beyond the Globalised Economy.* London: Zed Books.

Bichler, Shimshon and Jonathan Nitzan forthcoming. "Dominant Capital and the New Wars." *Journal of World-Systems Research.*

Brown, Donald 2000. "Kenyan Farm Take-Overs Spotlight Plight of Landless Poor." *Pacific News Service,* June 7.

Brownhill, Leigh S. 1994. "Struggle for the Soil: Mau Mau and the British War Against Women 1939–1956." Unpublished MA thesis, Department of Sociology and Anthropology, University of Guelph, Guelph, Ontario, Canada.

Brownhill, Leigh S., Wahu M. Kaara, and Terisa E. Turner 1997. "Gender Relations and Sustainable Agriculture: Rural Women's Resistance to Structural Adjustment in Kenya." *Canadian Woman Studies/Les Cahiers de la Femme* 17(2): 40–4.

CESNUR: Centre for Study of New Religions 2001. "Mungiki Movement (Kenya): 2001 Updates." Available at http://www.cesnur.org/testi/mungiki_001.htm.

Daily Nation 2000. "Invasion Calls Scare Investors, Says Envoy." May 17.
Daily Nation 2003a. "Police Foil Bid to Repossess." January 22.
Daily Nation 2003b. "17 Arrested after Houses Are Burnt on Disputed Farm." January 27.
Daily Nation 2003c. "300 City EPZ Workers Sacked as Row Persists." February 4.
Daily Nation 2003d. "Dzoro Rules out Land for Mau Mau Kin." March 26.
Daily Nation 2003e. "Slum Dwellers Merit Titles." June 14.
Daily Nation 2003f. "Nine Seized in Row over Biwott Farm." June 21.
Daily Nation 2003g. "Yes, Probe Land Allocations." July 2.
East African Standard 2001. "The Battle for Matatu Turf in the City." Special Report, *East African Standard* (Nairobi), November 18.
The Economist 2003. "The Global Menace of Local Strife." *The Economist,* May 22.
Federici, Silvia 2001. "Women, Globalization and the International Women's Movement." *Canadian Journal of Development Studies* XXII: 1025–36.
First Woman 1994. "Interviews with Njeri Kabeberi and Ruth Wangari wa Thungu" (Nairobi), July 16.
First Woman 1997. "Interviews with Wahu Kaara" (Nairobi), April 24.
First Woman 1998. "Interviews with *Muungano wa Wanavijiji:* Caroline Atieno, Livingstone Gichamo, Sabina Wanjiku" (Nairobi), July 25.
Freeman, Donald B. 1991. *A City of Farmers: Informal Urban Agriculture in the Open Spaces of Nairobi, Kenya.* Montreal: McGill-Queen's University Press.
Gatheru, Claire 2003. "Reject US Demands, Leaders Urge Kibaki." *Daily Nation* (Nairobi), June 23.
Harris, Paul 2000. "Mau Mau Returns to Kenya." *Sydney Morning Herald,* January 17.
Henderson, Ian 1958. *The Hunt for Kimathi.* London: H. Hamilton.
Inter-Church Coalition on Africa 2000. "Kenya in 1999: A Human Rights Report, 'Which Way Forward?'" Inter-Church Coalition on Africa, Toronto, March.
Kershaw, Greet 1997. *Mau Mau from Below.* Athens, OH: Ohio University Press.
Kimenyi, Mwangi S. 2002. "Agriculture, Economic Growth and Poverty Reduction." Kenya Institute for Public Policy Research and Analysis (KIPPRA), Occasional Paper No. 3, June.
Kisero, Jaindi 2003. "Unrest Reflects Desire for Change." *Daily Nation* (Nairobi), February 19.
Kithi, Ngumbao and Walker Mwandoto 2003. "Squatter Fury on MPs: Leaders Ejected from Meeting and asked to Free Suspects." *Daily Nation* (Nairobi), March 18.
Klein, Naomi 2003. "After Pulverizing Iraq, the U.S. Is Now Busy Privatizing It." *The Canadian Centre for Policy Alternatives Monitor,* June, p. 7.
Laxer, Gordon 2003. "Radical Transformative Nationalisms Confront the U.S. Empire," *Current Sociology* 51(2): 133–52.
Linebaugh, Peter and Marcus Redicker 2000. *The Many-Headed Hydra: Sailors, Slaves, Commoners, and the Hidden History of the Revolutionary Atlantic.* Boston, MA: Beacon Press.
Mackenzie, A. and D. Fiona 1990. "'Without a Woman There Is No Land': Marriage and Land Rights in Small-holder Agriculture, Kenya." *Resources for Feminist Research* 19(3/4): 68–73.
Mackenzie, A.F.D. 1998. *Land, Ecology and Resistance in Kenya, 1880–1952.* Portsmouth, NH: Heinemann.
Makokha, Kwamchetsi 2003. "Kenya Should Never Discover Oil." *Daily Nation* (Nairobi), March 21.
Marx, Karl [1887]1967. *Capital, Vol I.* New York: International Publishers.
McGhie, John 2003. "Mau Mau War Crime Inquiry." *Guardian Weekly,* May 22, p. 8.
McMurtry, John 2001. "The Life-Ground, the Civil Commons and the Corporate Male Gang." *Canadian Journal of Development Studies* XXII: 819–54.
Miring'uh, Eliud and Martin Masai 1992. "Pastor Denounces Women's Stripping." *East African Standard* (Nairobi), March 5, pp. 1 and 13.
Mugonyi, David and Kevin Kelly 2003. "Mystery of U.S. Base Plea to Kenya." *Daily Nation* (Nairobi), June 17.
Mulaa, Adieri and Peterson Githaiga 2003. "Chaos Rocks EPZ Firms: Textile Companies Forced to Close as Workers Damage Property and Battle Anti-Riot Police in Wave of Strikes." *Daily Nation* (Nairobi), January 21.

Mulama, Joyce 2003. "Former Freedom Fighters to Sue Britain for Compensation." *Inter Press Service News Agency,* September 17.

Muriuki, Muriithi 2003. "All Land Owners to Get New Title Deeds." *Daily Nation* (Nairobi), March 14.

Museka, Lillian 2003. "Anti-War Demonstrators Seek Poverty Alleviation." *Daily Nation* (Nairobi), February 17.

Mutonya, Njuguna 2001. "Row over Criticos Land Sale." *Daily Nation* (Nairobi), June 8.

Mutua, Makau 2003. "Kenyans Must Reject Anti-Terrorism Bill." *Daily Nation* (Nairobi), July 2.

Mwakenya 1987. The Draft Minimum Programme of MwaKenya. Nairobi: Union of Patriots for the Liberation of Kenya.

Njeru, Mugo and David Aduda 2003. "World Bank $5b Aid to Fight Hunger." *Daily Nation* (Nairobi), February 5.

Nyagah, Robert 2000. "Slump in Tourism Blamed on Marketing." *Daily Nation* (Nairobi), April 25.

Ochieng, Philip 2003. "A U.S. Base Would Be Suicidal." *Sunday Nation* (Nairobi), June 22.

Odhiambo, E., A. Atieno, and John Lonsdale, eds. 2003. *Mau Mau and Nationhood: Arms, Authority and Narration.* Oxford: James Currey.

Ogutu, Evelyne 2003. "Traders Storm Disputed Soko-Huru." *Daily Nation* (Nairobi), February 11.

Oketch, Willis and Mathias Ringa 2003. "Squatters Invade Kilifi Farm at Dawn." *Sunday Nation* (Nairobi), February 9.

Okoth-Ogendo, H.W.O. 1989. "Some Issues of Theory in the Study of Tenure Relations in African Agriculture." *Africa* 59(1): 6–17.

Onyango-Obbo, Charles 2003. "'Secrets Behind U.S., U.K. Anti-Terror War in Kenya." *Sunday Nation* (Nairobi), June 22.

Osoro, Jacque 2001. "The Kenyan Anti-Debt Crusade in the U.S." *Sunday Nation* (Nairobi), June 24.

Otieno, Jeff 2003. "Land Boards Will Be Ready in Two Months." *Daily Nation* (Nairobi), July 5.

Padmore, George 1953. *Pan-Africanism or Communism.* London: Dobson.

Palast, Greg 2001. "The Globalizer Who Came in from the Cold: Joe Stiglitz, Today's Winner of the Nobel Prize in Economics." *The Observer* (United Kingdom), October 10.

Robertson, Claire C. 1997. *Trouble Showed the Way: Women, Men, and Trade in the Nairobi Area, 1890–1990.* Bloomington, IN: Indiana University Press.

Ronald, Kefa A. 2003. "Africa Must Say NO to GM Foods." *Daily Nation* (Nairobi), June 17.

Rosberg, Carl and John Nottingham 1996. *The Myth of "Mau Mau": Nationalism in Kenya.* Nairobi: East African Publishing House.

Rosset, Peter 2001. "Tides Shift on Agrarian Reform: New Movements Show the Way." *Third World Resurgence* 129/130 (May/June): 43–8.

Shiva, Vandana 2003. "The Causes and Implications of the Failure of W.T.O. Ministerial in Cancun." Press Statement, Diverse Women for Diversity, 18 September.

Starhawk 2003. "Cancun Update 9/12/03 We Did It!", September 12.

Tamarkin, M. 1978. "The Loyalists in Nakuru During the Mau Mau Revolt." *Asian and African Studies* 12(2): 247–61.

Throup, David W. 1987. *Economic and Social Origins of Mau Mau 1945–1953.* London: James Currey.

Tomlinson, Chris 2003. "Africa Faces Hunger, Why Can't the Continent Feed Itself?" *East African Standard* (Nairobi), February 10–16.

Truglia, Elvira 2003. "Africa Is Not for Sale: The Resistance Continues in Cancun." *Indymedia,* (Mexico), September 13.

Turner, Terisa E. 1994. "Rastafari and the New Society: East African and Caribbean Feminist Roots of a Popular Movement to Reclaim the Earthly Commons." In *Arise Ye Mighty People!*

Gender, Class and Race in Popular Struggles, edited by Terisa E. Turner. Trenton, NJ: Africa World Press.

Turner, Terisa E. and C.S. Benjamin 1995. "Not in Our Nature: The Male Deal and Corporate Solutions to the Debt-Nature Crisis." *Review: Journal of the Fernand Braudel Center* XVIII(2): 209–58.

Turner, Terisa E. and Leigh S. Brownhill 2001a. "'Women Never Surrendered': The Mau Mau and Globalization from Below in Kenya, 1980–2000." In *There Is an Alternative: Subsistence and Worldwide Resistance to Corporate Globalization,* edited by V. Bennholdt-Thomsen, Nicholas Faraclas, and Claudia Von Werlhof. London: Zed Books.

Turner, Terisa E. and Leigh S. Brownhill 2001b. "African Jubilee: Mau Mau Resurgence and the Fight for Fertility in Kenya, 1986–2002." *Canadian Journal of Development Studies* XXII: 1037–88.

Turner, Terisa E., Wahu M. Kaara, and Leigh S. Brownhill 1997. "Social Reconstruction in Rural Africa: A Gendered Class Analysis of Women's Resistance to Cash Crop Production in Kenya." *Canadian Journal of Development Studies* XVIII(2): 213–38.

Turner, Terisa E., Sokari Ekine, Annie Brisbe, Leigh S. Brownhill, Diana Barikor-Wiwa, Emem J. Okon, Ifieniya Festavera Lott, and Annkio Opurum Briggs 2001. "Fightback from the Commons: Petroleum Industry and Environmental Racism." Paper presented at the United Nations World Conference Against Racism, Racial Discrimination, Xenophobia and Related Intolerance, Durban, South Africa, August 31–September 7.

Veltmeyer, Henry and James Petras 2002. "The Social Dynamics of Brazil's Rural Landless Workers' Movement: Ten Hypotheses on Successful Leadership." *The Canadian Review of Sociology and Anthropology* 39(1): 79–96.

Wa Kinyatti, Maina, ed. 1986. *Kimathi's Letters: A Profile of Patriotic Courage.* Nairobi: Heinemann.

Wa Wanjau, Gakaara 1983. *Mau Mau Author in Detention.* Nairobi: Heinemann.

Walsh, Janet 2003. "Double Standards: Women's Property Rights Violations in Kenya." *Human Rights Watch* 15(5A), March.

Walter, Natasha 2003. "Terror at Dol Dol." *Guardian Weekly,* May 29–June 4, p. 23.

Wamue, Grace Nyatugah 2001. "Revisiting Our Indigenous Shrines Through *Mungiki.*" *African Affairs* 100(400): 453–67.

White House 2002. *The National Security Strategy of the United States of America.* September.

Women's Edge Coalition 2003. "WTO Talks Collapse as Poor Nations Unite Against Rich Nations to Resist Unfair Trade Rules." September 15.

World History Archives 2000. *History of the Mungiki Movement of Kenya.* January–December.

Writers Bloc 2003. "Report from Cancun: We Are Winning." *Counterpunch,* September 15.

Zwartz, Hannah 1992. "Mothers Try to Free Political Sons." *The Dominion* (New Zealand), May 23.

8

Feminist Movements for Nonviolence and Peace

INTRODUCTION: FEMINIST MOVEMENTS FOR NONVIOLENCE AND PEACE, 1990 TO THE PRESENT

Men, of course, are responsible for most of the violence in the world. They initiate and wage almost all of the wars; adopt global and domestic policies that contribute to hunger and poverty; commit almost all of the murders, rapes, and violent crimes; and inflict domestic violence on women, wives, and children. In recent years, male violence in many places has increased, particularly against women.[1] We argue that the male violence develops within the intersecting hierarchies of a global class society, where men usually have control over households, neighborhoods, and localities. A number of developments have contributed to rising levels and new outbreaks of male violence around the world, and these developments have forced women-centered movements to confront multiplying forms of male violence.[2]

Although male violence is endemic in capitalism, developments associated with globalization have contributed to rising levels of male violence in different ways. The SAPs imposed by the International Monetary Fund on poor, debtor states and the policies and practices designed to cut commodity prices and labor costs around the world have contributed to growing hunger, poverty, and inequality. Of course, economic distress and hunger are structural forms of violence, which means that the assailants are not obvious but their activities nonetheless injure and cause pain and suffering to their many victims. Even though both women and men are victimized by poverty and hunger, women typically suffer more because in poor households men claim a greater share of food, education, health care, income, and household resources for themselves.[3] In general terms, growing poverty and inequality around the world have contributed to rising levels of social crime and violence. Criminal street gangs and bandit groups have emerged in cities and rural areas, and police have often conceded control of these areas to criminals and abandoned efforts to prosecute them. Poverty has also contributed to rising levels of intimate male violence, particularly where men have lost wage work. So, for example, in the gold-mining districts of South Africa, where the male wage labor force fell by half in the 1990s, rape, domestic violence against women and girls, and divorce all increased.[4] This is an all too common development in impoverished settings.

The economic crises and SAPs associated with contemporary globalization contributed to the collapse of violent, patriarchal dictatorships around the world, which was a good thing.[5] But the changes in capitalism that followed also led to a weakening or outright collapse of state structures in many countries. This often created a security void into which mafias and warlords have rushed. In Eastern Europe and the former Soviet Union, security forces reconfigured themselves into mafia groups and seized control of banks and businesses, smuggling and prostitution, extortion and drug trafficking. In Africa, where indebted and corrupt states collapsed—as they have in Somalia, the Congo, and Liberia—warlords have seized power in cities and substate territories. In Colombia and parts of Latin America, drug cartels, narco-guerrillas, and militias have seized control of many regions, and they have been joined in recent years by street gangs that consist of immigrant youths deported from the United States. At the same time that gangs and white supremacists have organized in the North, some gangs that originated on U.S. streets have essentially been transplanted to cities and towns in El Salvador.

Mafias, warlords, and criminal gangs use violence to establish economic monopolies and extract "protection" or taxes from local residents. They use violence to compete with their rivals. And they use violence to enforce discipline among workers—drug farmers, prostitutes—and prevent residents from becoming informants or testifying against them. Of course, many of the victims of mafia-warlord violence are other men, but women are particularly vulnerable to their predatory activities. And the threat of violence makes it difficult for women to engage in the wage, petty marketing and producing, and subsistence activities they need to survive.

The weakening, collapse, or division of states has contributed to another kind of male violence. In many places, ethnic groups have organized to demand states and battled with other ethnic groups for control of state institutions. The ethnic conflicts that erupted in the former Yugoslavia; in parts of the former Soviet Union, particularly in the Caucusus and Chechnya; in Lebanon and more recently Iraq; and across Africa and South Asia have resulted in widespread and destructive violence.[6] Of course, some of these conflicts in "divided states" can trace their origins to earlier periods.[7] Ethnic conflict in the Kashmir, for example, dates back to the partition of India in 1947, and conflict in Israel and the occupied territories back to 1948. But the violent and brutal *un*civil wars associated with ethnic struggles for power have wreaked havoc on local populations. Women and girls have been affected by the violence in several ways. They have seen their husbands, sons, and fathers killed in the wars, and they have suffered death, injury, and systematic rape by soldiers who regard civilians and women as legitimate targets of war. Of course, the rise of religious-ethnic movements determined to protect, reassert, and project patriarchy has also led to violence and war in Pakistan, Afghanistan, Iran, Iraq, and more recently Lebanon and the Israeli occupied territories. Again, women and civilians have been regarded as legitimate targets of male violence and, in some cases, have been pressed into service as suicide-bomber combatants, which makes women the servants of men who would master them.

The endemic male violence associated with the emergence of these "weird and terrifying warriors"—mafias, militias, warlords, gangs, armies, zealots, and irregulars— has been made more lethal by the global proliferation of small arms.[8] Capitalists and state officials in the United States and other states in the North have sold small arms to governments and individuals around the world. In addition to these massive arms sales, the fall of dictatorships in many countries opened arsenals to public looting and the subsequent sale and dispersal of military arms (many of them not so small) to groups of men around the world. The looting of military arsenals in Albania and Iraq has helped fuel violent insurgencies and made them more lethal. The ubiquitous display of AK-47s and rocket-propelled grenades by men and boys around the world is itself proof of rising levels of male violence. Where men are armed, they kill with greater alacrity and ferocity. And the violence they inflict helps them protect and project patriarchy.

This is a relatively recent development. In most countries, states discourage or prohibit the possession of firearms by men who are not servants of the state. The United States is an exception. The United States has emerged as one of the most violent societies in the world. And it is violent because people have guns, and they believe it is their right to be armed. Here, gun ownership is widespread, and murder rates are consequently higher than in most countries and comparable in real terms to countries where civil wars are waged.[9] And although school shootings and random massacres have become routine in the United States, they are virtually unheard of in most of the world, except in the borderland regions in the Congo. In the United States, most class struggle is expressed in terms of personal and social violence, and not through collective organizing for social change.

In social terms, the violence practiced by weird and terrifying male warriors harms men and women, destroys social institutions, creates conditions for ongoing and irremediable conflict, and makes it difficult for people to engage in the activities they need to survive—it is impossible to farm or work where violence is endemic, so violence condemns many to poverty and hunger. Male violence continues not only because men have banded together in all-male groups and armed themselves to lethal effect but also because violence is supported by patriarchal ideologies that treat violence as legitimate, effective, and purposeful.

IDEOLOGIES OF VIOLENCE

State officials have long argued that they should possess a monopoly on violence, and they have claimed a right to use violence to protect and project their power against enemies, both foreign and domestic. These ideologies have been used to justify war against other countries and against their own citizenry and to justify their use of capital punishment, according to judicial procedures in democracies and by fiat in dictatorships.

These ideologies and practices assume that violence is a legitimate, effective, and purposeful activity. But this is a dubious general assertion, given the fact that state officials have used their prerogatives to justify and defend colonial conquest, territorial expansion, the genocide of indigenous peoples, slavery, and the patriarchal institutions that maintain social inequality. Moreover, state-sponsored violence has had consequences that its defenders have not fully appreciated. When the state deploys and defends violence, it may unintentionally legitimize violence by men who practice it without legal authority. As Dane Archer and Rosemary Gartner discovered in *Violence and Crime in Cross-National Perspective,* men who live in states that engage in war come to see violence as a legitimate and purposeful activity and consequently commit more murders and violent crimes than men who live in peaceful states.[10] Where states have fought and *lost* wars, men murder infrequently. Archer and Gartner thought that men in defeated countries do not see violence as purposeful but as wasteful and ineffective. Likewise, men who live in states that practice capital punishment murder *more* frequently than men who live in states where the death penalty has been abolished. Again, Archer and Gartner argued that men murder more where capital punishment is practiced because they get the message that murder is a purposeful and legitimate activity.

What's different about the late twentieth and early twenty-first centuries is that many men have come to believe that violence is a legitimate and purposeful activity not only for states but also for *non*state actors who practice violence without license. Instead of looking to the practice of Gandhi and Martin Luther King Jr., violent male groups of the disenfranchised draw their inspiration from Mao Zedong, who argued that power comes out of the barrel of a gun, and from Che Guevara and Frantz Fanon. They accept the doctrine that the pursuit of a group's self-determination and state power permits the use of "any means necessary" to achieve their goals. This ideology is indirectly supported by state officials, particularly in the United States, France, the United Kingdom, and, previously, the Soviet Union, who argued that violence was an appropriate way to achieve revolutionary social change. Even when state officials do not condone violent revolution elsewhere, arms-bearing male warriors and seizers of state power rationalize their own violence, including the rape, torture, and abduction of potential laborers along with noncompliant people, by pointing to the example provided by great states.

In recent years, men have deployed violence in different forms to protect and project patriarchy, their own power and authority, in societies and in households. Because women are directly and indirectly the victims of male violence, women-centered movements have emerged to confront the many different expressions of violence around the world.

⊛   ⊛   ⊛

ENGAGING FEMINISTS AND PEACE ACTIVISTS IN COLLECTIVE CHANGE: "THE WOMEN'S ACTION AGENDA FOR A PEACEFUL AND HEALTHY PLANET 2015"

Feminist groups around the world often promote sustainable development that leads to peace and away from violence. Women-centered groups that reclaim the commons and create new relations of collective reproduction find that they need to address the most destructive, male-dominated force of all: war. War assumes many forms, and all warriors represent a real threat to security, especially when they threaten to pillage peaceful, unarmed community centers of reproduction. Sometimes states and conventional militaries engage in war, but increasingly war is perpetuated by irregular forces that fight to claim territories and redraw political boundaries in "uncivil" wars. War and violence are gendered, and this shapes how feminists work for peace, control of reproduction, gender equality, well-being, and security. War reflects the global North's expropriation of global labor, wealth, and resources. Although militarists often claim that war is a means of getting a larger share of the pie, war reflects and reinforces the unequal distribution of wealth and resources. War perpetuates the system's intersecting hierarchies of gender/sexuality/ age, ethnicity/"race," class, and global location, even when regional power shifts may occur. For these reasons, working effectively for peace necessarily requires that feminists engage in nonviolent movements.

PEACE

Violence is incompatible with sustainable development. Increased militarization and military expenditures (more than $800 billion per year), accompanied by rapid growth in the arms trade, have derailed sustainable development, diverting vital human, natural and financial resources away from pressing social needs and polluting land, water, and air. In war and conflict, women particularly experience displacement, widowhood, and loss of livelihoods and community support. Sustainability presupposes human security, and therefore protection of all human rights as well as steps to address the ecological, social, economic and political causes of conflicts, violence and terror.

GLOBALIZATION FOR SUSTAINABILITY

Left unchecked, economic globalization, driven by liberalized market forces, results in growing gaps between rich and poor, increasing poverty, violence and crime, and environmental degradation.... [W]omen bear the impact on multiple levels—juggling more work and household tasks with less income and less access to land. Women's economic inequity is further exacerbated by the failure of international institutions to formulate and evaluate financial and trade policies from a gender perspective, and the failure of governments to address working conditions in the informal sector, and wage inequalities in the formal sector, or to integrate women's unpaid work into national accounting systems.

ACCESS AND CONTROL OF RESOURCES

The earth's biological diversity is threatened ... due to production and consumption patterns driven by market forces. Women's contribution to biodiversity in terms of labour and skills, and their knowledge of how to use and manage natural resources, are most often overlooked.... A major cause of women's impoverishment and social insecurity is lack of equal property and inheritance rights.... Trade related intellectual property rights (TRIPS) ... further undermine women's autonomy and access to and control over vital resources.

ENVIRONMENTAL SECURITY AND HEALTH

Worldwide economic security of rural and urban communities is at risk, and people— especially those living in poverty—are exposed to toxic substances and radiation, lack clean, safe water and sanitation, or live in disaster prone areas. Global climate change contributes to these dangerous situations....

GOVERNANCE FOR SUSTAINABLE DEVELOPMENT

Governance for sustainable development includes, but is not limited to, full and proportional participation of all stakeholders/citizens at all levels of decision-making, accountability of governments to their citizens, transparency, inclusiveness, the rule of law, and equality.... [T]he concentration of global power in the hands of a few, mostly men, exclud[ed] large segments of global society, particularly women, from political and economic decision-making.

Source: Thais Corral. "The Women's Action Agenda for a Healthy and Peaceful Planet." *Development* 45, no. 3 (2002): 28–32, 31–32.

FEMINIST MOVEMENTS AGAINST VIOLENCE

The 1948 UN Declaration of Human Rights, which affirmed the equality and security of all women and men during peacetime and war, provided the grounding for subsequent feminist organizing on human rights. Feminist nonviolence movements gained momentum when women urged the United Nations to organize the Decade for Women (1975–1985) and to hold the First World Conference on Women in Mexico

City. In 1979 the UN General Assembly subsequently passed the Convention on the Elimination of All Forms of Discrimination Against Women (CEDAW), which came to include a number of appendices, including the 1994 Convention Against Sexual Exploitation. About one-third of the UN's members, including the United States, refused to sign this pro-woman, human rights document. In the United States, opposition to CEDAW was led by anti-equity conservatives, and government officials feared that tribunals might charge U.S. agents and soldiers with war crimes. After the fourth World Human Rights Conference, in 1993, delegates signed the breakthrough Vienna Declaration and Program of Action that declared, "Gender-based violence and all forms of sexual exploitation are incompatible with the dignity and worth of the human person, and must be eliminated."[11] At the 1995 Fourth World Conference on Women, in Beijing, national and NGO delegations challenged gender inequality, misogynist violence, violence directed at children, armed conflict, the impoverishment of women, environmental destruction, and the lack of women's health care.[12]

Women recognized that the interpenetration of social and gender violence was a growing concern because sexual torture, rape, and the denial of women's rights were regularly being used by men as weapons of war, genocide, or conquest. Aung San Suu Kyi argued that women and men should work "to liberate their own minds from apathy and fear" and "draw on their own inner resources to defend their inalienable rights as members of the human family."[13] After the Beijing Conference on Women, feminists defined human rights as a key part of gender equality and proposed nonviolent and peaceful alternatives to social violence and war.

THE SOCIAL CONTEXT OF CONTEMPORARY MOVEMENTS FOR PEACE

Feminist groups have worked to initiate projects that challenge interrelated forms of violence. Feminist movements for nonviolence have addressed various dimensions of socially embedded power relations. In recent years, they have advanced a number of nonviolent strategies to create a more peaceful world.

Feminist groups and movements have worked to end violence and establish peaceful ways of living in every sphere of social life. For diverse and accepting groups, feminism has come to mean the creation of peaceful and egalitarian relationships in all global social institutions. Inclusive feminists have worked to eliminate *ideologies* that promote conflict or justify inequality. As they have challenged injustice, feminist groups have worked to create *utopias,* or alternative, inclusive, and peaceful ways of thinking.[14] Sexism has been generated both through the world-system's global institutions and through unequal cultural relations and ideologies. Feminist groups argued that ongoing and systemic patterns of exclusion and inequality are forms of violence. Furthermore, activists should use nonviolent participatory engagement to work for gender inclusiveness as they work for peace. Many of the world's women have resolved to prevent power conflicts by building peaceful social relations, sustainable and ecological cultures, and inclusive ways of thinking.

Many of the women working for peace have bypassed organizing at the nation-state level and have instead focused on linking grassroots and global work. Nancy Fraser has asked whether it is useful for feminists to confine their organizations to single nation-states:

> [There] is a new appreciation of the role of transnational forces in maintaining gender injustice. Faced with global warning, the spread of AIDS, international terrorism, and superpower unilateralism, feminists in this phase believe that women's chances for living good lives depend at least as much on processes that trespass the borders of territorial states as on those contained within them. Under these conditions, important currents of feminism are challenging the state-territorial framing of political claims-making. As they see it, that frame is a major vehicle of injustice, as it partitions political space in ways that block many women from challenging the forces that oppress them ... effectively excluding transnational democratic decision-making on issues of gender justice. Today, accordingly, feminist claims for redistribution and recognition are linked increasingly to struggles to change the frame.[15]

To represent themselves, women have gone beyond seeking a voice in established institutions of the world-system and instead have sought justice by creating new political entities. As part of this, women-centered antiviolence movements have campaigned to rewrite not just international law, as mentioned by Fraser, but also the patterns and practices of grassroots change and the development of local-to-global networks. In this way, as we have suggested, women's movements often have gone above and beneath the radar of nation-states.

Feminists have rejected gendered violence on the global stage. This has widened and deepened connections between various nonviolence and peace movements, cross-fertilizing movements' knowledge-based understandings of violence. For some, this included an understanding of how the global hierarchy and world-systemic forces have contributed to violence. As Andrea Smith has written, "If sexual violence is not simply a tool of patriarchy but also a tool of colonialism and racism, then entire communities of color are the victims of sexual violence."[16] These understandings have enabled women to persuade global antiwar movements to start fighting social and intimate violence.

FEMINIST GROUPS WORK TO END VIOLENCE AND PROMOTE PEACEFUL RELATIONS

Antiviolence feminist movements have worked to end sterilization and forced abortion, domestic violence, virginity checks, female genital mutilation, rape, sexual enslavement, and murder, which occur within the contexts of the state, business, civil society, and the domestic sphere. Gender justice movements have addressed reproductive violence and pre- and postnatal gender selection. They have fought material acquisition and patriarchal movements opposed to female empowerment, which have triggered acid attacks and wife-killing. Women have taken on sexual harassment at work and rape and gendered violence during interrogation. They have resisted control over women's local and transnational movements and fought "honor killing" and adult men's control of wives and children. Women have fought to control their own reproduction and sexuality, and they have fought polygamy and male-dominated sexuality, which allow men to have multiple partners, and men's control over the sexuality of women.[17]

In Mexico, feminists there have joined with movements in Central America and the United States to bring an end to the brutal murders of more than 500 young women in Ciudad Juarez, Mexico, and to attack the global, racialized, and patriarchal causes of the young women's murders.[18] The victims were largely low-income, dark brown–skinned, long-haired Mexican women, many of whom had recently moved from southern Mexico's indigenous areas to work in global sweatshops along the border. This indicates, wrote Rosa Linda Fregoso, that transnational human rights organizing alone will not address the women's "intersectional identities as specific class, race, and gender subjects ... [who are] vulnerable to feminicide and state terrorism," connecting these movements to other disenfranchised people's movements that "eradicate all forms of violence."[19] Investigators found that some of the young women had been identified as prey when they had their pictures taken at the export zone's factories. Men appeared to select other young female victims when the workers took the bus, hailed a taxi after working late, or went to work in the evenings. Feminists and investigators have concluded that a number of very violent, male-dominated groups participated in group murders of young women. These violent, male groups included drug dealers, human traffickers, global sex-trade operators, policemen, other misogynists, and (according to news reports) possibly cross-border human organ dealers who kill to secure organs for high-paying customers in the United States and elsewhere. As Nancy Scheper-Hughes has noted, "The flow of organs follows the modern routes of capital: From South to North, from Third to First World, from poor to rich, from black and brown to white, and from female to male."[20]

The sexually violent murders of these young women have demonstrated how much patriarchal, ethnic, and class hatred has been directed at women of color who come from disenfranchised economic groups. Given the fact that these crimes have gone on since the early 1990s, these acts of hatred, which male policymakers and police have described as "inevitable" and "the fault of women who were out after dark," have essentially been permitted by officials on both sides of the border. Andrea Smith has argued that official ideology condones these murders: "The ideology of Native women's bodies as rapable is evident in the hundreds of missing indigenous women in Mexico and Canada. Since 1993, over 500 women have been murdered in Juarez, Mexico. The majority had been sexually mutilated, raped and tortured, including having their nipples cut off.... Similarly, in Canada, over 500 First Nations women have gone missing or have been murdered in the past 15 years, with little police investigation."[21]

To conceal evidence of physical and sexual violence in the violent Ciudad Juarez murders, the killers often burned women's cut-up bodies in huge bonfires in the desert. Although this misogynist torture, rape, and killing took place in Mexico, North-South inequalities set the stage for these crimes. And the consumerist, exploitative behavior of people in the North, who fail to examine their intimate connections with others, helped to perpetuate this violence.

Many women's movements have formed around the violence directed at young women in global assembly-line areas such as Ciudad Juarez. At the border, there have been many powerful women's groups that have organized across social and intergroup divisions to end violence. For example, according to Rosa Linda Fregoso, Grupo 8 de Marzo formed a nonprofit organization in Ciudad Juarez to maintain a record of the murdered and disappeared women. In 1999 the women's families formed Voces Sin Eco (Voices Without Echo) and placed black crosses on pink backgrounds on telephone poles.[22] And there have been many groups in North and Central America that have formed to end sexual violence, to address the ongoing murders of young women (especially at the border), and to create safe neighborhoods and workplaces. One of the most prominent groups has been Mujeres de Negro (Women in Black). According to ethnographer Melissa Wright, participants in the predominantly middle-class network Mujeres de Negro wear black tunics and pink hats and carry signs that protest the murders. Some of their actions have included blocking traffic at bridges between Mexico and the United States and stepping into state offices as though they were a moving funeral procession. In 2002, the group joined others in the Ni Una Más campaign, walking with other women across the desert from Chihuahua to Ciudad Juárez, protesting male violence against women on March 8, International Women's Day. This march was called Éxodo por la Vida, or Exodus for Life.[23] In the words of a poem that community members read at the Burial on the Border, "women are the protagonists of this grassroots movement" for peace and nonviolence.[24] "The fusion of traditional secular and religious iconography—pink for women, cross for mourning—contravenes against epistemic and real violence.... Crosses speak for women who cannot see, for women who can no longer speak, crosses marking the threshold of existence. In painting the crosses in public spaces, Voces Sin Eco forged a new public identity for women, claiming public space for them as citizens of the nation."[25]

In the coalition's march called Exodus for Life, the color black reminded participants and observers of images such as Argentina's Mothers of the Plaza de Mayo, who sought the return of their disappeared loved ones and protested authoritarian, brutal dictatorship.[26]

As a result of feminist actions and education, rape and gendered violence have been recognized as crimes, violations of human rights, and a way of committing genocide during ethnic conflict and war. For example, by testifying openly about the military squadron's use of rape, torture, and murder in the early 1980s, Guatemalan women and children documented how the state tried to control indigenous people and gain access to their land by using violence against women, children, and men.[27] During the 1998 International Criminal Tribunal for Rwanda, Judge Navaneetham

Pillay of South Africa changed the course of history when she ruled that rape was "an act of genocide when women were assaulted specifically because of their being members of a targeted ethnic group."[28] This judge, a member of Equality Now and the Sisterhood Is Global Institute, defined rape in a way that reflected an understanding of women's experiences. "Rape is a physical invasion of a sexual nature of a person under circumstances that are coercive."[29]

Noting that South Africa and Ecuador are the only countries that "have recognized sexual and reproductive rights in their constitutions," Sumati Nair expressed her appreciation of Carolyn Nordstrom's complex understanding of the connections between the treatment of women in times of "peace" and "war." "Somewhere between the frontlines and the sweatshops in which I have seen children exploited, between the girls raped in war and prostituted in peace, I have lost the clear distinction dividing war and peace. I think this is a positive step, a useful ambiguity. It is a step that leads us into questions of who profits from war, from silence, and from the lives and labour of girls on a global scale."[30]

The South-North and gender divides have also created economic and migration-related disparities that have become expressed in the structure of the global sex industry. In Europe, migrant women from non-European countries now constitute more than 50 percent of sex workers. The growth in international trafficking of migrant labor and enslaved sex workers has meant that 90 percent of sex workers in some parts of Europe have been brought from other areas.[31] The migration of workers from Indonesia, for example, has become feminized. "Migration, trafficking and exploitation intersect ... [bringing about] common experiences of confinement; violence, abuse and assault; poor working conditions and withheld wages; falsified and fake documents; bonded labour and debt bondage, and deception."[32]

Rebecca Surtees's research has shown that "[b]onded practices—loaning or renting out one's labour or that of a family member to pay off a debt or earn income—are common in migration from Indonesia."[33] As women's and men's lives become shaped by international labor traffickers who both respond to and cultivate the demand for low-cost laborers from the South, the separation of workers from their communities of origin places their safety and well-being at greater risk. Women, girls, and other wage working and enslaved workers come to be at the mercy of male-dominated, profit-seeking gangs, guerrilla and conventional military units, and illegal international businesses. To respond to these issues, and to the frequent connections between trafficking and migration, women-led groups have been working to understand these local and global changes and to define and implement effective interventions that will "prevent and redress trafficking and exploitative migration."[34] Prevention has been critical, Yayori Matsui has argued. She has emphasized the important interventionist role that women have played when they have brought girls to protective centers before they were sold or seized for the global sex trade.[35] As The Traffic in Women showed, women's groups in trafficked areas have discovered that participatory action research is an important way that they can work to educate, prevent recruiting, and create alternative economic practices that help people avoid recruiters, migration, sex work, and various kinds of enslavement.[36]

In her book *Sex Trafficking,* Kathryn Farr identified organizations that work to end the trafficking of women and girls. These antitrafficking organizations, which use Web sites to educate sex workers and activists, include Human Rights Watch, Global Survival Network, the International Organization for Migration, the International Labour Organization, Amnesty International's Women's Human Rights Network, the GABRIELA Network in the Philippines and the United States (see their Purple Rose Campaign, which started in 1999),[37] Terre des Hommes (see their Campaign to Stop Child Trafficking), Asia Pacific Center for Justice and Peace in Washington, D.C. (see their Burma Trafficking Project), Coalition Against Trafficking of Women (CATW), Coalition to Abolish Slavery and Trafficking, the Global Alliance Against Traffic in Women in Thailand, the Foundation Against Trafficking in Women (STV) in the Netherlands, and La Strada in Poland, the Czech Republic, Ukraine, and Bulgaria.[38] As she considered the work by these antitrafficking organizations, Farr did not call for a redistribution of global wealth or recognize the multiple benefits of participatory action research by people in areas that face aggressive recruiting and entrapment. Rather, Farr emphasized the central roles that could be played by strong antitrafficking networks and antitrafficking activists, some of them based in the global North. She suggested that people who are outside of trafficked populations can make a major difference by participating in antitrafficking networks:

> The most effective and far-reaching NGOs are networks and alliances themselves, are part of a larger network, or have formed important alliances with other organizations. Networking to deal with a global phenomenon should come as no surprise. Indeed, the very success of the sex trafficking industry has been predicated on its ability to develop and operate through flexible, sometimes overlapping networks.... The work of many of these organizations and alliances also addresses the root causes of sex trafficking. They recognize, for example, that until there is greater economic opportunity and justice for developing and poorer countries, and especially for women from these countries, we cannot hope to truly topple sex trafficking and the sex trade.[39]

In addition to these networking strategies, the authors of *The Traffic in Women* emphasized that local people who are engaged in participatory activism can lead the struggle against sex trafficking, as they help create alternative development.[40]

According to Jyoti Sanghera, it has been critical to examine migration and globalization from the perspective of the worker's country of origin and not from the point of view of the host country. She has argued that the human rights of migrants could be protected and strengthened by working with the Migrant Workers Convention. Rather than treating women's migration primarily as a form of trafficking and victimization, Sanghera has argued that most cross-border migration empowers women and enables them to make a living. But women's right to mobility and self-determination needs to be seen as distinct from women's actual experiences in migration. Those who abuse and commit violent acts against women need to be the focus of activists, rather than efforts to keep women from migrating. Sanghera argued that it is critical to stay engaged with the state, international human rights organizations, employers, and the military. "The transnational migrant is living the global reality," she wrote, "forcing us to revisit current legal responses to cross-border movements" and to recognize that migrants will cross borders illegally until their human rights are acknowledged by the formation of legal ways to cross.[41] Activists who work with women migrants need to deal with transnational social forces and see migration within that context.

In refugee camps, such as the Kakuma camp in northern Kenya, women and girls "live in daily fear of sexual abuse and other forms of violence [and] rape is endemic."[42] Although the United Nations has taken a stand against these abuses, it has been relatively unsuccessful prosecuting with its mobile courts, though some men have been convicted of rape and domestic violence. Local and global women's groups have tried to form protective groups and have worked to educate boys and men. But it has been very difficult to reduce the incidence of rape in refugee camps, as it has been in other parts of the world. In refugee camps, women and their families lack citizenship and security. Violent men and boys, armed with AK-47s, and sometimes violent UN and security personnel have assaulted women and girls. War and refugee camp conditions have sometimes forced women to use prostitution as a way to feed their children. Racialized and gender violence is widespread, as indicated by reports of gangs of men raping and sexually mutilating women and girls. In war and refugee camps, "[t]he abduction and sale of young girls as brides, the forced marriage of widows, and the physical and sexual abuse of women in mixed marriages are commonplace."[43]

According to researchers who have studied refugee camps, intersectional analysis can provide both an understanding of the effects of multiple subjugations and a road map forward. To begin ending violence against women who are in refugee situations, it will be necessary to address both the economic and cultural causes of violence, which grow out of noncitizenship status, ethnic racialization, and national conflict.[44] This development has persuaded some feminists to conclude that part of the answer is to "incorporate the rights of citizens into the rights of refugees everywhere."[45]

The dependence of women on men in households can place women and girls at tremendous risk of sexual violence. Even in places like Eritrea, where discrimination against women was eliminated and women were allowed to choose their marriage partners, more than 40 percent of women believe that female genital mutilation (FGM) should be eliminated, and 95 percent of Eritrean women have undergone FGM. The "partial or total removal of the female genitalia and/or injury to the female genital area or organs for cultural or nontherapeutic reasons" has been taking place in almost two-thirds of African countries and now places two million girls at risk each year.[46] In Egypt, about 85 percent of single teen girls between thirteen and nineteen have gone through female genital mutilation. Men and many women believe that FGM is a religious practice, that men should control and moderate women's sexuality, and that a girl who undergoes FGM is more marriageable. To help end this violent practice, men have joined with women's community education groups to educate men and women and persuade them to end this abusive practice.[47]

In parts of Bangladesh, rapid economic change has resulted in the loss of male jobs in industry and in growing employment for women. Global changes in the structure of the garment industry have led to a feminization of some occupations. Earnings from wages have enabled some women to become more independent, and this has contributed to the growth of female-headed households where women are the primary wage earners. Manufacturing changes also brought more male unemployment, growing economic stress, and a loss of land for many households. Some men have responded to changes in gender relations by attacking women in exceedingly violent ways. For example, there has been a dramatic increase in acid attacks against women by men. Within this shifting context, South Asian women's groups, U.S. organizations, and human rights groups have demanded that the state take action against men who throw sulfuric acid on women's faces. Men throw acid to cause disfiguring injuries and mark women as the victims of male retribution. The government of Bangladesh has built a burn unit to treat patients with acid burns and carried out training on domestic violence, and Bangladeshi women's groups have developed new linkages with antiviolence groups around the world.[48]

Since the United Nations' women's office (UNIFEM) began its global campaign against domestic violence in 1997, more countries have trained professionals to intervene where domestic violence occurs and to prosecute the perpetrators. In the United States, educational campaigns have been used to teach men not to commit violent acts against women and to keep other men from engaging in domestic violence. Some posters have displayed a man who assaulted his wife, another man who thought it was okay for his friend to hit his wife, and then a third man—wearing an anti–domestic violence ribbon—who thought it wasn't okay for men to assault women. In Surinam, almost 70 percent of women have experienced domestic violence, a fact that drove the Caribbean Association for Feminist Research and Action (CAFRA) to team up with women's advocates and the police to introduce intervention and prevention training.[49] Due to programmatic funding barriers and the divide among educators, domestic violence service providers, and law enforcement officials, it has been difficult for many urban programs to join together and provide the full range of services that would help women become safe and self-sufficient. To deal with Costa Rica's hidden domestic violence, activists have framed the grassroots movement as one for community participation and whole health, which has softened men's resistance to intervention by shifting the focus away from brutal men in households.[50]

During military occupation and rebellions, soldiers and interrogators have used sexual assault to control resistant populations. Torture, sexual assault, and the threat of both have been used as a form of social control. Rape also has been a common form of genocide during times of regional ethnic conflict and war.[51]

Sexual violence during war and colonial occupation has been a constant in global society.[52] But gendered violence is intimately tied with ethnic, class, and colonial violence, making the sexual assault of women also an assault and a crime against the entire group.

The inability to separate gender violence from other forms of violence has made it difficult for many groups even to articulate their struggle as one that includes the fight against male domination. For many women-centered movements, the struggle for human rights has become an overarching concept that includes work for gender equality. Mapuche women in Chile have found that it has been difficult to articulate how they integrate these struggles, particularly when they are speaking in Ladino and white contexts. Even when indigenous women are physically present at debates about human rights, their unique positions are frequently marginalized by those who set the terms of discussion. Nonindigenous feminists often attempt to subsume indigenous women's interests within their political views or accuse them of defending sexist cultural practices. And although women have been active in struggles for indigenous rights throughout history, they are often marginalized from leadership positions within indigenous movements.[53] "Mapuche men and some Mapuche women say that gender has no meaning in their cultural context. They refer to precolonial relationships of women's and men's complementary relationships and the community's reverence for the *machi* (or shamans), who often were women. Because the concept of gender is not always seen as useful, Mapuche women often talk about rights, including when they are referring to gender."[54]

The creation of linkages among various antiviolence movements has been part of the intertwining of feminist pathways that are leading to alternative development. Feminist groups have been addressing gendered and other social violence as they have become embedded in movements that are building a better world. According to ecofeminist Vandana Shiva, "ecology movements are a nonviolent intervention in this Third World War [of running for the mirage of unending growth] which threatens the survival of humanity."[55] The dominant development paradigm has led to hunger for one-quarter of the world's people, along with the erosion of land, water, and genetic diversity, argued Vandana Shiva. She agreed with Claude Alveres that the murder of nature has contributed to a "Third World War," which "involves the largest number of deaths and the largest number of soldiers without uniform."[56] Technologies of war have become the basis of production, and growing violence has stressed countries, ecosystems, and people, reaching new levels of ecological breakdown.[57] To stop this war and to establish sustainable and peaceful cultures, feminist women's and men's pathways to change have cultivated ecological, egalitarian, and peaceful ways of relating that will lead to a better world.

ALTERNATIVE DEVELOPMENT BASED ON FEMINIST NONVIOLENCE: PATHS TO GENUINE SECURITY

Okinawa Women Act Against Military Violence (OWAAMV) addresses many intertwined local and global feminist issues. Because this feminist movement develops an intergenerational stand against military violence, sexual violence, environmental degradation, and imperialism, it has caught the imagination of activists in the global North and South. Although the movement places little emphasis on partici-

patory engagement for regenerating the urban and rural commons, it does work to demilitarize land and production. As women have stepped up their struggles against military violence, OWAAMV has become a movement that has lit a fire under many Japanese and Asian movements and has created new connections among women's antiviolence movements across the world. For example, education on the Japanese military's past sexual enslavement of Okinawan women led to a resurgence of support for sexually enslaved women from Korea, the Philippines, the Netherlands, and other countries. They have sought a public apology and compensation from the Japanese state for its military's subjugation of "comfort women" in Japanese-controlled areas during and after World War II. The voices of the older women who were enslaved have become even stronger in recent years because Japanese leaders have tried to deny historical evidence that the government captured girls and women against their will, enslaved them, and organized their daily rape by countless Japanese soldiers throughout the war.

During the postwar period, the movement has also argued that the U.S. military bears responsibility for refusing to expose the Japanese subjugation of sexually enslaved women. Furthermore, the U.S. military and government encouraged similar practices to occur in postwar Japan, minimized U.S. male soldiers' rape of local women and U.S. female soldiers, intentionally built U.S. troops' "rest and recreation" enclaves as sex industry and prostitution centers, and contributed to the development of the global sex industry.

Through its activism, OWAAMV [Okinawa Women Act Against Military Violence] continues to point to the U.S. military's role in creating conditions of insecurity for women, children, and the environment. At the same time, the group recognizes that the military base lands held by the United States must be returned to local government control if alternative paths of development are to be achieved....

For Okinawan women, the opportunity to demonstrate these forms of alternative security [sustainability, connectedness, and true security] is fast approaching [as nine U.S. military posts are being returned to Japan, and a multi-media and resort industries are being planned]....

The alternative security framework put in practice by OWAAMV triggers a critique of such development approaches. It is unclear, for example, whether a "multi-media island" concept will address the key issues of meeting people's basic needs, ensuring that the environment will sustain human and natural life, honoring people's dignity and respect of cultural identities, and ensuring that people and the environment be protected from avoidable harm.... Three considerations in [creating development that will serve the local community] are (1) the cleanup of military toxics; (2) the need for an overall reuse plan that addresses the needs of local people, particularly women and children; and (3) a well-organized and powerful political force to ensure that cleanup and reuse processes are fully funded and implemented....

While OWAAMV has documented the impact of military toxics and begun to develop relationships with U.S.-based activists on issues of military toxics and cleanup, it is clear that more capacity must be developed in Okinawa to engage in activism specifically focused on issues of military toxics and cleanup.

Second, as former military land becomes available for local reuse, OWAAMV is poised to play a powerful leadership role in determining the scope and framework of the local development plan.... OWAAMV has helped develop community-serving projects including a Prefectural Women's Building that provides programs, services, and resources to and about women in Okinawa. Other efforts include a domestic violence and rape hotline and counseling center. Plans are under way to develop a women's shelter modeled after such successful shelters as the Asian Women's Shelter in San Francisco and My Sisters Place in South Korea.... [T]he models developed by women represent possible approaches to develop other community-based projects and the locally controlled institutions that will further these projects. They are tangible, physical and relevant examples of development that reflect the principles of alternative security and provide real critiques of development processes that have little to do with local resources....

Third, the struggle of military base cleanup and reuse requires broad political support that spans Okinawa, Japan and the United States. There are important lessons to be learned from earlier base conversion efforts. In the Philippines, women organized to develop a reuse plan for Subic that recognized the need for reuse activities that addressed the needs of women and children.... Having reviewed the citizen-initiated reuse plan developed for the Subic base in the Philippines and having met with activists involved in the Alameda [California] base closure, OWAAMV is aware of what it will take to organize and develop the political will to support a citizen-based plan. Currently the organizing strategies focus on mobilizing women around issues of women's rights as human rights, not on base conversion and reuse issues. Shifting focus to a base conversion agenda, even with women's issues as a central focus, will require a revisiting of organizing strategies.

Source: Yoko Fukumura and Martha Matsuoka. "Redefining Security: Okinawa Women's Resistance to U.S. Militarism." In Nancy Naples and Manisha Desai, eds. *Women's Activism and Globalization.* New York: Routledge, 2002, 239–263, 257–261.

Movements that have embraced gender equality and democracy have worked at ending all interconnecting forms of gendered, hierarchical, and social violence. Violence has assumed many forms, and male-dominated gender relations have been embedded in this violence. For this reason, feminist peacemaking has taken many forms, and women-centered struggles for a better world have included nonviolent change that will create a peaceful world. At this crucial moment in history, nonviolent feminist pathways to alternative development have begun to create powerful models for new ways of living together peacefully.

READINGS

By examining ways that women's movements have confronted violence, these selections explore complex connections between feminist social change movements. In addition, the writings show how women-centered movements are remaking the world at all levels, providing some closure on the interrelated issues that have been explored.

The first article, by Margaret Stetz, examined women's protests about Japanese military violence against enslaved sex workers during World War II.[58] This movement organized by Korean, Filipina, and other "comfort women" complements women's protests against U.S. military violence in Okinawa. As shown by recent protests organized by former sex slaves of the Japanese military, women work for peace and alternative development in a number of ways: through environmental activism, antiviolence activism and sexual assault service provision, the development of alternative cultures and artistic expressions, and movements directed at the state and corporations.

Next, an ethnographic study by Staudt and Coronado documented human rights work on the Mexico-U.S. border and presented holistic recommendations for promoting human rights and ending violence. This selection shows how feminist organizing against violence is a central part of many transformations, including the creation of alternative development in border areas and the questioning of dominant assumptions that accompanied the nation-state system.[59]

The third selection examined ways that diverse women's groups around the world have worked to end violence and war and to create the conditions for world peace.[60]

The last selection examined how women of color (and others, we add) can dismantle heteropatriarchy—the global system's base—if activists learn how to address heteropatriarchy in relation to the three pillars of white supremacy: the logic of slavery, the logic of genocide, and the logic of Orientalism.[61]

More feminists are learning how to address the global system's hierarchical violence. Some feminists are directly attacking and undermining the sources of violence, and others are initiating new, peaceful relations in spaces that are freer from dominant institutions.

NOTES

1. Maria Riley and Rocío Mejía, "Gender in the Global Trading System," *Development* 40, no. 3 (1997): 30–35, 35.

2. See Peter Linebaugh and Marcus Rediker, *The Many-Headed Hydra: Sailors, Slaves, Commoners, and the Hidden History of the Revolutionary Atlantic* (Boston: Beacon, 2000). Here the many-headed hydra refers to multiple groups of workers who struggle against the rule of capital and tyranny.

3. As the World Bank reported, "It is not uncommon for women and children's nutrition to deteriorate while wrist watches, radios and bicycles are acquired by the adult male household members." Lester Brown, *State of the World 1993* (New York: Norton, 1993), 64.

4. Donald G. McNeil Jr., "Gold Breaks Its Promise to Miners of Lesotho," *New York Times,* June 16, 1998; Rachel L. Swarns, "A Bleak Hour for South African Miners," *New York Times,* October 10, 1999.

5. Robert K. Schaeffer, *Power to the People: Democratization Around the World* (Boulder, CO: Westview Press, 1997).

6. Robert K. Schaeffer, *Understanding Globalization: The Social Consequences of Political, Economic, and Environmental Change,* 2nd ed. (Lanham, MD: Rowman and Littlefield, 2003), esp. chapter 12, "Division and War in Yugoslavia," 311–338; Robert K. Schaeffer, *Understanding Globalization: The Social Consequences of Political, Economic, and Environmental Change,* 3rd ed. (Lanham, MD: Rowman and Littlefield, 2005), 221–320.

7. Robert Schaeffer, *The Politics of Partition* (New York: Hill and Wang, 1990).

8. The term *weird and terrifying warriors* was coined by George Kennan, a state department policymaker during the Cold War. See ibid., 202.

9. Dane Archer and Rosemary Gartner, *Violence and Crime in Cross-National Perspective* (New Haven, CT: Yale University Press, 1984).

10. Dane Archer and Rosemary Gartner, *Violence and Crime in Cross-National Perspective* (New Haven: Yale University Press, 1984).

11. Estelle Freedman, *No Turning Back: The History of Feminism and the Future of Women* (New York: Ballantine, 2002), 288.

12. Michael Penn and Rahel Nardos, *Overcoming Violence Against Women and Girls: The International Campaign to Eradicate a Worldwide Problem* (Lanham, MD: Rowman and Littlefield, 2003), 215–216.

13. Aung San Suu Kyi, "Freedom from Fear," in Marjorie Agosín, ed., *A Map of Hope: Women's Writings on Human Rights—An International Anthology* (New Brunswick, NJ: Rutgers University Press, 1999), 80–84, 82.

14. Karl Mannheim, *Ideology and Utopia: An Introduction to the Sociology of Knowledge* (New York: Harcourt, Brace, 1936).

15. Nancy Fraser, "Mapping the Feminist Imagination: From Redistribution to Recognition to Representation," *Constellations* 12, no. 3 (2005): 295–307, 304.

16. Andrea Smith, *Conquest: Sexual Violence and American Indian Genocide* (Cambridge, MA: South End Press, 2005), 8.

17. Leonore Manderson, "Fighting Violence Against Women," *Development* 44, no. 3 (2001): 6–8.

18. Kathleen Staudt and Irasema Coronado, *Fronteras No Más: Toward Social Justice at the U.S.-Mexico Border* (New York: Palgrave, 2002).

19. Rosa Linda Fregoso, "The Complexities of 'Feminicide' on the Border," in Incite! Women of Color Against Violence, eds., *Color of Violence: The Incite! Anthology* (Cambridge, MA: South End Press, 2006), 134.

20. Nancy Scheper-Hughes, "The Global Traffic in Human Organs," in Mariam Fraser and Monica Greco, eds., *The Body: A Reader* (New York: Routledge, 2005), 208–215, 209. Also see the documentary film *Senorita Extraviada.*

21. Smith, *Conquest,* 30.

22. Fregoso, "The Complexities of 'Feminicide' on the Border," 130, 133.

23. Melissa W. Wright, *Disposable Women and Other Myths of Global Capitalism* (New York: Routledge, 2006), 155, 159–160.

24. Fregoso, "The Complexities of 'Feminicide' on the Border," 133, 288n11.

25. Ibid., 133.

26. Wright, *Disposable Women and Other Myths of Global Capitalism,* 155, 159–160.

27. Marion Ciborski, "Guatemala: 'We Thought It Was Only the Men They Would Kill,'" in Anne Llewellyn Barstow, ed., *War's Dirty Secret: Rape, Prostitution, and Other Crimes Against Women* (Cleveland, OH: Pilgrim Press, 2000), 124–138.

28. Sumati Nair, "Violence Against Women: Initiatives in the 1990s," *Development* 44, no. 3 (2001): 82–84, 82.

29. Ibid., 82.

30. Quoted in ibid., 83. See also Carolyn Nordstrom, "Visible Wars and Invisible Girls: Shadow Industries and the Politics of Not-Knowing," *International Feminist Journal of Politics* 1, no. 1 (June 1999): 2–15.

31. Laura Augustin, "Sex Workers and Violence Against Women: Utopic Visions or Battle of the Sexes?" *Development* 44, no. 3 (2001): 107–110, 108.

32. Rebecca Surtees, "Female Migration and Trafficking in Women: The Indonesian Context," *Development* 46, no. 3 (2003): 99–105, 99, 101.

33. Ibid., 103.

34. Ibid., 104.

35. Yatori Matsui, *Women in the New Asia: From Pain to Power,* trans. Noriko Toyokawa and Carolyn Francis (London: Zed Press, 1999), 17.

36. Siriporn Skrobanek, Nattaya Boonpakdi, and Chutima Janthakeero, "From Research to Action," Skrobanek, Boonpakdi, and Janthakeer, in *The Traffic in Women: Human Realities of the International Sex Trade* (London: Zed, 1997), 80–97.

37. GABRIELA Network (GABnet) is a Philippine-U.S. network of feminists named after Gabriela Silang, a woman who led the longest revolt against the Spanish colonizers. GABRIELA also stands for General Assembly Binding Women for Reform, Integrity, Equality, Leadership, and Action.

38. Kathryn Farr, *Sex Trafficking: The Global Market in Women and Children* (New York: Worth Publishers, 2005), 242–243.

39. Ibid.

40. Skrobanek, Boonpakdi, and Janthakeero, "From Research to Action," 80–97.

41. Jyoti Sanghera, "Unpacking the Trafficking Discourse," in Kamala Kempadoo with Jyoti Sanghera and Bandana Pattanaik, eds., *Trafficking and Prostitution Reconsidered: New Perspectives on Migration, Sex Work, and Human Rights* (Boulder: Paradigm, 2005), 3–24, 35–39.

42. Linda Bartolomei, Eileen Pittaway, and Emma Elizabeth Pittaway, "Who Am I? Identity and Citizenship in Kakuma Refugee Camp in Northern Kenya," *Development* 46, no. 3 (2003): 87–93, 87–88.

43. Ibid., 88.

44. Ibid., 91–92.

45. Ibid., 92.

46. Rachel Odede and Eden Asghedom, "The Continuum of Violence Against Women in Eritrea," *Development* 44, no. 3 (2001): 69–73, 70.

47. Fatma Khafagi, "Breaking Cultural and Social Taboos: The Fight Against FGM in Egypt," *Development* 44, no. 3 (2001): 74–76.

48. Afroza Anwary, "Acid Violence and Medical Care in Bangladesh: Women's Activism as Casework," *Gender and Society* 17, no. 2 (April 2003): 305–313.

49. Carla Bakboord, "Domestic Violence Strategies and Actions in Surinam," *Development* 44, no. 3 (2001): 59–63 and poster on 68.

50. Rita K. Noonan, "Gender and the Politics of Needs: Broadening the Scope of Welfare State Provision in Costa Rica," *Gender and Society* 16, no. 2 (April 2002): 216–239, 237.

51. Elham Bayour, "Occupied Territories, Resisting Women: Palestinian Women Political Prisoners," in Julia Sudbury, ed., *Global Lockdown: Race, Gender, and the Prison-Industrial Complex* (New York: Routledge, 2005), 201–214, 205.

52. For a related writing, also see Suzuyo Takazato, "Report from Okinawa (1997): Long-Term U.S. Military Presence and Violence Against Women," in Gywn Kirk and

Margo Okazawa-Rey, eds., *Women's Lives: Multicultural Perspectives,* 2nd ed. (Boston: McGraw Hill, 2001), 260–263.

53. Patricia Richards, "The Politics of Gender, Human Rights, and Being Indigenous in Chile," *Gender and Society* 19, no. 2 (April 2005): 199–220, 201.

54. Ibid., 200–202.

55. Vandana Shiva, "Ecology Movements in India," *Alternatives* 11 (1986): 255–273, 272.

56. Ibid., 272; C. Alvares, "Deadly Development," *Development Forum* 11, no. 7 (1973): 3–4.

57. Vandana Shiva, "Violence of Globalization," *Canadian Women's Studies* 21, no. 4 (Spring 2002): 15.

58. Margaret D. Stetz, "Representing 'Comfort Women': Activism Through Law and Art," *Iris: A Journal About Women* (Fall 2002): 26.

59. Staudt and Coronado, "Human Rights and Wrongs" and "What, Then, Is to Be Done?" in *Fronteras No Más,* 150–159, 171–173.

60. Shelley Anderson, "Crossing the Lines: Women's Organizations in Conflict Resolutions," *Development,* special issue, *Community and Conflict* 43, no. 3 (2000): 34–39.

61. Andrea Smith, "Heteropatriarchy and the Three Pillars of White Supremacy: Rethinking Women of Color Organizing," in Incite! Women of Color Against Violence, eds., *Color of Violence: The Incite! Anthology* (Cambridge, MA: South End Press, 2006), 66–73.

❁

Representing "Comfort Women": Activism through Law and Art

Margaret D. Stetz

Before and during World War II, some 200,000 Asian women were used by the Japanese government as sexual slaves for the Imperial Army and euphemistically called "comfort women." Since the early 1990s, the struggles of the few aging survivors of this war crime to obtain official apologies and financial reparations have proved a magnet for feminist activism. The title of my essay emphasizes the word *representing,* in order to indicate two of the different spheres in which important new initiatives have been appearing every year on behalf of those who have come forward and identified themselves as former "comfort women." Yet the different spheres are, in the end, connected. Over the past decade, the remaining "comfort women," along with the issues of accountability raised by their situations, have been represented by attorneys and legal scholars in actions brought before courts of law in several nations. At the same time, the survivors' histories have been represented in the worlds of publishing, through growing bodies of nonfiction and fiction, and also in the visual arts—through painting, printmaking, multi-media installations, and film. Some of the latter sort of representations have been produced by the "comfort women" themselves. But many more of them have been generated by the scholars and artists—large numbers of whom also are women—who have come forward to collect their testimonies or to interpret and disseminate their stories and, in doing so, have taken an activist stance.

Both forms of representation—the legal and the artistic—have been essential, not only to advocate on behalf of the survivors' demands for apologies and compensation from the Japanese government, but to assert the reality of the history these women bear and to make that history widely known. For, unlike the experiences of European Holocaust survivors, which have been contested only by small groups of "deniers" whose efforts have been condemned and discredited, the experiences of the "comfort women" are being erased or ignored, even as their claims for redress are still being dismissed. Thus, the term *production of documents,* which is part of standard U.S. court procedure, also describes, I believe, the aim and function of much of the work that academics, editors, novelists, filmmakers, and visual artists have been doing recently in Asia and North America.

I will start with the question of legal representation: on September 18, 2000, a group of fifteen survivors of the "comfort system"—Asian women who are not American citizens—filed a class-action suit in U.S. District Court against the Japanese government for its forcible recruitment and use of women as military sex slaves in World War II. They did so under the Alien Tort Claims Act, a 1789 federal law that "gives foreigners the right to file federal lawsuits for crimes committed in violation of international law" (Miller, "'Comfort Women' Suit" A7). It is no coincidence that one of the lawyers who handled the plaintiffs' action—Agnieska M. Fryszman, an attorney with the Washington, D.C.–based firm of Cohen, Milstein, Hausfeld & Toll—has, like many of those involved in devising legal strategies to advance the "comfort women's" claims, moved into this area of representation after working on cases involving the Holocaust. There are clear overlaps between the precedents that have been set in recent victories on behalf of Holocaust survivors—for instance, reparations paid out to individuals by German corporations that employed slave labor; the return, with interest, by Swiss banks of assets from the account-holders who were murdered in concentration camps; or the surrender by American and European museums of works of art seized illegally from their owners by the Nazis—and the demands for financial compensation to the "comfort women" for the trampling of their human rights, the violation of the sanctity of their bodies, the irreparable damage done to their mental and physical health, and the forcible exploitation of their labor as sexual slaves. What these European cases have demonstrated is that there should be no statute of limitations when it comes to crimes against humanity; and that there are many such crimes against individuals that were not covered by the treaties signed between nations after the Second World War. Numerous crimes against individual Holocaust victims are receiving the redress of compensation and damages.

So far, where there have been legal and political advances already for the "comfort women's" cause, especially in the West, these have tended to come through mechanisms put into place to address European Holocaust issues. On December 3, 1996, for example, the U.S. Justice Department, under the Clinton administration, put the names of "sixteen Japanese citizens … on the U.S. government's Watch List of aliens who are ineligible to enter the United States," on the grounds that they are war criminals, whose crimes included the administration of the "comfort system" during World War II (Lee, 153). The Justice Department was able to do this by applying the terms of the Holtzman Amendment (named for former U.S. Representative Elizabeth Holtzman, who was herself an activist politician). This amendment, passed by Congress in 1978, states that anyone who "has participated in, under the direction of the Nazi government or any other government that was an ally of the Nazi government, the persecution of any person because of race, religion, national origin, or political opinion is prohibited from entry into the United States" or is subject to deportation (Lee, 152). In 1996, U.S. officials ruled unequivocally that the enslavement, rape, torture, and murder of thousands of women from Korea, the Philippines, Taiwan, China, Indonesia, Malaysia, and Burma—who were reduced to the status of sexual chattel and expendable war supplies because of their alleged racial and national inferiority to the Japanese—constituted an instance of "persecution" under an Amendment that was originally devised to rid the U.S. of Nazi war criminals.

More recently, a new effort at political and legal representation was undertaken—a largely symbolic act, initiated by a white, American-born man representing the cause of the surviving Asian "comfort women" before an American legislative body—in the U.S. House of Representatives. In June 2001, Congressman Lane Evans, a Democrat who serves a district in Illinois, brought a resolution to the floor of the House. This resolution calls upon Congress to urge Japan to make full disclosure of its past enslavement of the "comfort women" and at last to take legal, as well as moral, responsibility for this crime against humanity, even as it asks for American support of the survivors' initiatives in seeking the official apologies and reparations that the Japanese government has refused to offer. Rep. Evans's measure follows upon the heels of House Resolution 126, introduced in July 1997 by Congressman William O. Lipinski (also a Democrat from Illinois), which addressed Japanese war crimes in general, including the abuse of and medical experimentation upon prisoners of war, rather than those against "comfort women" in particular. After gaining dozens of signatures from other House members, that earlier resolution, so far, has produced no tangible results.

Indeed, the chances that these attempts to represent the "comfort women" in the sphere of U.S. law and politics will meet with more success than similar efforts in Japan have encountered are very slim, or perhaps slim to none. In November 1994, Professor Tanaka Hiroshi, from Hitotsubashi University, tried to represent the "comfort women's" cause to a Japanese government subcommittee holding investigative hearings. At the time, Professor Tanaka argued in favor of paying official, government-authorized reparations to the survivors, on the grounds that fifteen laws had been enacted "to compensate or provide pensions to former Japanese soldiers and civilians drafted into the military," including a "one-time payment totaling [yen]500 billion in condolence money ... to relatives of those who served and died in the military, commemorating the 50th anniversary of Japan's surrender in World War II"; yet nothing was done directly by the government for the "comfort women," even after then–Prime Minister Murayama had expressed his wish to find ways of showing "remorse" for their past suffering (Hirakawa, 3). Professor Tanaka's recommendations were rejected by Japan's version of Congress, the Diet.

So, too, the Japanese courts almost unanimously have supported their government's resistance to accepting legal responsibility: The sole exception came in April 1998, when a Japanese court ruled in favor of three Korean "comfort system survivors who sought damages. This unique decision by a judge in Yamaguchi District Court was welcomed by Gay McDougall, who was then the U.N.'s Special Rapporteur on the issue of sexual slavery during armed conflict. As the newsletter produced by the Korean Council for the Women Drafted for Military Sexual Slavery by Japan (one of several female-dominated Asian NGOs working on this matter) announced in March 1999, Ms. McDougall's official report to the United Nations had viewed this development with optimism, "saying that it would serve as a momentum for former sexual slaves to get legal reparation through the courts of Japan" (Korean Council, 7). But the favorable ruling for those women was overturned on appeal by a higher Japanese court three years later in March 2001, on the grounds that "no constitutional violations occurred" (Associated Press, A6).

The recent case in U.S. District Court, involving fifteen survivors, faced an even greater hurdle—not merely the opposition of the Japanese government, but of our own government. In May 2001, the Bush administration took a public stand against the "comfort women's" lawsuit. Filing a "statement of interest" with the court, John Ashcroft's Justice Department and Colin Powell's State Department asserted jointly that "Japan is entitled to sovereign immunity, and its wartime activities were dealt with decades ago" (Miller, "U.S. Resists," A19). Therefore, this document argued, the court lacked jurisdiction, and the women's class-action lawsuit deserved to be dismissed. As Bill Miller, writing for the *Washington Post,* reported at the time, "The government also warned that court action 'could have a potentially serious negative impact on U.S.-Japan relations'" (Miller, A19). In the weeks immediately following the September 11th attacks in America, President Bush welcomed the visit of Japan's Prime Minister Koizumi and made it clear that Japan would be asked to play ever-larger strategic roles in the global campaign against terrorism, working closely with the United States. In light of this new reason for cooperation and harmonious political relations between the two nations, it is probably safe to say that the Bush administration, unlike its predecessor, will be putting no more former Japanese officials involved in the "comfort system" on a Watch List. Those activists who have been representing "comfort women" in their legal and political struggles have, therefore, little reason for optimism. On the other hand, those who have been and are still attempting to represent the "comfort women" in other ways—especially by creating, producing, and disseminating linguistic or pictorial representations—have every incentive to work toward victory in the court of public opinion around the world. In that other sort of court, they have, in fact, already been tremendously successful. Over the protests of small groups of right-wing nationalists in Japan, who continue to insist that the women in the "comfort system" were willing and well-paid sex workers, not sexual slaves, the supporters of the "comfort women" have taken control of the issue internationally. Through a variety of media, they have burned into the consciousness of millions the image of young Asian girls coerced or abducted and then subjected to an organized system of brutal, repeated rape. Even those in the U.S. Justice Department and State Department, for instance, who opposed the "comfort women's" recent class-action lawsuit have been quick to endorse the credibility of the survivors' accounts of forced subjection within a system of abuse run by the Japanese Imperial Army and to express their own outrage. As they wrote in the "statement of interest" filed with U.S. District Judge Henry H. Kennedy, Jr., "The horror of the plaintiffs' ordeal can scarcely be overstated" (Miller, "'Comfort Women' Suit," A7).

On October 4, 2001, Judge Kennedy, Jr., dismissed the "comfort women" survivors' lawsuit. But it was obvious nonetheless that he had been persuaded by what he had learned about their history and that he believed they were victims deserving of redress by other means. Bill Miller reported the following day in the *Washington Post* that the judge "condemned the women's treatment" by Japan and in his written opinion noted with disgust that "The 'comfort women' were treated as mere military supplies ... and were even catalogued on supply lists under the heading of 'ammunition'" (Miller, "'Comfort Women' Suit," A7). Indeed, so clear was Judge Kennedy, Jr.'s support for their cause that he said "reparations should be sought through diplomatic channels," albeit "without the court's intervention" (Miller, A7). Wherever and whenever the "comfort women's" stories are disseminated by activists in the West, those narratives have proved both powerful and convincing.

The body of material, moreover, around "comfort women" issues has grown so rapidly, over just the last decade, that we can now speak of there being a "'comfort women's' literature," in the same way that we refer to a "Holocaust literature." Its size and scope suggest that the day is not far off when we may also be able to talk of "Comfort Women" Studies as an academic subject. This would institute a formal means to acknowledge the continuing importance of the women themselves and the significance of their experiences; it would also mirror the development of Holocaust Studies programs at many universities. So far, there have been many overlaps between Holocaust representations and "comfort women" representations, yet also interesting differences. Holocaust literature, which exists in a variety of media—from poetry, to exhibitions in museums dedicated to the Shoah, to pop-culture versions made for cinema and television—is, of course, the result of nearly sixty years of cultural work in every Western and Eastern European nation. Its aims might be summed up in two phrases: "Never forget" and "Never again." Thus, it has been concerned first with memorializing the six million victims murdered by the Nazis; with preserving accounts of the pre-War cultures that were destroyed (whether those were the cultures of whole towns and villages populated by Jews or of Romany populations, or of gay men and lesbians in German cities); with detailing the fates that these cultures met; and with recording the survivors' ordeals before, during, and after the War, as well as the continuing effects of these experiences upon the next generations. While building this work of communal memory, it has insisted upon the importance of individual lives and of individual accounts. At the same time, Holocaust literature, whether based in verbal or visual forms, has taken the prevention of future group persecution and genocide as its goal, studying the historical contexts of anti-Semitism, racism, and homophobia that enabled mass murder to occur, and also insisting upon the role of moral education and the advancement of respect for human rights as deterrents.

"Comfort women" literature has had similar aims. It, too, memorializes the 200,000 women who were used as military sex slaves and records the accounts of the few hundred survivors who have come forward to identify themselves and testify since the early 1990s, when former "comfort woman" Kim Hak Soon spoke out in Korea.

It also works toward the prevention of future war crimes, by exposing the ideologies that underpinned atrocities such as these. But it differs from Holocaust literature in two important respects. Nazi war atrocities were followed immediately by the Nuremberg Trials. During these trials, the details of the concentration camp system were published widely throughout the West, and the crimes against victims were detailed through the testimony of witnesses and also documented with corroborative evidence, especially through displays of photographs and films from the Allies' liberation of the camps. This first round of prosecution set up the climate in which many later kinds of legal action have been possible. This was work, therefore, that art did not have to do later.

But in the absence of any such attention to or punishment for the "comfort system" at the Tokyo War Crimes Tribunal, which followed the end of World War II, the field of representation has had to assume the burden of documenting and indicting in retrospect. As well as reviewing the past, "comfort women" literature—from lithographs to films to fiction—has, moreover, served the interests of advocacy in the present, placing in a sympathetic light the survivors' demands for apologies and reparations from an unwilling Japanese government. It has also self-consciously positioned itself as a counterweight to other sorts of representations circulating in Japan, such as school history textbooks, which have been approved by Japanese authorities, despite their erasure of any mention of the "comfort system." "Comfort women" literature, in other words, has had to be propaganda art—a term that I am using not pejoratively, but positively, to acknowledge the work that art can and often must do in the political realm. And unlike Holocaust literature, which until lately has tended to ignore issues of gender and (as Joan Ringelheim found in the 1980s, through her groundbreaking work with women survivors) often refused to acknowledge the experiences of women as in any way different or as worthy of special study, "comfort women" literature has, throughout its more than ten-year development, put questions of gender and of sexism front and center, since the nature of the war crimes was gender-based. "Comfort women" literature has been informed by feminist perspectives on such questions as wartime rape as a crime against humanity and, in many cases, has been driven by the passionate commitment of artists who are themselves feminists. The majority of these activist-artists so far have been Asian or Asian-American, including a number of Japanese women, giving lie to the myth of feminism as a white Western phenomenon, interested only in middle-class, domestic concerns.

REFERENCES

Associated Press. "Japan: Wartime Brothel Case." In "World Briefing." *New York Times,* 30 March 2001, A6.

Hirakawa, Naomi. "'Comfort Women' Debate Rages On." *Japan Times,* 9 November 1994, 3.

Korean Council for the Women Drafted for Military Sexual Slavery by Japan. "Activities in the UN: Publication of Gay/McDougall Report." *International Activities Against Military Sexual Slavery by Japan* 1 (1999): 6–8.

Lee, John Y. "Placing Japanese War Criminals on the U.S. Justice Department's 'Watch List' of 3 December 1996: The Legal and Political Background." In Margaret Stetz and Bonnie B.C. Oh, eds., *Legacies of the Comfort Women of World War II.* Armonk, NY: M.E. Sharpe, 2001, 152–167.

Miller, Bill. "'Comfort Women' Suit Against Japan Dismissed." *Washington Post,* 5 October 2001, A7.

HUMAN RIGHTS AND HUMAN WRONGS

Kathleen Staudt and Irasema Coronado

SUCCESSFUL ENDEAVORS IN THE HUMAN RIGHTS ARENA

In Ciudad Juárez/El Paso there are several organizations that address human rights issues. It is difficult to say that any one of these organizations is a "successful" organization because success in this arena would mean that these organizations would have no need to exist because, idealistically, government officials and law enforcement agents would respect human rights. One organization is binational, vocal, and has been able to survive amidst great adversity. It is the Asociación de Familiares y Amigos de Personas "Desaparecidas," also known as the Association of Relatives and Friends of "Disappeared" Persons. It is headed by a resident of El Paso, Texas, and was officially founded four years ago. The organization emerged with a couple's disappearance "from the face of the earth" in Ciudad Juarez. The disappeared man's father is a friend of one of the activist/founders of the organization, who is the present co-director of the association. "Well my friend's son was providing listening devices to the federal police, he was helping to catch criminals and it was top secret, but still it was leaked to the cartels and now they are missing." He said that this was the event that brought him into the business of advocating the investigation of the disappeared.

When newspapers and the media started publicizing the disappearance of this young couple, many other people started to come forward with their own stories of disappeared relatives and friends. Relatives and friends of disappeared people indicated that they had negative experiences with the authorities and that they were reluctant to continue pressing them for information. Under the guise of the war on drugs, authorities attributed disappearances and murders to the *ajuste de cuentas* (adjustment of an account involving a drug deal). "These people are afraid of the Mexican police and consider the American Drug Enforcement Agency (DEA) a dirty agency. The association has 'busted' the attorney general in Ciudad Juarez who didn't want to know about the 200 files of adults that have disappeared and over 164[1] women that have been raped, violated and murdered" according to the association informant.

Under the guise of the "War on Drugs," Mexican law enforcement agents tend to justify actions even if they are gross egressions of a basic human right. In Mexico, there is a growing concern that under the pretext of the war on drugs, people's human rights are being violated and people are afraid to go to the authorities to report crimes or disappearances. In some instances, relatives of disappeared people report that police and law enforcement agents start interrogating them when they report a crime to the authorities. The power of the authorities to validate or invalidate a crime has strong psychological implications, especially when one attempts to report a crime committed against a son or a daughter and is humiliatingly asked, "what kind of person was your son or daughter?" Imagine the mixed emotions that people experience: on the one hand your loved one has disappeared and on the other hand people are questioning their moral character. People have reported that officials at times have demanded bribes to pursue a case.

The spokesperson for the association of the relatives and friends of the disappeared claimed that:

> the government of Chihuahua stopped these investigations because they were leading to the young, middle management in the *maquila* industry that has money and power and the government does not want to do anything to scare the *maquiladoras* away. *Maquiladoras* are making families rich in Ciudad Juarez. If you investigated certain prominent families, you will see that they own much of the land in the city and probably all the way to Chihuahua City.

He went on to add that the government, in the case of the disappearances, does not move investigations forward. They claim that witnesses are afraid and that they do not have clues, so there is nothing that the government can do. According to the spokesperson of this organization, at the time (in the summer of 2001), there were 236 women dead and over 500 executions in Ciudad Juarez that were unresolved. However, public officials make statements such as "Ciudad Juarez is doing ok because Sinaloa has over 2,000 executions." According to the spokesperson for the association, "over 2,200 files have been reported missing from the new district attorney's office."

We are acutely aware of the discrepancies in the number of disappeared people, the number of murdered women, and the incidences of rape; there are various reasons for the discrepancy in the number of crimes. Human rights organizations claim that the authorities want to "keep the numbers" down because of the negative publicity that Ciudad Juarez received both nationally and internationally. Additionally, they believe that many young people come to the border because of the economic hardships in their families, or because they want to leave their homes and do not tell their families where they are going. This leads people to believe that when a young woman disappears in Ciudad Juarez, no one is looking for her because her family may not know her whereabouts. The authorities claim that human rights organizations inflate the figures of the disappeared and the murdered women to make them look bad.

With the discovery of the narco-cemeteries (in a ranch located outside of Ciudad Juarez), many bodies were found buried in a common grave. Initially, the media reported that there were hundreds of bodies (but in the end nine bodies were found) in 1999; this led members of the association to launch a campaign about the deaths. Letters were faxed and sent to local, state, and federal officials in both countries. A local law enforcement officer from El Paso responded to the fax by saying "you know Mexico is another country, and we cannot tell Ciudad Juarez how to run their city. El Paso is ok." During the unearthing of nine bodies in a ranch outside of Ciudad Juarez in 1999, the Federal Bureau of Investigation (FBI) was asked to help with the investigation due to the fact that they had expertise and the technical wherewithal for the forensic studies that were needed. The U.S.-Mexican "mass graves" investigation was halted when Mexican politicians and others complained (presumably nationalistic Mexicans) that the FBI presence was a violation of Mexico's sovereignty.[2]

Joint binational efforts are at times complicated and difficult to carry out because of the perception that someone is stepping on someone else's toes. Also, the fact that joint efforts are usually a north-south phenomenon, not the other way around, is seen as suspect. How would people in the United States feel if Mexican law enforcement officers were invited into the United States to assist with an investigation? Nevertheless, many *Mexicanos* welcomed the involvement of the Americans in the investigation because of the mistrust that they have of their own institutions and their ability to conduct investigations honestly and well. During this time, the head of the association sent a fax three times a day to the attorney general in Mexico City until he finally got a response. This activism has had a cost since members of the association have received various death threats. However, membership in the organization continues to grow as more people disappear or are found murdered. Again, an increased membership role is another indicator of success but is that really a good way to measure a successful human rights organization? Membership in this organization is growing because the association has started working with people in Tijuana, Baja California Norte and in Matamoros, Tamaulipas. This organization is organizing vertically along the border.

Membership in this organization is a source of moral support for family members who have lost loved ones. Being able to share one's plight with another person who is similarly situated must be helpful to anyone who experiences this kind of personal tragedy. The support network offered by the association as well as the growing membership allows for more people to work on this together and make demands of the authorities in unison rather than individually; after all, there is power in numbers. Membership and participation in this organization are very personal and in order to protect people's privacy they are reluctant to publicly publish a member directory.

In Ciudad Juarez, the *asociación* also has a co-director of this binational organization. She became involved in this struggle in the early 1990s when her brother-in-law, who went out one evening, disappeared. Her work focuses on asking the authorities in Mexico to "help them find" their loved ones, who are both Mexican and American citizens. She states that there are over 198 people who have disappeared in Ciudad Juarez, 22 of whom are U.S. citizens. She was interviewed in the early spring of 2001. According to a member of the *asociación,* this is an emotional struggle because it is difficult to live with the uncertainty of not knowing if your loved one is dead or alive. "A person cannot disappear from the face of the earth just because something had to happen to these people and logically there has to exist someone who is culpable" said a spokesperson for the *asociación.* At this point the group's strategy is to ensure that these disappearances, murders, and rapes are investigated. Allegations that the authorities are dragging their feet on the investigations are well documented.

Women's groups nationwide and internationally started to support the efforts of local women's organizations with the launching of the *Ni una más* (not one more) campaign in 1998. "Before the null response of the State of Chihuahua authorities to finish and resolve the deaths of women in Ciudad Juarez that now number 133 [this was the figure in 1998], the NGOs and feminist movement, . . . have launched a national and international campaign: *"A parar la lista: Ni una más* [Let's stop the list: Not one more]."[3]

An anonymous source from an NGO hired by the government to help out with the investigation of the murdered women stated that she felt that either the investigators needed more experience and training in the investigation of sexually violent crimes or else they were dragging their feet. "When I was asked to come off board I started asking obvious questions regarding basic procedures. At first I thought that they were really naïve and inexperienced; it finally dawned on me that they were overlooking the obvious in some instances. At that point, I decided to depart gracefully from the investigation," lamented a highly respected psychologist whom we interviewed.

Activists and family members of victims blame the lack of progress made in the investigations of the disappeared and murdered women on the authorities. Family members of the victims have accused the police of being part of a cover up or protecting someone prominent and wealthy. A famous *Televisa* show, *Círculo Rojo,* aired in late November 2001, close to the site where eight women had been found, documented the concerns the victims' families had vis-à-vis the authorities. An aunt of one of the victims stated how she had sent six e-mails to Vicente Fox. "First I asked him to think of his daughters and then I mentioned our concerns and asked him to address the situation by providing more federal resources to the investigation. I have received an acknowledgement that my emails have been received," the woman said on the television show.

In Mexico human rights work is not an easy endeavor. In October 2001, Digna Ochoa y Placido, a human rights attorney in Mexico City, was shot to death at her office. The culprits left behind a message to other human rights defenders that they could meet similar fates.[4] Unfortunately, there have been other human rights workers and journalists who have been threatened or killed in the line of duty. Death threats, assassinations, and kidnappings are deterrents to people who work in the human rights arena in Mexico and preclude people from getting involved in similar work. In Ciudad Juarez, women's issues are of concern to many human rights organizations and have become a focal point for human rights organizations to rally around.

Diana Washington Valdez, a leading reporter on border issues, reported that she had been on the telephone with a member of *Votes Sin Eco* (Voices Without Echo), a nongovernmental organization that advocates justice for the more than 300[5] women who have been killed in Juarez since 1993. (The number of disappeared was provided in 2001.)

> The sound quality was unusually poor that day. There were strange and scratching noises in the background. We were on touchy ground. The call went dead immediately at the mention of a National Action Party member who was questioned by police about one of the victims. The line remained "blocked" for three straight days. I could not call that number, and the other party could not call me back.[6]

Various organizations have held rallies in Ciudad Juarez to raise awareness and bring attention to the issue of the disappeared women. Black crosses on pink backgrounds appear on walls, telephone and electricity posts to commemorate the deceased women. In downtown El Paso, there is a mural on the side of a building where this black cross on pink stands out to remind everyone that the plight of these women is a binational concern.

LAS AMIGAS—LOS AMIGOS Y LAS CASAS DE LA FRONTERA

Casa Amiga

In Ciudad Juarez, there is an institution that is helping address the challenges that women face in the community—Casa Amiga (Friendly Home, fem.) has received local, national, and international attention for its work in this arena. Casa Amiga has been able to establish many binational and international linkages throughout the course of its existence.

In 1992 women's raped and mutilated bodies were found in Ciudad Juarez. A group of women came together and formed Grupo 8 de Marzo (the 8th of March Group), named after International Women's day in order to raise awareness of the crimes and to promote women's rights. In 1996 La Coordinadora de Organismos no Gubernamentales/ The Coordinating Group of NGOs was founded to defend women's rights. The impetus for this organization emanated from a proposed change in article 219 of the Penal Code of the state of Chihuahua, which proposed outlawing abortion.[7]

Members of Grupo 8 de Marzo determined that there was great need for a shelter that would provide women who were victims of crime and sexual abuse [with] support, counseling and legal assistance to victims. Hence, Casa Amiga opened in 1999 with the help of a CNN reporter, the municipal government, institutions and people from El Paso, Texas, and a few *maquilas*. Women who have been raped, assaulted, or physically abused can avail themselves of medical assistance, counseling, social services and legal aid at Casa Amiga. There is more demand for their services than what they are able to provide. This help is for victims as well as for their families. Additionally, they give workshops at schools and places of work regarding sexual harassment.

Casa Amiga is only one of four rape crisis centers in Mexico, and the only one in Ciudad Juarez. It has numerous links to organizations in the United States. The Texas attorney general's office agreed to fund the training of rape crisis volunteers; a businesswoman's organization in El Paso donated $5,000 for the printing of needed educational materials. The El Paso Police Department's Crimes Against Persons Unit has provided training for police officers in Ciudad Juarez. The training involves police officers examining their own views about criminal sexual conduct, then work toward building a new trust between victims and police.[8] Private individuals from El Paso and other communities in the United States send donations to Casa Amiga. A fast-food chain from the United States has also donated money to Casa Amiga. Lots of organizations on both sides of the border support Casa Amiga.

Cross-border activity is common in the health care arena. Organizations that serve women in the United States report that they also have clients that come from Ciudad Juarez. Estimates indicate that one-third of all abortions reported in El Paso are performed on women who come from Mexico. American women also have been known to avail themselves of abortions in Mexico. American women had been traveling to Tijuana for abortions since at least the 1950s.[9]

The work of Casa Amiga and the success that it has had in raising awareness in the community is commendable because of the adversity it faces: hostility from the government, increasing public pressure to not air the community's "dirty laundry," sexist and patriarchical attitudes, limited funding, and an ever-increasing work load. It is important to note that the leadership of Casa Amiga has not gone unnoticed by other groups in the community who have expressed concern that they are monopolizing resources and using the organization.

The challenges that women face in the border region are many. The issues they encounter run the gamut from the legal, criminal, and medical to work-related concerns. Another *Casa* that is open to help migrants is the Casa del Migrante (House of the Immigrant).

Casa del Migrante

La Casa del Migrante in Ciudad Juarez is one of five homes dedicated to helping immigrants. The other homes are located in Tijuana and on the southern border with Guatemala. La Casa del Migrante is part of a religious organization that was founded by Beato Juan Bautista Scalabrini in 1987 to provide services to immigrants and refugees. A Catholic priest runs La Casa del Migrante in Ciudad Juarez.

This home provides shelter, food, clothing, medical services, and spiritual guidance to people who have left their place of origin to seek a better life, either within Mexico or abroad. Many of those seeking services at the Casa del Migrante, deported from the United States, are victims of discrimination and abuse. The house has been in existence for 11 years in Ciudad Juarez and has never been closed "thanks in part to institutions and people of good will and heart."[10]

Casa del Migrante also has ties with a binational group, "Solidaridad Fronteriza" (Border Solidarity), which is also a religious organization in El Paso and Ciudad Juarez. Casa del Migrante also works with other border communities to collaborate on information sharing, for example, in Nogales, Tucson, and Douglas, Arizona. Again, this is an example of linking border people.

The priest who runs Casa del Migrante never misses an opportunity to raise people's awareness to the plight of immigrants. Whether it is a public hearing or a meeting, he always welcomes the opportunity to share the Casa's mission with others and to elaborate on the root causes of migration. He feels that U.S. organizations have more technical wherewithal, economic resources, and legal staff to work with immigrants. In Mexico, many of the human rights organizations rely on volunteers; in the United States, there are paid staff, attorneys, and other professionals who can help the cause of immigrants. In Mexico, that is not the case.

Casa del Migrante provides services to approximately 250–300 people a month. They are always seeking to collaborate with other organizations to bring about social justice on the border when dealing with issues of immigration, access to water and other environmental issues, and in raising wages in the *maquiladora* industry. According to the priest at Casa del Migrante *"la division fronteriza es teórica"* (the border exists only in theory). This organization is a friend to the immigrant, regardless of where they come from or where they are going. Other friends of immigrants also exist in the region.

American Friends Service Committee

The American Friends Service Committee (AFSC), through their U.S.-Mexico Border Program (USMBP), works to end human and civil rights abuses in the region. This is a purposive and religious organization that also works nationally and internationally. The American Friends work to link border residents vertically as well. Throughout the region, the American Friends have offices, staff, and programs from San Diego/Tijuana to Brownsville/Matamoros. They monitor and document abuses and work together with a network of local human and civil rights organizations on both sides of the border. Human rights violations occur on both sides of the border. In Mexico, *coyotes* (people who smuggle people into the United States for a fee), drug dealers, law enforcement officers, and *bandidos* (Mexicanos who prey on migrants in Mexico, desperate to cross into the United States); all have been known to violate people's rights. Reports of robbery, rape, and assault have been documented in many areas. Unscrupulous *coyotes* offer their services to help unsuspecting migrants enter the United States and then abandon them either in the middle of the desert or in the back of a rented truck without water or food. *Coyotes* and *bandidos* are some of the main culprits in the human rights arena.[11]

The AFSC/USMBP has more resources available to them when compared with organizations in Mexico. Their modus operandi is also multifaceted; they work within the legal system, through educational outreach efforts and in the development of policy. The AFSC/USMBP files complaints on behalf of the migrants, secures legal representation, and increases public awareness of human and civil rights violations. Additionally, they monitor immigration law enforcement practices and make recommendations on policy to representatives of both the United States and Mexico. Their binational work is easily carried out because many of their staff are bilingual and bicultural. A staff person of the AFSC explained how she was able to work both sides of the fence so to speak on this issue:

> I can work both sides on these issues. When I testify before the U.S. Congress I exclaim, "As an American citizen, I am deeply troubled by what we are witnessing in the border region in terms of senseless deaths." And when I testify in Mexico, I also exclaim *"Nosotros los Mexicanos, merecemos un trato digno ..."* (We Mexicans deserve to be treated with dignity).
>
> —Staff Member of AFSC

The work of this organization has had a profound effect in the human rights arena throughout the border region in raising the human rights issue in a binational context and in educating the public at large about these issues. Irasema has witnessed how people in border communities leave meetings where AFSC personnel have spoken: Participants leave with a new awareness and an increased sense of community self-esteem, a sense of empowerment just because their rights have been reaffirmed.

NOTES

1. The number of disappeared women varies depending on the source and the time frame that we conducted interviews. Hence, the discrepancy in the figures.

2. Diana Washington Valdez, "Bodies Everywhere," *El Paso Times,* June 25, 2000, B1.

3. Sonia Del Valle, "A parar la lista: Ni una más," www.nodo50.org/mujeresred/mexico-juarez-htm, May 18, 1998.

4. Amnesty International, www.amnesty-volunteer.org/usa/group137/org/usa/group137/digna.html.

5. Again, the inconsistency in reported number of disappeared women from another source.

6. Diana Washington Valdez, "Phone Taps in Mexico Uncovered," *El Paso Times,* July 9, 2001: B1.

7. Carlton Stowers, "The Angel of Juarez," *Dallas Observer,* January 4, 2001.

8. Ibid.

9. Leslie Reagan, "Crossing the Border for Abortion: California Activists, Mexican Clinics and the Creation of a Feminist Health Agency in the 1960s," *Feminist Studies* 26: 2, Summer 2000, pp. 323–48.

10. Red Casa del Migrante www.migrante.com.mx/ciudadjuarez.html.

11. Irasema Coronado, "Who Governs in a Binational Context? The Role of Transnational Political Elites," unpublished dissertation, University of Arizona, 1998.

WHAT, THEN, IS TO BE DONE?

Cross-border organizing is a daunting prospect. We celebrate its emergence and sustenance, for more factors block it than facilitate it. As the book and our brief summary show, cross-border organizing is possible and concrete outcomes are achievable. It can grow, strengthen, and deepen through collaborative work. But these collaborations need to occur across borders: institutional, territorial, and cultural; they need to span the local and the global to combine strong and weak ties, including the resources and networks that come with weak ties. Without growth in cross-border organizing, the power and authority of business and commerce in the officially sanctioned regional and globalized economy will overwhelm civic capacity. If global NGOs are to have real legitimacy beyond consciousness-raising, electronic listservs, and protests, they must be grounded in real people and personal ties.

We extract kernels of wisdom from the analysis and list them below as strategies for change. These strategies contain equally profound implications at the national, regional, and international levels at the levels of policy and law.

- Relevant both to NGOs and official institutions, we urge people to conceptualize interdependent and integrated regions and communities while acknowledging still-existent territorial lines. States in federal systems govern with "difference" in their nations. Nations within the European Union govern with difference within their fifteen-country community. Canada, Mexico, and the United States should begin thinking and acting along these lines.

- Border regions should be as open to civic activists and their movements as border regions are open to business, commerce and trade. With civic activists encompassing potentially large numbers, we necessarily imply movement toward more open borders for work and civic action.

- Schools should open up civic education, both to transnational common interests and to connecting ideas to action, in the communities. Civic and social studies curricula are focused on the nation and nationalist interpretations of national histories. Students should get wider and comparative exposure to other cultures and institutions. Student learning should be connected to community action, including the binational community in borderlands contexts. At least bilingual capacity should be prized and valued, and taught at all educational levels. Optimally, multilingual capacity should prevail in the North American multilingual community. Residents of the European community live in this complex, but rich reality and learn languages from childhood on into adulthood.

- Just as business gets cues, incentives, and subsidies for transnational activities, so also should NGOs and civic organizations. Democracy should be elevated to the level of free trade in policy and budgets.

- Funders should acknowledge borderlands and remove budgetary restrictions that hinder spending beyond national borders. A North American transnational service, beyond Servicio Social and AmeriCorps/Vista, would develop a leadership corps for the future.

- Borderland NGOs should make it common practice to include members and leaders from both sides in their ranks. Much is to be learned about common agendas and creative strategies to use spaces in the democratic openings that prevail on both sides of the border.

- People in borderland NGOs and public agencies should engage with one another in relationships characterized by civility. They should engage with respect. They should listen to and observe cultural subtleties and nuances. They should be open and think outside historic memories and nationalist boxes.

- People should acknowledge the personal and build relationships of trust as they proceed to work on reasoned, ideological, principled, and purposive agendas. Once the purpose of organizing has taken hold, they should be able to agree to disagree and to move beyond friendships and "enemyships" in pursuit of common agendas. They should avoid gossip and use new democratic spaces for open and transparent dialogues.

- Institutional shrouds must change in ways that open access to NGOs and democratic voice. Rule of law should prevail, and when political strategies are exhausted, lawsuit mechanisms should be available to provoke accountability.

- Minimum wages must increase on both sides of the border, but especially in Mexico. Border wages seem to be centuries away from social justice in wage terms, but employers can begin by acknowledging the reality that four times Mexico's current minimum wage is a minimal standard.

- NGOs and businesses should work together to encourage employment standards, as did some employers under apartheid in South Africa with Sullivan guidelines. Transnational standards should be adopted and enforced within governments as well.
- Global NGOs should ground their loose networking with strong personal ties at borderlands. Listservs that claim a global reach should sort names and contacts by geographic region to facilitate local contacts and personal relationship building.
- Portable insurance should be available to citizens and noncitizens with preferred provider lists to ensure quality and accountability of healthcare.
- Human rights agreements should be developed and elevated to the levels of La Paz (environmental) and NAFTA (trade) agreements in terms of their enforcement authority.
- Immigration law enforcement should take family unification seriously, including people without the wherewithal and resources for expensive lawyers.
- Crimes against people should be elevated to the level of drug crimes. The murdered girls and women deserve cross-national attention from local police and national investigation agencies.
- National agencies would do well to utilize one office or department to deal with border issues rather than fragment efforts within a single organization.
- Borderlanders deserve "living wages" with health benefits. Poverty and its special bordered dimensions also need attention. Living wages would go a long way in reducing poverty at the border.

The U.S.-Mexico borderlands are now visible to the national heartlands and to North America as a whole. Power relations between the border and the interior, and between the more and less privileged, must change with the move toward social justice. North American institutional shrouds, coupled with strong, cross-border NGOs, provide the framework in which to address problems with the environment, living wages, and human rights. The North American Union (NAU) is an imagined future, but we can seize the structures of opportunity to begin building the bridges and transcending the divisions to act on common interests now.

Crossing the Lines: Women's Organizations in Conflict Resolutions

Shelley Anderson

Women's organizations are playing an increasingly important role in nonviolent conflict resolution. They are frequently the first to take the risks necessary to promote dialogue across divided communities and move towards reconciliation. This work includes small local initiatives which often involve an income generating component. One example of this is a café and pastry shop women have organized in an ethnically divided town in Bosnia-Herzegovina. Situated on the unofficial border that separates the two communities, the café and pastry shop is the only safe place within miles where members from the different communities can meet and talk with each other. It was started by Croat, Serb and Bosnian women together as a way to both provide employment for women and to help heal ethnic enmity. The women also collect the names and addresses of possible returnees from the "wrong" ethnic group, and help provide returnees with practical necessities such as tools and milk cows (Cockburn, forthcoming).

Women's work for dialogue also reaches to the highest political levels. The Northern Ireland Women's Coalition (NIWC), after mobilizing broad cross-community support, played a key role in the talks leading up to the 1998 Good Friday Agreement. and conducted a successful door-to-door election campaign that sent two members to the Northern Ireland Assembly. In a radical departure from partisan politics, the NIWC has refused to take a stand on issues such as a constitution for Northern Ireland, emphasizing instead the need for inclusive dialogue and decision-making (Fearon, 1999).

The Liberian Women's Initiative (LWI) likewise helped to transform a previously male-dominated political process by demanding a voice at the 1994 Accra Clarifications Conference. By insisting that all parties disarm before the election, by publishing lists of women qualified to take up positions in government ministries if appointed, and by conducting an energetic voter education programme that emphasized the need for women to be actively involved in peace-building, the LWI helped build stability and peace in Liberia. LWI's efforts also laid the groundwork for a founding LWI member, Ruth Perry, to be elected as Liberia's head of state (Fearon, 2000).

Several common understandings—and paradoxes—inform the work of all these groups. The first understanding is the necessity of involving as many ordinary people as possible in building peace. For peace to be sustainable, peace processes and reconstruction must be owned by the communities involved. Women's engagement in such peace processes is especially critical. Women's political marginalization paradoxically often provides them a wider space for peace-building. Women's motivation in becoming involved in peace-building often stems from, or is perceived as, the desire or need to provide for their family, especially children. This concern for their family gives many women the permission to enter formerly forbidden male political territory. Because of their previous marginalized position, women may be perceived as outside the influence of a conflict's major stakeholders. This means that women's peace-making initiatives may be trusted more by a community than those of peace-makers coming from the political elite. Angela E.V. King, Special Adviser on Gender Issues and Advancement of Women to the United Nations, pointed out some of these perceptions in analysing the role of women in the United Nations Observer Mission in South Africa (UNOMSA), in which she served as Chief of Mission. While she writes of foreign women in the role of observers, women inside a particular community may also be perceived in the same way.

> The presence of women seems to be a potent ingredient in fostering and maintaining confidence and trust among the local population. In performing their tasks with their male colleagues, women were perceived to be more compassionate, less threatening or insistent on status, less willing to opt for force or confrontation over conciliation, even it is said less egocentric, more willing to listen and learn—though not always—and

to contribute to an environment of stability which fostered the peace process. (King, 1997)

Conflict can thus lead to social transformation. In some post-conflict situations, such as in Cambodia and Rwanda, male death rates during the armed violence mean that the surviving population may be 60 to 70 percent women. Reconstruction in such societies often demands that women take on new roles. Whether women keep this new ground and/or use it to promote improvements in women's status, after the crisis that has made such an opening possible is over, is an unanswered question. In western history, during World War II, women in the UK, Canada and the USA were mobilized in unprecedented numbers to work in jobs and decision-making functions formerly restricted to men. After the war, women were immediately sacked and told to return to their kitchens and more traditional gender roles.

In what ways are community-based women's peace groups promoting dialogue and rebuilding societies destroyed by armed conflict? To answer this question we will first look at the work of the International Fellowship of Reconciliation's (IFOR) Women Peacemakers Program.

EMPOWERING WOMEN PEACEMAKERS

The International Fellowship of Reconciliation's Women Peacemakers Program (WPP) began in 1997, though its roots go back much further. The WPP's operating assumptions include the belief that, without peace, development is impossible —and that without women, neither peace nor development can take place. Other assumptions include the belief that peace-building, especially in a post-conflict situation, is a long-term process, and that the principal actors in such reconstruction should be the affected communities themselves.

The WPP's main goal is to support and strengthen women's peace-making initiatives and capacities. The WPP does this in four ways: by helping women's groups to organize trainings in active non-violence and conflict resolution (as has been done with tribal women in the Chittagong Hill Tracts, along the Thai-Burma border, in Romania, Azerbaijan, India, Nepal, Nigeria and Zimbabwe); by organizing regional consultations where women from different sides of conflicts can safely meet to discuss strategies for de-escalating the violence, and to deepen their understanding of nonviolent conflict resolution (as has been done for the European, Asian and African regions); by publishing materials that document and analyse the successes and failures of women's efforts in reconciliation and peace-making (such as the annual 24 May International Women's Day for Peace and Disarmament action pack, and the WPP newsletter "Cross the Lines"); and by helping to promote self-sustaining women's organizations (primarily by linking women's groups with resources and organizations that can provide technical and financial support for peace initiatives). Some practical examples of how the WPP works are given below.

THE SUDANESE WOMEN'S VOICE FOR PEACE

"Peace comes from talking to your enemies," says Teody Lotto of the peace non-governmental organization (NGO) Sudanese Women's Voice for Peace (IFOR Women's

Peacemakers Program, 2000). The Sudanese Women's Voice for Peace (SWVP) is a good example of the role community-based women can play in the peaceful resolution of armed conflicts. It also exemplifies the role dialogue on all levels—between communities in violent conflict, between different factions inside particular communities, and between conflictants and the international community—plays in nonviolent conflict resolution.

Lotto's attitude reflects SWVP's approach to its work of transforming Sudanese society through peace-building and human rights advocacy. Such an attitude is a key element towards a dialogue that makes for reconciliation. "I am not interested in revenge. Will revenge bring back my loved ones? No!" she states. SWVP teaches conflict resolution skills to villagers. Lotto says: "We have trained 66 women trainers so far. When we come to an area we ask the women to select the women with influence in the village. These leaders are trained in non-violence and reconciliation so they can train others. We teach women to promote traditional peacemaking, to bring different villages to forgive one another."

Village women have been empowered to begin a dialogue with guerrilla leaders.

Sometimes the women come together to talk to rebels who have been raping, looting and burning houses. When the women oppose this, they have made some rebel leaders change. The leaders see how some soldiers took advantage to loot, pretending that they are under orders. Some leaders say even the military needs peace training. They have given us the okay to build peace demonstration centres.

In some areas women stopped the recruitment of child soldiers by negotiating agreements from guerrilla leaders to stop abducting children from schools.

The Sudanese conflict has provided some women an opportunity to explore public space and power negotiations with men in a way that peace time society did not. This opening up of possibilities for positive social transformation during a period of conflict resolution is not unique. The Wajir Peace and Development Committee, a community-based group in Northeastern Kenya composed primarily of women, is also creating a public political role and voice for women. The women's ongoing work to prevent violence between different clans has mobilized both youth, a group not normally listened to, and the traditional decision-makers, older men, to work together to create peace and stability. One committee activist says: "When one elder asked me how a woman dared to speak in public, I asked him, "If your house was on fire would you wait to put it out until a neighbour came? My house is on fire and I must put it out."

The WPP helped the SWVP make critical international links during its formation, in order to secure non-violence training, office support and funding. SWVP members were invited by IFOR to international gatherings, such as the 1994 "Women, Religion and Peace" seminar in Sweden; the 1995 United Nations Fourth World Conference on Women in Beijing, China; and the 1999 Hague Appeal for Peace conference in the Netherlands, in order to put Sudan on the international agenda.

Other international peace organizations are also cooperating with the SWVP. In 1997, Pax Christi started a pilot trauma counselling project in Nairobi for Sudanese refugee women and inside Sudan in Mapel. In this project "We help women to feel free to tell of their suffering," says Lotto. "We ask women not to hold bitterness in their hearts, but to go to trained women to be healed of trauma and aggression. You cannot amend the past but you can correct the future."

WORK IN FORMER YUGOSLAVIA AND THE CAUCASUS

Women, like the Women in Black in Belgrade and the Anti-War Coalition in Zagreb, were among the first to publicly oppose nationalist and ethnic violence when war first broke out in former Yugoslavia in the early 1990s. IFOR supported these groups in practical ways by distributing their statements and manifestos; publicizing their work with dissidents, military deserters, conscientious objectors and refugees; helping to relay messages between the two groups when telephone and fax communications between Belgrade and Zagreb were cut; providing safe spaces where Serbian and Croatian and Slovenian activists could meet; and eventually helping these and other anti-war groups to secure computer equipment and getting on-line.

IFOR was also a founding member of the Balkan Peace Team (BPT, a cooperative project by some 11 peace NGOs, including War Resisters International and Peace Brigades International). BPT has been sending trained volunteers to Bosnia, Croatia, Kosovo, and Serbia since 1994 to support local civil society groups and to assist with dialogue and community conflict resolution projects. One example of how BPT works occurred in 1998 when students in southern Serbia wanted to do something about the growing tensions in Kosovo. The students approached BPT to help make connections with ethnic Albanians in Kosovo. BPT organized a prejudice reduction workshop for the Serbian students, then accompanied the students on a visit to an Albanian youth group inside Kosovo. As the crisis increased the Serb students attended a non-violent march in Kosovo as observers. They were able to report back to their community on the Serbian police's aggression against the marchers.

After the 1999 NATO bombing campaign, the BPT office in Belgrade was shut down. The BPT in Pristina continues to assist local groups in working for a multi-ethnic Kosovo. In order to counter the rigid emerging ethnic enemy images that will perpetuate inter-ethnic violence, BPT is now working on a project to collect and publicize stories of how individuals from one community, whether Serbian, Albanian, Slav or Roma, saved the lives of members from the "other" community. BPT volunteer Erik Torch writes:

> In working on peace building there are several important points that we need to bear in mind. First and foremost, peace (and conflict) is based on the relationship. Therefore, building peace needs to be focused on the relationship ... [there is] overwhelming pressure within Albanian society to portray all Serbs and Slavs and Roma as inherently evil ... how does one begin to deconstruct such attitudes in others? It requires a relationship that is strong enough to challenge such attitudes. (Torch, 1999)

Similar challenges to enemy images have been undertaken by other community-based peace groups. The IDP Women's Association of Georgia specifically focuses on children and youth in this regard, bringing together Georgian, Abkhazian, and Ossetian children in peace camps where they will have a chance to build personal relationships with their "enemy" counterparts, and learn peace-building skills. The IDP Women's Association has also been involved in documenting stories where people from one community saved individuals from the opposite side. "Ethnically induced armed confrontation had one more side: a humane one. The facts are ... people at the risk of their own lives rescued the lives of other people, belonging to the opposite, 'hostile' side of the conflict," explains the introduction to *Restoring the Culture of Peace in the Caucasus: A Human Solidarity Document* (Pagava, 1999). This 86-page book records the testimonies of some 60 women and men during the conflicts in Georgia, Abkhazia, South Ossetia, Armenia, and Azerbaijan.

The testimonies were collected by the non-governmental organization Assist Yourself, an organization of internally displaced people (mostly women) from Abkhazia, explicitly because "there exists a risk that it [the stories] might disappear some time, and information of a different, negative kind, used by the destructive forces, would promote further separation and distrust" and the creation of enemy images.

During the WPP European consultation, Gulnara Shaninian of Armenia emphasized the importance of such attempts. "My generation had personal relationships with Azeris, lived side by side as neighbours, had friendships. This generation only knows enemy images and war. This will make it harder to build peace for the future" (Anderson, 1998).

IFOR members remain committed to working with community groups throughout the Balkans. The Fellowship of Reconciliation (FOR) and the IFOR branch in the USA helped several hundred young Bosnians to continue their secondary school and university education in the USA during the war, placing the students with American families, securing scholarships, and helping the participants in the FOR's Bosnian Student Project (BSP) return after the war's end. The FOR also organizes annual work camps throughout the former Yugoslavia, which focus on practical work such as rebuilding homes, sharing experiences in peace organizing and multi-cultural living, and teaching English.

The FOR also supports the work of Bosnia activists such as Emsuda Mujagic, a survivor of the Trnopolje concentration camp. Mujagic is founder of From Hearts to Peace, which works for dialogue between Bosnians and Serbs. Among other work, From Hearts to Peace organizes an annual dialogue group where Bosnian and Serb educators can meet to discuss reconciliation. Dolores Gunter, a FOR staff member who participates in the BSP, wrote about a party Mujagic organized for a FOR work camp in Bosnia:

> Emsuda and others prepared a big barbecue of roast lamb and invited the few Serbs who live in town (their homes were not destroyed) and who will someday be their neighbours again. The Serbs did not come—but some of their children did. Emsuda packed up meat and sent it home with them to their parents. And so, in the small gestures of women, the work of reconciliation proceeds. (Gunter, 1998)

STRENGTHS, WEAKNESSES, AND CONTRADICTIONS

Women are playing a leading role in reconciliation. This fact is being recognized more and more by conflict resolution specialists, government officials and development agencies. Despite this growing awareness, women's peace-making initiatives remain underresourced. There is a danger that women's work for reconciliation and reconstruction can be seen as a "natural" extension of women's role in society. This means that such work goes unrecognized and inadequately resourced. It is stripped of its political meaning and rendered, like much of women's work, invisible. Women remain marginalized, their problems ignored, their experiences unanalysed, and their skills underutilized. When does capitalizing on women's strengths in peacemaking, such as good listening and communication skills, flexibility, and a concern for people above abstract principles, become perpetuating traditional sex role stereotypes?

The functions women have in reconciliation processes are complex, reflecting the multiple roles women have in society. Like women's lives, such functions must be viewed holistically. Women are peace educators inside the family, in schools, in women's and mixed organizations and elsewhere. Their networks and knowledge of local affairs make them effective early warning monitors, alert for rumours, increasing tensions, a sudden influx of weapons and other signs of potential conflict. Their sometimes extensive kinship links, social expectations and training can make women highly effective mediators. Their status as outsiders, the perception that they are not primary stakeholders in conflict, also reveal a role as negotiators and originators of new approaches to peace.

The challenge for people interested in reconciliation is to explore this complexity and to develop an integrated gender approach. Such an approach would investigate both the ways in which women contribute to and oppose armed conflict. Most of all such an approach needs to discover concrete ways to support community-based women's work for peace.

REFERENCES

Anderson. S. (1998) "Women Peacemakers: Healing and Reconciliation," *Reconciliation International,* June: 22.

Cockburn, C. (forthcoming) "Picking Up the Pieces: Women's Organizations in Post-war Reconstruction in Bosnia-Herzegovina." Keynote address to the Trinity College Euroconference on Women, Violence and Reconciliation. 10–12 March 2000, Dublin, Ireland.

Fearon, K. (1999) Women's Work: *The Story of the Northern Ireland Women's Coalition.* Belfast: The Blackstaff Press.

Fearon, K. (2000) 'The Liberian Women's Initiative," International Women's Day for Peace and Disarmament, 24 May, pack 9.

Gunter, D. (1998) "Women Reconcilers in Bosnia," *Fellowship* 64, 11–12: 28.

IFOR Women Peacemakers Program (2000) *Sudan: As Long as You Are Alive You Must Have Hope.* International Women's Day for Peace and Disarmament, 24 May.

King, A. (1997) "Success in South Africa," *UN Chronicle,* 3.

Pagava, M (ed.) (1999) *Restoring the Culture of Peace in the Caucasus: A Human Solidarity Document.* Georgia: International Center on Conflict and Negotiation.

Torch. E. (1999) "The Paradoxes I See: A Letter from a Volunteer," *Balkan Peace Team Newsletter,* No. 17.

HETEROPATRIARCHY AND THE THREE PILLARS OF WHITE SUPREMACY: RETHINKING WOMEN OF COLOR ORGANIZING

Andrea Smith

SCENARIO 1

A group of women of color come together to organize. An argument ensues about whether or not Arab women should be included. Some argue that Arab women are "white" since they have been classified as such in the US census. Another argument erupts over whether or not Latinas qualify as "women of color," since some may be classified as "white" in their Latin American countries of origin and/or "pass" as white in the United States.

SCENARIO 2

In a discussion on racism, some people argue that Native peoples suffer from less racism than other people of color because they generally do not reside in segregated neighborhoods within the United States. In addition, some argue that since tribes now have gaming, Native peoples are no longer "oppressed."

SCENARIO 3

A multiracial campaign develops involving diverse communities of color in which some participants charge that we must stop the black/white binary, and end Black hegemony over people of color politics to develop a more "multicultural" framework. However, this campaign continues to rely on strategies and cultural motifs developed by the Black Civil Rights struggle in the United States.

These incidents, which happen quite frequently in "women of color" or "people of color" political organizing struggles, are often explained as a consequence of "oppression Olympics." That is to say, one problem we have is that we are too busy fighting over who is more oppressed. In this essay, I want to argue that these incidents are not so much the result of "oppression Olympics" but are more about how we have inadequately framed "women of color" or "people of color" politics. That is, the premise behind much "women of color" organizing is that women from communities victimized by white supremacy should unite together around their shared oppression. This framework might be represented by a diagram of five overlapping circles, each marked Native women, Black women, Arab/Muslim women, Latinas, and Asian American women, overlapping like a Venn diagram.

This framework has proven to be limited for women of color and people of color organizing. First, it tends to presume that our communities have been impacted by white supremacy in the same way. Consequently, we often assume that all of our communities will share similar strategies for liberation. In fact, however, our strategies often run into conflict. For example, one strategy that many people in US-born communities of color adopt, in order to advance economically out of impoverished communities, is to join the military. We then become complicit in oppressing and colonizing communities from other countries. Meanwhile, people from other countries often adopt the strategy of moving to the United States to advance economically, without considering their complicity in settling on the lands of indigenous peoples that are being colonized by the United States.

Consequently, it may be more helpful to adopt an alternative framework for women of color and people of color organizing. I call one such framework the "Three Pillars of White Supremacy." This framework does not assume that racism and white supremacy is enacted in a singular fashion; rather, white supremacy is constituted by separate and distinct, but still interrelated, logics. Envision three pillars, one labeled Slavery/Capitalism, another labeled Genocide/Capitalism, and the last one labeled Orientalism/War, as well as arrows connecting each of the pillars together.

SLAVERY/CAPITALISM

One pillar of white supremacy is the logic of slavery. As Sora Han, Jared Sexton, and Angela P. Harris note, this logic renders Black people as inherently slaveable—as nothing more than property.[1] That is, in this logic of white supremacy, Blackness becomes equated with slaveability. The forms of slavery may change—whether it is through the formal system of slavery, sharecropping, or through the current prison-industrial complex—but the logic itself has remained consistent.

This logic is the anchor of capitalism. That is, the capitalist system ultimately commodifies all workers—one's own person becomes a commodity that one must sell in the labor market while the profits of one's work are taken by someone else. To keep this capitalist system in place—which ultimately commodifies most people—the logic of slavery applies a racial hierarchy to this system. This racial hierarchy tells people that as long as you are not Black, you have the opportunity to escape the commodification of capitalism. This helps people who are not Black to accept their lot in life, because they can feel that at least they are not at the very bottom of the racial hierarchy—at least they are not property; at least they are not slaveable.

The logic of slavery can be seen clearly in the current prison industrial complex (PIC). While the PIC generally incarcerates communities of color, it seems to be structured primarily on an anti-Black racism. That is, prior to the Civil War, most people in prison where white. However, after the thirteenth amendment was passed—which banned slavery, except for those in prison—Black people previously enslaved through the slavery system were reenslaved through the prison system. Black people who had been the property of slave owners became state property, through the conflict leasing system. Thus, we can actually look at the criminalization of Blackness as a logical extension of Blackness as property.

GENOCIDE/COLONIALISM

A second pillar of white supremacy is the logic of genocide. This logic holds that indigenous peoples must disappear. In fact, they must *always* be disappearing, in order to allow non-indigenous peoples rightful claim over this land. Through this logic of genocide, non-Native peoples then become the rightful inheritors of all that was indigenous—land, resources, indigenous spirituality, or culture. As Kate Shanley notes, Native peoples are a permanent "present absence" in the US colonial imagination, an "absence" that reinforces, at every turn, the conviction that Native peoples are indeed vanishing and that the conquest of Native lands is justified. Ella Shoat and Robert Stam describe this absence as "an ambivalently repressive mechanism [which] dispels the anxiety in the face of the Indian, whose very presence is a reminder of the initially precarious grounding of the American nation-state itself ... In a temporal paradox, living Indians were induced to 'play dead,' as it were, in order to perform a narrative of manifest destiny in which their role, ultimately, was to disappear."[2]

Rayna Green further elaborates that the current Indian "wannabe" phenomenon is based on a logic of genocide: non-Native peoples imagine themselves as the rightful inheritors of all that previously belonged to "vanished" Indians, thus entitling them to ownership of this land. "The living performance of 'playing Indian' by non-Indian peoples depends upon the physical and psychological removal, even the death, of real Indians.

In that sense, the performance, purportedly often done out of a stated and implicit love for Indians, is really the obverse of another well-known cultural phenomenon, 'Indian hating,' as most often expressed in another, deadly performance genre called 'genocide.'"[3] After all, why would non-Native peoples need to play Indian—which often includes acts of spiritual appropriation and land theft—if they thought Indians were still alive and perfectly capable of being Indian themselves? The pillar of genocide serves as the anchor for colonialism—it is what allows non-Native peoples to feel they can rightfully own indigenous peoples' land. It is okay to take land from indigenous peoples, because indigenous peoples have disappeared.

ORIENTALISM/WAR

A third pillar of white supremacy is the logic of Orientalism. Orientalism was defined by Edward Said as the process of the West defining itself as a superior civilization by constructing itself in opposition to an "exotic" but inferior "Orient." (Here I am using the term "Orientalism" more broadly than to solely signify what has been historically named as the Orient or Asia.) The logic of Orientalism marks certain peoples or nations as inferior and as posing a constant threat to the well-being of empire. These peoples are still seen as "civilizations"—they are not property or "disappeared"—however, they will always be imaged as permanent foreign threats to empire. This logic is evident in the anti-immigration movements within the United States that target immigrants of color. It does not matter how long immigrants of color reside in the United States, they generally become targeted as foreign threats, particularly during war time. Consequently, Orientalism serves as the anchor for war, because it allows the United States to justify being in a constant state of war to protect itself from its enemies.

For example, the United States feels entitled to use Orientalist logic to justify racial profiling of Arab Americans so that it can be strong enough to fight the "war on terror." Orientalism also allows the United States to defend the logics of slavery and genocide, as these practices enable the United States to stay "strong enough" to fight these constant wars. What becomes clear then is what Sora Han states—the United States is not at war; the United States *is* war.[4] For the system of white supremacy to stay in place, the United States must always be at war.

Because we are situated within different logics of white supremacy, we may misunderstand a racial dynamic if we simplistically try to explain one logic of white supremacy with another logic. For instance, think about the first scenario that opens this essay: if we simply dismiss Latino/as or Arab peoples as "white," we fail to understand how a racial logic of Orientalism is in operation. That is, Latino/as and Arabs are often situated in a racial hierarchy that privileges them over Black people. However, while Orientalist logic may bestow them some racial privilege, they are still cast as inferior yet threatening "civilizations" in the United States. Their privilege is not a signal that they will be assimilated, but that they will be marked as perpetual foreign threats to the US world order.

ORGANIZING IMPLICATIONS

Under the old but still potent and dominant model, people of color organizing was based on the notion of organizing around shared victimhood. In this model, however, we see that we are victims of white supremacy, but complicit in it as well. Our survival strategies and resistance to white supremacy are set by the system of white supremacy itself. What keeps us trapped within our particular pillars of white supremacy is that we are seduced with the prospect of being able to participate in the other pillars. For example, all non-Native peoples are promised the ability to join in the colonial project of settling indigenous lands. All non-Black peoples are promised that if they comply, they will not be at the bottom of the racial hierarchy. And Black, Native, Latino, and Asian peoples are promised that they will economically and politically advance if they join US wars to spread "democracy." Thus, people of color organizing must be premised on making strategic alliances with each other, based on where we are situated within the larger political economy. Thus, for example, Native peoples who are organizing against the colonial and genocidal practices committed by the US government will be more effective in their struggle if they also organize against US militarism, particularly the military recruitment of indigenous peoples to support US imperial wars. If we try to end US colonial practices at home, but support US empire by joining the military, we are strengthening the state's ability to carry out genocidal policies against people of color here and all over the world.

This way, our alliances would not be solely based on shared victimization, but where we are complicit in the victimization of others. These approaches might help us to develop resistance strategies that do not inadvertently keep the system in place for all of us, and keep all of us accountable. In all of these cases, we would check our aspirations against the aspirations of other communities to ensure that our model of liberation does not become the model of oppression for others.

These practices require us to be more vigilant in how we may have internalized some of these logics in our own organizing practice. For instance, much racial justice organizing within the United States has rested on a civil rights framework that fights for equality under the law. An assumption behind this organizing is that the United States is a democracy with some flaws, but is otherwise admirable. Despite the fact that it rendered slaves three-fifths of a person, the US Constitution is presented as the model document from which to build a flourishing democracy. However, as Luana Ross notes, it has never been against US law to commit genocide against indigenous peoples—in fact, genocide *is* the law of the country. The United States could not exist without it. In the United States, democracy is actually the alibi for genocide—it is the practice that covers up United States colonial control over indigenous lands.

Our organizing can also reflect anti-Black racism. Recently, with the outgrowth of "multiculturalism" there have been calls to "go beyond the black/white binary" and include other communities of color in our analysis, as presented in the third scenario. There are a number of flaws with this analysis. First, it replaces an analysis of white supremacy with a politics of multicultural representation; if we just *include* more people, then our practice will be less racist. Not true. This model does not address the nuanced structure of white supremacy, such as through these distinct logics of slavery, genocide, and Orientalism. Second, it obscures the centrality of the slavery logic in the system of white supremacy, which is *based on a black/white binary.* The black/white binary is not the *only* binary which characterizes white supremacy, but it is still a central one that we cannot "go beyond" in our racial justice organizing efforts.

If we do not look at how the logic of slaveability inflects our society and our thinking, it will be evident in our work as well. For example, other communities of color often appropriate the cultural work and organizing strategies of African American civil rights or Black Power movements without corresponding assumptions that we should also be in solidarity with Black communities. We assume that this work is the common "property" of all oppressed groups, and we can appopriate it without being accountable.

Angela P. Harris and Juan Perea debate the usefulness of the black/white binary in the book, *Critical Race Theory*. Perea complains that the black/white binary fails to *include* the experiences of other people of color. However, he fails to identify alternative racializing logics to the black/white paradigm.[5] Meanwhile, Angela P. Harris argues that "the story of 'race' itself is that of the construction of Blackness and whiteness. In this story, Indians, Asian Americans, and Latinos/as do exist. But their roles are subsidiary to the fundamental binary national drama. As a political claim, Black exceptionalism exposes the deep mistrust and tensions among American ethnic groups racialized as nonwhite."[6]

Let's examine these statements in conversation with each other. Simply saying we need to move beyond the black/white binary (or perhaps, the "black/nonblack" binary) in US racism obfuscates the racializing logic of slavery, and prevents us from seeing that this binary constitutes Blackness as the bottom of a color hierarchy. However, this is not the *only* binary that fundamentally constitutes white supremacy. There is also an indigenous/settler binary, where Native genocide is central to the logic of white supremacy and other non-indigenous people of color also form a "subsidiary" role. We also face another Orientalist logic that fundamentally constitutes Asians, Arabs, and Latino/as as foreign threats, requiring the United States to be at permanent war with these peoples. In this construction, Black and Native peoples play subsidiary roles.

Clearly the black/white binary is central to racial and political thought and practice in the United States, and any understanding of white supremacy must take it into consideration. However, if we look at only this binary, we may misread the dynamics of white supremacy in different contexts. For example, critical race theorist Cheryl Harris's analysis of whiteness as property reveals this weakness. In *Critical Race Theory*, Harris contends that whites have a property interest in the preservation of whiteness, and seek to deprive those who are "tainted" by Black or Indian blood from these same white property interests. Harris simply assumes that the positions of African Americans and American Indians are the same, failing to consider US policies of forced assimilation and forced whiteness on American Indians. These policies have become so entrenched that when Native peoples make political claims, they have been accused of being white. When Andrew Jackson removed the Cherokee along the Trail of Tears, he argued that those who did not want removal were really white.[7] In contemporary times, when I was a non-violent witness for the Chippewa spearfishers in the late 1980s, one of the more frequent slurs whites hurled when the Chippewa attempted to exercise their treaty-protected right to fish was that they had white parents, or they were really white.

Status differences between Blacks and Natives are informed by the different economic positions African Americans and American Indians have in US society. African Americans have been traditionally valued for their labor, hence it is in the interest of the dominant society to have as many people marked "Black" as possible, thereby maintaining a cheap labor pool; by contrast, American Indians have been valued for the land base they occupy, so it is in the interest of dominant society to have as few people marked "Indian" as possible, facilitating access to Native lands. "Whiteness" operates differently under a logic of genocide than it does from a logic of slavery.

Another failure of US-based people of color in organizing is that we often fall back on a "US-centricism," believing that what is happening "over there" is less important than what is happening here. We fail to see how the United States maintains the system of oppression here precisely by tying our allegiances to the interests of US empire "over there."

HETEROPATRIARCHY AND WHITE SUPREMACY

Heteropatriarchy is the building block of US empire. In fact, it is the building block of the nation-state form of governance. Christian Right authors make these links in their analysis of imperialism and empire. For example, Christian Right activist and founder of Prison Fellowship Charles Colson makes the connection between homosexuality and the nation-state in his analysis of the war on terror, explaining that one of the causes of terrorism is same-sex marriage:

> Marriage is the traditional building block of human society, intended both to unite couples and bring children into the world.... There is a natural moral order for the family ... the family, led by a married mother and father, is the best available structure for both child-rearing and cultural health. Marriage is not a private institution designed solely for the individual gratification of its participants. If we fail to enact a Federal Marriage Amendment, we can expect not just more family breakdown, but also more criminals behind bars and more chaos in our streets.[8]

Colson is linking the well-being of US empire to the well-being of the heteropatriarchal family. He continues: "When radical Islamists see American women abusing Muslim men, as they did in the Abu Ghraib prison, and when they see news coverage of same-sex couples being 'married' in US towns, we make this kind of freedom abhorrent—the kind they see as a blot on Allah's creation. We must preserve traditional marriage in order to protect the United States from those who would use our depravity to destroy us."[9]

As Ann Burlein argues in *Lift High the Cross,* it may be a mistake to argue that the goal of Christian Right politics is to create a theocracy in the United States. Rather, Christian Right politics work through the private family (which is coded as white, patriarchal, and middle class) to create a "Christian America." She notes that the investment in the private family makes it difficult for people to invest in more public forms of social connection. In addition, investment in the suburban private family serves to mask the public disinvestment in urban areas that makes the suburban lifestyle possible. The social decay in urban areas that results from this disinvestment is then construed as the result of deviance from the Christian family ideal rather than as the result of political and economic forces. As former head of the Christian Coalition, Ralph Reed, states: "The only true solution to crime is to restore the family,"[10] and "Family break-up causes poverty."[11] Concludes Burlein, "'The family' is no mere metaphor but a crucial technology by which modern power is produced and exercised."[12]

As I have argued elsewhere, in order to colonize peoples whose societies are not based on social hierarchy, colonizers must first naturalize hierarchy through instituting patriarchy.[13] In turn, patriarchy rests on a gender binary system in which only two genders exist, one dominating the other. Consequently, Charles Colson is correct when he says that the colonial world order depends on heteronormativity. Just as the patriarchs rule the family, the elites of the nation-state rule their citizens. Any liberation struggle that does not challenge heteronormativity cannot substantially challenge colonialism or white supremacy. Rather, as Cathy Cohen contends, such struggles will maintain colonialism based on a politics of secondary marginalization where the most elite class of these groups will further their aspirations on the backs of those most marginalized within the community.[14]

Through this process of secondary marginalization, the national or racial justice struggle takes on either implicitly or explicitly a nation-state model as the end point of its struggle—a model of governance in which the elites govern the rest through violence and domination, as well as exclude those who are not members of "the nation." Thus, national liberation politics become less vulnerable to being co-opted by the Right when we base them on a model of liberation that fundamentally challenges right-wing conceptions of the nation. We need a model based on community relationships and on mutual respect.

CONCLUSION

Women of color–centered organizing points to the centrality of gender politics within antiracist, anticolonial struggles. Unfortunately, in our efforts to organize against white, Christian America, racial justice struggles often articulate an equally heteropatriarchal racial nationalism. This model of organizing either hopes to assimilate into white America, or to replicate it within an equally hierarchical and oppressive racial nationalism in which the elites of the community rule everyone else. Such struggles often call on the importance of preserving the "Black family" or the "Native family" as the bulwark of this nationalist project, the family being conceived of in capitalist and heteropatriarchal terms. The response is often increased homophobia, with lesbian and gay community members construed as "threats" to the family. But, perhaps we should challenge the "concept" of the family itself. Perhaps, instead, we can reconstitute alternative ways of living together in which "families" are not seen as islands on their own. Certainly, indigenous communities were not ordered on the basis of a nuclear family structure—[this] is the result of colonialism, not the antidote to it.

In proposing this model, I am speaking from my particular position in indigenous struggles. Other peoples might flesh out these logics more fully from different vantage points. Others might also argue that there are other logics of white supremacy [that] are missing. Still others might complicate how they relate to each other. But I see this as a starting point for women of color organizers that will allow us to reenvision a politics of solidarity that goes beyond multiculturalism, and develop more complicated strategies that can really transform the political and economic status quo.

NOTES

1. Angela P. Harris, "Embracing the Tar-Baby: LatCrit Theory and the Sticky Mess of Race," in *Critical Race Theory,* eds. Richard Delgado and Jean Stefancic, 2nd ed. (Philadelphia: Temple University Press, 2000), 440–7. I also thank Sora Han and Jared Sexton for their illuminating analysis of Blackness.

2. Ella Shoat and Robert Stam, *Unthinking Eurocentricism* (London: Routledge, 1994), 118–119.

3. Rayna Green, "The Tribe Called Wannabee," *Folklore* 99, no. 1 (1988): 30–55.

4. Sora Han, *Bonds of Representation: Vision, Race and Law in Post–Civil Rights America* (Santa Cruz: University of California–Santa Cruz, 2006).

5. Juan Perea, "The Black/White Binary Paradigm of Race," in *Critical Race Theory,* Delgado and Stefancic, 2nd ed.

6. Angela P. Harris, "Embracing the Tar-Baby."

7. William McLoughlin, *Cherokees and Missionaries, 1789–1839* (Norman, OK: University of Oklahoma Press, 1995).

8. Charles Colson, "Societal Suicide," *Christianity Today* 48, no. 6 (June 2004): 72.

9. Charles Colson and Anne Morse, "The Moral Home Front," *Christianity Today* 48, no. 10 (October 2004): 152.

10. Ralph Reed, *After the Revolution* (Dallas: Word, 1990).

11. Ibid.

12. Ann Burlein, *Lift High the Cross* (Raleigh, NC: Duke University Press, 2002).

13. Andrea Smith, *Conquest, Sexual Violence and American Indian Genocide* (Cambridge, MA: South End Press, 2005).

14. Cathy Cohen, *The Boundaries of Blackness* (Chicago: University of Chicago Press, 1999).

9

Pathfinders: Women-Centered Movements Discover Intersecting Routes to Global Change

CONCLUSION: GLOBAL THEORIES, THE HISTORICAL WORLD-SYSTEM, AND INTERSECTING WOMEN-CENTERED MOVEMENTS

It is important now to draw some conclusions about feminist theories of global change and about the global, women-centered movements that have emerged in recent years, "pathfinders" that are looking for ways to make constructive change.

A key development for both theory and politics has been that the intersection of different global hierarchies has led to the rise of global, intersecting social movements. Many of the movements that have emerged are feminist-inspired and women-centered because women have been targeted by male-dominated institutions as new sources of accumulation, profit, and power in this period.

Feminist theorists have long argued that hierarchies of oppression—age, sexuality, gender, class, ethnicity, geography, or coloniality—overlap and intersect with others, creating what they call a "matrix of oppression." But most feminists study these hierarchies outside of the context of a historical, global system. Many feminists express reluctance to "privilege" any one, arguing that they be given equal analytical weight and insisting that no hierarchy is more important or politically significant than another. Other feminist scholars, such as those engaged in postcolonial research, place the study of gender and feminism within the contexts of race, class, and colonial hierarchies and seem less hesitant to order the study of intersections. Intersectional feminist scholars have not used world-systems theory to frame comparative, historical studies on the relative weight of gender, race, class, and coloniality and their influence on local and global movements. Feminists are aware of ongoing research conducted by white, northern, middle-class academics that abstracts gender from racial, class, and colonial contexts, ignoring how women's lives have been shaped by more than gender and sexuality. There continue to be important concerns about how to end the reproduction of white supremacist and colonial understandings of women's and men's lives. But a lack of understanding about how to develop an inclusive, global history of movements may have limited how theories are developed to examine changes in gender, intersecting global hierarchies, and the development of women-led movements and feminisms. Within the specific historical context of today's global society, we ask whether the construction of gender and gendered politics has assumed enough primacy that some global movements may become heavily influenced by the gendered politics of women, girls, and feminists.

The feminist intersectional approach has made important theoretical and empirical contributions to our study of oppression. But it is limited by its focus on separate hierarchies and an unwillingness to look at the intersection of the *whole*—how separate hierarchies are joined. In this regard, some theorists are reluctant to take their own argument about the importance of intersectionality to its logical conclusion, which would be to examine the whole grid, not just single intersections. This perspective is also limited by its proponents' insistence that no oppressive hierarchy is more salient at any given time than any other, which is a profoundly ahistorical view. There is a reluctance here to examine how, in different ways, separate hierarchies were constructed historically in relation to the others or explain why some were more salient at different periods—for example, how global racism was particularly significant during slavery. In the contemporary period, for reasons we have explored, ageist-heterosexist institutions have made the global gender hierarchy (which of course intersects with other hierarchies) particularly salient, which is why women-inclusive, feminist-inspired global movements have become more prominent in recent years. To deny this and to insist that women-centered movements that are trying to deal with the gender hierarchy and its intersecting connections with other hierarchies are no more significant than other hierarchies seems determinedly obtuse.

For these reasons, we think it is important to join feminist intersectional analysis with world-systems analysis, creating a new "intersection" or theoretical crossroads through which ideas from both perspectives can meet.[1] World-systems analysis is important for feminist intersectional theory and practice for many reasons, some of which we highlight here. First, world-systems theorists insist on the study of the *whole*, not just its constituent parts, and examine how separate hierarchies are joined and articulated into a global structure. Second, they urge theorists to use a global historical perspective, providing a view of system-wide trends and secular and cyclical patterns, which gives scholars the analytical tools for determining how and why intersecting hierarchies were created and why some hierarchies become more salient at particular times in different settings. Third, by highlighting the importance of in-kind and market values generated by women in the laboring household—the smallest and most overlooked global institution—world-systems analysis identifies accumulators' and states' secret, largely nonmonetized source for reproducing greatly underpaid, unequal work-forces, a central issue raised by the world's women who have reorganized work to keep households going.[2] Fourth, as the contradictory impacts of intersections are explored in the future, world-systems analysis can offer profound insights into ways to create new social relations that eliminate apartheid and separatism and promote the democratic integration of people.

It is not enough to study separate hierarchies in a particular social formation at one particular moment in time. It is crucial now to examine the construction of hierarchies, as a whole, on a world scale and to do so in a long-term, historical context so that its shared and distinctive features, its past development, and its possible future trajectories can be appreciated. The construction of hierarchies and feminist pathways to global change can only be fully understood within the context of the long-term transformations of the world-system as a whole. By examining global transformations that affect gender, it is possible to see why women-centered movements have recently emerged to challenge ageist-heterosexist institutions the world over.

This is *not* a totalizing, universalist project. It is instead a way to explain "difference" by examining its historical development, the reasons why and how hierarchies and unequal positions in the world (at both the microlevel of households and the macrolevel of states and world-economy) were created and how contemporary institutions and movements transform social relations. It is only by looking at the *whole,* from a *historical perspective,* that one can understand "difference" and identify strategies that have promoted or could advance "equality."

The world-system perspective is *not* synonymous with globalization, which *is* a totalizing, universalist approach. Indeed, the world-system perspective is exactly the *opposite* of globalization. Proponents of globalization argue that a process of homogenization, which is driven by the global market (in combination with complementary political and culture developments), will eliminate "difference" and promote "equality." But this is a false promise because it is the global market, in association with collaborative ageist, heterosexist institutions in households and states, that for 500 years has *differentiated* people by age, gender, ethnicity, class, and geography and assigned them subordinate places in separate and intersecting hierarchies. By contrast, world-system theorists examine the *whole* as a way to understand how these different hierarchies were *historically* constructed, linking divided groups of the world's people through multiple bonds of inequality. By examining the construction of "difference" in relation to the whole, it is possible to advance strategies that deconstruct difference and the intersecting hierarchies that maintain it and promote real "equality," democracy, environmental regeneration, humanizing work relations, and peace.

CONNECTING GLOBAL THEORIES: FEMINIST WORLD-SYSTEMS, POSTCOLONIAL, AND EMPIRE ANALYSIS

Theories are not fixed and finished. Instead, feminist and other theories can best be seen as open approaches or explanatory roadmaps for conducting more research and new actions. Theories, in this sense, always form part of ongoing critical inquiry and serve as a guide to recognizing, understanding, and interpreting empirical processes that relate to feminist pathways to social change. Just as global frameworks need to be grounded in feminist, antiracist, and anticolonialist theories, feminist theories remain abstract and disconnected without global theories and intersectional understandings.

In the twenty-first century, global thinkers often refer to three global theories as if they were all the same, when they are actually quite different. But when cross-cultural feminist theorists combine ideas from postcolonial (or neocolonial) and empire perspectives, it is possible to arrive at a world-systemic view. We argue that world-systems analysis contains other global frameworks' most useful components and adds critical new elements, leading to a more comprehensive approach for determining how society is changing and how complementary movements contribute to new, more inclusive social relations and institutional arrangements.

Here the differences and overlaps among these three general approaches can be considered in a general, schematic way. Although there are important differences within each of these general perspectives—postcolonialism, empire, and world-systems analysis—these theories are potentially complementary and can contribute useful ideas to diverse social change movements.

Postcolonial theory has allowed feminists to explain how colonialism and postcolonialism have reconfigured people's lives by changing intersectional hierarchies, such as gender/sexuality, "race"/ethnicity, and class.[3] Although some postcolonial analysis, such as Chandra Talpade Mohanty's work, has extended the social construction of gender/sexuality and race to cross-border work in the global South and North, feminist scholars generally have applied postcolonial theories to the study of gendered and racialized groups in particular times and places in the global South.[4] Postcolonial scholars have also examined the other side of racism: the social construction of whiteness and privilege. Feminist scholars combined feminist and postcolonial theories in ways that reveal how culturally subordinate groups of women resisted and how they created affirmative cultures. But although postcolonial scholars provided a sustained analysis of the social construction of gender and sexuality within colonized and other racialized groups, most still did not provide a framework that would allow scholars and activists to see beyond intersecting hierarchies in particular precolonial, colonial, and postcolonial areas. They did not examine long-term and holistic perspectives, which meant their understanding of historical capitalism and resistance was fragmentary.

Recently empire theorists have provided a way to contextualize change. Empire theories focus on the present and the future. By opening up the global as a legitimate area of research for scholars coming out of postmodern, cultural traditions, empire theorists have had a big impact on feminist scholars. According to Michael Hardt and Antonio Negri, authors of *Empire* and *Multitude,* empire is a "new form of global sovereignty" that consists of a "series of national and supranational organisms united under a single logic of rule."[5] As the following quotation from Hardt and Negri suggests, the importance of cultural fragmentation and hybridity—concepts of major importance to postmodern thinkers—is reinforced by Hardt and Negri's new conceptions of empire. But unlike their structuralist predecessors, who emphasized the intracapitalist conflict within and between states,[6] the new regulatory rulers of empire are everywhere.

> The passage to Empire emerges from the twilight of modern sovereignty. In contrast to imperialism, Empire establishes no territorial center of power and does not rely on fixed boundaries or barriers. It is a decentered and deterritorializing apparatus of rule that progressively incorporates the entire global realm within its open, expanding frontiers. Empire manages hybrid identities, flexible hierarchies, and plural exchanges through modulating networks of command. These distinct colors of the imperialist map of the world have merged and blended in the imperial global rainbow.... *The United States does not, and indeed no nation-state can today, form the center of an imperialist project....* The concept of Empire is characterized fundamentally by a lack of boundaries: Empire's rule has no limits. First and foremost then, the concept of Empire posits a regime that effectively encompasses the spatial totality, or really that rules over the entire "civilized" world.... Second, the concept of Empire presents itself not as a historical regime originating in conquest, but rather as an order that effectively suspends history and thereby fixes the existing state of affairs for eternity.... Third, the rule of Empire operates on all registers of the social order extending down to the depths of the social world. [emphasis added][7]

Through diffuse networks, empire governs the world by regulating a "global market and global circuits of production," which Hardt and Negri call a new global order and "a new logic and new structure of rule."[8] But their concept of empire is monolithic and removed from its historical antecedents, both in terms of the construction of global society in the past and in terms of conflicts between anticapitalist and other antisystemic forces.

Although many intellectuals used to have a historical understanding of empire (partly as a result of Eric Hobsbawm's analysis of the era that began with Britain's industrial rule over the world),[9] empire theorists tend to minimize the importance of its ties to the past. Today's empire theorists forget that the past still shapes us, as they try to "discover the commonality that enables us to communicate and act together."[10] Although this idea of empire provides an appreciation of overlapping global movements, the emphasis is placed on looking forward, not on understanding how the future is a product of the past. At some level feminists and other excluded groups know that their movements emerged in response to historical inequalities. Ending divisions in and between social movements requires addressing the systemic intersecting hierarchies that have divided and segregated people. But although these intersecting hierarchies have divided working people, they have also created conditions that led to the development of overlapping social movements, which now challenge the system.

Empire theorists have provided a broader global framework that has helped academic feminists to confront their fears of being labeled "essentialists" and to become more comfortable with the study of global change. In *War Talk,* for example, Arundhati Roy provided a useful critique of empire, which she sees as emanating from imperialism, corporate globalization, and the global search for "money, goods, patents, and services." In her view, empire is a "loyal confederation" made up of the countries in the North; it is "this obscene accumulation of power, this greatly increased distance between those who make decisions and those who have to suffer them."[11] Roy argued that "[e]mpire is out in the open now—too ugly to behold its own reflection. Too ugly to even rally its own people." To lay siege to empire, Roy argued that "we can hone our memory, we can learn from our history." Organizers of civil disobedience must work to "deprive [Empire] of oxygen. To shame it. To mock it." Resisters from the North and South should do this with "our art, our music, our literature, our stubbornness, our joy, our brilliance, our sheer relentless—and our ability to tell our own stories." She concluded that "the corporate revolution will collapse if we refuse to buy what they are selling—their ideas, their version of history, their wars, their weapons, their notion of inevitability."[12] To bring empire to its knees, Roy wrote, we must "isolate Empire's working parts and disable them one by one," and we must "battle to reclaim democracy."[13] Although she argued that the anticorporate, antiglobalization multitudes can use democracy to "stop Empire in its tracks," she did not say how they can address divisions between people (which they still carry) or how to build better societies and a better world.[14] bell hooks might step in here and say that informed activists need to both take a good look at themselves and create equal and loving relationships as they move forward with the democratic processes of change.[15]

Although she did not focus on the global capitalist system and how movements can undo it, Zillah Eisenstein provided a gutsy understanding of empire that complements the humanistic thrust of world-systems analysis. By being emotional and analytical, Eisenstein broke new ground in *Against Empire: Feminisms, Racism, and the West.* Eisenstein took on postmodernists' fears of universalizing discourse and shaping other women's bodies by "rewriting universalized rights for polyvocal needs" and using the human body as her "inclusive site for humanity."[16]

> The notion of the global must be reclaimed—taken from capitalist hegemony— for a radically inclusive humanity. The notion of inclusivity recognizes a unity among people that is hard to fathom.... Diversity and not uniformity underlies life's "complex oneness."
>
> The self must be present if an earnest commitment to community is to be embraced. The love of humanity—as an inclusive polyversal—must therefore start close to home, and home is the body.[17]

The idea of confronting empire to build humanity is reinforced by Eisenstein's reading of global history, where "history is never just simply the 'past'" and where much of it has been told only through oral and other traditions. Feminist, globalization, and empire thinkers frequently overlook feminist struggles of women in culturally subordinated groups and in previously colonized countries. Furthermore, by defining globalization as new, they fail to appreciate the fact that globalization occurred for centuries.[18] As women carry out political acts in particular places, such as fighting for democracy in Afghanistan and protecting rural Mexicans' land from being expropriated by airport builders, Eisenstein argued that women challenge patriarchal divisions between the private and public, expose capitalism's push for consumerism, and address male privilege.[19] All are seen as part of the humanistic, polyvocal struggle for democracy.

As part of her work on the construction of empire and people's struggles against it, Jacqui Alexander analyzed heteropatriarchy as an integral dimension of intersecting hierarchies. Alexander distinguished between white imperial heteropatriarchy, created as part of white colonial rule, and black heteropatriarchy, created as part of political independence and recolonization. The current period of recolonization in the Caribbean rests on multinationals' accumulation of profits, largely through tourism.[20] To promote tourism, the state uses women's bodies, their sexual labor, and women's service work. Alexander defined white imperial and black heteropatriarchy as part of the history of "the enforced Crossing of the millions of Africans that serviced from the fifteenth century through the twentieth the consolidation of British, French, Spanish, and Dutch empires."[21]

In order to understand empire and nation-building, Alexander argued that the sexual hierarchy needs to be studied as an integral part of domination and the construction of intersecting hierarchies. As she reinterpreted the history of the Bahamas, Alexander showed that the state made heterosexuality the standard for citizenship by tying property ownership to heterosexist marriage, enacting state reductions of social services on the backs of women, making most women become poor and disadvantaged, and initiating domestic violence at home by organizing state economic violence against women.[22] These inequalities can be challenged on a deeper level when feminists and activists in queer movements examine heterosexism in relation to "colonialism, racial formation, and political economy." By including the fight against heterosexism in the struggle against intersecting hierarchies, feminists will find that they are better prepared to engage in the "praxis of the Sacred."[23] Alexander asked her readers to "reimagine wholeness as a necessary part of the pedagogy of crossing" and to "use Spirit knowing as the mechanism of making the world intelligible."[24]

Seeing all aspects of intersecting hierarchies, locating them in a long-term historical perspective, and knowing where you want to go (in terms of equality, democracy, peace, ecological balance, humanism, and spirituality) enables feminists and inclusive activists to move forward, regardless of the theories that inform their work. It is helpful to see the present and future in relation to historical continuities and to see that fragmented cultures and movements grew out of global society's production of heterosexist supremacy, white supremacy, corporate rule, and periods of hegemonic domination. If they focus only on the present and future, scholars and activists may develop a blindness that keeps them from breaking with past inequalities. Both postmodern feminists and empire analysts tend to focus on the political hope that comes from today's ongoing social fragmentation, without confronting the fact that global profit-making generated unequal groups and produced the very fragmentation that has become the basis for so many movements. This requires the formation of new ways of living and the conscious replacement of the old, not simply the celebration of fragmented hybrid cultures that coalesce in the heart of, or even at the margins of, global society.

Combining feminist theories with world-systems analysis can provide both a more comprehensive framework that helps activists analyze the ongoing creation of overlapping and fragmented labor forces and cultures and insights into ways that movements and projects can build new sets of inclusive social relations at local and global levels.

WOMEN-CENTERED MOVEMENTS

Contemporary women-centered movements share a number of distinguishing features. They are socially diverse and organizationally diversified, they intersect and cooperate with other movements, they set institutional and alternative goals, and they are motivated by both medium- to long-term self-interest and collective altruism that extend beyond healthy fragmented identity group, locality, country, continent, and global North or South constructions.

Diverse and Diversified

Women-centered movements are extraordinarily diverse. This social diversity grows out of the very different situations in which women find themselves in settings around the world. Feminist theorists have celebrated this diversity, and with good reason. But it is also important to recognize that these movements have resisted organizational centralization and remained diversified, even though they cooperate with one another.

Contrast this organizational diversity with some of the global social movements that were prominent 100 years ago. The First, Second, and Third Internationals organized diverse socialist movements into a centralized organizational structure, a model widely adopted by male "labor" movements and by "nationalist" and anticolonial movements. Movement leaders drew movements into centralized political or economic organizations because they thought they would be more effective against the centralized power of states and of capital.

But contemporary movements take a rather different view. They resist constructing or joining centralized organizations. They do so in part because these centralized organizations lend themselves to domination by political elites and "vanguard" parties, in part because they prize the flexibility, independence, adaptability, and democratic decisionmaking of movements that take diversified organizational forms. By taking a don't-put-all-the-eggs-in-one-basket approach to movement organization, contemporary movements can move forward even if one organizational expression falters.

Intersecting and Cooperative

Although women-centered movements have diversified in organizational terms, they still intersect and cooperate with other movements. They do so in part because each movement typically consists of people with hybrid, multiple, and overlapping identities, which makes it easy for them to cooperate with or participate in *other* movements. Women who participate in movements today do not insist that their political activity and social engagement be *restricted* to a single movement based on a single social identity. Instead, they often participate in a variety of movements that express different facets of their identities as women. For their part, many movements seek to address issues that speak to women's different identities and needs. For example, women-inclusive rural cooperatives, which grow a variety of organic crops for fair trade export, local markets, and direct consumption, do not just seek to address their members' economic needs (one facet of poor women's identity); they also try to address housing needs, family violence, literacy and education, reproductive choice, and democratic decisionmaking, issues that speak to their members' identities as wives, mothers, learners, and decisionmakers. Of course, movements find ways to cooperate and collaborate with each other, but this is based on a relationship that has been negotiated, not imposed.

Contrast this intersecting, cooperative approach with the kind of single-identity movements that emerged in the late 1960s and 1970s. These movements were based on the idea that movements should represent women (or other members of distinct hierarchies) with a singular identity and that the movements should focus on problems specific to this identity and work on these problems alone. Today, movements recognize that women participants have multiple and overlapping identities and work on a range of issues that address different needs and advance solutions to different sets of problems. This kind of approach tends to broaden the definition of the "problem" and widen the range of issues that individual movements address. This is a positive development because this enables people to see how problems "intersect" and how different groups of people are needed to address local and global issues. Once again, the development of a family of movements, a family of antisystemic forces, enables activists and intellectuals to invent collaborative ways of developing knowledge and addressing issues.[25]

Institutional and Alternative Goals

Many women-centered movements seek to capture or change state and market institutions in order to secure social and reproductive rights, obtain access to education and employment, and secure economic benefits that would help women and households. In addition to these "institutional" goals, movements have decided to push for economic, social, and political change outside these institutional settings, creating "alternative" institutions to promote change.

This alternative arena is sometimes called "civil society." But the term *civil society* has been narrowed by political scientists to mean the NGOs and institutions—schools, churches, media—that collaborate with or buttress state and market institutions. By contrast, Antonio Gramsci, the Italian theorist who coined the term, used it to describe nongovernmental institutions that could challenge the state and provide democratic alternatives to hierarchical institutions, both governmental and nongovernmental alike.

Many women-centered movements have worked to create alternative institutions in a broadly defined civil society as a way to promote change. They have done so in part because state institutions have shed important responsibilities and transferred them to less accountable market institutions (privatization); because many state institutions are corrupt, dysfunctional, or collapsed; and because states by themselves have not been able to promote the kind of change or "development" that would actually improve conditions for their citizenry. Because it is difficult to rely on state institutions to promote real change, women-centered movements have worked to create alternative institutions that could help them weather the global, systemic crises that beset individual state and market institutions and promote genuine development and democracy.

These objectives contrast sharply with the kind of goals set by prominent movements in times past. A century ago, socialist and also nationalist movements set the capture of state power (either by democratic means or by force) as their central objective. They did so because they believed that state power was the key to change. If they seized state power, they thought they could use it as an instrument of change.

Of course, this proved much more difficult than movement leaders imagined. As Immanuel Wallerstein and others have argued, movements that assumed power soon learned that state power was a relatively *in*efficient way to promote change, given the existence of a larger world-economy and interstate system.[26] Socialists in Cuba and nationalists in Egypt found they could not use the state to make Cuba the equal of Japan or Egypt the equal of Germany. Not only is state power an ineffective tool of movements in poor countries, it is also ineffective for leaders of powerful states. Leaders in Great Britain and in the United States have discovered that the enormous power of these "hegemonic" states could *not* arrest their own decline or prevent defeat in "minor" wars.

Given these realities, feminist movements have largely abandoned the Marxist and ethnonationalist fascination with state power as a central objective or as an end in itself. They have instead developed theories that value other approaches to change, ones that rely less on institutional objectives and more on "alternative" goals.

Self-Interested and Interconnected

Most social movement theorists—Marxist, capitalist, ethnonationalist, feminist—assume that people organize movements to represent and advance their collective self-interest. These theorists then go on to explain why gender, race, religion, class, and other identities become salient for self-interested actors. Of course, women *do* organize movements to protect and promote their interests as women. They do so to protect themselves from assault by men or to improve their access to education and employment. But women-centered movements *also* act with *others*. They are motivated not only by collective "self-interest" but also by caring for others and developing a more humanistic world. Unfortunately, world-systemic and hybridic-generated, self-interested, interconnected collective altruism has not been adequately theorized as a motivation that animates many contemporary women-centered movements.

Altruistic, women-centered movements sometimes act on behalf of others because these people may be unable to organize effectively or act on their own behalf. For example, children, the disenfranchised, and immigrants may not possess the legal standing that would enable them to organize movements that could act in their collective self-interest. Participants in women-centered movements often assume responsibility for changing the world with others and for working with people who are locked out of power in different ways. For example, the idea of ending inequality by addressing one's own class, racial, and global privilege, as one works with less privileged women and men, is a practice found in past and contemporary movements. This collaborative, transclass, transracial, and transglobal approach has taken different forms. In the eighteenth and nineteenth centuries, black and white abolitionists, for example, organized to end the enslavement of fellow Americans and people held in bondage elsewhere. Environmental activists in the global North and South are joining hands to protect local commons by building solar and wind energy systems and by restoring endangered prairie and cloud forest ecosystems. And today women and men step forward in different countries to end war and anti-immigrant violence, even though their own countries may charge them with treason. All of these actions require compassion for others and openness about learning from others.

Women-centered movements also act in a self-organized, globally sensitive, collective altruistic fashion because they are motivated by ideas and practices that value others, not just themselves. Fair trade movements in the core work with producers in the periphery not because they want a "cheap" cup of coffee (which would be in their own self-interest), but because they value a "good" cup of coffee, one that embodies not just good flavor but also values social equality, environmental protection, sustainable development, and the development of democratically run, women-inclusive producer co-ops in the tropics. If fair trade movements were only motivated by self-interest, they would not insist that the cup of coffee include values of "collective altruism."

This, we think, is a significant development. The capacity to empathize with and act on behalf of others, the ability to act in a nurturing and humanizing manner, not just with family and friends but also with strangers in distant reaches of the world, enhances the capacity of others to act, to organize movements and promote real change. Collective altruism, compassion, and love are *intersectional* values. They help join diverse movements in common cause.

NOTES

1. Many scholars and practitioners of social change use world-systems analysis and develop the theoretical perspective associated with world-systems analysis. Key works have

been written by Immanuel Wallerstein, founder of the world-system school and founder of the Braudel Center for the Study of Economies, Historical Systems, and Civilizations at Binghamton University. Professor Wallerstein works with the Sociology Department at Yale University. Three basic world-systems texts are *The Modern World-System* (a series), *Historical Capitalism,* and *World-Systems Analysis.* Two collections that address households and gender are *Households and the World-Economy* and *Creating and Transforming Households.* Immanuel Wallerstein's students and colleagues can be found at different universities and organizations. For example, Giovanni Arrighi and Beverley Silver teach at Johns Hopkins University. Written by T. Dickinson and R. Schaeffer, the most recent world-systems analysis of gender and households is *Fast Forward: Work, Gender, and Protest in a Changing World.*

2. The world-system's institutions assume different forms in the changing global society. For example, in different parts of the world, in different locales, and at different points in time, the household takes different forms. Laboring households in a large, contemporary city may take a variety of forms, including an extended family form, a nuclear form (perhaps for both gay and heterosexual couples), and a polygamous form. There also may be labor-defined households, such as multifamily cooperatives. But what is common across time is that profit makers and states both try to shape households so that one worker assumes responsibility for sharing his/her wages with other household members, thereby lowering the costs of reproduction for employers. The ideology of heterosexism tries to justify why the adult, heterosexual male is privileged and why women, girls, boys, and elders should be "dependent" on the socially constructed "head of the household." As world-systems research reveals, the male household head is often a myth, as women and girls have served, and currently serve, as primary wage earners (as they simultaneously engage in unpaid, use-value generation to sustain low-paid and unpaid members of laboring households). Rather than being structural functionalist, as some have suggested, world-systems researchers examine the processes that shape the world-systems' key institutions and the unequal relations that link the world's groups together. The ties that have bound the world's labor forces together become transformed into the ties that build movements for global change.

3. Key feminist writings show the development of these critiques: The Combahee River Collective, "A Black Feminist Statement," in Carole R. McCann and Seung-Kyung Kim, eds., *Feminist Theory Reader* (New York: Routledge, 2003), 164–171; Audre Lorde, "Age, Race, Class, and Sex: Women Redefining Difference," in Amy Kesselman, Lily McNair, and Nancy Schniedewind, eds., *Women: Images and Realities* (Boston: McGraw Hill, 2003), 427–433; Gloria Anzaldúa, ed., *Making Face, Making Soul: Creative and Critical Perspectives of Women of Color* (San Francisco: Aunt Lute Books, 1990), esp. the writings in "'Doing' Theory in Other Modes of Consciousness," including those by Barbara Christian: "The Race for Theory"; by Norma Alarcón: "The Theoretical Subject(s) of This Bridge Called My Back and Anglo-American Feminism"; and by Gloria Anzaldúa: "La conciencia de la mestiza: Towards a New Consciousness," 335–402; and Sharlene Nagy Hesse-Biber and Michelle Yaeger, "Feminist Approaches to Research as a *Process,*" in *Feminist Perspectives on Social Research* (New York: Oxford University Press, 2004), 3–26, 18–19.

4. Chandra Talpade Mohanty, *Feminism Without Borders: Decolonizing Theory, Practicing Solidarity* (Durham, NC: Duke University Press, 2003).

5. Michael Hardt and Antonio Negri, *Empire* (Cambridge, MA: Harvard University Press, 2000), xii.

6. In the 1970s, debates took place between those who saw highly fractured upper-class governance and those who saw great coherence within the ruling class, even though

governance was never unified. Postmodernism's predecessors, such as structuralist Nicole Polantzas, studied contradictory class positions in the state and the ongoing struggle between differentiated ruling blocs. In contrast, Ralph Miliband and the proponents of the instrumentalist state argued that the ruling class was more united and that it took action to benefit the extension of capital's rule.

7. Hardt and Negri, *Empire,* xii–xiii.

8. Ibid., xi.

9. E. J. Hobsbawm, *Industry and Empire* (Harmondsworth, England: Penguin, 1977). See also Eric Hobsbawm, *The Age of Extremes: A History of the World, 1914–1991* (New York: Pantheon, 1994). As part of his historical and global examination of empire in *The Age of Extremes,* Hobsbawm defined the period between 1914 and 1991 as the age of extremes. He broke this period into three stages that centered on World War I and World War II, decolonization and the rise of Third World power, and the decades of crisis, including the decline of U.S. power and the disintegration of the Soviet Union. He wrote, "The future cannot be a continuation of the past, and there are signs, both externally and, as it were, internally, that we have reached a period of historic crisis" (584). Furthermore, he concluded that humanity can only have a "recognizable future" if we decide not to prolong the past or present. "If we try to build the third millennium on [the basis of prolonging the past], we shall fail. And the price of that failure, that is to say, the alternative to a changed society, is darkness" (585).

10. Michael Hardt and Antonio Negri, *Multitude: War and Democracy in the Age of Empire* (New York: Penguin, 2004), xiii.

11. Arundhati Roy, *War Talk* (Cambridge, MA: South End Press, 2003), 107.

12. Ibid., 109–112.

13. Arundhati Roy, *An Ordinary Person's Guide to Empire* (Cambridge, MA: South End Press, 2004), 66.

14. Roy, *War Talk,* 109.

15. bell hooks, *Teaching Community: A Pedagogy of Hope* (New York: Routledge, 2003).

16. Zillan Eisenstein. *Against Empire: Feminisms, Racism, and the West* (New York: Zed, 2004), xvi.

17. Ibid., 65.

18. Ibid., 128. See also pp. 78, 240.

19. Ibid., 78. See also pp. 150, 192, 221.

20. M. Jaqui Alexander, *Pedagogies of Crossing: Meditations on Feminism, Sexual Politics, Memory, and the Sacred* (Durham, NC: Duke University Press, 2005), 25–27, 36.

21. Ibid., 2. See also pp. 36, 50–51.

22. Ibid., 27, 32–37, 52.

23. Ibid., 12, 328.

24. Ibid., 14, 15.

25. Immanuel Wallerstein, *After Liberalism* (New York: The New Press, 1995), 248–251; Immanuel Wallerstein, *World-Systems Analysis: An Introduction* (Durham, NC: Duke University Press, 2004), 84–90.

26. Immanuel Wallerstein, *Anti-Systemic Movements* (London: Verso, 1989).

About the Editors

Torry Dickinson is Professor of Women's Studies at Kansas State University and coauthor of *Fast Forward: Work, Gender, and Protest in a Changing World,* which was identified as a core reading in Women's Studies and Sociology by the Association of College and Research Libraries.

Robert Schaeffer is Professor of Sociology at Kansas State University, author of *Understanding Globalization,* and coauthor of *Fast Forward.*